ORTHODOX CHRISTIANITY

Volume IV:

The Worship and Liturgical Life of the Orthodox Church

METROPOLITAN HILARION ALFEYEV

ORTHODOX CHRISTIANITY

Volume IV:
The Worship and
Liturgical Life of
the Orthodox
Church

Translated from the Russian by Andrei Tepper

ST VLADIMIR'S SEMINARY PRESS
YONKERS, NEW YORK 10707
2016

Library of Congress Cataloging-in-Publication Data

Ilarion, Hieromonk.
  [Pravoslavie. English]
  Orthodox Christianity / Metropolitan Hilarion Alfeyev.
    p. cm.
  Includes bibliographical references.
  ISBN 978–0–88141–878–1
    1. Russkaia pravoslavnaia tserkov'—History.   2. Orthodox Eastern Church—Russia
(Federation)—History.   3. Russkaia pravoslavnaia tserkov'—Doctrines.   4. Orthodox
Eastern Church—Russia (Federation)—Doctrines.   5. Russkaia pravoslavnaia tserkov'.
6. Orthodox Eastern Church—Russia (Federation).   I. Title.
  BX485.I4313 2011
  281.9'47—dc22

                                              2011002385

Pravoslavie, Tom II.
originally published by Sretensky Monastery, 2008

ST VLADIMIR'S SEMINARY PRESS
575 Scarsdale Rd, Yonkers, NY 10707
1-800-204-2665
www.svspress.com

ISBN 978-0-88141-552-0

PRINTED IN THE UNITED STATES OF AMERICA

Table of Contents

Preface

THIS IS THE FOURTH VOLUME of a detailed and systematic exposition of the history, canonical structure, doctrine, moral and social teaching, liturgical services, and spiritual life of the Orthodox Church.

The basic idea of this work is to present Orthodox Christianity as an integrated theological and liturgical system—a world view. In this system all elements are interconnected: theology is based on liturgical experience, and the basic characteristics of church art—including icons, singing, and architecture—are shaped by theology and the liturgy. Theology and the services, in their turn, influence the ascetic practice and the personal piety of each Christian. They shape the moral and social teaching of the Church as well as its relation to other Christian confessions, non-Christian religions, and the secular world.

Orthodoxy is traditional and even conservative (we use this term in a positive sense, to emphasize Orthodoxy's reverence for church tradition). The contemporary life of the Orthodox Church is based on its historical experience. Orthodoxy is historic in its very essence: it is deeply rooted in history, which is why it is impossible to understand the uniqueness of the Orthodox Church—its dogmatic teaching and canonical structure, its liturgical system and social doctrine—outside of a historical context. Thus, the reference to history—to the sources—is one of the organizing principles of this book.

This series covers a wide range of themes relating to the history and contemporary life of the Orthodox Church. It contains many quotations from works of the church fathers, liturgical and historical sources, and works of contemporary theologians. Nevertheless, we do not claim to give an exhaustive account of the subjects discussed: this work is not an encyclopedia, a dictionary, or a reference work. It is rather an attempt to understand Orthodoxy in all its diversity, in its historical and contemporary existence—an understanding through the prism of the author's personal perception.

A special feature of these books is that they strive to provide a sufficiently detailed wealth of material. It is addressed to readers who are already acquainted with the basics of Orthodoxy and who desire to deepen their knowledge and, above all, to systematize it.

The first volume focused on the history and canonical structure of the Orthodox Church, and the second volume on the fundamental teachings of the Church, grounded in Scripture and Tradition. The third volume delved into the unique aspects of Orthodox art as expressed in its architecture, icons, and liturgical music.

The current fourth volume is dedicated to the liturgical life of the Orthodox Church in all its variety and richness.[1] The history, structure, and meaning of the Church's liturgical services—including the daily, weekly, yearly, and festal—are explored and explained. Both beginners and experts can benefit from this examination of Orthodox worship and liturgical life. Special attention will be paid to the divine liturgy, which is the heart of Orthodox worship, its true spiritual center.

---

[1]Unfortunately, there is no single standard translation of the services of the Orthodox Church in the English language. For the daily services, the Priest's Service Books published by St. Tikhon's Monastery Press—the *Hieratikon* (2014) and the *Divine Liturgy* book (2013 ed.)—were used, with the publisher's kind permission. Likewise, material from the *The Lenten Triodion* and *The Festal Menaion* were taken from Mother Mary and Met. Kallistos' translations, also published by St. Tikhon's. For texts from the Octoechos, the Pentecostarion, and parts of the Menaion not found in *The Festal Menaion*, we often drew upon translations used by the Orthodox Church in America, found in the liturgical booklets published by the Department of Religious Education (now republished by SVS Press), or used the working translation heard in the Three Hierarch's Chapel at St Vladimir's Seminary. In several instances, SVS Press commissioned new translations, which were produced by Fr John Mikitish for the present volume.—*Ed.*

PART ONE

CERTAIN FEATURES OF WORSHIP
IN THE ORTHODOX CHURCH

W ORSHIP IS SO IMPORTANT in the life of the Orthodox Church that many
non-Orthodox Christians associate Orthodoxy mainly with liturgical
services, singing, and icons. Protopresbyter John Meyendorff wrote:

> In our day millions of people are being nourished spiritually by Orthodox wor-
> ship. Very many . . . in the West . . . are beginning to understand Orthodoxy
> through the liturgical tradition not only of the Christian East, but also of the
> ancient Christian West. They are finding in Orthodox worship a connection
> with the apostolic faith of the first centuries of Christendom and the experience
> of the coming kingdom of God. It is for this reason that we Orthodox must
> preserve worship not only as a necessary link with the past, but also as a living

9

testimony of the faith. We need both a good knowledge of the history of this testimony as well as a theological and spiritual experience of the core of prayer in the Church—in which the past, present, and future are united in the life of the body of Christ.[1]

In terms of content, length of services, and theological richness, Orthodox worship differs noticeably from worship in non-Orthodox Christian communities, both Protestant and Catholic. Even outward distinctions are plain to see. For example, modern-day Protestant worship is generally a series of disjointed, unrelated prayer actions. First, a clergyman utters a benediction; everyone then opens a book to a certain page and sings a particular hymn; later, following a break, a minister delivers a sermon; then a prayer is read and someone plays the organ. Parishioners generally sit and only occasionally stand—for a short time before sitting down again. Worship services may be accompanied by a clergyman's explanations, such as where (in what book and on what page) a particular hymn can be found, and whether the hymn ought to be sung while sitting or standing. Many worship services last about thirty or forty minutes. In some Protestant communities rock music is performed during the services.

After the liturgical reforms of the Second Vatican Council, worship in many Catholic churches differs little from Protestant worship. It is marked by the same absence of wholeness and the same alternation of unconnected, unrelated prayers and hymns.

Things are done differently in the Orthodox Church. From the very first exclamation of every service—be it the divine liturgy, vespers, matins, the hours, the midnight office, or compline—the faithful are immersed in an environment of prayer, interrupted by nothing. Psalms, litanies, troparia, prayers, and the priest's exclamations—these elements follow one another uninterrupted. The entire service takes place in one breath as an integrated and constantly unfolding mystery. Everything is carried out in the same rhythm and nothing takes away from prayer. Byzantine liturgical texts, rich in profound theological and mystical content, alternate with the prayerful breathing of the psalms. Even those elements of "choreography" that are characteristic of Orthodox divine services—the ceremonious entrances and processions, prostrations, and censing—are intended not to divert the attention of the faithful but, on the contrary, to establish the faithful in a prayerful mood and to

---

[1]John Meyendorff, *Pravoslavie v sovremennom mire* [Orthodoxy in the contemporary world] (Moscow: Izdatel'skoe predpriiatie Put', 1997), 240–241. Previously published as in English as *Orthodoxy in the Contemporary World* (New York, NY: Chalidze Publications, 1981).

draw them into that *theourgia*[2] in which not only the earthly Church participates, but the heavenly Church as well—not only people, but also angels.

WORSHIP AND THEOLOGY

The divine service texts used in the Orthodox Church were written, for the most part, in great antiquity—roughly between the third and seventh centuries. Many of these texts are so replete with profound theological content and interspersed with so many biblical allusions that their meaning may be extremely difficult to grasp for contemporary people who do not have any special training. Some have spoken in favor of simplifying worship with a liturgical reform, while some have even called for an outright "surgical operation" in Orthodox worship with the goal of updating it to make it more understandable and more in accordance with the mindset of the contemporary person. Not a single local Orthodox Church, however, has deemed it possible to revise the liturgical Typikon, even though in the Church's practical experience, certain essential changes have been made in the Typikon's use (these will be described later). The texts used in Orthodox worship services are both profound and rich in content, even if they are not always understandable and contemporary. For the faithful, the presence of these texts in the divine services helps to make Orthodox worship a veritable school of theology and contemplation of God.

Furthermore, worship in its primordial and unchanged form represents the basic criterion of life in the Church—the criterion of theological development. It is necessary to confirm theology in worship, the liturgy, and the Eucharist. "Our opinion is in accordance with the Eucharist, and the Eucharist in turn establishes our opinion," said Saint Irenaeus of Lyons.[3] The principle of agreement between worship and theology is solidly rooted in the Orthodox consciousness. For this very reason, a theology which is not founded on liturgical experience, or which clearly contradicts this experience, cannot be regarded as truly Orthodox. Similarly,

---

[2]Originally this was a pagan word: "theurgy was a form of religious magic associated with the Chaldean Oracles and taken up by the later Neoplatonists. . . . Theurgy was . . . believed to promote the union of the human soul with the divine." *The Oxford Classical Dictionary*, 3rd ed., Simon Hornblower and Antony Spawforth, eds. (Oxford: Oxford University Press, 1996), 1512. This word was "baptized" and came to refer to the liturgical rites of the Church, which unite God and man. The word appears in the original Greek of the pre-communion prayers, and the related word *hierourgia* appears as a noun and a verb in the priest's prayer before the Cherubic hymn.—*Ed.*

[3]Irenaeus of Lyons, *Against Heresies* 4.18.5 (*ANF* 1:486).

worship that has lost its original theological content ceases to be a criterion of truth for the faithful. Such worship ceases to be a school of theology and contemplation of God.

In his lecture "Concerning the Mutability and Immutability of Orthodox Worship," delivered in 1988, Protopresbyter John Meyendorff put forth three basic principles relating to the connection between worship and theology:

1. *Worship expresses the tradition of the Church*—that is, the confession of the Church's faith in history, in various cultures and epochs. We believe this tradition to be a "holy tradition." It changes through the centuries, yet it remains unchanged in its essence. We ought to perform the divine services in such a way that they always reflect holy tradition. . . .

2. *Worship reflects the unity of the Church*—unity with the patristic past and unity with all those who now confess the same Orthodox faith.

3. *Worship is the witness of conscious faith*: it must not develop separately from theology, faith, teaching or the experience of the fathers.[4]

A rupture between theology and worship has a negative impact on both. Theology, deprived of its primordial liturgical substance, turns into a dry academic science that is disconnected from true spiritual life. Long ago this is what came to be of "professional" theology in both the Catholic and Protestant West. (This process did not fail to affect Orthodox theology, which was under the intermittent influence of both Catholic and Protestant theology in the eighteenth and nineteenth centuries.) Contemporary theologians are categorized in specialized groups: Old or New Testament, patristics, liturgics, history of dogmatics. Generally, the focus of specialization in each group can be narrowed down to a single concrete subject: one scholar may specialize in the study of a particular father of the Church or the teaching of a certain period in the life of that Church father. As a result, scientific theological literature is not written for the public at large, nor the community of the Church, but for the same limited circle of specialists engaged in studying similar questions. A theologian may write a book for what may be, in the best case, a few hundred people similar to himself. The book then occupies a place on the shelves of specialized libraries and does not exercise any influence on the life of the Church. Exceptions to this rule are quite rare.

---

[4]Meyendorff, *Orthodoxy*, 245.

Inevitably, the break between worship and theology, between *lex orandi* and *lex credendi*, has a most pernicious effect on the course of liturgical life. Wherever "worship ceases to be fed by the living Tradition of the Church," there arises an "amnesia of liturgical customs and a loss of understanding of their meaning."[5] The preservation of liturgical forms—while lacking an understanding of their content—has especially taken place in certain "priestless" Old-Rite communities.

But the detachment of worship from true Orthodox theological tradition may have the opposite effect as well: worship may become subject to mutations that fundamentally distort its essence and render it unrecognizable. This process takes place in Protestant communities in which theology underwent a radical transformation and essentially departed from original Christian tradition. In some Protestant communities worship is adapted to accommodate a particular group of the faithful. For example, there are feminist services with specially composed texts. In this case, *lex orandi* may be in full agreement with *lex credendi*, but the *lex credendi* itself is the result of a major "surgical operation" on the very substance of Christian Tradition. And

Sinai Euchologion (Service Book)—Glagolitic Old Slavonic Manuscript. 13th c.

this operation comes not so much from within the church community as from outside of it—from the secular world in which the feminist movement was born and grew.

It seems that the Orthodox tradition is securely protected from such phenomena because it possesses a large enough number of "defense mechanisms" which do not allow outside forces to encroach upon its liturgical practice. These mechanisms were effective in those cases when there were attempts to introduce into the Church erroneous or heretical opinions under the guise of the revision of liturgical texts. For example, Nestorianism arose from the proposal of replacing the commonly-used term "Theotokos" with what Nestorius considered to be a more logical term—"Christotokos." When this proposal was made, one of the Church's defense mechanisms snapped into action: Orthodox people were indignant. Later, another mechanism was set in motion: theologians took part in discussing the problem. Finally, an ecumenical council was called (in AD 431). It turned out that a dangerous christological heresy was concealed behind this seemingly innocuous

---

[5]Ibid., 240.

"surgical operation" in the practice of the Church's worship—a heresy which was condemned by the council.

Orthodox worship is precious in this way. It gives a definite criterion of theological truth. And it is necessary to confirm theology with worship, not to correct worship on some kind of theological premise. *Lex credendi* springs from *lex orandi*, and dogmas are "God-revealing" for the very reason that dogmas were born in prayer and were revealed to the Church through worship.

LITURGICAL LANGUAGES

Certain obsolete languages are used in the worship of some local Orthodox churches while worship in other churches are conducted in contemporary languages. In the Greek Church the so-called "Byzantine Greek" language is used, which is similar to the language of the New Testament and profoundly different from conversational modern Greek. The Georgian Church uses the Old Georgian language which has been recorded using a special script called *khutsuri*.[6] Worship in the Russian Orthodox Church is conducted in the Church Slavonic language. In the past, the Serbian and Bulgarian Churches also used the Slavonic language, but in the last decades of the twentieth century both Churches changed to the use of contemporary languages—Serbian and Bulgarian, respectively.

The use of the Church Slavonic language in the worship of the Russian Church can be traced back to the holy enlighteners and brothers Cyril and Methodius, who produced translations in Slavic countries in the ninth century. Following the baptism of Rus' by the holy equal-to-the-apostles Prince Vladimir at the end of the tenth century, the systematic translation of Byzantine liturgical texts into the Slavonic language began. Translation and editing continued right up to the twelfth century. The corpus of Greek liturgical texts was completely translated into the Slavonic language over the course of centuries.

The "literal method" was used in the process of translating. This method allowed for the preservation not only of words, but also of the syntax in which they appear in a sentence. In Byzantine poetic texts, word order was stipulated by the need to conform to a particular meter; due to this fact, words often traded places. Furthermore, words were sometimes chosen not for their meaning but for their

---

[6]At the present time, liturgical texts in the Old Georgian language are published using the civilian script called *mkhedruli*, which is similar to the case in Russia, where Church Slavonic texts are often printed using Russian letters.

mutual rhythmic agreement. As a result, in some cases the impression was given of an arbitrary selection of words. In this poetic speech, clarity of meaning and correctness of a phrase's construction could be sacrificed for the sake of phonetic euphony and the rhythmic harmony of the verse. When translated into another language, the poetry was transformed into prose, euphony disappeared, and the rhythm was broken, while the absence of logic in the phrase's construction and the unnatural word order was preserved. This all creates the impression that Slavonic texts are difficult to understand, exceedingly pompous, and complicated.

The use of an obsolete language in the divine services is a subject of controversy that has continued within the Russian Church for more than one hundred years. And among both clergy and laity there are those who favor the preservation of the Church Slavonic language as something untouchable and those who favor translating the divine services into the Russian language. There are also those who call for a partial replacement of Church Slavonic texts with Russian texts, or a new edition of the divine services books which would make Slavonic liturgical texts easier to understand.

Slavonic-Greek Text of Service to Holy Great Martyr Panteleimon. Mount Athos. Middle of 14th c.

The question of liturgical language was widely discussed during the preparations for the Local Council of 1917–1918. By that time the problem of difficulty in comprehending the divine services was already very acute. Archbishop Tikhon of the Aleutian Islands and North America (later Patriarch of All Russia) wrote in 1906: "For the Russian Church it is important to have a new Slavonic translation of the divine service books (the one we have now has grown old and in many instances is incorrect), by which it may be possible to forestall the demands of others to serve in the Russian vernacular language."[8] Another hierarch, Bishop Seraphim of Polotsk, also spoke of the need to improve the Slavonic translation in the worship services:

> In polemics with the Catholic Church, Orthodox theologians always make mention of our worship as one of the advantages of the Orthodox Church in view of its ability to edify the faithful. But in practice it hardly achieves this purpose for which it was created by the grace-filled bearers of Orthodoxy. The

[8] *Responses from the diocesan hierarchs on the question of church reform* [in Russian] (St. Petersburg: Sinodal'naia tip., 1906), pt. 1, 530.

reason for this lies primarily in the fact that it is not understood by the majority of the faithful. In view of this, it is necessary first of all to improve the language of worship, to make it clearer and understandable in its individual words and constructions.[9]

An "experimental" publication of newly edited liturgical texts in the Slavonic language was made and published with a small circulation not long before the Local Council of 1917–1918, but it never reached the majority of Orthodox Churches. The discussion about liturgical language undertaken at the Council also remained unconcluded. The events which followed are well-known: the attempts of reformers to Russify the divine services and the rejection of these attempts by the church community. Similar attempts in our own day are decisively halted by the faithful, who stand as guardians of the Church Slavonic language as of a bulwark of churchliness.

Nevertheless, the problem of the Church Slavonic language being difficult to understand continues to await a solution. While it is just to speak of the necessity of preserving Church Slavonic, it is also evident that worship services are meant to be understood to the fullest extent possible; otherwise they lose their ability to edify the faithful. But at the same time, special care and attention is required when initiating any changes to the existing liturgical practice, including the translation or editing of the liturgical texts. It is worth remembering that a new edition of the Slavonic texts of the divine services was precisely one of the causes of the emergence of the Old Rite schism in the seventeenth century, which gripped millions of Russian people and persists to this day. The conservative nature of the Church's consciousness must be considered, as well as the fact that the practice of using particular texts, expressions, and phrases has endured for many centuries, even though they are not understood by all.

Moreover, the issue is not limited to the mere translation of the liturgical texts into Russian or of a new edition of the Slavonic texts. The task set before the Russian Orthodox Church and especially its theologians is more global in nature. This task was formulated by His Holiness Patriarch of Moscow Alexei II:

> The Church Slavonic language is not understood by all: for this reason the question has stood before many liturgists of our Church concerning the translation of the entire cycle of liturgical texts into Russian. But attempts to translate the worship services into modern Russian have shown that the issue is not limited

[9]Ibid., pt. 1, 148.

to the replacement of one lexicon with another, of one set of grammatical forms with others. The liturgical texts used in the Orthodox Church are the inheritance of Byzantine antiquity: even translated into a modern language, they require of a person a special preparedness. . . . Therefore the problem of the divine services being unintelligible is not limited to the question of language, which undoubtedly must be considered and resolved. Set before us is a more global and truly missionary task: to teach people to understand the meaning of worship.[10]

One of the means of fulfilling this missionary task is a new edition of the Slavonic texts of the divine services. The work begun on the eve of the Local Council of 1917–1918 should be continued. His Holiness Patriarch Alexei II spoke concerning this:

> . . . We should think about an organization of the Church's liturgical life that would give new impetus to the didactic and missionary element of this life. In this connection we pay special attention to the work that was begun but left unfinished by the Local Council of 1917–1918 in putting liturgical practices in good order, and complete the editorial process of the Slavonic liturgical texts, also begun in our Church.[11]

It is obviously necessary to pose the question of whether or not it is acceptable to use the Russian language for at least some parts of the worship services, in particular, for the readings from the gospel, the book of epistles, and the Psalter. The Local Council of 1917–1918, in the results of its discussions concerning the use of the Russian and Ukrainian languages during the divine services, made the following recommendation:

> 1. The Slavonic language used during the divine services is a great and sacred inheritance passed down to us by our native, ecclesiastic antiquity, and for this reason it should be preserved and supported as the basic language of our worship services;

> 2. In order to bring the worship of the Church closer to the understanding of ordinary people, the right to use the Great Russian language and Small Russian languages during services is recognized;

---

[10]Aleksii II, "Concerning the mission of the Russian Orthodox Church in the contemporary world" [in Russian], *Church and Time* 4 (1998): 8–14, at 12.

[11]Ibid., at 13.

3. The immediate and universal replacement of the Church Slavonic language during divine services by the Great Russian or Small Russian languages is neither desirable nor possible to implement;

4. The partial application of the Great Russian language and Small Russian languages in the divine services (the reading of the word of God and individual hymns and prayers, the replacement of individual words and phrases, etc.) to allow for a greater understanding of the divine services, approved by the ecclesiastical authorities, is desirable at the present time.[12]

Moreover, an understanding of the worship services by the faithful would be made significantly easier if booklets containing the main liturgical texts in the Slavonic language, with a parallel Russian translation and explanations, could be freely obtained in every church. In this way it is necessary to create a text of the divine liturgy, the texts of the all-night vigil, the major Christian feasts, the rites[13] of baptism, matrimony, and other sacraments. Churches should have such texts in large numbers so that every person desiring to know the meaning of the worship service might be able to follow the service by reading the booklet.

LITURGICAL CEREMONY: HIERARCHICAL SERVICES

Orthodox worship differs from non-Orthodox worship not only in its duration and theological richness, but also in its rich liturgical ceremony. Some people consider this ceremony outdated, that it does not correspond with the present day and requires simplification. The splendor of the Orthodox ritual is contrasted with the simplicity and clarity of Protestant worship. Some people consider the hierarchical services in the Orthodox Church overly pompous. But the Orthodox Church does not undertake any reforms that would simplify the liturgical ritual or make the hierarchical service less festive. Quite the opposite: Orthodox tradition conveys the understanding that, while a hierarch may be humble and unpretentious in everyday life, in the performance of the worship services he should be presented in all the grandeur of his hierarchical rank. As such, liturgical attributes—such as expensive vestments, precious stones on the mitre or *zhezl*, dikirion and trikirion—are

---

[12]Cited in Nikolai Balashov, *On the path towards a liturgical rebirth* [in Russian] (Moscow: Kruglyi stol po religioznomu obrazovaniiu i diakonii, 2001), 153.

[13]The term "rite" signifies the combination of both prayers and liturgical actions that make up a given worship service or sacrament.

perceived as relating not to the person of the hierarch, but exclusively to his lofty rank.

All artificiality is foreign to Orthodox worship. There is nothing and must be nothing theatrical or merely entertaining. The rites of the hierarchical services were developed in detail and are not meant to entertain the faithful or distract them from prayer; rather, on the contrary, they are meant to draw the faithful into the "theourgic" mystery of the heavenly Eucharist. In Orthodox worship everything is symbolic, iconic, and significant: not only the iconostasis and the liturgical singing, but also the entire liturgical rite, the whole ceremony. At the little entrance, when the subdeacons, deacons, and other clergy exit the sanctuary one after another, carrying candles, staff, dikirion, trikirion, and fans, and the hierarch at that time prays to God with the words, "Grant that with our entrance there may be an entrance of holy angels, serving with us and glorifying Thy goodness," this entire liturgical procession is an iconic, symbolic depiction of that magnificent, rapt, and pious procession of angels that accompanies the King of glory in heaven. The same is the case during the great entrance when "the King of kings and the Lord of

Set of Hierarch's Vestments. Belonged to Patriarch Sergius (Stragorodsky).

lords comes to be slain, to give Himself as food to the faithful. Before Him go the ranks of angels: all the principalities and powers; the many-eyed cherubim and the six-winged seraphim. . . ."[14] The "ranks of angels" are symbolized by the subdeacons, deacons and priests who enter into the sanctuary to perform the bloodless service.

The grandeur of the hierarchical service in the Orthodox Church was inherited from the Byzantine cathedral liturgies and retained several elements of the Constantinopolitan imperial ritual. Even so, the hierarchical service is based on a liturgical order that is older than Byzantium and more ancient than Constantinople, and which dates back to the first centuries of the Church's existence:

[14]This is sung in place of the Cherubic hymn on Great and Holy Saturday, and in the Liturgy of Saint James.—*Ed.*

When the liturgy is performed by a bishop, the people gather in the church first and are already there to greet him when he enters, the vesting takes place amidst the congregation, the bishop does not proceed to the altar until the little entrance and, finally, the prosthesis is, as it were, repeated just before the offertory—i.e., what we now term the "great entrance." It would be wrong to suppose that all this arose as the result of a special "solemnity" being attached to the pontifical service, which we sometimes hear in the protests of proponents of a "primitive Christian simplicity." On the contrary . . . the pontifical service goes much further in preserving the form and spirit of the early Eucharistic practice, because in the early Church it was precisely the bishop who customarily presided over the eucharistic assembly.[15]

To this it may be added that the hierarchical service is in itself a liturgical school for those who participate in it, especially for subdeacons. Before every service they are required to iron the hierarch's vestments carefully and prepare the dikirion and trikirion as well as other sacred objects and to prepare for the arrival of the hierarch. All of this is a part of the sacred service—a type of subdeacons' proskomedia. The overall mood and impression created upon the faithful depends to a great extent on the performance of the subdeacons during the hierarchical service. In no way are subdeacons to be considered the hierarch's servants—rather, they serve God on high. Subdeacons, as well as the hierarch and the faithful, must bear this fact in mind. An attitude of servility to the hierarch, as if to a "boss," must be completely replaced with a new attitude: above all, subdeacons must learn a pious attitude towards God, the Church, and the altar. The hierarch must not be a demanding and faultfinding boss to his subdeacons, but rather a father and teacher. Thanks to him and through their common service to God—and not mere subservience—they enter into the mystical depths of the liturgy and commune in the sacraments of the kingdom of God.

The Church Calendar

The liturgical year of the Orthodox Church is based on two calendars—solar and lunar. The dates of the fixed feasts are determined according to the solar calendar, while the dates of the movable feasts are determined according to the lunar calendar.

---

[15] Alexander Schmemann, *The Eucharist: Sacrament of the Kingdom*, trans. Paul Kachur (Crestwood, NY: St Vladimir's Seminary Press, 1987), 16.

At the present time in the Orthodox Church one may encounter the use of three calendar styles. In the overwhelming majority of parishes of the Russian Orthodox Church (excluding some parishes in Western Europe) the Julian calendar is in effect. This is the calendar used in the Jerusalem Church, Georgian Church, and Serbian Church, and also on the holy Mount Athos. In other Local Orthodox Churches the so-called new Julian calendar—or revised Gregorian calendar—is used. In this way the date of Pascha is calculated on the basis of the Julian calendar in all the Orthodox Churches with the exception of the Church of Finland, in which the western date of Easter is accepted.

The Julian calendar, named after Julius Caesar, was developed by a group of Alexandrian astronomers headed by Sosigenes and introduced in the Roman Empire in 45 BC. According to this calendar a year comprises 365 days, but each fourth year becomes a leap year and an additional day is added to it. In this way, the average duration of a Julian year is 365 and a quarter days (i.e., 365 days and 6 hours), which is approximately 11 minutes and 46 seconds more than the actual solar (astronomical) year.[16] The imprecision of the Julian calendar adds up to an entire day once in approximately every 128 years. The error of the Julian calendar presently comprises nearly thirteen days, and by the year 2100 it will comprise fourteen days and grow larger in the future.

A new calendar was introduced in the year 1582 by Pope Gregory XII of Rome and was given the name Gregorian. The reason given for its creation was the merging of the vernal equinox, according to which the date of Pascha was determined. In order to reduce the inexactitude of the calendar, ten days were skipped (from the fifth through the fourteenth of October) in 1582. Also, a new scheme was devised to determine the leap year: every fourth year was to be considered a leap year, if it *was not* divisible by 100, or if it *was* divisible by 400.[17] The error of the Gregorian calendar compared to the solar year comprises approximately one day every 3,280 years.

The Orthodox Church at first sharply rejected the reform of the Gregorian calendar. But the question of the calendar's reform was newly examined in Constantinople in the 1920s. In 1922 the Yugoslavian geophysicist Milutin Milanković proposed a calendar system that was named the "revised Julian" calendar. The error of the new Julian calendar was even less than the error of the Gregorian calendar,

---

[16]The solar year is equal to 365.242199 days (365 days, 5 hours, 48 minutes and 46 seconds). The length of the solar year conforms to the gap between two successive passings of the sun through the point of the vernal equinox.

[17]In this way, the years 1700, 1800, 1900 were not leap years, but the year 2000 was.

comprising less than two seconds per year.[18] A discrepancy of one day accumulates about once every 43,500 years. The revised Julian calendar, or "new calendar," will concur with the Gregorian calendar until the year 2800, after which a discrepancy of one day will occur.

Milanković's calendar was approved in May–June of 1923 at the so-called "Pan-Orthodox Congress," which was chaired by the patriarch of Constantinople, Meletius IV (Metaxakis).[19] The congress decreed: (1) to switch from the Julian calendar to the "revised Julian" calendar, eliminating thirteen days, and (2) to use true astronomical data for the Jerusalem meridian for the determination of the paschal full moon.[20]

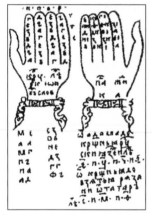

Calendar Tables from the Priest's Service Book of 14th c.

In practice, however, only the first part of the decree was carried out—and this took place neither immediately nor in all Orthodox churches. People switched to the new style in determining the dates of the fixed feasts but preserved the old Alexandrian Paschalion, based on the Julian calendar. According to this Paschalion, the date of Pascha is the first Sunday after the first vernal equinox, as long as that Sunday does not coincide with the Jewish Passover or come before it.[21]

The mechanical superimposition of the old Paschalion onto the new calendar resulted in a breach of the relationship between the fixed and movable liturgical cycles formulated in the Orthodox Typikon. An evident sign of this disparity is the reduction—and in some years the complete disappearance—of the Apostles' Fast.[22] By preserving the new Julian calendar together with the Alexandrian Paschalion, the feast of the Nativity of Christ may fall during Great Lent sometime in the future (although, it is true, it will take approximately five thousand years for this to happen).

---

[18]The average length of a year according to the new Julian calendar is 365.242222 days.

[19]Actually the congress was not "pan-Orthodox" since, besides the representatives of the Patriarchate of Constantinople, only representatives of the Churches of Greece, Serbia, and Romania participated.

[20]Liverii Voronov, "The calendar problem" [in Russian], *Theological Writings* 7 (1971): 170–203, at 175.

[21]Concerning the Orthodox Paschalion, see, in particular, D. P. Ogitskii, "Canonical norms of the Orthodox Easter computation and the problem of the dating of Pascha in our time" [in Russian], *Theological Writings* 7 (1971): 201–211; Voronov, "The Calendar Problem," 177–203.

[22]According to the current Greek edition of the Typikon, if the Apostles' Fast is reduced to nothing or even a negative number, it must still be observed: the Feast of Saints Peter and Paul is transferred to the Week of All Saints and the fast begins on the Wednesday following Pentecost.

Following the "Pan-Orthodox Congress" of 1923, the Churches of Constantinople, Greece, and Romania switched to the New Calendar. Later, the Churches of Alexandria, Antioch, Bulgaria, Cyprus, and Albania joined them.[23] The Churches of Jerusalem, Georgia, and Serbia preserved the Old Calendar.

The Russian Church also preserved the Old Calendar, but an attempt to introduce the New Calendar took place in 1923 by the decision of His Holiness Patriarch Tikhon and the Patriarch's Synod of September 23, 1923 (Old Style) (in the New Style, October 7). On October 1 (O.S.) (October 14, N.S.), Patriarch Tikhon issued an encyclical in which the reasons for this decision were given:

> Having examined together with our God-favored bishops the decree of the Ecumenical Patriarch with great attention and, with discussion from all sides, acknowledging that the ecclesial calculation of time decreed by him: (1) is introduced by legal ecclesial authority; (2) in no way affects the dogmas and sacred canons of the Orthodox Church; (3) leaves the celebration of the day of Holy Pascha, according to the decree of the First Ecumenical Council, on the first Sunday following the first full-moon after the vernal equinox, i.e. later than the Jewish Passover; (4) is in precise agreement with the data of contemporary astronomical science; (5) is not an introduction of the western Gregorian calendar but merely a revision of the old Paschalion with the calculation of the days of Pascha according to the time of the mother of God's churches—the Jerusalem Church, and (6) it is necessary and convenient for Russian ecclesial life to agree with the calculation of time already decreed in our own country and in all Christian countries; we and our bishops unanimously decree: first, to skip in time the calculation of thirteen days so that following October 1 of the Old Style instead of October 2 the day will be October 15 and (2) the issue of time of the celebration of Holy Pascha is to be decided in agreement with the Orthodox churches according to the decrees of the Pan-Orthodox Meeting that took place in this year in Constantinople. Informing our God-protected Orthodox flock of this our decree, we appeal to all the beloved in the Lord archpastors and pastors and faithful laymen to accept this revision of the ecclesial calendar without any confusion or hesitation.[24]

---

[23]I. Z. Iakimchuk, " 'All-Orthodox Congress' "[in Russian], in *Orthodox Encyclopedia*, vol. 9 (Moscow: Tserkovno-nauchnyi tsentr "Pravoslavnaia entsiklopediia," 2005), 683.

[24]"Epistle of Patriarch Tikhon to the Orthodox people concerning the reform of the calendar in the Russian Orthodox Church" [in Russian], in *Investigatory matter of Patriarch Tikhon: Collection of documents* (Moscow: PSTBI, 2000), 361–362.

But a little more than a month later a new patriarchal order followed, in which it was explained that "by circumstances outside of our control, the encyclical concerning the introduction of a new calculation of time was released only at the beginning of November, when the convenient time for transitioning to the New Style had already passed." According to the patriarch, "at the time of the printing of the encyclical, it became known that other Orthodox Churches, with which the Russian Church always must be in union, temporarily postponed the introduction of the New Style. Therefore, we too considered it necessary to postpone the universal and mandatory introduction into ecclesial usage of the New Style."[25]

His Holiness Patriarch Tikhon made the decision to repeal the decree on the transition to the New Calendar due to numerous protests of the faithful, as he himself later explained in his statement of September 30, 1924.[26] The saint's prudence concerning this issue and his desire not to instigate a conflict within the Church were the more justified by the fact that, in some local Orthodox churches that transitioned to the New Calendar, a broad movement protesting the decision resulted after the meeting in Constantinople in 1923. In Greece the protest grew into the Old Calendarist schism, which endures to the present day.[27]

The issue of calendar reform was also raised at the conference of heads and representatives of the local Orthodox churches that was held in Moscow in 1948. The conference decreed that (1) the celebration of Pascha must universally take place according to the Old Calendar and according to the Alexandrian Paschalion; (2) for the fixed feasts, each autocephalous Church may use the calendar style being used by that Church, and (3) clergy and laymen must follow the style of the Local Church in which they find themselves.[28]

In practice, however, it is possible at the present time for two calendar styles to coexist not only within a single Local Church, but even within a single diocese, and even a single parish.[29]

[25]"Order of Patriarch Tikhon to repeal the decree introducing the new calendar style into ecclesial use" [in Russian], in *Investigatory matter*, 362–363.

[26]Balashov, "Towards a liturgical rebirth," 334.

[27]See Volume One, pp. 164–166.

[28]*Acts of the Conference of heads and representatives of the Autocephalous Orthodox Churches in connection with the celebration of 500 years of autocephaly of the Russian Orthodox Church, 8–18 July 1948* [in Russian] (Moscow: Moskovskaia Patriarkhiia, 1948), 2:432–433.

[29]An example of the coexistence of two calendar styles in a single local church is the Patriarchate of Constantinople, which follows the New Calendar but includes Mount Athos, on which the Old Calendar is in effect. Two calendar styles are in effect also in the Orthodox Church of the Czech Lands and Slovakia, as well as in the Orthodox Church in America. The Hungarian Diocese of the Moscow Patriarchate serves as an example of the coexistence of two styles in a single diocese: Hungarian parishes (which have been a part of

The coexistence of two calendar styles most certainly creates discomfort. The main discomfort is that the fixed feasts are celebrated by Orthodox Christians at different times and, correspondingly, fasting periods do not coincide. While some have celebrated Christmas on December 25, others continue to fast until January 7. Emperor Constantine wrote to the fathers of the First Ecumenical Council in 325: "Reflect how grievous and scandalous it is that on the self-same days some should be engaged in fasting, others in festive enjoyment."[30] During Constantine's time the given situation was created by a difference in the date of celebrating Pascha, and the emperor's words concerned Great Lent. At present all Orthodox (with the exception of the Church of Finland) observe Great Lent at the same time. Other fasts, however, do not coincide: for those who follow the New Calendar, the Nativity and Dormition fasts begin and end thirteen days earlier than for those who follow the Old Calendar, while the Apostles' Fast, though beginning on the same day, ends thirteen days earlier.

In the contemporary Orthodox Church there are opponents and apologists for both the Old and New Calendars. The main argument in support of the New Calendar is its greater accuracy in relation to the solar year. The main argument in support of the Old Calendar is the fact that it was used during apostolic times and became the main calendar of the Christian Church from the moment of its creation. Many even maintain that the Julian calendar is "ecclesial" while the Gregorian calendar is "secular," but it is obvious that the Julian calendar in itself does not possess any sacred characteristics. At the same time, it is no less obvious that the introduction of the New Calendar at the price of a schism, as occurred in Greece, cannot be justified. The unity of the Church must stand higher than the issue of the calendar, whose resolution may be postponed for as many years or even centuries as is needed to ensure peace and harmony of thought within each local Orthodox Church.

---

the Russian Orthodox Church since 1950) preserved the New Calendar, introduced earlier in the 1920s, while Russian parishes celebrate the divine services according to the Old Calendar. Examples of the coexistence of two calendar styles in a single parish are the Dormition Cathedral in Budapest (where divine services in the Hungarian language are performed according to the New Calendar, while services in Slavonic are performed according to the Old Calendar) and the Orthodox church in Oxford (where the Greek community uses the New Calendar while Russians use the Old Calendar.)

[30]Eusebius Pamphilius, *Life of Constantine* 3.18 (*NPNF²* 1:525). Cf. Socrates Scholasticus, *Church History* 1.9 (*NPNF²* 2:15); Theodoret of Cyrus, *Ecclesiastical History* 1.9 (*NPNF²* 3:48).

LITURGICAL CYCLES AND LITURGICAL BOOKS

Priest's Service Book. Serbian Edition. c. 1624.

At the root of the Orthodox liturgical cycle is the notion of the combination of four liturgical cycles, each of which was formed over the course of many centuries: the daily, weekly, annual fixed, and annual movable cycles. Like the wheels of a mechanical clock, these cycles regulate the liturgical time of the Orthodox Church.[31]

The daily cycle includes the divine services of the midnight office, matins, first, third, sixth, and ninth hours, vespers, compline, and the divine liturgy. The major liturgical books used in performing these orders are the *Horologion* and the *Priest's Service Book*. They contain the main framework of each of the services, including the prayers and hymns that remain unchangeable during each day throughout the year. Into this framework texts and hymns are added from other books, depending on the combination of a specific day with other liturgical cycles. For the hierarchical service a book called the *Chinovnik* [Gr. *Archieratikon*] is used, which contains the texts of liturgies, as well as the order for ordinations, the consecration of temples, and other sacred services performed by a hierarch.

The weekly[32] cycle of worship is regulated by the *Octoechos*. The basis of the Octoechos is a system in which worship is divided into eight tones (the system of the eight tones). Each of the tones represents a collection of texts and also a special collection of melodic formulae used to sing the texts. One tone is heard during the course of a single week, while a new tone is heard during the next week, and so on. At the end of the eighth week, the cycle of eight tones begins anew.

The fixed yearly cycle, oriented on the solar calendar, includes feasts and commemorations of saints which occur every year on the same day. In particular, the Nativity of Christ, Theophany, the Meeting of the Lord, Transfiguration, and the Nativity and Dormition of the Most-Holy Theotokos are numbered among the great feasts of the fixed yearly cycle. For the majority of saints the dates of commemoration are also fixed. The divine services of the fixed yearly cycle are regulated

---

[31] See Mary Cunningham, *Faith in the Byzantine World* (Downers Growe, IL: InterVarsity Press, 2002), 112–113.

[32] The Slavonic is "*sedmichny*" from the Slavonic word "*sedmitsa*" meaning "week."

by the *Festal Menaion* and the *Service Menaia* (in twelve volumes according to the months of the year).

The movable yearly cycle, oriented on the lunar calendar, incorporates the entire cycle of worship services comprising Great Lent, the feast of the Entrance of the Lord into Jerusalem, and Holy Week, as well as the entire paschal cycle—including the feasts of Pascha (the Resurrection of Christ), the Ascension of the Lord, and Pentecost. The texts of the divine services of Great Lent and Holy Week are contained in the *Lenten Triodion*, and the texts of the services for the paschal cycle are in the *Pentecostarion*.

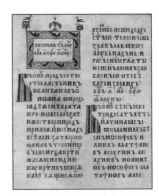

Aprakos Gospel. Rostov (?). 1220s.

There are also cycles for the reading of Scripture in church. These cycles govern the fixed readings of the sacred books of the Old and New Testaments. The book read most often in church is the Psalter. Aside from the fact that every divine service includes the reading of certain psalms, the entire Psalter ought to be read each week over the course of the divine services. During Great Lent, the Psalter ought to be read twice per week.

The four Gospels are read in their entirety during the divine liturgy over the course of each year. With this goal in mind, the gospel is divided into pericopes— small, thematically coherent passages. The reading of the Gospel according to John begins at the liturgy on

Illuminated Psalter. Bulgaria. 3rd quarter of 14th c.

the first day of Pascha and ends at the liturgy on the feast of Pentecost. During the period from Pentecost to the Exaltation of the Cross, the Gospel according to Matthew is read; from the Exaltation to the weeks preceding Great Lent, the Gospel according to Luke is read. During Great Lent, the Gospel according to Mark is read.

Furthermore, every other book of the New Testament, with the exception of Revelation, is read during the course of each year. The primary books of the Old Testament read in church are Genesis, the Book of Job, and the Wisdom of Solomon, which are read during Great Lent. Moreover, other readings from the Old Testament, selected for their special thematic content, are read on certain feast days.

Heirmologion with Notation.
Old Russian Edition.
Beginning of 8th c.

Jerusalem Typikon.
Mount Athos. c. 1372.

The number of passages read at a given service ranges from three to fifteen.

The worship services of any given day are constructed by taking into account both the cycles of liturgical services and the cycles of readings from sacred Scripture, which have been described. So, for example, if the commemoration of a certain saint were to fall on a Thursday, the divine service would be composed from the Horologion, the services of the Octoechos (for Thursday in the tone of the week in which the saint's commemoration falls), and the monthly Menaion (which contains texts for the divine service in honor of the saint). Further, there may be two readings from the Book of Epistles and the Gospel Book: one "ordinary" reading, called for by the calendar date for the given day, and another, dedicated to the celebrated saint. For example, should the feast of the Annunciation of the Most-Holy Theotokos coincide with one of the days of Great Lent, in addition to the Horologion, the Gospel Book, and the Book of Epistles, the Menaion (which contains the service for the Annunciation) and the Lenten Triodion (which contains the service for the given day of Great Lent) are also necessary to compile the divine services for the feast. The rules governing the combination of separate services are contained in the Typikon.

PART TWO

Worship Services of the Daily Cycle

Formation of the Daily Liturgical Cycle

W E MUST LOOK FOR THE ORIGINS of Christian worship in the daily and weekly cycles of temple and synagogue worship at the time of Jesus Christ. It has already been stated that it was Jesus' custom to attend the synagogue on Sabbath days; moreover, no less than once per year, he participated in the temple worship in Jerusalem together with his disciples on the feast of Passover.

THE MYSTICAL SUPPER

Hebrew Priest Pouring Oil into the Menorah (Seven-branched Candelabrum). Miniature. 13th c.

The Mystical Supper, celebrated by Christ on the eve of his death on the cross, was a special, unique, and fateful event in the life of the disciples. It was precisely this paschal meal—at which Christ broke bread and shared with his disciples the cup of wine—which became the basis of eucharistic worship in the early Christian community. Moreover, the entire liturgical life of the Church came to grow steadily around the celebration of the Eucharist.

The Book of Exodus relates to us how the paschal supper was carried out during the time of Christ (see Ex 12.1–20). It describes how God ordained the feast of Passover, and lists the basic rules by which the paschal meal ought to be celebrated. The meal is a family dinner that takes place on the fourteenth day of the month of Nissan. The basic food of the paschal meal is the lamb "unblemished, a male of a year old." It must be roasted over a fire and eaten by all the members of the family with unleavened bread and bitter herbs. It must be eaten "in haste"; that is, the members of the family must be girded and shod, with staves in their hands. The paschal celebration that follows the supper should last for seven days, during which time there ought to be no leavened bread in the home.

The first paschal meal was eaten by the Jews right before their flight from Egypt; the meal's "journey" character (staves in hands, sandals on feet, eating "in haste") came to be determined by this fact. After the flight from Egypt, Passover came to be a remembrance of the exodus as the most glorious event in Israel's history. The paschal meal possessed a liturgical character: "One may call it a sacred meal because religious feelings predominated from the beginning of the supper to its conclusion, and traditional festal foods were subjected to a religious idea."[1]

The gospel account of the Mystical Supper (see Mt 26.26–29; Mk 14.22–25; Lk 22.19–20; Jn 13.1–30; 1 Cor 11.23–25) does not contain a clear description of the rite of the paschal meal. This is probably because this rite was well known to all. However, several details of the narrative indicate that the Mystical Supper was indeed the paschal meal. In particular, the Gospels make reference to the preparation of the paschal meal (see Mt 26.19; Mk 14.16; Lk 22.13), the blessing before eating the bread, the breaking of bread (see Mk 14.22; Mt 26.27; Lk 22.17), the dipping of a piece of bread into a sauce of bitter herbs (see Jn 13.26), and the singing of a psalm at the conclusion of the meal (see Mt 26.30; Mk 14.26)

A special point of interest is the question of the divergence between the synoptic Gospels and the Gospel according to John, regarding the exact time of the celebration of Passover. According to the synoptic Gospels, the Mystical Supper took place "on the first day of Unleavened Bread, when they killed the Passover lamb" (Mk 14.12; see Mt 26.17; Lk 22.7), that is, on the fourteenth day of Nissan. But John says that the meal took place "before the Feast of the Passover" (Jn 13.1) and that Jesus was arrested on the eve of the Passover and he was brought to the trial before Pilate in the morning on the day of the Passover; for this very reason the Jews did not enter into the Praetorium so as to not defile themselves and so as to eat the Passover (see Jn 18.28). This divergence lay at the basis of a dispute concerning the days of Unleavened Bread between the Latins and Byzantines.[2] The former, on the basis of the synoptic gospels, asserted that the Mystical Supper took place on the first day of Unleavened Bread, when in the homes of the Hebrews there should not be any leavened bread. The latter asserted that the Mystical Supper took place on the eve of the Jewish Passover and, consequently, there may have been leavened bread in the house in which Jesus was reclining with his disciples.

The discrepancy between the synoptic Gospels and Saint John's Gospel is described in a variety of ways in scholarly literature. The most common explanation

---

[1]Nikolai Uspenskii, *The Orthodox liturgy: Historical-liturgical studies. Feasts, texts, Ustav*, vol. 3 of *Works on liturgics* [in Russian] (Moscow: Izdatel'stvo Moskovskoi Patriarkhii, 2007), 9–10.

[2]This controversy was discussed in vol. 1 on pp. 112–115.

Mystical Supper. Miniature. Dionysiou Monastery. Mount Athos.

derives from the fact that because the fourteenth of Nissan coincided with a Sabbath Day in the year of Jesus' crucifixion (see Jn 19.31), Jesus could not celebrate the paschal supper on the eve of the Sabbath, but rather he would celebrate it one evening earlier—on the eve of Friday. Nevertheless, in both form and content this was precisely the paschal meal, even if leavened bread was used.

The Eucharist that was fulfilled by Christ also became a part of the paschal meal. Based on the narrative of the evangelists, it follows that Christ gave his body and blood to his disciples at the conclusion of the evening. According to Apostle Paul it was even "after supper" (1 Cor 11.25). In this way, the traditional Old Testament Passover was celebrated first and then Christ celebrated the new Pascha—the mystery of the Eucharist. A new Pascha was established, following the form of the paschal supper that contained a remembrance of Israel's exodus from Egypt, but its basic semantic focus became the crucifixion and resurrection of Christ. And the Savior commanded his disciples to celebrate Pascha not in remembrance of the exodus, but in remembrance of him (see Lk 22.19; 1 Cor 11.24).

THE EUCHARIST IN THE EARLY CHURCH

Catacombs of Saints Marcellinus and Peter in Rome—A Gathering Place for Prayer for the First Christians.

The eucharistic service in the early Christian Church preserved many characteristics of the Jewish paschal supper, and the Christian Pascha preserved the symbolism of the Jewish Passover. In form, each Eucharist was a likeness of the Jewish paschal meal. It began in the evening and could continue until morning (see Acts 20.7–11). The meal bore a festive, ritual-liturgical character. Its basic tone was of thanksgiving. The books of the Old Testament were read during it; prolonged teachings were delivered (see Acts 20.7–11); psalms and hymns and "spiritual songs" were performed (see Col 3.16; Eph 5.19). The Eucharist itself—the breaking of bread and the remembrance of Jesus—was celebrated at the end of the meal, after the main meal was eaten.

It is difficult to say what Apostle Paul meant by "psalms, hymns, and spiritual songs," but it is evident that, apart from psalms, the beginnings of real Christian hymnography were already taking shape in his time. Moreover, early Christian worship was familiar with the phenomenon of speaking in tongues, a practice that later fell out of use.[3]

In the apostolic community, the Eucharist was celebrated on the "first day of the week" (Acts 20.7; 1 Cor 16.2), or "the day of the sun"[4]—that is, the day following the Sabbath. This is the day that became the major day of worship in the Christian Church and came to replace the Jewish Sabbath as the day of rest.

In the apostolic period, celebrants of the eucharistic service were the apostles themselves and also those appointed by them: presbyter-bishops. (In Paul's letters the two terms signified the same service.) In certain cases, the Eucharist could be celebrated by so-called "prophets"—preachers who possessed the gift of foretelling

[3]Glossolalia—speaking in tongues—was widely practiced in Christian churches in the time of the Apostle Paul. There are a great number of testimonies to it in the Acts of the Apostles and the apostolic epistles. (See Acts 2.1–11; 10.44–48; 19.1–6; 1 Cor 12.10, 28, 30; 14.2–19, and others). The phenomenon of glossolalia is connected with the descent of the Holy Spirit upon the apostles on the day of Pentecost. However, at the moment of the descent of the Holy Spirit, the apostles presumably spoke in one language while those who had come to the city heard them speak in other languages, such that everyone heard his own language spoken (see Acts 2.6; 8.11). In the period which followed, speaking in other, unknown languages became widespread in the Church. The Apostle Paul considered prophecy more important than speaking in tongues (see 1 Cor 14.1–6) and called the latter "speaking into the air" (see 1 Cor 14.9), comparing it to the indistinct sound of musical instruments (see 1 Cor 14.7–8).

[4]Justin Martyr, *First Apology* 67 (*ANF* 1:186).

the future.[5] At any rate, one person always presided over the celebration of the Eucharist, thereby occupying the place of Christ at the Mystical Supper. At the same time, the Eucharist was always a collective act in which all members of the local Church community participated.

A Page from a Manuscript of the Didache. 14th c.

Insofar as it is possible to determine from the sources that have come down to us, an element of improvisation predominated in Christian worship during the first three centuries after the Savior's resurrection. In this period, though, formulae of prayers, which gradually acquired the significance of a canon [or anaphora], were already beginning to take shape alongside the improvised prayers. These formulae came to be firmly established in written sources. One of the earliest witnesses of Christian worship is contained in the *Teaching of the Twelve Apostles* (the *Didache*), which presumably dates back to the turn of the second century. Christians are directed in it to say the Lord's Prayer three times per day, and the rite of the celebration of the Eucharist is described:

> Regarding the Eucharist. Give thanks as follows: First, concerning the cup: "We give thee thanks, our Father, for the life and knowledge which thou hast made known to us through Jesus, thy Servant. To thee be the glory for evermore." Next, concerning the broken bread: "We give thee thanks, our Father, for the life and knowledge which thou hast made known to us through Jesus, thy Servant. To thee be the glory for evermore. As this broken bread was scattered over the hills and then, when gathered, became one mass, so may thy Church be gathered from the ends of the earth into thy kingdom. For thine is the glory and the power through Jesus Christ for evermore." . . . After you have taken your fill of food, give thanks as follows: "We give thee thanks, O holy Father, for thy holy name which thou hast enshrined in our hearts, and for the knowledge and faith and immortality which thou hast made known to us through Jesus, thy Servant. To thee be the glory for evermore. Thou, Lord Almighty, hast created all things for the sake of thy name and hast given food and drink for men to enjoy, and they may give thanks to thee; but to us thou hast vouchsafed spiritual food and drink and eternal life through <Jesus>, thy

[5]Concerning prophets, see Nikolai Afanas'ev, *The Church of the Holy Spirit* [in Russian] (Paris: YMCA-Press, 1971).

Servant. Above all, we give thee thanks because thou art mighty. To thee be the glory for evermore. Remember, O Lord, thy Church: deliver her from all evil, perfect her in thy love, and from the four winds assemble her, the sanctified, in thy kingdom which thou hast prepared for her. For thine is the power and the glory for evermore. May grace come, and this world pass away! Hosanna to the God of David! If anyone is holy, let him advance; if anyone is not, let him be converted. *Marana tha!* Amen." But permit the prophets to give thanks as much as they desire.[6]

The citation represents an extremely simple and brief eucharistic rite, characteristic of that period in which a universally recognized and clearly established rite for celebrating the Eucharist did not exist: each Christian community preserved and developed its own liturgical customs. While recommending certain liturgical formulae, the source does not insist on their use, and permits "prophets" to celebrate an improvised Eucharist. We note that the eucharistic prayer in the *Didache* does not contain the Savior's words "Take, eat" and "Drink of it, all of you", and does not make mention of the death and resurrection of Christ.[7]

Saint Justin Martyr.
Contemporary Icon.

An account by Saint Justin Martyr, concerning the celebration of the Eucharist in the Roman church community, dates to the second half of the second century:

And on the day called Sunday, all who live in cities or in the country gather together to one place, and the memoirs of the apostles or the writings of the prophets are read, as long as time permits; then, when the reader has ceased, the president verbally instructs, and exhorts to the imitation of these good things. Then we all rise together and pray, and, as we before said, when our prayer is ended, bread and wine and water are brought, and the president in like manner offers prayers and thanksgivings, according to his ability, and the people assent, saying "Amen"; and there is a distribution to each, and a participation of that over which thanks have been given, and to those who are absent a portion is sent by the deacons.[8]

---

[6]*Didache* 9–10 (Kleist, ACW).

[7]Cf. Enrico Mazza, *The Origins of the Eucharistic Prayer* (Collegeville, MN: The Liturgical Press, 1995), 15.

[8]Justin Martyr, *First Apology* 67 (*ANF* 1:186).

In this, the eucharistic prayer still possesses a character of improvisation (the celebrant offers up thanksgivings "according to his ability"). Also, the Eucharist is preceded by readings whose content and number are not fixed (scriptures are read "as long as time permits"). It was also characteristic for all Christians residing "in cities or in the country" to gather "to one place." That is to say that one Eucharist, presided over by the bishop, was celebrated for a city and its surrounding settlements. A multitude of parishes did not yet exist, in which the Eucharist would be celebrated by presbyters, delegated by the bishop.

A description of the Eucharist found in the *Apostolic Tradition*, ascribed to Saint Hippolytus of Rome, dates to the third century:[9]

Martyrdom of Saint Hippolytus of Rome. Miniature. 15th c.

When he has been made bishop let everyone offer him the kiss of peace, greeting him because he has been made worthy. Let the deacons present the oblations to him and, laying hands on it with the whole presbytery, let him say, giving thanks: "The Lord be with you." And all shall say: "And with your spirit." "Let us lift up our hearts." "We lift them up to the Lord." "Let us give thanks." "It is meet and right." And then he shall continue thus: "We give thanks to you God, through your beloved child Jesus Christ, whom, in the last times, you sent to us as savior and redeemer and angel of your will, who is your inseparable Word through whom you made all things and who was well pleasing to you. You sent him from heaven into the womb of a virgin, and he was conceived and made flesh in the womb and shown to be your Son, born of the Holy Spirit and the virgin. He fulfilled your will and won for you a holy people, opening wide his hands when he suffered that he might set free from suffering those who believed in you. When he was handed over to voluntary suffering, in order to dissolve death and break the chains of the devil and harrow hell and illuminate the just and fix a boundary and manifest the resurrection, he took bread and giving thanks to you he said: "Take, eat, this is my body which will be broken for you." Likewise with the cup saying: "This is my blood which is poured out for you. Whenever you do this, you perform my commemoration." Remembering therefore his death and resurrection, we offer you bread and cup, giving thanks to you because you have held us worthy to stand before you and minister to you as priest. And we ask

---

[9]Most contemporary scholars consider this work to be spurious.

that you should send your Holy Spirit on the presbytery of the holy church. Gathering ‹us› into one, may you grant to all the saints who receive for the fullness of the Holy Spirit, for the confirmation of their faith in truth, that we may praise and glorify you through your child Jesus Christ, through whom be glory and honor to you, with the Holy Spirit in your holy church both now and to the ages of the ages. Amen.[10]

Despite all the subsequent development of eucharistic worship in the Christian East, the main elements of the rite cited above have been preserved in the Orthodox liturgy up to the present day. The major elements include the giving of the kiss of peace, the opening exclamations "Let us lift up our hearts," "Let us give thanks unto the Lord," "It is meet and right," the address to God the Father, the uttering of Christ's "words of institution" ("Take, eat" and "This is my blood"), the overall character of a thanksgiving prayer and its basic content, as well as the concluding doxology.[11] For this reason, it may be said that the basic core of the eucharistic worship of the Orthodox Church had already taken shape in the third century.

The simplicity of worship in the early Christian community is explained in large part by the restrained conditions in which the Christian Church found itself during the first three centuries. Still it was precisely in this time that the liturgical ceremony began to take shape. This ceremony would become the basis of worship in the Christian East in the post-Constantinian period in a significantly more developed and detailed form.

THE EUCHARIST OF THE EARLY BYZANTINE PERIOD

With Emperor Constantine's Edict of Milan (AD 313) a new epoch began, not only in the life of the Church, but also in the history of Christian worship. The years following the promulgation of the edict were "a time of unparalleled liturgical revision all over Christendom, when the churches everywhere were taking stock of their own local traditions, sifting their devotional value and borrowing freely from each other whatever seemed most expressive or attractive in the rites of other churches."[12] This systematization primarily pertained to the eucharistic rites that were set in writing and received a finished form in each local church. Numerous

---

[10]Hippolytus of Rome, *On the Apostolic Tradition* 4 (Stewart, PPS).

[11]We may note that the eucharistic prayer from the *Apostolic Tradition* is used in the Roman Catholic Church. It lay at the basis of the second eucharistic rite, which entered into the Roman Missal of 1970.

[12]Gregory Dix, *The Shape of the Liturgy* (London: A & C Black, 1960), 304.

rites of the Eucharist that have survived to the present day date to the fourth and fifth centuries. Several of them are used in the present day, while others have fallen out of use and have been preserved only in collections of ancient liturgies, which are of historical interest.

Of all the ancient liturgical rites of the Orthodox Church, those that remain in use today are the Liturgies of Saint Basil the Great, Saint John Chrysostom, and also the Liturgy of the Presanctified Gifts. The Liturgy of Saint Basil the Great is celebrated ten times per year (on the eves of the Nativity of Christ and of Theophany, on Holy Thursday and Holy Saturday, on the day of the commemoration of Saint Basil the Great and on the Sundays of Great Lent). The Liturgy of Saint John Chrysostom is celebrated on all the other days of the church year with the exception of the weekdays of Great Lent. The Liturgy of the Presanctified Gifts is celebrated on Wednesdays and Fridays of Great Lent. The liturgy ascribed to Apostle James is celebrated on the day of his commemoration (October 23) in the church of Jerusalem, and also in individual parishes of several other local Orthodox churches.[13]

Saint John Chrysostom. Illumination from the Service Book of Saint Barlaam of Khutyn. Turn of 13th c.

Saint Basil the Great. Illumination from the Service Book of Patriarch Job. Moscow. 1604.

The difference between the liturgies of Saint Basil the Great and Saint John Chrysostom consists mainly of the prayers that in contemporary practice are read secretly by the priest, especially the Anaphora Prayers. Therefore, except for the fact that the singing during Saint Basil's liturgy is more drawn out, the difference between the two liturgies is nearly imperceptible to the majority of parishioners, because they do not hear these prayers. In Byzantium, tradition held that Basil shortened the liturgy of the Apostle James, and that Chrysostom shortened the liturgy of Basil,[14] or that both Basil and Chrystostom shortened the liturgy of the

[13]In the Russian Orthodox Church, for example, this liturgy is celebrated in Budapest's Dormition Cathedral.

[14]Proclus of Constantinople, *Homily on Tradition* (PG 65:850b–852c).

Apostle James.[15] But a comparative analysis of the texts shows this is not the case: we are talking about two distinct orders of liturgies, in which certain prayers coincide completely but others differ quite considerably in their content, form and length. Indeed, the prayers of the eucharistic canon in the Liturgy of Saint Basil the Great are considerably longer than the corresponding prayers in Chrysostom's liturgy. Nevertheless, the prayers of Chrysostom's liturgy can in no way be considered an abridgement of Basil's version.

To what extent were Saints Basil the Great and John Chrysostom the authors of the liturgies which bear their names? Various opinions exist among scholars concerning this question. It is clear that the liturgies were not the products of their individual creative work, but it is perfectly likely that Basil the Great and John Chrysostom were the authors of individual prayers, and that they organized and systematized the eucharistic rites that had preceded them. It is also evident that over the course of time the liturgies ascribed to Basil and John were enhanced with new hymns and prayers; therefore, the liturgies appear differently today than they did in the fourth century. Only the basic core, which includes the Anaphora Prayers (the so-called "eucharistic canon"), has remained unchanged.

The liturgical reform of the fourth century involved not only liturgical texts but also the Church's ceremony, which became considerably richer in the post-Constantinian period. After transitioning from private to public services, Christian worship gained a splendor it previously lacked during the age of persecutions. As the well-known historian of worship Dom Gregory Dix notes, the heavenly worship that Saint John the Theologian describes in Revelation is a reality that is reflected in the earthly worship of the Christian community only to the smallest degree. When the Church was granted the freedom of public worship, it was deemed possible to incarnate heavenly ideals in the life of the earthly church community. "It was part of the general translation of worship from the idiom of eschatology into that of time,"[16] the scholar notes.

The *Apostolic Constitutions*, dating to the second half of the fourth century, are collections of considerably earlier fragments that reveal the Syrian practice of worship. An extremely detailed liturgical ceremonial is described in these documents.

---

[15]Saint Mark of Ephesus, for example, was of the latter opinion. See his *Essay on how the Divine Gifts are consecrated not only by the recitation of the Savior's words* (chapter 4) [in Russian], in Amvrosii (Pogodin), *St Mark of Ephesus and the Union of Florence* [in Russian] (Jordanville, NY: Holy Trinity Monastery, 1963; Moscow: Posad, 1994), 297.

[16]Dix, *Liturgy*, 314. Moreover, certain characteristics of ancient Jewish temple worship re-emerged in Christian worship of the post-Constantinian period, either consciously or unconsciously. For more on this subject, see, in particular, Margaret Barker, *The Revelation of Jesus Christ* (Edinburgh: T & T Clark, 2000), 373–378.

The first segment of eucharistic worship—the liturgy of the catechumens—begins with readings from the Old Testament. The readings are interspersed with the singing of King David's psalms. A singer exclaims the psalm verses while the congregation sings the remaining words of the verses. Then, a deacon or presbyter reads the gospel, and those present stand "in great silence" and listen to the reading. One at a time, each of the presbyters delivers a homily, and the bishop is the last to preach. The people remain seated during the homilies. At the conclusion of the homilies, the catechumens and penitents depart and the liturgy of the faithful begins:

> After this, let all rise up with one consent, and looking towards the east, after the catechumens and penitents are gone out, pray to God eastward, who ascended up to the heaven of heavens to the east; remembering also the ancient situation of paradise in the east, from whence the first man, when he had yielded to the persuasion of the serpent, and disobeyed the command of God, was expelled. As to the deacons, after the prayer is over, let some of them attend upon the oblation of the Eucharist, ministering to the Lord's body with fear. Let others of them watch the multitude, and keep them silent. But let that deacon who is at the high priest's hand say to the people, "Let no one have any quarrel against another; let no one come in hypocrisy." Then let the men give the men, and the women give the women, the Lord's kiss. But let no one do it with deceit, as Judas betrayed the Lord with a kiss. After this let the deacon pray for the whole Church, for the whole world, and the several parts of it, and the fruits of it; for the priests and the rulers, for the high priest and the king, and the peace of the universe. After this let the high priest pray for peace upon the people, and bless them, as Moses commanded the priests to bless the people, in these words: "The Lord bless thee, and keep thee: the Lord make His face to shine upon thee, and give thee peace" [Num 6.24]. Let the bishop pray for the people, and say: "Save Thy people, O Lord, and bless Thine inheritance, which Thou hast obtained with the precious blood of Thy Christ, and hast called a royal priesthood, and an holy nation." After this let the sacrifice follow, the people standing, and praying silently; and when the oblation has been made, let every rank by itself partake of the Lord's body and precious blood in order, and approach with reverence and holy fear, as to the body of their king. Let the women approach with their heads covered, as is becoming the order of women; but let the door be watched, lest any unbeliever, or one not yet initiated, come in.[17]

---

[17]*Apostolic Constitutions* 2.57 (*ANF* 7:421–422).

The systematization and unification of the divine services in the fourth century took place around the major cultural centers of the empire, such as Jerusalem, Alexandria, Antioch, and Constantinople. So-called "liturgical families" emerged, in which liturgical rites characteristic of various regions were united. Scholars distinguish between Antiochian, Alexandrian, Jerusalemite, East Syrian, West Syrian, Cappadocean, Constantinopolitan, and other rites, each of which used its own form of the eucharistic service.[18]

One of the centers of liturgical work in the fourth century was Jerusalem, which was transformed by Emperor Constantine into a massive center of pilgrimage. The eucharistic worship in the Jerusalemite rite was described in detail in one of

the mystagogical lectures of Saint Cyril of Jerusalem (c. 315–386). In his description, the liturgy of the faithful commences with the washing of the hands of the presiding hierarch and the priests. The kiss of peace then follows after the proclamation of the deacon: "Embrace one another and let us kiss one another." Then the priest exclaims, "Let us lift up our hearts." The people answer, "We lift them up unto the Lord." The priest says, "Let us give thanks unto the Lord," and the people say, "It is meet and right." It is evident that all of these formulae encountered in the *Apostolic Tradition* became an integral part of the liturgy of the fourth century.

Saint Cyril, Archbishop of Jerusalem. Fresco.

Saint Cyril of Jerusalem does not cite the eucharistic prayer in its entirety, but he does give a short description of it:

> After this we make mention of heaven, and earth, and sea; of the sun and moon; of the stars and all the creation, rational and irrational, visible and invisible; of angels, archangels, virtues, dominions, principalities, powers, thrones; of the cherubim with many faces. . . . We make mention also of the seraphim, whom Isaiah by the Holy Spirit beheld encircling the throne of God, and with two of their wings veiling their countenances, and with two their feet, and with two flying, who cried, "Holy, Holy, Holy, Lord God of Sabaoth" (Is 6.3). For this cause rehearse we this confession of God, delivered down to us from the seraphim that we may join in hymns with the host of the world above. Then having sanctified ourselves by these spiritual hymns, we call upon the merciful

[18]"Worship" [in Russian], in *Orthodox Encyclopedia*, vol. 5 (Moscow: Tserkovno-nauchnyi tsentr "Pravoslavnaia entsiklopediia," 2002), 539.

God to send forth his Holy Spirit upon the gifts lying before him; that he may make the bread the body of Christ, and the wine the blood of Christ; for whatsoever the Holy Spirit has touched, is sanctified and changed. Then, after the spiritual sacrifice is perfected, the bloodless service upon that sacrifice of propitiation, we entreat God for the common peace of the Church, for the tranquility of the world; for kings; for soldiers and allies; for the sick; for the afflicted; and, in a word, for all who stand in need of succor we all supplicate and offer this sacrifice. Then we commemorate also those who have fallen asleep before us, first, patriarchs, prophets, apostles, martyrs, that at their prayers and intervention God would receive our petition. Afterwards also on behalf of the holy fathers and bishops who have fallen asleep before us, and in a word of all who in past years have fallen asleep among us, believing that it will be a very great advantage to the souls, for whom the supplication is put up, while that holy and most awful sacrifice is presented.[19]

The Lord's Prayer follows after the prayers for the living and the departed, after which the priest exclaims, "The holy things are for the holy." The people respond, "One is holy, one is the Lord Jesus Christ." The hymn *Taste and see that the Lord is good* follows and the communion takes place: the faithful receive into their hands a particle of the sacred bread which has become the body of Christ and afterwards approach the holy chalice of the blood of Christ. The worship service concludes with a prayer of thanksgiving.[20]

In the subsequent period Jerusalem retained its significance as one of the major liturgical centers of the Orthodox East. In 478, the venerable Sabba the Sanctified (439–532) founded a monastery relatively close to Jerusalem, which was later given the name of the Great Lavra. Liturgical work was undertaken vigorously in this monastery, typika (manuals) of church services were compiled, and original works of liturgical poetry were composed.

Saint Sabba the Sanctified.
Icon. Novgorod. 15th c.

[19]Cyril of Jerusalem, *Mystagogical Catecheses* 5.6–9 (Church, PPS).
[20]Ibid. 5.19–22.

The Non-Eucharistic Services of the Daily Cycle

Besides the Eucharist, other worship services were performed in the early Christian Church that likely took shape earlier, in the apostolic period. An innate link exists between these worship services and the divine rite of the Jerusalem temple in the time of Jesus Christ. Divine services were performed in the temple three times per day: before the rising of the sun, around noon, and before the setting of the sun. The apostles preserved the custom of praying at established times (see Acts 10.9). This custom later became established in the Christian services of the third, sixth, and ninth hours.

Horologion. Ancient Rus'. 15th c.

Material concerning non-eucharistic worship services in the pre-Constantinian period is rather scant. However, what does exist allows for a certain understanding of the formation of vespers, matins, and the hours, as well as the composition of these services.

We find mention of prayers offered at established times of the day beginning with Saint Clement of Rome.[21] Clement of Alexandria makes mention of a prayer at the third, sixth, and ninth hours.[22] In another place, he speaks about a prayer after rising, before sleep, in the night, and also before and after meals.[23] Origen makes mention of prayer in the morning, at noonday, in the evening, and at night.[24] Tertullian spoke of prayers at the third, sixth, and ninth hours[25] and prayer during the night.[26] Tertullian's account of prayer at the third, sixth, and ninth hours is confirmed by Saint Cyprian of Carthage, who also mentions prayer in the morning, at the setting of the sun, and during the night.[27]

Tertullian was the first author to make reference to the evening ceremony of the lighting of lamps. Sources of this rite date back to Old Testament worship. The Bible speaks of the lighting of lamps in the evening, accompanied by the burning of incense

[21]Clement of Rome, *First Epistle to the Corinthians* 40 (*ANF* 1:16).

[22]Clement of Alexandria, *The Stromata* 7.7.49 (*ANF* 2:534).

[23]Clement of Alexandria, *The Instructor* 2.9–10 (*ANF* 2:257–263); *The Stromata* 7.7.49 (*ANF* 2:537)

[24]Origen, *De Orationes* [On Prayer] 12 (PG 11:452–453).

[25]Tertullian, *On Prayer* 25 (*ANF* 3:689–690).

[26]Tertullian, *To His Wife* 2.5 (*ANF* 4:46–47).

[27]Cyprian of Carthage, *On the Lord's Prayer* 34–36 (*ANF* 5:456–457).

(see Ex 30.8; Lev 24.1–4). Tertullian describes the ceremony of the lighting of lamps in this way: "After manual ablution, and the bringing in of lights, each is asked to stand forth and sing, as he can, a hymn to God, either one from the holy Scriptures or one of his own composing."[28] A description of the evening rite of bringing the lamp into the assembly of prayer has been preserved in the *Apostolic Tradition*:

> When the bishop is present and evening is come the deacon brings in a lamp and standing among all the believers who are present he shall give thanks. Firstly he greets them as he says: "The Lord be with you." And the people shall say: "And with your spirit." "Let us give thanks to the Lord." And they shall say: "It is meet and right. Greatness and exaltation with praise is fitting to him." And he shall not say "Let us lift up our hearts," for it is to be said at the offering. And he shall pray in this way as he says: "We give you thanks, O God, through your child Jesus Christ our Lord, through whom you have illuminated us, revealing to us the incorruptible light. Therefore we have completed the length of the day and we have arrived at the beginning of the night, being sated with the day's light which you created for our satisfaction. And now, having arrived at the light of evening through your grace, we give you praise and glorify you through your child Jesus Christ, our Lord, through whom to you be power and honor together with the Holy Spirit, now and always and to the ages of ages. Amen." And all shall say: "Amen."[29]

In the fourth century, Saint Basil the Great wrote concerning thanksgiving at the time of the coming of the evening light, which was called a "thanksgiving at the lighting of the lamp."[30] It is clear that Saint John Chrysostom had this ceremony in mind when he stated that listening to a homily is more important than watching the lamp lighter:

> Wake up there, and dispel indifference. Why do I say this? Becaue while we are discoursing to you on the Scriptures, you instead are averting your eyes from us and fixing them on the lamps and the man lighting the lamps. What extreme indifference is this, to ignore us

Saint John Chrysostom.
Homilies on Genesis.
Constantinople. 10th–11th c.

[28]Tertullian, *Apology* 39.18 (*ANF* 3:47).
[29]Hippolytus of Rome, *Apostolic Tradition* 25 (Stewart, PPS).
[30]Basil the Great, *On the Holy Spirit* 73 (PG 32:205a; Hildebrand, PPS).

and attend to him! Here am I, lighting the fire that comes from the Scriptures, and the light of its teaching is burning on our tongue. This light is brighter and better than that light: we are not kindling a wick saturated in oil, like him: souls bedewed with piety we set alight with the desire for listening.[31]

Two descriptions of non-eucharistic worship services of the daily cycle dating to the end of the fourth century have come down to us. The first is found in the *Apostolic Constitutions*:

Offer up your prayers in the morning, at the third hour, the sixth, the ninth, the evening, and at cock-crowing: in the morning, returning thanks that the Lord has sent you light, that he has brought you past the night, and brought on the day; at the third hour, because at that hour the Lord received the sentence of condemnation from Pilate; at the sixth, because at that hour he was crucified; at the ninth, because all things were in commotion at the crucifixion of the Lord, as trembling at the bold attempt of the impious Jews, and not bearing the injury offered to their Lord; in the evening, giving thanks that he has given you the night to rest from the daily labors; at cock-crowing, because that hour brings the good news of the coming on of the day for the operations proper for the light.[32]

In all, six worship services of the daily circle are mentioned in this source. The order for celebrating vespers is described in detail:

When it is evening, thou, O bishop, shall assemble the church; and after the repetition of the psalm [Ps 140] at the lighting up the lights, the deacon shall bid prayers for the catechumens, the energumens [i.e. those undergoing exorcism], the illuminated, and the penitents. . . . But after the dismissal of these,[33] the deacon shall say: "As many as are of the faithful, let us pray to the Lord." And after the bidding prayer, which is formerly set down, he shall say, "Save us, O God, and raise us up by thy Christ. Let us stand up, and beg for the mercies of the Lord, and his compassions, for the angel of peace, for what things are good and profitable, for a Christian departure out of this life, an evening and

---

[31]John Chrysostom, *Eight Homilies on Genesis* 4.3 (PG 54:597). English translation from *St. John Chrysostom: Eight Sermons on the Book of Genesis,* trans. Robert Charles Hill (Brookline, MA: Holy Cross Orthodox Press, 2004), 72–73.

[32]*Apostolic Constitutions* 8.34 (*ANF* 7:496).

[33]That is, the prayers described separately—in chapter ten of the eighth book of *Apostolic Constitutions*. These prayers were rather lengthy and were used not only in the evening worship service, but also in the liturgy of the catechumens.

a night of peace, and free from sin; and let us beg that the whole course of our life may be blameless. Let us dedicate ourselves and one another to the living God through His Christ."[34]

Next, two prayers are offered by the bishop. In the first, he asks God to send down an "evening of peace" and a "night free from sin." The prayer is followed by the deacon's exclamation, "Bow down for the laying on of hands." The prayer of the bowing down of heads is read:

Do thou now also look down, O Lord Almighty, and cause thy face to shine upon thy people, who bow down the neck of their heart, and bless them by Christ; through whom thou hast enlightened us with the light of knowledge, and hast revealed thyself to us; with whom worthy adoration is due from every rational and holy nature to thee, and to the Spirit, who is the Comforter, forever.

Judging from the exclamation that precedes this prayer, it follows that upon the conclusion of this prayer, the bishop would lay his hands on all those present. Then the deacon would say, "Depart in peace."[35] And with this, the evening service would be concluded.

Apostolic Constitutions states the following about the order of the morning service:

In like manner, in the morning, after the repetition of the morning psalm [Ps 62], and his dismissal of the catechumens, the energumens, the candidates for baptism, and the penitents, and after the usual bidding of prayers, that we may not again repeat the same things, let the deacon add after the words, "Save us, O God, and raise us up by thy grace: Let us beg of the Lord his mercies and his compassions, that this morning and this day may be with peace and without sin, as also all the time of our sojourning; that he will grant us his angel of peace, a Christian departure out of this life, and that God will be merciful and gracious. Let us dedicate ourselves and one another to the living God through his Only-begotten."[36]

As in the order for vespers, two prayers of the bishop follow. The first contains the morning thanksgiving and doxology:

[34]*Apostolic Constitutions* 8.35–36 (*ANF* 7:496).
[35]Ibid. 8.36 (*ANF* 7:496–497).
[36]Ibid. 8.37 (*ANF* 7:497).

O God, the God of spirits and of all flesh, who is beyond compare, and standeth in need of nothing, who hast given the sun to have rule over the day, and the moon and the stars to have rule over the night, do thou now also look down upon us with gracious eyes, and receive our morning thanksgivings, and have mercy upon us; for we have not spread out our hands unto a strange God; for there is not among us any new God, but thou, the eternal God, who is without end, who hast given us our being through Christ, and given us our well-being through him. Do thou vouchsafe us also, through him, eternal life; with whom glory, and honor, and worship be to thee and to the Holy Spirit forever. Amen.[37]

Before the second prayer, the deacon exclaims, "Bow down for the laying on of hands." The public listens to the second prayer at the bowing of heads:

O God, who art faithful and true, who "hast mercy on thousands and ten thousands of them that love thee," the lover of the humble, and the protector of the needy, of whom all things stand in need, for all things are subject to thee; look down upon this thy people, who bow down their heads to thee, and bless them with spiritual blessing. "Keep them as the apple of an eye," preserve them in piety and righteousness, and vouchsafe them eternal life in Christ Jesus thy beloved Son, with whom glory, honor, and worship be to thee and to the Holy Spirit, now and always, and for ever and ever. Amen.[38]

Like vespers, matins is concluded with the laying on of hands by the bishop and the deacon's exclamation, "Depart in peace."[39]

Before us are two liturgical orders that have a similar structure. Both include the singing of a psalm, prayers for the catechumens, penitents, energumens, two prayers of the bishop preceded by the deacon's exclamation, and then the deacon's concluding exclamation, "Depart in peace." The relative simplicity and brevity of both services were characteristic of the early Christian period.

Another rather detailed description of the divine services of the daily cycle, including the non-eucharistic services, comes down to us from the pilgrim Egeria. According to her account, the Jerusalemite worship consisted of a daily order of services, lasting many hours and comprised of several services per day. By the time of her writing, this order of services had been worked out in great detail.

[37]Ibid. 8.38 (ANF 7:497).
[38]Ibid. 8.39 (ANF 7:497).
[39]Ibid.

Divine services began every day in the Church of the Holy Sepulchre before cockcrow. The doors of the church were opened, and a large number of monks and laymen of both genders entered the church, after which hymns were performed in the antiphonal manner—interspersed with prayers—right up to sunrise. Matins began at sunrise, after which the bishop entered the church and offered prayers for the catechumens and the faithful, and bestowed his blessing upon all present.

The Church of the Holy Sepulchre. Jerusalem.

The services of the sixth and ninth hours also included antiphonal singing of psalms and ended with the blessing of the bishop.

Vespers was served at the tenth hour (around 4:00 PM), beginning with the lighting of the lamps throughout the church and the singing of "psalms and antiphons." Towards the end of vespers, the bishop entered the church, and "hymns and antiphons" were performed in his presence. Then prayers said by the bishop alternated with petitions offered by the deacon, and a boys' choir responded to these prayers with the singing of "Lord, have mercy." As with other services, vespers ended with the bishop's blessing. The veneration of the cross and the reading of prayers for the catechumens and faithful took place after vespers.

The worship service on Sundays differed significantly in its great solemnity and length, compared to the services conducted during the week. In particular, Sunday matins included the censing of the entire church and a series of sermons given by the presbyters, followed by the preaching of the bishop. According to the pilgrim Egeria, the sermons added considerable length to the morning service. Because of the sermons, the service lasted until the fourth or fifth hour (ten or eleven o'clock), after which the bishop and faithful conducted a procession to Golgotha.

The divine services of the daily cycle in the Christian East of the fourth century were marked by their great diversity of rites, traditions, and orders. The church historian Socrates Scholasticus even held that it was impossible to find two churches in which the divine services were conducted in exactly the same way. According to him, "to give a complete catalogue of all the various customs and ceremonial observances in use throughout every city and country would be difficult—rather, impossible."[40]

---

[40]Socrates Scholasticus, *Church History* 5.22 (*NPNF*² 2:133).

The existence of different rites and traditions is observed in the period that followed. But the basic framework of the divine services, conducted at the established times—sunrise, third, sixth, and ninth hours, the setting of the sun, and at night—remained unchanged and universal.

The divine services of the daily cycle were performed both in cathedrals and in monasteries. Saint Basil the Great's *Long Rules* shed light on the liturgical customs of the Cappadocian monasteries:

> Prayers are recited early in the morning so that the first movements of the soul and the mind may be consecrated to God and that we may take up no other consideration before we have been cheered and heartened by the thought of God, as it is written: "I remembered God and was delighted" [Ps 76.4], and that the body may not busy itself with tasks before we have fulfilled the words: "To thee will I pray, O Lord; in the morning thou shalt hear my voice. In the morning I will stand before thee and will see" [Ps 5.4–5]. Again at the third hour the brethren must assemble and betake themselves to prayer, even if they may have dispersed to their various employments. Recalling to mind the gift of the Spirit bestowed upon the apostles at this third hour, all should worship together, so that they also may become worthy to receive the gift of sanctity, and they should implore the guidance of the Holy Spirit and his instruction in what is good and useful, according to the words: "Create a clean heart in me, O God, and renew a right spirit within my bowels. Cast me not away from thy face; and take not thy Holy Spirit from me. Restore unto me the joy of thy salvation and strengthen me with a guiding spirit" [Ps 50.12–14]. Again, it is said elsewhere, "Thy good spirit shall lead me into the right land" [Ps 142.10]; and having prayed thus, we should again apply ourselves to our tasks.
>
> But, if some, perhaps, are not in attendance because the nature or place of their work keeps them at too great a distance, they are strictly obliged to carry out wherever they are, with promptitude, all that is prescribed for common observance, for "where there are two or three gathered together in my name," says the Lord, "there am I in the midst of them" [Mt 18.20]. It is also our judgment that prayer is necessary at the sixth hour, in imitation of the saints who say: "Evening and morning and at noon I will speak and declare; and he shall hear my voice" [Ps 54.18]. And so that we may be saved from invasion and the noonday devil [Ps 90.6], at this time, also, the nineteenth psalm will be recited.
>
> The ninth hour, however, was appointed as a compulsory time for prayer by the

apostles themselves in the Acts where it is related that "Peter and John went up to the temple at the ninth hour of prayer" (Acts 3.1). When the day's work is ended, thanksgiving should be offered for what has been granted us or for what we have done rightly therein and confession made of our omissions whether voluntary or involuntary, or of a secret fault, if we chance to have committed any in words or deeds, or in the heart itself; for by prayer we propitiate God for all our misdemeanors. The examination of our past actions is a great help toward not falling into like faults again; wherefore the Psalmist says: "the things you say in your hearts, be sorry for them upon your beds" [Ps 4.5]. Again, at nightfall, we must ask that our rest be sinless and untroubled by dreams. At this hour, also, the ninetieth Psalm should be recited. Paul and Silas, furthermore, have handed down to us the practice of compulsory prayer at midnight, as the history of the Acts declares: "And at midnight Paul and Silas praised God" [Acts 16.25]. The Psalmist also says: "I rose at midnight to give praise to thee for the judgments of thy justifications" [Ps 118.62]. Then, too, we must anticipate the dawn by prayer, so that the day may not find us in slumber and in bed, according to the words: "My eyes have prevented the morning; that I might meditate on thy words" [Ps 118.148]. None of these hours for prayer should be unobserved by those who have chosen a life devoted to the glory of God and His Christ. Moreover, I think that variety and diversity in the prayers and psalms recited at appointed hours are desirable for the reason that routine and boredom, somehow, often cause distraction in the soul, while by change and variety in the psalmody and prayers said at the stated hours it is refreshed in devotion and renewed in sobriety.[41]

In the instructions to the Cappadocian ascetics Saint Basil the Great recommended performing seven services each day, interpreting literally the words of verse 164 of Psalm 118:

Prayer time should cover the whole of life, but since there is absolute need at certain intervals to interrupt the bending of the knee and the chanting of psalms, the hours appointed for prayer by the saints should be observed. The mighty David says: "I rose at midnight to give praise to thee for the judgments of thy justification" [Ps 118.62]; and we find Paul and Silas following his example, for they praised God in prison at midnight [Acts 16.25]. Then too, the same prophet

[41]Basil the Great, *The Long Rules* 37.2–5 (PG 31:1031a–1016c). The above translation is found in Basil the Great, *Ascetical Works*, trans. Monica Wagner, Fathers of the Church 9 (Washington, DC: Catholic University of America Press, 1999), 309–311.

says: "Evening and morning and at noon" [Ps 54.18]. Moreover, the coming of the Holy Spirit took place at the third hour, as we learn in the Acts when, in answer to the Pharisees who were jeering at the disciples because of the diversity of tongues, Peter said that they were not drunk who were speaking these words: "seeing that it is but the third hour" [Acts 2.15]. Again, the ninth hour recalls the Lord's passion, which took place that we might live [cf. Mt 27.45; Mk 15.33–34]. But, since David says: "Seven times a day I have given praise to thee for the judgments of thy justice," and the times for prayer which have been mentioned do not make up this seven-fold apportionment, the mid-day prayer should be divided, one part being recited before the noon repast and the other afterward. In this way, the daily seven-fold praise of God distributed throughout the whole period of the day may become a pattern for us also.[42]

Saint Basil the Great. On Fasting.
Mount Athos. End of 14th–Middle of 15th c.

Clearly this indication corresponded to a practice already adopted by the Cappadocian communities of ascetics in Basil's time. Later this practice was strengthened by the theory of the "Seven Prayers" service as the structural basis for monastery services. According to this theory, the "Seven Prayers" are made up of vespers, compline, midnight office, matins (with first hour), third hour, sixth, and ninth hours. The liturgy is not included because it is not a daily worship service, and also because it symbolizes "the age to come."[43]

Information concerning monastic worship services in Antioch in the fourth century is found in the works of Saint John Chrysostom. In one of his commentaries on Saint Paul's first epistle to Timothy, Chrysostom, speaking about worship services in monasteries, makes mention of the nocturnal prayer, third, sixth, and ninth hours, vespers, and the prayer after supper. The nocturnal prayer is described in the following way:

[42]Basil the Great, *Ascetical Discourse* 40.4 (PG 31:877a–c). The above translation is found in *Ascetical Works*, trans. Wagner, 212–213.

[43]A. van der Mensbrugghe, "Prayer-Time in Egyptian Monasticism (320–450)," *Studia Patristica* 2, Texte und Untersuchungen zur Geschichte der altchristlichen Literatur 64 (Berlin: Akademie-Verlag, 1957), 453. Cf. Armand Veilleux, *La liturgie dans le cénobitisme pachomien au quatrième siècle*, Studia Anselmiana 57 (Rome: Herder, 1968), 281–282.

At the crowing of the cock their president comes, and . . . rouses them all. . . . Then as soon as they have arisen they stand up, and sing the prophetic hymns with much harmony, and well composed tunes. And neither harp nor pipe nor other musical instrument utters such sweet melodies, as you hear from the singing of these saints. . . . Having performed their morning prayers and hymns, (they) proceed to the reading of the Scriptures. . . . Then at the third, sixth, and ninth hours, and in the evening, they perform their devotions, having divided the day into four parts, and at the conclusion of each they honor God with psalms and hymns.[44]

In Homily 68 on the Gospel according to Matthew, Chrysostom again describes the order of the nocturnal worship service in monasteries:

These that are the lights of the world, as soon as the sun is up, or rather even long before its rise, rise up from their bed, healthy, and wakeful, and sober (for neither doth any sorrow and care, nor headache, and toil, and multitude of business, nor any other such thing trouble them, but as angels live they in heaven); having risen then straightway from their bed cheerful and glad, and having made one choir, with their conscience bright, with one voice all, like as out of one mouth, they sing hymns unto the God of all, honoring him and thanking him for all his benefits, both particular, and common. . . . Then, after they have said those songs, they bow their knees, and entreat the God who was the object of their hymns for things. . . . And he leads them in their prayers, who is their father, and their ruler. After this, when they have risen up and finished those holy and continual prayers, the sun being risen, they depart each one to their work, gathering thence a large supply for the needy.[45]

Monastery of Saint Anthony the Great in Egypt. Contemporary View.

Saint John Cassian the Roman witnesses to how the worship services of the daily cycle were performed in the monasteries of Egypt, Palestine, and Mesopotamia at the turn of the fifth century. His description of the nocturnal divine services begins with the words: "We have found that many in different countries, according to the fancy of their mind (having, indeed, as the Apostle says, "a zeal for God but not according to knowledge" [Rom 10.2]), have made for themselves different rules

[44]John Chrysostom, *Homilies on 1 Timothy* 14.4 (*NPNF*[1] 13:456–457).
[45]John Chrysostom, *Homilies on Matthew* 68.3 (*NPNF*[1] 10:400).

and arrangements in this matter (the nocturnal singing of psalms). . . . In this way we have found . . . the system and regulations . . . are almost as many in number as the monasteries and cells which we have visited."[46] In particular, in Egypt and Thebaid, twelve psalms with an additional two readings from the Old and New Testaments are read both at vespers and in the nocturnal gatherings.[47] John Cassian notes that psalms are not all read at once, but rather they are divided into two or three "stases." During the reading of psalms, only one reader stands, while all the others sit on low stools.[48] The author of the narrative especially notes the quietness which reigned in the monasteries of Egypt during worship services. "When they gather to pray, in the churches such silence reigns that, despite the innumerable multitude of those present, it is as if nobody is there save for the one reading the psalms, and especially when prayers are spoken, there is not heard any expectoration, coughing, yawning, sighing, and not even any words save those uttered by the serving clergy."[49]

According to John Cassian's account, there were no daily general worship services in the monasteries of Egypt, with the exception of Saturdays and Sundays. All the services of the daily cycle were read by monks in their cells.[50] In the monasteries of Palestine and Mesopotamia, there were general worship services of the third, sixth, and ninth hours, and at every service three psalms were read.[51] Cassian considered these three divine services to have been established in antiquity, while, according to him, the service performed at the rising of the sun (first hour) "was established in our time and originally in the monastery in Bethlehem." The service of the first hour "completes the Seven Prayers with the praises which David performed continuously throughout the entire day (see Ps 118.164). Including this divine service, we truly give praise to the Lord seven times during the course of each day."[52]

During the night from Saturday to Sunday, the all-night vigil was performed, which concluded during the winter months with the fourth crowing of the cock, so that the next two hours could be used for sleeping.[53] John Cassian considered the all-night vigil an ancient institution dating back to apostolic times.[54] On Sundays

---

[46]John Cassian, *The Institutes of the Coenobia* 2.2 (*NPNF²* 11:205).
[47]Ibid. 2.4 (*NPNF²* 11:206).
[48]Ibid. 2.11–12 (*NPNF²* 11:209–210).
[49]Ibid. 2.10 (*NPNF²* 11:209).
[50]Ibid. 3.2 (*NPNF²* 11:212–213).
[51]Ibid. 3.3 (*NPNF²* 11:213–214).
[52]Ibid. 3.4 (*NPNF²* 11:215).
[53]Ibid. 3.8 (*NPNF²* 11:216–217).
[54]Ibid. 3.9 (*NPNF²* 11:217).

before lunch, all the monks gathered for the divine liturgy, but they did not gather at the third and sixth hours.[55]

THE GROWTH OF CHRISTIAN HYMNOGRAPHY

The basis of monastic worship services in the fourth and fifth centuries was the singing (or reading) of psalms. In fact, Christian hymnography at first occupied an extremely modest place in monastery worship services, especially in Egypt. The Egyptian recluse Pambo, answering the question of why he did not sing troparia and canons,[56] as they did in Alexandria's parishes, replied with a smile, "Not for this reason did monks depart into the desert—to display themselves before God, invent things, sing songs, make faces, flail one's arms about and shift from one foot to the other."[57]

But later it was precisely the monasteries that became the major centers of liturgical composition. Between the sixth and ninth centuries, a great number of troparia, canons, and other works of liturgical poetry were created in the monasteries of the Orthodox East, and these entered into the daily cycle of services.

The start of the rapid growth of liturgical poetry was already taking place in the fourth century. This development occurred both in the large centers of the Byzantine Empire as well as in its outskirts, and even beyond its borders, especially in the Persian Sassanid Empire. This is precisely where the great hymnographer of the Church, the venerable Ephraim the Syrian, lived (c. 306–373). Saint Ephraim wrote in the Syriac language, but many of his poetic works were translated into Greek. Later, following his death, a huge corpus of theological and liturgical works in Greek was ascribed to his name. The creative output of Saint Ephraim (and also the Greek pseudo-Ephraim) became the "binding link" between the Palestinian-Aramaic tradition and Byzantine instructive literature.[58]

---

[55]Ibid. 3.11 (*NPNF*[2] 11:218).

[56]Troparion—originally (around the 4th c.) a short prayer written in rhythmic prose and performed following each verse of a psalm; in the later Byzantine rite (6th–9th c.), the troparion was set apart from the psalms and came to be a separate genre of hymnography in worship. The canon consists of nine songs, each containing several troparia. Cf. Egon Wellesz, *A History of Byzantine Music and Hymnography*, 2nd ed. (Oxford: Clarendon Press, 1961), 171, 198. [The dismissal hymn, called a "troparion" by Russians and many English speaking Orthodox, is called an "apolytikion" by the Greeks (from the Greek *apolysis*, "dismissal").—*Ed.*]

[57]Wilhelm Christ and Matthaios Paranikas, *Anthologia graeca carminum christianorum* (Leipzig: B. G. Teubner, 1871), XXIX–XXX.

[58]Sergei Averintsev, *The poetics of early Byzantine literature* [in Russian] (Moscow: CODA, 1997), 188–189.

Saint Ephraim the Syrian. Fresco. Dormition Cathedral of the Moscow Kremlin. 16th c.

Among the church fathers of the fourth century, Saint Ephraim the Syrian occupies such a singular place primarily because he belonged to a tradition that greatly differed from that represented by the Greek fathers of his day. The growth of Greek theology of that period was moved by the effort to find a maximally precise and full expression of Christian doctrine, and to establish boundaries to separate Orthodoxy from heresy. For the attainment of this goal it was necessary, first, to work out a precise theological terminology and, second, to express the basic truths of the Christian faith in the language of dogmatic definitions. Precisely these tasks were solved by the Ecumenical Councils, which stood up in opposition to heresies and formulated the Christian doctrine in special instructive documents called "*horoi*" (definitions) for the teaching of the faith.

Saint Ephraim set for himself the same task as his Greek contemporaries. He also opposed heresies and formulated for his readers (listeners) the theological teaching of the Church. But the arsenal of tools that he used was different. He vested theological truths not in the armor of precise dogmatic definitions, but rather in the colorful finery of poetic symbols and metaphors.[59] This difference in the selection of tools reveals a difference in the theological method itself. For Saint Ephraim, theology is not an attempt to define or prove something; rather, for him, to theologize does not mean to speak about God or to contemplate about him—it is to praise God in prayer. It was more important for him that the truths of the Christian faith be lived out by the faithful in prayerful experience than for these truths to be thoroughly comprehended, considered, defined, and proven.

This very approach was characteristic of the Byzantine hymnographers of the following period, among whom the venerable Romanos the Melodist (sixth century)[60] occupies the leading place. This legendary personality stands at the source

---

[59]See Sebastian Brock, *The Luminous Eye: The Spiritual World of Saint Ephrem the Syrian* (Kalamazoo, MI: Cistercian Publications, 1985), 10–11.

[60]The precise dates of Saint Romanos' life are unknown. Allegedly he was born at the end of the fifth century and died no later than 555 (insofar as his fifty-first kontakion establishes this *terminus post quem*.) See William Lawrence Petersen, *The Diatessaron and Ephrem Syrus as Sources of Romanos the Melodist*, CSCO 475, Subsidia 74 (Louvain: Peeters, 1985), 3.

of the creation of the yearly cycle of Orthodox liturgical poetry. His compositions were the foundation of many liturgical texts used in the Orthodox Church.

Saint Romanos was familiar with the compositions of Saint Ephraim the Syrian, and he borrowed much from him, both in poetic craft and in terms of developing individual liturgical subjects and theological themes. The compositions of Saint Ephraim were well known to Saint Romanos, not only in the Greek translation, but also in the Syriac original.[61] Having equal mastery of both languages, Saint Romanos was able in his works to assimilate the successes of the Semitic hymnographical tradition and transfer them to a Byzantine realm. This resulted in the emergence of a unique poetic style, in which elements of national Greek poetry and traditional genres of Syriac poetry were interwoven.[62]

Saint Romanos the Melodist. Contemporary Icon.

Despite the fact that a major portion of the poetic inheritance left by Saint Romanos the Melodist has not remained in the worship services of the Orthodox Church, it is difficult to overestimate the influence of this poet on the formation of the entire cycle of liturgical texts. With his kontakia[63] dedicated to various dates of the church year, he set the tone, so to speak, for the many works of subsequent generations of Byzantine hymnographers. In the canons and stichera created by them, the same themes are worked out that appear in Saint Romanos' kontakia. It is therefore justified that many consider him to be the father of Byzantine church hymnography.

One of the most characteristic features of Saint Romanos the Melodist's kontakia is the existence (in the majority of them) of a plot that supposes the participation of several acting characters, entering into dialogues either with the author or with one another. Saint Romanos does not set for himself the task of reproducing historical events with the closest resemblance to how they may have occurred in reality. Rather, he gives a certain iconographic reproduction of these events, placing

---

[61]See William Lawrence Petersen, "The Dependence of Romanos the Melodist upon the Syriac Ephrem: Its Importance for the Origin of the Kontakion," *Vigiliae Christianae* 39, no. 2 (June 1985): 171–187. See also Petersen, *Diatessaron*, 16.

[62]Wellesz, *History*, 184–185.

[63]For Saint Romanos a kontakion (from the Greek κοντάκιον–"stick") is a poetic work composed of separate hymns (stanzas), united by a common thematic and rhythmic character. Each hymn concludes with a refrain.

words in the mouths of the characters that correspond to the theological content of the event described, and not those words which the character would have spoken in the real circumstance. In Saint Romanos' kontakia, all of the characters acting in a particular dramatic scene fully know its final result; moreover, bad characters appear to acknowledge their own wrongdoing and by their words emphasize this fact all the more.

Refrains played an important compositional role in Saint Romanos' kontakia. Often they were not connected directly with the subject of the kontakion, and appear artificially "stuck on" to the individual parts of the kontakion. Sometimes the overall tone of the refrain directly contradicted the overall mood of the kontakion: a kontakion possessing a tone of remorse might have a joyful refrain, or vice versa. In this way, the antinomic and paradoxical character of subjects to which kontakia are dedicated was emphasized, and "one semantic pole of philosophical-theological antinomy is localized in the general text while others—in the refrain."[64]

Saint Romanos' poetic style is genetically linked with the Semitic tradition to which Saint Ephraim the Syrian belonged. The influence of the Semitic tradition explains, in particular, the fact that Saint Romanos utilized not the classical quantitative meter, which is based on the alternation of long and short vowels, but accentual meter, which is built on the principle of alternating lines with a recurring number of syllables and with stress consistently in the same places. Owing to the use of accentual meter, liturgical poetry could be understood by simple people,[65] in contrast to the poetry of Saint Gregory the Theologian, for example, whose reading was the lot of the intellectual elite.[66]

In the sixth and seventh centuries, the kontakia of Saint Romanos were greatly popular, but beginning in the eighth century new genres of liturgical works, especially canons, began to supplant kontakia in use during worship services. As a rule, only the opening stanzas of former kontakia remained in the divine services.

Following the removal of kontakia from liturgical usage,[67] the term "kontakion" came to be used to describe the opening stanzas of kontakia, which were preserved in liturgical books. The famous *Akathist Hymn to the Most Holy Theotokos*—some

[64]Averintsev, *Poetics*, 230.

[65]A. Vasil'ev, "Concerning Greek church hymns" [in Russian], *Byzantine Chronicle* 3 (1896): 582–633, at 623.

[66]Saint Gregory the Theologian used classical quantitative meter but in his time the difference between long and short vowels was already not audibly perceptible. Saint Gregory's poetry was not intended for liturgical use; rather, it bore a didactic character.

[67]Only two full kontakia were preserved in use: a service for the departed (*Rite for the Burial of Priests*) and the kontakion for the Expulsion of Adam (in the service of Forgiveness Sunday).

scholars consider Saint Romanos the author of this work—represents a development of the genre of the kontakion (as this term was understood in the time of Saint Romanos the Melodist).[68] This akathist later served as a model for the creation of other akathists. These included the akathists to the Most Sweet Jesus, to Saint Nicholas, and to many saints.

The development of the genre of the canon is linked with the name of Saint Andrew of Crete (*c.* 660–*c.* 750). He is the author of the *Great Canon of Repentance*, which is read in the Orthodox Church twice during the year. It is read once in parts during the first four days of Great Lent, and again, in its entirety, on the Wednesday of the fifth week of the fast. Written in verse, this canon is a comprehensive poetic composition on the theme of repentance, in which the illustrative material is based on biblical subjects. The canon is made up of nine "odes"; the content of each ode has something in common with one of the biblical canticles performed during matins.[69] The verses of the *Great Canon of Repentance* are inserted into the verses of the biblical canticles in such a way that each verse has the same number of syllables as the corresponding verse from the biblical canticle; its content resonates with the canticle as well.

Saint Andrew of Crete. Contemporary Icon.

This rather complicated form of liturgical composition was most popular among Byzantine hymnographers, and Saint Andrew had many imitators. The young contemporaries of Saint Andrew—Saint John of Damascus and Saint Cosmas of Maiuma (*c.* 685–*c.* 750)—were authors of liturgical canons dedicated to feasts of the Church.[70] The most famous of Saint John's poetic works is the paschal canon performed during matins on the night of holy Pascha.

[68]Concerning the Akathist Hymn, see Egon Wellesz, *The Akathistos Hymn*, Monumenta Musicae Byzantinae Transcripta 9 (Copenhagen: Munksgaard, 1957); Wellesz, *History*, 191–197; Averintsev, *Poetics*, 243–249.

[69]The biblical canticles will be discussed in more detail in the section on matins.

[70]Scholars do not agree concerning the question of which of these three cited hymnographers deserves pride of place in the creation of the genre of the canon. E. Wellesz considers Andrew of Crete the creator of this genre. See Wellesz, *History*, 204. But a number of contemporary scholars think that all three hymnographers should be considered the creators of the genre. See Andrew Louth, *St John Damascene: Tradition and Originality in Byzantine Theology*, Oxford Early Christian Studies (Oxford: Oxford University Press, 2002), 257.

Worship in Constantinople

Constantinople occupies a special place in the development of Orthodox liturgical rites and church hymnography. The very layout of this grandiose city and its abundance of churches and monasteries facilitated its transformation into one of the major centers of liturgical composition in the Orthodox East in the fourth

through sixth centuries.[71] Constantinople's significance increased as that of other centers—Alexandria, Antioch, Jeursalem, and Edessa—diminished. It was precisely in Constantinople, the "new Rome" of Emperor Constantine and his successors, that the liturgical rite acquired that "blinding magnificence"[72] that has left a mark on Orthodox worship even to the present day.

Collection of Byzantine Hymnody. Constantinople. 1360s.

In particular, the many liturgical processions and cross processions—which had become quite widespread and greatly popular—had an influence on the development of the Constantinopolitan rite. Because of these processions, Orthodox worship acquired forever a character of dynamic sacred action. This action was to take place in several places and required movement within the temple or even outside of its walls. (This was certainly not a static act of motionless prayer.) The liturgy's small and great entrances, as well as the cross processions performed on Pascha, altar feasts (parish feast days), and other most significant days for the church community, have been preserved in contemporary liturgical practice from these ancient festal actions.

An event of unprecedented significance in the development of Constantinople's liturgical Typikon was the sixth-century construction of the Hagia Sophia Church, in which the divine services were performed by the patriarch, often in the presence of the emperor. In Hagia Sophia, worship acquired a character not only of "common work" but also of mass action, in which hundreds of clergy and thousands of laypersons participated. The roster of the temple's clergy and church servers alone numbered more than four hundred. Emperor Justinian determined that the size

---

[71]See, in particular, John F. Baldovin, *The Urban Character of Christian Worship: The Origins, Development, and Meaning of Stational Liturgy*, Orientalia Christiana Analecta 228 (Rome: Pontificio Istituto Orientale, 1987), 167–181.

[72]Robert F. Taft, *The Byzantine Rite: A Short History*, American Essays in Liturgy (Collegeville, MN: Liturgical Press, 1992), 31.

of the clerical staff of Hagia Sophia should not exceed sixty presbyters, one hundred deacons, forty deaconesses, ninety sub-deacons, one hundred and ten readers, twenty-five singers, and one hundred doorkeepers.[73] In reality, there could have been considerably more clergy because clergy from other churches in Constantinople as well as a great number of guests participated in the worship services.[74]

Church of Hagia Sophia in Constantinople. Contemporary view.

Magnificent worship—whose composition was regulated by the Typikon of the Great Church—befitted this magnificent temple. One of the characteristic features of this Typikon and the Typika of other cathedrals in Constantinople was the direction to perform festive "all-night vigils" or "panikhidas"[75] on the eves of great feasts and several Sundays. All-night vigils were lengthy liturgical rites which began at the setting of the sun and continued until sunrise. A brief description of the all-night vigil performed in the Church of the Most-Holy Theotokos in Blachernae is given in *The Book of Ceremonies* of Emperor Constantine VIII Porphyrogenitus ("the Purple-born," 913–959). From this description, it follows that the all-night vigil was a public event that encompassed the entire city. A single all-night vigil was served for the entire city, at which clergy and laypersons from other churches congregated:

> The patriarch goes away on the Saturday evening to the Church of the Most Holy Theotokos at Blacherni. With him go metropolitans, archbishops and bishops, as many as happen to be in the City on the said day, and likewise the clergy of the Great Church and those from churches outside, and as many as practise the solitary life in all the monasteries in this God-guarded City, and they all complete the all-night vigil's hymn of praise in the venerable church.[76]

[73]Justinian, *Novellae Constitutiones* 3.1, in *Corpus Juris Civilis* 3.21.

[74]Robert F. Taft, *The Great Entrance: A History of the Transfer of Gifts and other Preanaphoral Rites of the Liturgy of St. John Chrysostom*, Orientalia Christiana Analecta 200 (Rome: Pontificium Institutum Studiorum Orientalium, 1975), 201.

[75]The Greek word *pannychēs* means "all-night." In contemporary Russian practice this word is used to describe the liturgical service for the departed, but in the Byzantine period it was used in accordance with its literal meaning.

[76]Constantine VII, *The Book of Ceremonies* 1.28.1 (PG 112:393–396a). The above translation from Constantine VII, *The Book of Ceremonies*, trans. Ann Moffatt and Maxeme Tall, Byzantina Australiensia 18 (Canberra: Australian Association for Byzantine Studies, 2012), 1:156–157.

Alongside Hagia Sophia, liturgical composition actively developed in the monasteries of Constantinople and its vicinities. The famous Studion Monastery was one of the centers for the composition of hymns. The great work of collecting and editing ancient liturgical texts, and also the creation of new texts, was conducted in this monastery from the eighth to the ninth century. The liturgical books mentioned earlier and used up to the present day in the Orthodox Church—the Octoechos, Lenten Triodion, and Pentecostarion—were the result of this activity.

The corpus of texts that entered into these books was formulated in the sixth through ninth centuries. (However, certain texts belong to both later and earlier periods). Several texts were written by great Byzantine hymnographers such as Saint Romanos the Melodist, Saint Sophronius of Jerusalem (†638), the Venerable Andrew of Crete, Saints John of Damascus, Cosmas of Maiuma, Theodore the Studite (759–826), Joseph the Studite (762–832), Theophanes Graptus (778–845), and Joseph the Hymnographer (c. 816–c. 886).[77] These authors, as well as many others whose works entered into the liturgical books but whose names have not been recorded in history, were not only "professional" poet-hymnographers, but also exceptional theologians, capable of capturing the richness of Orthodox dogma in poetic form.

Not only venerable monks were among the Byzantine hymnographers whose works entered into the liturgical books of the Orthodox Church. Emperors participated in creating liturgical works as well. Emperor Justinian (r. 527–565), in particular, is the author of the hymn *Only-begotten Son and Immortal Word of God*, which is sung at the liturgy. Leo VI the Wise (r. 886–912) was the author of the eleven gospel stichera that correspond to the eleven gospel narratives read at Sunday matins.[78] His son Constantine VII "the Purple-born" (r. 913–959) is credited with the authorship of the exapostilaria to the gospel stichera written by his father.

A woman also ranks among the hymnographers—the nun Saint Cassia (c. 805–c. 867), whose fate was extremely unusual.[79] In her youth, she was presented as a potential bride to the Emperor Theophilus (r. 829–842), but Theophilus preferred another girl, Theodora, who later entered into the ranks of saints. Cassia founded

[77]Kallistos (Ware), "The Meaning of the Great Fast," in *The Lenten Triodion*, trans. Mother Mary and Kallistos (Ware) (London: Faber & Faber, 1977), 40–43.

[78]Leo the Wise also wrote stichera for Lazarus Saturday and hymns for the Exaltation of the Cross. He also delivered festal homilies that remain extant.—*Ed.*

[79]There is a great deal of literature concerning Cassia. In particular, see Ilse Rochow, *Studien zu der Person, den Werken und dem Nachleben der Dichterin Kassia*, Berliner byzantinistische Arbeiten 38 (Berlin: Akademie-Verlag, 1967); and Antonia Tripolitis ed. and trans., *Kassia: The Legend, the Woman, and her Work* (New York: Garland, 1992).

a monastery at which she became a nun and engaged in literary labors. She was the author of numerous epigrams and also a great number of stichera and canons. In particular, she is the author of the sticheron for the Nativity of Christ "When Augustus reigned alone upon the earth,"[80] and also the sticheron performed on Holy Wednesday dedicated to the sinful woman who anointed Christ's feet with fragrant oil, "When the sinful woman brought oil of myrrh. . . ."[81]

Saint Cassia. Icon. Greece.

In the liturgical texts that entered into the service books of the Orthodox Church, there are interpretations of many episodes in the life of Christ and many aspects of his teaching. In this sense, it is possible to say that liturgical texts are a "gospel according to the Church." Liturgical texts give the faithful the opportunity to come into contact with the gospel story and to make it a part of their spiritual experience.

In several cases, the liturgical texts represent a detailed poetic commentary on a specific gospel subject. The canon for the Annunciation, written in the form of a dialogue between Archangel Gabriel and the Theotokos, serves as an example:

The Angel: "In gladness I cry to thee: incline thine ear and give heed unto me, as I tell thee of God's conception without seed. For thou, O Most Pure, hast found grace before the Lord such as no other woman ever found."

The Theotokos: "O Angel, help me to understand the meaning of thy words. How shall what thou sayest come to pass? Tell me clearly, how shall I conceive, who am a virgin maid? And how shall I become the Mother of my Maker?"

The Angel: "O Virgin, thou dost seek to know from me the manner of thy conceiving, but this is beyond all interpretation. The Holy Spirit shall overshadow thee in His creative power and shall make this come to pass."

The Theotokos: "My mother Eve, accepting the suggestion of the serpent, was banished from divine delight: and therefore I fear thy strange salutation, for I take heed lest I slip."

---

[80]Menaion. The Nativity of Christ. Vespers. Stichera on "Lord, I call."
[81]Lenten Triodion. Great Wednesday. Matins. Stichera on the Praises.

Annunciation of the Most-Holy Theotokos.
Miniature from the Gospel. 13th c. Mount Athos.

The Angel: "I am sent as the envoy of God to disclose to thee the divine will. Why art thou, O Undefiled, afraid of me, who rather am afraid of thee? Why, O Lady, dost thou stand in awe of me, who stand in reverent awe of thee?" (Menaion. Annunciation of the Most Holy Theotokos. Matins. Canon.)

The liturgical texts are not merely commentaries on the Gospels. Often they speak of things on which the Gospels are silent. The divine service for the feast of the Nativity of Christ may be cited as an example. The Gospel is very laconic concerning the Nativity: "Now the birth of Jesus Christ was as follows: After his mother Mary was betrothed to Joseph, before they came together, she was found with child of the Holy Spirit. Then Joseph her husband, being a just man, and not wanting to make her a public example, was minded to put her away secretly" (Mt 1.18–19). In this narrative, much has remained behind the scenes. In particular, the Gospel is silent regarding the private drama of Joseph. One can only guess at his worries, doubts, and what he might have said to his bride when he learned that she was with child. The liturgical texts attempt to reconstruct the dialogue between Joseph and Mary in poetic form:

> Joseph spoke thus to the Virgin: 'What is this doing, O Mary, that I see in thee? I fail to understand and am amazed, and my mind is struck with dismay. Go from my sight, therefore, with all speed. What is this doing, O Mary, that I see in thee? Instead of honour, thou hast brought me shame; instead of gladness, sorrow; instead of praise, reproof. No further shall I bear the reproach of men. I received thee from the priests of the temple, as one blameless before the Lord. And what is this that I now see? (Menaion. The Eve of the Nativity of Christ. First Hour. Troparion.)

> O Virgin, when Joseph went up to Bethlehem wounded by sorrow, thou didst cry to him: 'Why art thou downcast and troubled, seeing me great with child? Why art thou wholly ignorant of the fearful mystery that comes to pass in me? Henceforth, cast every fear aside and understand this strange marvel: for in my womb God now descends upon earth for mercy's sake, and He has taken flesh. Thou shalt see Him according to His good pleasure, when He is born;

and filled with joy thou shalt worship Him as Thy Creator. (Menaion. The Eve of the Nativity of Christ. Ninth Hour. Troparion.)

It is possible to regard these kinds of texts as poetic invention or church rhetoric, but it is also possible to see in them something more—an attempt to delve into the feelings and emotional experiences of the people by whose hands this sacred history was played out. Byzantine hymnographers had the richest arsenal of literary methods at their disposal for expressing the truths of God's revelation. This entire arsenal was necessary for them because they spoke of things which the eye did not see, the ear did not hear, and which did not enter into the hearts of people (see 1 Cor 2.9); things which were outside the boundaries of possibility for human reason, which lay in the realm of faith. In Christianity there are many mystical truths that are difficult to expound with the language of prose. Poetry is needed to help people connect with these truths.

The activity of the eastern Christian hymnographers—Saint Ephraim the Syrian in the fourth century, Saint Romanos the Melodist in the sixth century, Saint John of Damascus in the eighth century, or Studite monks in the eighth through tenth centuries—determined once and for all the overall structure and content of the worship services of the Orthodox Church. An exceptional form of expressing theological truth, which greatly differs from a prosaic form, as well as a distinct system of images, which facilitates not so much an emotional perception of the truths of the faith as a spiritual understanding of them—all of this has been preserved in the Orthodox divine services up to the present day. At the same time, a high level of intellectualism, characteristic of liturgical poetry, has remained in the divine services, which makes it difficult for the contemporary listener to understand.

Saint John of Damascus. Illuminated Manuscript of the Festal Menaion. 1760–1764.

The development of the liturgical rite in Constantinople over the course of five centuries led to the use in the tenth century of two Typika, the Typikon of the Great Church and the Studite Typikon, in the imperial capital. The Typikon of the Great Church reflected the particularities of ceremonial worship in cathedrals, whereas the Studite Typikon was in fact the Typikon of monastic services. Their differences pertained not so much to the divine liturgy, which was celebrated the same way in cathedrals and in monasteries, as to the other services of the daily cycle. In particular, the Studite Typikon differed from the Typikon of the Great Church in that it called for kathismata, readings, stichera, and canons, which were part of Studite worship, had replaced more ancient elements such as antiphons and troparia.

In cathedrals, the services of the daily cycle were formed into a so-called "sung office." In this, the main elements were the priest's prayers, deacon's litanies, psalms performed in the antiphonal manner, and chanting. There were few troparia and stichera, and canons were altogether absent. In monastery worship, on the other hand, a significant place was occupied by readings and the singing of proper Christian hymns—stichera and canons—composed by Studite monks or inherited from hymnographers of previous generations. The collections of Christian hymns—the Octoechos, Lenten Triodion, Pentecostarion, and Menaion—were created precisely in a monastic setting, because the Euchologion (the analogue of the contemporary Horologion and Priest's Service Book) was predominantly used in cathedral worship.

Saint Symeon the New Theologian. Miniature. Archimandrite Zenon. 1996.

Moreover, monastery worship differed from cathedral practice in that the lives of saints and the writings of the church fathers were read during the divine services.

At the turn of the eleventh century, the daily cycle of worship in Constantinople's monasteries corresponded to the principle of the "Seven Prayers" and included the midnight office, matins with first hour, third, sixth, and ninth hours, vespers, and compline. Detailed information concerning the liturgical life of Constantinople's monasteries at the start of the eleventh century is contained in the *Life of Venerable Symeon the New Theologian*, compiled by his disciple Saint Niketas Stethatos. Describing the life of Saint Symeon in Saint Mammas Monastery, Saint Niketas records that "on Sunday and the feast the cell saw him laboring from evening until morning."[82] Niketas' remark confirms that vigils were not performed in the monastery, even on important feast days. On weekdays Symeon woke at "the seventh hour after midnight" (around one o'clock in the morning) and went to the church to sing "morning songs" (*heōthēnoi hymnoi*); then he was present at matins (*orthros*).[83] Evidently, *mesonyktikon* (the midnight office) is meant by the term "morning songs";

---

[82]Niketas Stethatos, *The Life of Symeon the New Theologian* 25.13–14.
[83]Ibid. 28.1–3.

matins probably followed it. A long break came at the end of matins: Symeon could spend a little time in his cell, and then he could sit outside, after which he returned to his cell where he read holy Scripture and the lives of the saints and also "copied God-inspired books."[84] The liturgy (*hē hagia anaphora*—"the divine offering") followed.[85] Niketas also mentions (though only obliquely) the evening service.[86]

In the works of Saint Symeon the New Theologian himself, we find references to matins (*orthros*) with the reading of the Six Psalms, the singing or reading of psalms with refrains (Gr. *stichologia*, Sl. *stichoslovie*), readings (*anagnōseis*), and a final troparion.[87] He also mentions vespers (*lychnikon*)[88] and compline ("evening prayers").[89] He probably had the midnight office in mind when he speaks of the *amōmoi* ("blameless"—the reading of Psalm 118), which is the basic component of the midnight office. The saint recommends reading this service in the cell, from which we may conclude that in his monastery, *mesonyktikon* (the midnight office) was read by monks in the cells.[90] This sentence confirms the allusion to the cell prayer before matins.[91]

When he spoke of the monastery's services of the daily cycle, Symeon the New Theologian emphasizes how important they are for the spiritual perfection of monks. Instructing new novices, he writes:

[A monk] should rise up before matins and pray the appointed prayer, and thus after that rouse himself to the morning service [*doxologia*] with all [the others], and with understanding and watchfulness stay through the whole of it, giving great heed to the beginning of the hymnody, that is to the six psalms, the psalms with refrains [*stichologia*], and the readings; [and he should do this] without hesitation, not relaxing his body, not shifting from one foot to the other or leaning against the walls and columns, but he ought to keep his arms firmly folded, his feet resting flat on the floor, his head not nodding this way and that; his thought not frivolous nor his mind distracted . . . to the extent that he is able, [he ought to keep] his eyes and his soul attentive solely to the psalmody and the reading and the power of the words of holy Scripture, whether read

---

[84]Ibid. 26.20–27.2.
[85]Ibid. 27.5.
[86]Ibid. 19–20.
[87]Symeon the New Theologian, *Catechetical Discourse* 26.114–115 (SC 113).
[88]Ibid. 26.257–261 (SC 113).
[89]Ibid. 26.268 (SC 113).
[90]Ibid. 26.294–298 (SC 113).
[91]Ibid. 26.294–298 (SC 113).

or sung, so that no word in it pass unnoticed, but that his soul, enriched by all of these, may come to compunction and humility and the illumination of the Holy Spirit.[92]

Two Typika—Cathedral and Monastery—continued to exist in the period after the tenth century, but their gradual integration was observed. In the period of the Crusades, when Constantinople was sacked [AD 1204] and magnificent worship in cathedrals became impossible, the Monastery Typikon took root in cathedral practice as well. In the thirteenth century, one of the editions of the Monastery Typikon, created in Palestine and named the Jerusalem Typikon,[93] spread throughout all the monasteries of Asia Minor. From there it came to Mount Athos and Constantinople, where it completely replaced the "sung office." At the turn of the fifteenth century, the Russian Church adopted the Jerusalem Typikon, having earlier used the Studite Typikon in worship.[94] The development of the Orthodox liturgical Typikon virtually ended after the fall of Constantinople in 1453. After this, the only additions to the divine services were services compiled in honor of newly glorified saints and certain liturgical customs of local significance.

The Monastic Character of Orthodox Worship

The coexistence and integration of various liturgical typika as a historical phenomenon is probably of interest at present only to specialists in the field of liturgics. But in order to have an understanding of the meaning of worship, every Orthodox Christian must be aware of the fact that contemporary Orthodox worship, including that which is performed in city or village parish churches, is—in its primal Typikon—monastic worship. Even the Typikon which is used in the Orthodox Church up to the present day for uniting the services of daily, weekly, and yearly cycles is a monastic Typikon and contains directions intended for monks, not laymen. While in the eighth through the tenth centuries there was one Typikon for cathedral and parish churches and another for monasteries, after the tenth century the parish Typikon completely fell out of use, and only the monastic Typikon remained.

[92]Ibid. 26.23–38 (SC 113).

[93]Tradition traces the compilation of the Jerusalem Typikon to Venerable Sabba the Sanctified, but in reality this Typikon, as well as other Monastery Typika, were the fruit of collective work of many generations of monks. For more detail, see Nikolai Uspenskii, *Orthodox vespers: A historical-liturgical overview. The order of the all-night vigil in the Orthodox East and in the Russian Church*, vol. 1 of *Works on liturgics* [in Russian] (Moscow: Izdatel'stvo Moskovskoi Patriarkhii, 2004), 155–175.

[94]"Worship," *Orthodox Encyclopedia*, 541.

This situation gave rise to—and continues to give rise to—several obvious inconveniences. First of all, the Typikon of monastic services is intended for a community of people whose major occupation is to participate in worship services. It is impossible to demand daily attendance at services that last many hours from a person in a secular position, who is supporting a family and raising children. While monks are able to pray throughout the entire night, regular participation in "all-night vigils" (in the literal sense) is not possible for laymen.

As a result, church practice, both in Greece and in Russia as well as in other countries with Orthodox traditions, created its own order of parish services, which is not established in any Typikon. This order is essentially the monastic order of services, albeit significantly reduced. For example, in the contemporary parish practice of the Greek Church, the all-night vigil is hardly practiced, while in the Russian Church the "all-night vigil" is the name given to the service performed in the evening that lasts two or three hours—by no means the entire night, as prescribed in the Typikon. Matins, the service intended to be served at the hour before the rising of the sun, is performed in the evening. Of the two kathismata prescribed by the Typikon, only one is read during the divine services in some churches, while only a single psalm is read in others, and in yet other churches the kathismata are altogether omitted. In the place of the intended eight stichera, four or two are often performed; in place of the intended fourteen troparia of the canon, four are sung, and so forth. Many parts of matins are altogether omitted—the "biblical canticles," for example, and also

*Cross Procession in
Tobolsk Diocese.*

numerous teachings that the Typikon prescribes to be read in the church. Worship is abridged even in monasteries, although not to the same degree as in parishes.

Abridgements of the church Typikon have been made unequally in the various services. For instance, compline and midnight office[95] are performed only in monasteries and have been almost completely removed from parish practice. Matins

---

[95]An exception is great compline, which is part of the office of the all-night vigil on the eve of a few great feasts (Nativity, Theophany) and is performed during Great Lent. Another exception is the midnight office at Pascha. [In Greek practice, small compline is served on the first four Fridays of Great Lent, along with portions of the akathist to the Theotokos. Small compline also forms an important part of everyday piety for many in the Greek tradition. Since Greek prayerbooks do not contain "evening prayers," many of the faithful pray compline in their homes every evening.—*Ed.*]

and vespers are performed in parish churches regularly, but their composition has been radically shortened. The divine liturgy, on the other hand, is served almost without any abridgements. The hours (first, third, sixth, and ninth) are also served without abridgements. But while they once were separate services performed at a certain time of the day, the hours are now services that have been joined to other services. First hour is joined to matins, third and sixth hours are read before the liturgy, and ninth hour is either read before vespers or omitted completely.

Despite all the abridgements, Orthodox worship remains extremely lengthy. In a normal parish, the liturgy lasts about two hours, and the all-night vigil lasts two to three hours (always in the evening). Festal services and services during Great Lent often last more than three hours. Services are longer in monasteries and may last five or six hours. (An example is the all-night vigil, or matins, joined with the liturgy).

The length of worship services is one of the factors that make it difficult for some people to attend church services. At the same time, there is no information which would confirm that the level of attendance at church services is considerably higher in Catholic or Protestant communities, where services often last between twenty and sixty minutes. Moreover, the Orthodox faithful who do not consider it possible to stand for the duration of a two- or three-hour-long service often do not arrive by the beginning of the service, or they leave early, not waiting for the end. But when this is the case, it is difficult to completely immerse oneself in the atmosphere of worship, which requires attendance in the church from the beginning to the end of the service.

The divergence between the Typikon and today's practice is so significant that it would require great initial preparation to serve matins or the all-night vigil in their entirety according to the Typikon. At the beginning of the twentieth century, a reconstruction of the all-night vigil in full accordance with the Typikon was attempted in Kiev Theological Academy. The preparation lasted several months and required significant material expense. The all-night vigil itself lasted nearly eight hours. Of this, the reading of the canon lasted more than two hours. Plain chant in four-part harmony was used. Mikhail Skaballanovich, the organizer of this unusual enterprise, recalled:

Words can hardly describe the impact this "historic all-night service" had on those who listened to it. . . . Two of those leading the service, who knew the second chapter of the Typikon by heart . . . took turns in getting confused during the service and needed to check with one another to be sure what part came next. It was as if most of the participants in the service . . . were drunk during it. . . . One student, who liked to nap, exited the church several times to undress and get into bed, but, being unable to fall asleep from the thought that such an original and unprecedented concert was taking place a few steps away, returned to the church. One female student learned all the psalms, stichera, canons, and biblical canticles that would be sung before coming to the all-night vigil. . . . It is proposed that everything should be sung in Great Znamenny Chant the next time, which would extend the all-night vigil by about three to four hours.[96]

As far as we know, there was no "next time." This curious event only confirmed that the Typikon, with respect to the all-night vigil and especially matins, is impracticable under modern conditions, and if someone tried to fulfill it, it would be received as an "original, unprecedented concert." It is true that all-night vigils, similar to this, and even more lengthy, are performed on Mount Athos to the present day. The author of this book had the opportunity to be present at such a service in the Great Lavra of Saint Athanasius of Mount Athos on the day of the commemoration of the founder of the monastery in 1992. Altogether, the worship lasted nearly fifteen hours, from evening until noon. It included vespers, matins, first, third, and sixth hours, the mysteries of baptism and the divine liturgy. But it is evident that in parish conditions the performance of such worship services is unthinkable.

The radical divergence between the Typikon and liturgical practice leads one to consider the necessity of the "legalization" of current practice by formulating a typikon that would take into account the particularities of parish life.

[96]Mikhail Skaballanovich, "The practical feasibility of the entire observation of the all-night vigil" [in Russian], in *The Typikon Interpreted: An explanatory presentation of the Typikon with a historical introduction* [in Russian], 2nd ed. (Kiev, 1913), 330–336, at 336.

2

Vespers, Compline, Midnight Office, Matins, the Hours

VESPERS

IN ACCORDANCE WITH THE TRADITION inherited from the Old Testament, in the Christian Church the liturgical day begins in the evening. The Typikon distinguishes between several types of vespers services—daily, great, little, and also vespers combined with the liturgy. Daily vespers is celebrated on weekdays; great vespers is served on the eves of Sundays and feast days (as part of the all-night vigil); little vespers is only served in some monasteries before the evening meal and prior to the all-night vigil. Vespers is united with the liturgy in those cases where the Typikon calls for the liturgy to be served in the evening: on Wednesdays and Fridays of Great Lent, on the eves of the Nativity and Theophany, and on Great Thursday and Great Saturday. When this is the case, only the beginning of vespers is used because it replaces the beginning of the liturgy (the service of the antiphons).

Contemporary vespers includes elements taken from Constantinople's "sung office" and the monastic evening rule of prayer. The confluence of these two rules, disparate in origin, took place back in the seventh century.[1]

Daily vespers begins with the words, "Come, let us worship God our king. Come, let us worship and fall down before Christ, our king and our God. Come, let us worship and fall down before Christ himself, our king and our God." In the accepted tradition of the Orthodox Church, these exclamations are spoken before the reading of the psalms. They indicate that the Church understands psalms, despite their origin in the Old Testament, to be christocentric prayers that the faithful experience through the prism of worshipping Christ as King and God.

When great vespers is part of the all-night vigil, it begins with the deacon's exclamation, "Arise," after which the Typikon calls for the priest to perform a full

---

[1] Uspenskii, *Orthodox Vespers*, 57.

Evening Worship in Saint Panteleimon Monastery. Mount Athos.

censing of the temple. Then the choir sings, "Lord, bless,"[2] and the priest exclaims, "Glory to the holy, consubstantial, life-creating, and undivided Trinity, always, now and ever, and unto ages of ages." Following "Amen," the usual beginning is omitted and "Come, let us worship" is sung, as is the custom, by the clergy in the sanctuary. In practice, however, the censing takes place not before the opening exclamation of the priest, but after the singing of "Come, let us worship," during the singing of Psalm 103.

It is supposed that this psalm entered into the order of vespers from the Palestinian monastic rule. (It is contained in the Horologion of the Lavra of Saint Sabba the Sanctified, dating to the eight or ninth century.)[3] At daily vespers Psalm 103 is read, and at great vespers it is sung by the choir. It is selected to be performed at vespers not only for the reason that the evening and night are mentioned in its verses ("the sun knows its going down. Thou madest darkness, and it is night"), but also for the reason that its overall content of praise corresponds with the beginning of the liturgical day. The general tone of the psalm is one of delight in God's

---

[2] There are two contemporary practices: in some churches the choir sings "Lord, bless," but in others the deacon says "Arise" while facing westward on the solea, then turning to the east he says, "Lord, bless." The latter is more common in American churches that follow the Russian tradition.—*Ed.*

[3] Uspenskii, *Orthodox Vespers*, 46.

wisdom and the diversity of the created world. In the practice of the Greek Church, a considerable part of Psalm 103 is read at great vespers and only the final verses are sung. In the tradition of the Russian Church, the psalm is chanted, but in parish practice it is sung in a significantly abridged form.

During the singing of the psalm, the priest reads the so-called "prayers of light." These prayers were part of vespers in Constantinople's "sung office." Each prayer of light is thematically connected to a particular psalm. The first three prayers of light, "O Lord, compassionate and merciful," "O Lord, rebuke us not in thine anger," and "O Lord our God, remember us, thy sinful and unprofitable servants," are called in the liturgical manuscripts of the tenth through twelfth centuries the "prayers of the three antiphons" (which comprise the first set of three psalms). The fourth prayer ("O thou who, with never-silent hymns") was performed during the singing of Psalm 129. The fifth and sixth prayers ("O Lord, O Lord, who upholdest all things in the undefiled hollow of thy hand" and "O God, great and wonderful") are possibly ancient versions of liturgical prayers of the faithful. Ancient liturgical sources refer to the seventh prayer ("O great and most high God") as the dismissal prayer (that is, it was read at the end of vespers). Thematically, it is closer to the prayers from the eighth book of the *Apostolic Constitutions.*[4]

Illustration for Psalm 103. Chludov Psalter. Byzantium. c. 840s–850s.

As the order of vespers developed and some psalms and antiphons were substituted with others, the prayers of light gradually stood out as a separate order, and today they are read all at once in succession by the priest. Their content reveals the meaning of vespers as a service focused on thanksgiving as well as repentance and supplication. A particularly vesperal theme is present in the final two prayers ("who hast given us a pledge of the promised kingdom through the good things already bestowed upon us, and hast made us to shun all evil during that part of the day which is past," "who hast vouchsafed unto us sinners at this present hour also to come before thy presence with confession and to offer unto thee our evening hymn of glory," "grant that we may pass the present evening and the coming night in peace. Endue us with the armor of light. Deliver us from the terror of the night

[4]Uspenskii, *Orthodox Vespers*, 29–32.

and from everything that walks in darkness, and grant that the sleep which thou hast appointed for the repose of our infirmity may be free from every imagination of the devil").

The great litany follows Psalm 103 and the prayers of light, and does not differ from the great litany pronounced during other services, specifically during the liturgy and matins.

The Typikon then calls for the performance of a kathisma.[5] In the Orthodox Church, the Psalter is read in its entirety in worship services over the course of a single week, and the reading of kathismata is appointed during vespers and matins. One kathisma is read during vespers, two during matins. The reading of the Psalter begins at the resurrectional vespers (performed on Saturday evening), at which it is proper to read the first kathisma (Psalms 1–8). Accordingly, the second and third kathismata are read at the resurrectional matins (Psalms 9–16 and 17–23). At vespers on the eve of Monday (performed on Sunday evening), the kathisma is omitted, and from Monday matins right up to Saturday matins kathismata are read.[6] At the resurrectional vespers an antiphon is sung, "Blessed is the man," which is composed of separate verses selected from the first kathisma.

Next, following the little litany, the Typikon calls for the singing of Psalms 140, 141, 129, and 116. In contemporary monastic practice the first several verses of Psalm 140, beginning with the words "Lord, I call upon Thee, hear me," are sung by the choir while the subsequent verses are read. In parish practice a portion of the verses is often omitted. The psalms are sung in a particular melody determined by the tone of the week. During the singing of "Lord, I call," the deacon performs a full censing of the temple.

Stichera—referred to as "'Lord, I call' verses"—are added to the final verses of Psalm 141 and the verses of Psalms 129 and 116. Depending on the day, the number of stichera may be six, eight, or ten. Weekday vespers services usually have six verses, a festal all-night vigil has eight, and the resurrectional vespers has ten. It is often necessary to combine verses. For example, if Sunday coincides with the afterfeast of one of the major twelve feasts and the commemoration of a great saint, three resurrectional stichera are taken from the Octoechos, three festal stichera from the Menaion, and four stichera to the saint are also taken from the Menaion (but from

---

[5]The Typikon prescribes the singing of kathismata, but in practice they are read.

[6]Outside of Great Lent, the kathismata are read in order up to the fifteenth kathisma on Thurday at vespers. On Friday at matins, the nineteenth and twentieth kathismata are read; finally, on Saturday at matins the weekly cycle of Psalter readings ends with the sixteenth and seventeenth kathismata.—Ed.

a different service.) The final sticheron is always dedicated to the Theotokos and is called the "Theotokion."

Stichera represent an ancient poetic genre whose completed form dates to the seventh or eighth century. A considerable number of stichera that entered into the liturgical books of the Orthodox Church were written by the hymnographers of Studion Monastery from that period. Stichera are thematically connected with the event that is being celebrated. As such, resurrectional stichera are dedicated to the resurrection of Christ, festal stichera are dedicated to the celebrated event, and stichera to saints are dedicated to the life and ascetic works of the saint whose memory is commemorated on a given day.

An entrance made with the censer follows the stichera on "Lord, I call" at the resurrectional and festal vespers. It is done in the same way as the little entrance during the liturgy, the only difference being that the Gospel Book remains on the altar table.[7] The prayer of the entrance at vespers ("In the evening and in the morning and at noonday we praise thee, we bless thee, we give thanks to thee, and we pray unto thee, O Master of all . . .") differs from the prayer of the entrance at the liturgy ("O Master, Lord our God, who hast appointed in heaven orders and hosts of angels and archangels for the service of Thy glory . . .").

Following the entrance or directly following the completion of the stichera (when an entrance is not performed), the hymn *O Gladsome Light* is sung, whose text originates in the early Christian period:

O Gladsome Light of the holy glory of the immortal Father, heavenly, holy, blessed Jesus Christ, now that we have come to the setting of the sun and behold the light of evening, we praise Father, Son, and Holy Spirit: God. For meet it is at all times to worship thee with voices of praise, O Son of God and Giver of life, wherefore all the world glorifies thee.

In the Slavonic Horologia the authorship of the hymn is ascribed to Saint Sophronius, Patriarch of Jerusalem (patriarch from 634–644), but the hymn is actually significantly more ancient. The text of the hymn is cited in the Alexandrian codex of the Bible (fifth century). Even earlier, in the fourth century, Saint Basil the Great referred to this hymn as an "ancient" song and cited it as a testimony to the ancient Church's faith in the divinity of the Holy Spirit:

---

[7]At vespers, the entrance procession is performed with the gospel book only if a gospel reading will follow. This occurs only in special cases; for instance, during the combined service of vespers and the liturgy of Saint Basil the Great.

In addition, I will now add this point, which perhaps would be insignificant to introduce, but necessary as an ancient witness against someone who accuses us of novelty. It seemed good to our fathers that the grace of evening light not be receieved in silence; rather, it seemed good to them to give thanks at its first appearance. And we cannot say who is the father of those words of thanksgiving at the lighting of the lamp. Yet the people put forth the expression as an ancient one, and no one ever considered them impious when they said, "we glorify the Father and the Son and the Holy Spirit: God."

Now, if someone knows the hymn of Athenogenes, which he left to those who were with him as a kind of departing gift as he hastened toward perfection through fire, then he knows also the opinion that the martyrs held on the Spirit. And for this sort of argument, these points suffice.[8]

Greek Horologia refer to *O Gladsome Light* as "an ancient work, or, as some say, the work of the martyr Athenagoras." Some Greek Horologia call it the work of "the martyr Athenogenes," which is clearly based on the words of Saint Basil the Great cited above (although it is as if he is speaking about two separate hymns, one containing the words "We praise the Father and the Son and the Holy Spirit: God" and another, composed by the martyr Athenogenes).[9]

In the early Church the singing of the hymn *O Gladsome Light* was accompanied by the rite of the lighting of lamps. In the hymn, Jesus Christ is referred to as the gladsome light of the holy glory of the heavenly Father. Slavonic translations chose the word "gentle" to convey the Greek *hilaros*, which signifies not only "gentle" but also "bright" and "joyful." The words "now that we have come to the setting of the sun and behold the light of evening" expose the hymn's thematic link with the vesperal time of day (i.e. evening). The hymn is directed to Christ, but simultaneously contains a Trinitarian doxology ("we praise the Father and the Son and the Holy Spirit: God").

The prokeimenon follows *O Gladsome Light*. This incorporates several verses from the psalms. Each day of the week has its own prokeimenon. Special prokeimena are dedicated to feasts. Specially selected readings from the Old Testament are read following the prokeimenon on feast days and days which commemorate various especially revered saints. As a rule, there are three Old Testament readings. The Old Testament readings are followed by the litany of fervent supplication and

---

[8]Basil the Great, *On the Holy Spirit* 29.73 (PG 32:205a; Hildebrand, PPS).
[9]Mikhail Skaballanovich, *The Typikon Interpreted* [in Russian] (Moscow: Izdatel'stvo Stretenskogo monastyria, 2004), 559.

the litany of supplication, whose content does not differ from the corresponding litanies as they appear in the liturgy.

Between the two litanies (when vespers is served with an entrance) or before the first litany (when there is no entrance) the prayer "Vouchsafe, O Lord to keep us this evening without sin" is read. This prayer is composed of several biblical verses. In particular, the verse "Blessed art thou, O Lord God of our fathers, and praised and glorified be thy name forever" is taken from the song of the three children in the Book of the Prophet Daniel (3.26).[10] The verses "Let thy mercy, O Lord, be upon us even as we have placed our hope on thee" (Ps 32.22), "Blessed art thou, O Lord, teach me thy statutes" (Ps 118.12), and "Thy mercy, O Lord, endureth forever; despise not the works of thy hands" (Ps 137.8) all come from the Psalter. It is customary in the practice of the Russian Orthodox Church to sing this prayer at resurrectional and festal vespers.

The *aposticha* are performed after the litany of supplication. These verses number no more than six, but they are thematically linked with the feast being celebrated. The final verse is dedicated to the Theotokos.

Following the aposticha, the Typikon prescribes the reading of the prayer, "Lord, now lettest thou thy servant depart in peace"—the song of Saint Simeon from the Gospel according to Luke (see Lk 2.29–32).[11] The Prayer of Saint Simeon is mentioned as an evening prayer in the *Apostolic Constitutions*.[12] In the context of the evening worship service, the song of Saint Simeon is thematically linked to the end of the day and the approaching time of sleep. At the same time, it serves as a reminder of every person's final days and departure to the life of eternity. According to the Christian understanding, life is not lived in vain if a person has met Christ on life's path, as Saint Simeon did. Christ is

Righteous Saint Simeon the God-Receiver. Icon. Mount Sinai. 15th c.

[10] This is only found in the Greek Bible (Septuagint).

[11] The tradition in the Russian Church calls for the choir to sing this prayer, whereas in the Greek Church it is read. [This is also true of "Vouchsafe, O Lord."—*Ed.*]

[12] *Apostolic Constitutions* 7.48 (*ANF* 7:478).

the salvation that the Lord prepared "before the face of all people." And the day is not spent in vain if a person, during the course of the day, has not forgotten about Christ, but has turned to him in prayer.

Next, the Trisagion prayers are read up to and including the Lord's Prayer.[13] Following the priest's exclamation, the concluding ("dismissal") troparion is sung. At resurrectional vespers the dismissal troparion is the hymn "Rejoice, O Virgin Theotokos," sung thrice. This hymn is composed of the words addressed to the Theotokos by the Archangel Gabriel (see Lk 1.28) and the words of the righteous Elizabeth (see Lk 1.42). This is one of the most ancient and most widely used Christian prayers to address the Theotokos. A similar prayer (*Ave Maria, gratia plena,* "Hail Mary, full of grace") is used in the Western Church.[14]

Resurrectional and festal vespers conclude (as is the case with the liturgy) with the singing of "Blessed be the Name of the Lord," Psalm 33, and the blessing of the priest, followed by the dismissal. When vespers is celebrated as part of the all-night vigil, the dismissal is omitted and matins begins directly following the blessing of the priest.

On Sundays and feast days, the Typikon calls for a special rite called the *litiya* to be inserted into vespers. In contemporary parish practice, the litiya is added to vespers only during the all-night vigil for great feasts and days of commemoration of especially revered saints. The litiya is conducted in the narthex of the church, where the serving clergy go after leaving the sanctuary. The contemporary litiya is a remnant of the ancient liturgical processions that were a part of the nighttime vigils. Similar processions are mentioned by Saint John Chrysostom at the end of the fourth century and by Constantinopolitan liturgical records of the tenth century.[15] In the Jerusalemite Church of the fourth century, festal processions were a part of every resurrectional vespers. The contemporary litiya is a synthesis of the traditions of Constantinople and Jerusalem.[16]

The exit to the litiya is conducted during the singing of stichera called, in the Typikon, "stichera at the litiya." At festal vespers these stichera are dedicated to the

[13]It is customary to call this short series of prayers the "Trisagion prayers." They consist of the "usual beginning" and include the prayer of the Thrice-Holy, "O Most Holy Trinity" and the Lord's Prayer. The Church Typikon calls this series of prayers the "Trisagion."

[14]These prayers consist of a nearly identical combination of Lk 1.28 and 1.42, and differ in the second half. The eastern prayer ends simply with "for thou hast borne the Savior of our souls," while the western prayer ends with the words: "holy Mary, Mother of God, pray for us sinners, now and in the hour of our death."—*Ed.*

[15]For more on this, see Robert F. Taft, *The Liturgy of the Hours in East and West: The Origins of the Divine Office and its Meaning for Today* (Collegeville, MN: Liturgical Press, 1986), 169–173.

[16]Skaballanovich, *Typikon* (2004), 586.

feast. When the litiya is conducted on a regular Sunday, the Typikon calls for the singing of "the sticheron of the temple" (that is, the sticheron dedicated to the saint or feast to whom or to which the temple is dedicated).

At the conclusion of the stichera, four diaconal petitions and two prayers of the priest follow. The first diaconal petition, beginning with the words, "O God, save thy people and bless thine inheritance" (Ps 27.9), is a prayer that salvation may be granted to Christians, by the prayers of the Theotokos and the saints. In this prayer, the most revered saints are commemorated by name. The second petition contains a prayer for the spiritual and secular authorities and also for groups of people who are normally mentioned in the fervent supplication. In the third petition, the deacon prays for the preservation of the city and temple from natural calamities. The fourth petition is the shortest: "Again we pray also that the Lord God may hearken unto the voice of supplication of us sinners and have mercy on us." After each of the deacon's petitions, the choir sings "Lord, have mercy" many times: after the first petition—forty times, after the second petition—fifty times, and after the third and fourth petitions—three times each.[17]

Next, the priest says the prayer, "Hearken unto us, O God our Savior, thou hope of all the ends of the earth and of them that be far off at sea." The frequent mention of "those who are at sea" or "travelers by sea" in the liturgical petitions arises from the fact that in the period when the order of services was being compiled, seafaring was a most dangerous and risky means of traveling; therefore, it was considered necessary to offer a fervent prayer for those traveling by sea. In our day, in those countries where the divine services use the contemporary language, a petition is added for "those who fly" (for example, in English the petition reads, "For those who travel by land, by sea, and by air"). But in the Slavonic and Byzantine Greek languages there is no word which would denote the idea of travelling in an airplane.

Following the prayer, "Hearken unto us, O God," the priest blesses the people and says one more prayer beginning with the words, "O Master plenteous in mercy." This prayer is closer in its content to one of the four petitions of the deacon in the litiya; in it, too, the saints are commemorated by name.

[17] The Typikon calls for five petitions at the litiya, including a separate petition for the tsar and a separate petition for the ecclesial authorities. In contemporary practice, these two petitions are combined in one. Accordingly, the Typikon calls for the singing of "Lord, have mercy" following each petition in the following quantities: forty, thirty, fifty, three, and three. Ancient liturgical manuscripts varied greatly in their recommendations of how many times to sing "Lord, have mercy."

The Blessing of the Loaves, Wheat, Wine, and Oil.

At the conclusion of the prayers, the litiya procession moves from the narthex to the center of the church where the serving clergy remain until the blessing of the loaves, wheat, wine, and oil. This order has ancient origins; the prayer read by the priest mentions the miracle of the feeding of the five thousand men with five loaves (see Mt 14.13–21; Mk 6.31–44; Lk 9.11–17; Jn 6.1–14). It is an essential part of the all-night vigil, and has as its aim the bodily strengthening of the participants in the all-night vigil at the end of vespers and before the beginning of matins. In the parish practice of the Russian Church, where the vigil lasts between two and three hours, this order has lost its practical meaning to a significant degree and is seen as a symbolic action. In monasteries on Mount Athos, where to this day all-night vigils lasting many hours are celebrated, the order has preserved its practical significance and the all-night vigil is interrupted by the partaking of the loaves, wheat, wine, and oil.

COMPLINE

The Church Typikon knows two forms of compline—great and small. The name of this service indicates that it is celebrated following the evening meal (Gr. *apodeipnon*, Sl. *po vecheri,* "after dinner"). Great compline is celebrated only on the feasts of the Nativity and Theophany (in this case it replaces vespers in the all-night vigil), and also during the period of the fast. Small compline is a daily service which is celebrated in several monasteries and enters into the cell rule of prayer for monks. On days in which the all-night vigil is served, the Typikon calls for the omission of compline.

Saint Basil the Great mentioned the prayer before sleep, with the reading of Psalm 90, as one of the monastic services.[18] Psalm 90 remained one of the psalms read during great compline. Great compline begins with the exclamation, "Blessed is our God." Then, after the "usual beginning," Psalms 4, 6, 12, 24, 30, and 90 are read. Following these, the "Six Psalms" are read, and on great feasts the hymn is sung that begins with the words, "God is with us, understand all ye people and submit yourselves, for God is with us." This hymn is composed of verses from the

[18]See p. 51.

book of the Prophet Isaiah (see Is 8.9–18; 9.2–7). The performance of this hymn at great compline on the feasts of the Nativity and Theophany has a special significance, as it contains the prophecy of the birth of the Messiah. The festive and exalted character of the hymn coincides with the meaning of both feasts.

Next, three troparia follow, the first of which begins with the words, "The day now passed, I give thanks unto thee, O Lord." In these prayers, the worshippers beseech God to grant them a favorable evening and night. Then a hymn is read which begins with the words, "The bodiless nature of the cherubim glorifies thee with hymns unceasing," and ends with the hymn "Holy, holy, holy, thrice-holy Lord, have mercy on us and save us. Amen." The reading of the Nicene-Constantinopolitan Creed follows. Then, the priest addresses short prayers to the Theotokos, angels, and saints (the saints of the church and of the day are commemorated by name). The choir repeats the prayers of the priest, and the Trisagion prayers are read up to and including the Lord's Prayer.

After the Lord's Prayer, the troparion of the feast is sung on feast days; on ordinary days, other troparia are read, in which death and the Last Judgment are remembered. Then a prayer is read that is ascribed to Saint Basil the Great, which begins with the words, "O Lord, Lord, who deliverest us from all the arrows that fly by day." This prayer entered into the composition of the Constantinopolitan "sung office" as the prayer of the second antiphon.[19] It appears also in vespers for the feast of Pentecost. On behalf of the community, the priest prayerfully asks God to accept "our evening sacrifice—the lifting up of our hands" (which indicates the ancient custom of praying with raised hands) and to aid the worshippers "to pass through the course of the night without blemish, untempted by evil things."

The second part of great compline follows, including Psalms 50 and 101, and also "the Prayer of Manasseh, King of Judah." A special commentary on this prayer is necessary. The Second Book of Kings mentions King Manasseh, who "did evil in the eyes of the Lord," raised up altars in honor of pagan gods, did other "abominations," and "poured out large quantities of innocent blood" (2 Kg 21.2–17). Similar information about Manasseh is contained in the Second Book of Chronicles, but there is also a story about the capture of Manasseh: "And the Lord spoke to Manasseh and his people, but they would not listen.

The Repentance of King Manasseh. Chludov Psalter. Byzantium. c. 840s–850s.

---

[19]Uspenskii, *Orthodox Vespers*, 30.

Therefore the Lord brought against them the captains of the army of the king of Assyria, who took Manasseh with bonds, bound him with fetters, and carried him to Babylon. Now when he was in affliction, he sought the face of the Lord his God and humbled himself greatly before the God of his fathers, and prayed to him. And the Lord received his entreaty, heard his cry, and brought him back to Jerusalem into his kingdom" (2 Chr 33.10–13). Later, in the same book, it reads, "The rest of the acts of Manasseh and his prayer to his God . . . is written among the kings of Israel." These references clearly show that Manasseh composed the prayer that was known to the author of the Second Book of Chronicles. This prayer is not found in the Hebrew text of the book, but it is found in the Septuagint, where it appears as an appendix to the Second Book of Chronicles. (Specifically, it is found in the famous Alexandrian codex of the Bible from the fourth century.) The prayer is also cited in the *Apostolic Constitutions*.[20] Clearly, the prayer was originally formulated in the Greek language, and it may have been composed by a Palestinian Jew of the epoch of the Maccabees. One way or another, the prayer has pre-Christian origins.

In its content the prayer is a brilliant example of a sinner's penitential turning to God. Manasseh prayerfully recalls his sins and transgressions, which are "multiplied" and "more in number than the sand of the sea." The shackles and fetters with which Manasseh is bound ("I am weighed down with many an iron fetter") become an image of spiritual imprisonment: the sinful man finds himself in captivity with his sins and passions. The prayer is penetrated with hope in the mercy of "the God of them that repent," the God who is "of great compassion, long-suffering, and very merciful." The rare term "great compassion" (Sl. *blagoutrobie*, Gr. *eusplanch-nia*)—which literally means "good innards" and is usually translated as "compassion"—solidly entered into the eastern Christian theological lexicon because of this prayer.[21] It points to God's love for man, which is similar to a mother's love for her child. The book of Isaiah speaks of this love: " 'Will a woman forget her child, so as not to have mercy on the offspring of her womb? But even if a woman should forget these things, nevertheless, I shall not forget you,' says the Lord" (Is 49.15). Owing to such content, the prayer became widespread in the eastern Christian tradition and entered into the Greek and Slavonic manuscripts of the Bible and was included in the divine services.

---

[20]*Apostolic Constitutions* 2.22 (*ANF* 7:406–407).
[21]See Sergei Averintsev, "Eusplanchnia," *Al'fa i omega* [Alpha and omega] 4 (1995): 11–14.

After the Prayer of Manasseh come the Trisagion prayers up to and including the Lord's Prayer and then, on festal days, the kontakion of the feast. On other days the troparia "Have mercy on us, O Lord, have mercy on us" are read.

The third part of great compline includes Psalms 69 and 142 and also the "great doxology." Psalm 142 is the final psalm of the Six Psalms read at matins. The great doxology is also a feature of matins: its origin and content will be discussed in the section on matins.

When compline is served as a part of the all-night vigil, the choir exits to the litiya directly following the reading of the great doxology, and matins begins following the litiya. When compline is celebrated separately (for example, during Great Lent), the concluding portion of great compline follows the doxology. It includes a hymn made up of verses from Psalm 150 joined to the refrain, "Remain with us O Lord of hosts, in affliction we have no other helper but Thee. O Lord of hosts, have mercy on us." Penitential troparia are joined to the hymn, then "Lord, have mercy" is prayed forty times followed by the prayer, "Thou who at every season and every hour. . . ." (This prayer will be discussed in the section on the hours.) In conclusion, two prayers are read: one is directed to the Theotokos and the other to Jesus Christ; the latter is thematically linked to the approaching night's sleep ("And grant rest, O Master, to our souls and bodies as we sleep"). Compline ends with the dismissal prayer, after which the priest asks for forgiveness from "the brethren" and says a short litany for the health of the civil and church authorities.

In its contemporary form, great compline is an order composed of several heterogeneous elements. Several of its prayers had previously been parts of other services, and, even today, several of its prayers are parts of other services. Both in content and composition, great compline partially duplicates vespers and partially (especially in its third part) duplicates matins. Great compline is overall one of the fullest and spiritually richest of all the orders of divine services. Texts from the Old Testament are predominant in it, while Christian hymnography occupies an unassuming position.

MIDNIGHT OFFICE

Rising for prayer at midnight is an ancient tradition dating back to pre-Christian times. The psalmist says, "At midnight I will rise to give thanks to you because of your righteous judgments." (Ps 118.62). When in prison, Paul and Silas praised God "at midnight" (Acts 16.25). We recall that Saint Basil referred to both of these texts as justification of the monastic practice of midnight prayer.

In antiquity, when electric lighting did not exist and the rhythm of life conformed to the natural rhythm of alternating day and night, it was customary to lie down to sleep right after the setting of the sun and to rise at sunrise. Monks sought to reduce the time of sleep as much as possible, and for this reason monastic services were performed after the setting of the sun, at midnight, and in the early morning. A "full" eight- or even six-hour night was not possible for a monk who would have to interrupt his sleep with prayer at midnight. Some monks slept without getting undressed and without lying down on a bed, similar to warriors ready for battle. Abstinence from sleep was perceived as one of the important ascetic feats that constituted the monastic way of life.

In its contemporary form, the midnight office is the fruit of a long development. Scholars have various opinions regarding the origin of the midnight office, insofar as the diversity of liturgical sources does not allow us to make definitive conclusions regarding these questions.[22] But the primeval bond of the midnight service with the monastic tradition is indisputable. This link has been preserved to the present day, insofar as the midnight office is performed only in monasteries (and not at midnight, but in the early morning hours). The only exception is the paschal midnight office, which is performed in parish churches before the beginning of the paschal service.

There are three forms of the midnight office—daily, Saturday, and Sunday. The basic element of the daily midnight office is the reading of Psalm 118, divided into three parts. The attitude towards Psalm 118 in the eastern Christian tradition was especially reverent. This psalm was perceived as messianic, uttered by the person of Christ. At the same time, Psalm 118 is a kind of compendium of the ascetic life:

> In this psalm David describes the life of the saints, their ascetic feats, sorrows, and labors, also the attack of demons, thousands of tempting thoughts, nets and other means of ensnaring, and together with this, how the saints gain the victory: the law, the divine words, patience, help from above, and finally, what follows after the labors: awards, laurels, recompenses.[23]

The semantic content of the midnight office is expressed most fully in the troparion borrowed from the divine service of Holy Week:

[22]Taft, *The Liturgy of the Hours*, 191–209.
[23]Athanasius of Alexandria, *Commentary on Psalm 118* (PG 27:480c).

Behold the Bridegroom comes in the middle of the night; and blessed is the servant whom He shall find watching, but unworthy is he whom He shall find in slothfulness. Beware, then, O my soul, and be not overcome by sleep, lest thou be given over to death and be shut out from the Kingdom. But return to soberness and cry aloud: Holy, holy, holy art Thou, O God: through the Theotokos have mercy upon us.

This troparion is based on the parable of the ten virgins who came to the wedding feast but forgot to buy oil for their lamps; when the bridegroom came, they were unprepared and remained outside of the bridal chamber (see Mt 25.1–13). At the same time, the troparion contains an allusion to Christ's parable of the servants who are awaiting the return of their master from the wedding feast (see Lk 12.35–40). In the eastern Christian tradition, both parables are treated as a call to spiritual vigilance. The major content of the midnight office is the expectation of the Second Coming of the Son of Man.

Parable of the Ten Virgins. Fresco. Ferapontov Monastery. Beginning of 16th c.

Two more troparia are added to this troparion, followed by the concluding part of the midnight office, which includes several morning prayers, Psalms 120 and 132, two troparia for the departed, and one prayer for the departed.

On Saturday, the midnight office differs almost completely from the daily midnight office. Instead of Psalm 118, the ninth kathisma, including Psalms 64–69, is found in the service. Also, the prayer of Saint Eustratius is read. This prayer, according to tradition, is ascribed to the martyr who was condemned to be burnt alive during the rule of Emperors Diocletian and Maximian. According to the life of the saint, Saint Eustratius uttered the prayer, "I magnify, magnify thee, O Lord," on the way to his execution.

On Sunday, the midnight office differs from the daily midnight office and the office served on Saturday, in that the kathisma is not read and a canon is performed in the place of the kathisma. The Octoechos calls for the reading of canons to the Trinity, written by Metrophanes II, Patriarch of Constantinople (patriarch from 1440 to 1443).

MATINS

Matins is the longest service and also the most diverse in content of all the non-eucharistic services of the daily cycle. According to the Typikon, matins should begin before daybreak and should end after the rising of the sun. This is stipulated to a significant degree by the overall dynamic of this service. It begins at twilight, with lamps extinguished, and the beginning portion bears a penitential character. The overall mood of the service gradually changes and the concluding portion is penetrated with a spirit of thanksgiving and praise of God, "who hast shown us the light."

When matins is celebrated separately from vespers and is not part of the all-night vigil, it begins with the "two psalms," Psalms 19 and 20, followed by a short litany with petitions for the church and civil authorities. The litany is followed by the exclamation, "Glory to the holy, consubstantial, life-creating, and undivided Trinity, always, now and ever, and unto ages of ages." This opening exclamation is a characteristic feature of matins and distinguishes it from all the other divine services. In the case when matins is part of the all-night vigil, this exclamation is transferred to the beginning of vespers, and the "two psalms" and litany at the beginning of matins are omitted.

The so-called "little doxology" is said the beginning of matins. This follows the exclamation "Glory to the holy . . ." and includes the reading (thrice) of the angels' praise, "Glory to God in the highest, and on earth peace, good will towards men," (Lk 2.14) and the reading (twice) of the verse, "O Lord, open thou my lips and my mouth shall show forth thy praise" (Psalm 50.17). The Six Psalms immediately follow this doxology; they include Psalms 3, 37, 62, 87, 102, and 142. The psalms are read by a single reader standing in the middle of the temple. According to the Typikon, lamps should be extinguished at the beginning of the reading of the Six Psalms.

The Six Psalms constitute a selection from the entire Psalter—a selection of the most representative psalms, in tone and mood, of repentance and praise. Psalms 3 and 37 express a feeling of internal confusion, which grows into hope in the Lord. Psalm 62 is penetrated with a feeling of a great thirst for communion with God, of being drawn to God. Psalm 87 is a morning prayer joined with the remembrance of death. Psalm 102 contains triumphant praise of God, the Creator of the visible world. Psalm 142 again returns to the mood of Psalm 3 and concludes with a petition for aid and deliverance from sorrow and despondency. One or two of the most expressive verses is repeated at the end of each psalm, as if summarizing the psalm's content.

The reason that these psalms, and not others, are part of matins is the fact that they many times make mention of night, morning, and waking: "I lay down and slept" (Ps 3.5); "Early will I seek thee" (Ps 62.1); "When I remember thee on my bed, I meditate on you in the night watches" (Ps 62.6); "I have cried out day and night before thee" (Ps 87.1); "in the morning my prayer comes before thee" (Ps 87.13); "Cause me to hear thy lovingkindness in the morning" (Ps 142.8). The Six Psalms acquired their final form in about the seventh century.[24] Certain individual psalms had been part of matins in a considerably earlier period. An example is Psalm 62, which was already indicated as being part of the morning service in the *Apostolic Constitutions*.[25]

While the Six Psalms are being read, the priest, standing before the royal doors, quietly reads the twelve prayers of light. These prayers were once found throughout the entire text of matins, and each prayer corresponded to a particular moment of the service. Ancient Euchologia, including the Barberini Euchologion (ms. Barberini gr. 336), dating to the end of the eighth century, include almost a full selection of these prayers (except for the ninth). The prayers are even found in the same order as in the contemporary Priest's Service Book.[26]

As for the question of where in matins the prayers of light were read, we can judge from the exclamations, which have remained in the contemporary order of matins. Each of the exclamations was the conclusion of a particular prayer. The first of the prayers of light expresses thanksgiving to God for having woken us from sleep. It concludes with the exclamation, "For unto thee is due all glory . . . ," and was spoken by the priest subsequently, at the great litany. The second and third prayers begin with the words, "Out of the night our spirit waketh at dawn unto thee . . ." Thematically these words are linked with the song of the prophet Isaiah (cf. Is 26.9–19); these prayers could be spoken at the little litanies, following the kathismata. The fourth prayer is a supplicatory prayer and in its content is linked with the litany of fervent supplication; its exclamation, "for thou art a merciful God . . . ," also points to this link. "Incense" is mentioned in the fifth prayer; it was probably said before the censing or at the time of the censing at the beginning of the canon.[27] The concluding exclamation of this prayer, "For thou art our God," is now heard after the third ode of the canon. The sixth prayer concludes with the

[24]Skaballanovich, *Typikon* (2004), 618.
[25]*Apostolic Constitutions* 8.38 (*ANF* 7:497).
[26]Skaballanovich, *Typikon* (2004), 622.
[27]The ancient typika prescribe this type of censing. At the present time, it has fallen out of use in the Russian Church but has been preserved, for instance, on Mount Athos. See Skaballanovich, *Typikon* (2004), 686.

exclamation, "For thou art the King of peace . . . ," which is heard in contemporary matins following the sixth ode of the canon. The seventh and tenth prayers are thematically connected with Psalm 50 and are partly made up of verses from this psalm. The exclamation of the tenth prayer, "Through the mercy and compassion . . . ," is heard in contemporary matins following the reading of Psalm 50. The eighth prayer concludes with the exclamation, "For blessed is thy name . . ." The corresponding exclamation in contemporary matins is heard at the litany before the Gospel reading. The ninth prayer, "Make to shine in our hearts . . . ," is borrowed from the liturgies of Saints Basil the Great and Saint John Chrysostom, in which it precedes the gospel reading. The eleventh prayer thematically corresponds with the praises and the great doxology. Its concluding exclamation, "For all the hosts of heaven praise thee," is heard in the contemporary matins following the ninth ode of the canon, before the praises. The rising of the sun and the beginning of the day are mentioned in the twelfth prayer, which corresponds with the end of matins.

After the reading of the Six Psalms, the great litany is said, followed by "God is the Lord"—selected verses from Psalm 117. After this, the troparion of the feast is sung: either the resurrectional troparion or the troparion to the saint, depending on the event being celebrated. The troparion is one of the most ancient genres of liturgical composition. The troparion expresses in condensed form the basic content of the feast. It is sung twice at "God is the Lord," and the Theotokion (a troparion dedicated to the Theotokos) is added to it. When the divine service is conducted during Great Lent, and also in several other cases (for instance, during a matins service for the departed/panikhida), the Typikon calls for the singing of "Alleluia" with verses and troparia in the place of "God is the Lord."

Two kathismata are read following "God is the Lord" or "Alleluia."[28] After this, the little litany is said, followed by a sessional hymn (Sl. *sedalen*)—a short hymn in a form resembling a troparion. The word "kathisma," which in the Greek practice signifies the divisions of the Psalter, stems from the verb *kathixō*—"to sit." It points to the custom of listening to the psalms while sitting. The term "kathisma" is also used for those troparia which are sung after the reading of the psalms. In Slavonic this type of troparion is called a "sedalen," which indicates the custom of sitting during their performance.

During the resurrectional and festal matins, after the kathismata and sessional hymns the *polyeleos*—Psalms 134 and 135—is sung. In parish practice, only four

---

[28]Outside of Great Lent, two kathismata are read after "God is the Lord." Three kathismata are read after the "Alleluia" on every weekday of Great Lent (except for Thursday of the fifth week, or Tuesday of the fifth week if Annunciation falls on Thursday).—*Ed.*

verses of these psalms are sung: "Praise the name of the Lord" (Ps 134.1); "Blessed be the Lord out of Zion, who dwells in Jerusalem!" (Ps 134.21); "Oh, give thanks to the Lord, for he is good!" (Ps 135.1); "Oh, give thanks to the God of heaven! For his mercy endures forever" (Ps 135.26). To each verse is added a threefold "Alleluia." All the lamps in the temple are lit at the beginning of the singing of the polyeleos; the royal doors are opened, and the serving clergy exit the sanctuary and proceed to the center of the temple holding lit candles.

The magnification—a short verse that glorifies the event being celebrated—comes right after the polyeleos at festal matins. At resurrectional matins the *evlogetaria* is sung.[29] During the singing of the magnification or resurrectional troparia (i.e. the evlogetaria), the priest and deacon perform a full censing of the church. On the three Sundays that precede Great Lent, Psalm 136 ("By the waters of Babylon") is added to the psalms of the polyeleos. This psalm expresses a mood of repentance.

The Church Typikon calls for the performance of the polyeleos on Sundays only during a specific period of the year (from September 22 through December 20 and from January 14 through Cheesefare Sunday). On the other Sundays, Psalm 118 ("Blessed are the blameless") should be sung.[30]

At resurrectional matins, directly following the polyeleos and the resurrectional troparia the little litany is said, followed by the reading of the *hypakoë* (from the Greek *hypakoē*, meaning "attentive listening"). It is a short refrain glorifying the resurrection of Christ. This is followed by the "Hymns of Ascent" [Gr. *anabathmoi*]—verses whose authorship is attributed to Saint Theodore the Studite. The "Hymns of Ascent" are so called because they were written as refrains for verses of those psalms that are called "songs of ascent" in the Greek Bible (see Psalms 119–133). The prokeimenon—selected verses of a psalm—is sung following these hymns, followed by "Let every breath praise the Lord" (verses drawn from Psalm 150). The prokeimenon and "Let every breath" are performed by the deacon and choir in an alternating fashion.

It is customary for the gospel to be read at all matins services at which the polyeleos is performed. At festal matins, the gospel reading is thematically connected to the feast. At resurrectional matins, gospel pericopes concerning the resurrection

---

[29]In the Russian tradition, this is referred to by the opening line: "The angelic assembly was amazed." The word "evlogetaria" comes from the first word of the refrain in Greek: "Blessed [*eulogētos*] art thou, O Lord, teach me thy statutes."—*Ed.*

[30]In parish practice, however, this Typikon directive is rarely observed and Psalm 118, as a rule, is replaced by the polyeleos throughout the entire year.

of Christ are read. Eleven such pericopes are selected from the four Gospels: one from Matthew (see Mt 26.16–20), two from Mark (see Mk 16.1–8 and 9–20), three from Luke (see Lk 24.1–12, 12–35, and 36–53), and five from John (see Jn 20.1–10, 11–18, 19–31; 21.1–14, 15–25.) They are read in their entirety over the course of eleven Sundays; a new cycle begins when all the pericopes have been read.

After the reading of the gospel at the resurrectional matins, the hymn "Having beheld the resurrection of Christ" is sung. This hymn stems from the paschal divine service. After this, Psalm 50 is read, according to the Typikon. Refrains which recall the theme of the celebrated event are added to it. For example, "Jesus rose from the dead as he foretold, giving us eternal life and great mercy" is sung on Sundays. This is followed by the prayer, "O God, save thy people," with the commemoration of the saints by name.[31]

Illustration of the First Biblical Canticle. Chludov Psalter. Byzantine. c. 840s–850s.

Next, according to the Typikon, it is customary to perform the "biblical canticles." These are selected prayers from various books of the Old and New Testaments, read in various contexts. Ten biblical canticles entered into church practice: the first—the prayer of Moses after the Jews crossed the Red Sea (see Ex 15.1–18); the second—Moses' song before his death in Deuteronomy (see Deut 32.1–43); the third—Hannah's song for the birth of Samuel (see 1 Sam 2.1–10); the fourth—the Prophet Habbakuk's song (see Hab 3.1–19); the fifth—the Prophet Isaiah's song (Is 26.9–19); the sixth—the Prophet Jonah's song (see Jon 2.3–10); the seventh and eighth—the song of the three youths in the furnace (see Dan 3.26–45 and Dan 3.52–88); the ninth—the song of the most-holy Theotokos (see Lk 1.46–55); and the tenth—Zachariah's song of the birth of Saint John the Baptist (see Lk 1. 68–79).

It is customary to add troparia to the concluding verses of nine of the ten biblical canticles (the second to last—the song of the Theotokos—is not counted as one of these nine canticles). Together, these form the canon. Consequently, there ought to be nine odes in the canon as well. However, in the majority of the canons used in the divine services, the third ode immediately follows the first ode. This is due to the fact that the content of the second biblical canticle is distinguished by its extreme severity, and for this reason it is only used during the services of Great Lent. Accordingly, the second ode is present only in Saint Andrew of Crete's *Great*

---

[31]This prayer is found also in the order of the litiya. In this case, when matins is served as part of the all-night vigil with litiya at vespers, the prayer "O God, save thy people" is customarily omitted at matins.

Canon of Repentance and in several other canons of Great Lent, while it is absent in other canons.

As a rule, each ode of the canon consists of four troparia. They are preceded by an *irmos*—the troparion most closely connected with the content of the biblical canticle and at the same time serving as an image for the subsequent troparia of the canon. Insofar as canons were performed in a singing voice in the Byzantine Church, the same melody was used for the irmos and the troparia of the canon. Therefore, both the number and arrangement of syllables in the irmos and troparia had to be identical. This rhythmic correspondence is a characteristic feature of the genre of the canon. In the process of translation into Slavonic and other languages, this correspondence is lost, and because of this the understanding of the canon as a work of poetry is also lost.

Two, three, or four canons are usually performed together at matins. For example, at resurrectional matins, the resurrectional canon of the Octoechos, the canon to the cross and the resurrection, and the canon to the Theotokos are read. The canon to the saint being celebrated, from the Menaion, is added to these. In this case, four troparia are taken from the resurrectional canon, three from the canon to the cross and the resurrection, three from the canon to the Theotokos, and four from the canon to the saint, for a total of fourteen troparia. The irmos is performed at the beginning of the canticle, while the katavasia is performed at the end.[32] Correspondingly, the irmos and katavasia ought to be joined to the fourteen final verses of each of the biblical canticles. When each of the canons has eight odes, the overall number of performed troparia should comprise one hundred and twelve, and together with the irmoi and katavasias—one hundred and twenty-eight.

In combination with the canons, the biblical canticles form the most complicated part of matins, in terms of structure. They are also the longest part and the most difficult to understand. This is clearly the reason for the fact that in contemporary practice, with the exception of the eighth canticle (the Song of the Theotokos), the biblical canticles have completely gone out of use, both in parishes and in monasteries. They are performed in their entirety only during Great Lent. On regular Sundays and feast days, and also at matins on weekdays, only the canons are read, and in parish practice they are considerably abridged. As a rule, only four troparia remain out of the fourteen troparia for each canticle. In this way, at resurrectional matins in a normal parish, one troparion from each ode of

---

[32]Katavasia (from the Greek *katabaino*, meaning "to descend") is the name given to the irmos repeated at the end of each ode of the canon. It owes its name to the way it was performed: two choirs descended from their places to the middle of the church to perform this hymn.

each canon is heard: one resurrectional, one to the cross and to the resurrection, one to the Theotokos, and one to the saint.

A refrain is read before each troparion of the canon. "Glory to thy holy resurrection, O Lord" is read before the troparia of the resurrectional canon; "Glory to thy precious cross and resurrection, O Lord" is read before the troparia of the canon to the cross and the resurrection; "Most-Holy Theotokos, save us" is read before the troparia of the canon to the Theotokos; "Holy Saint (name), pray to God for us" is read before the troparia of the canon to a saint. These refrains are not stipulated by the Typikon; they entered into use as replacements for the verses of the biblical canticles.

Following the third, sixth, and ninth odes of the canon, the little litany is said. After the sixth ode, the kontakion and ikos are performed. These make up the first pair of hymns in the ancient genre of the kontakion, which was discussed earlier. On several feast days, the Typikon calls for the "synaxarion"—a teaching shedding light on the meaning of the feast—to be read after the ikos. These synaxaria are contained in the Festal Menaion, Lenten Triodion, and Pentecostarion, as well as in several services of the monthy Menaia. On saints' days of commemoration, it is proper at this point in the service to read the life of the particular saint from the Prologue, a collection of the lives of the saints. In practice, these readings are omitted everywhere.

Following the eighth ode, the deacon says, "The Theotokos and the Mother of the Light, let us magnify in song." The choir then sings the Song of the Theotokos, "My soul magnifies the Lord." This is the only one of the biblical canticles that has remained in universal use. On certain feasts, the singing of this song is replaced with the singing of certain other special refrains.

In the Russian Orthodox Church, the custom emerged of anointing the faithful with holy oil during the reading of the canon. This is done in the following way: the faithful venerate the Gospel Book or the icon of the feast that lays on an analogion in the center of the church. After this, they approach the priest, who anoints the foreheads of the faithful in a crosswise fashion. The Typikon does not call for this order to take place at this part of matins. Rather, the Typikon simply mentions the anointing with oil "from the lampada" following the completion of matins on certain feasts.

Following the canon on the day of the resurrection, the verse "Holy is the Lord our God" is sung. Then, at the resurrectional matins, the "exapostilarion"—a hymn dedicated to the resurrection of Christ and thematically linked with the matins

Gospel reading—is read.[33] There are eleven exapostilaria in all, one for each of the resurrectional Gospel readings. It has already been mentioned that the author of the exapostilaria was the Byzantine emperor Constantine VII Porphyrogenitus ("born in the purple").

The exapostilarion is followed by the psalms of praise—Psalms 148, 149, and 150—which were a component of the morning worship service in the synagogues. In the Christian monastic matins service, they are mentioned as early as the fifth century by Saint John Cassian of Rome.[34] Stichera on the praises—normally six or eight—are added to the final verses of Psalm 149 and Psalm 150. Afterwards, the so-called "gospel sticheron" and Theotokion are sung. The gospel sticheron is thematically linked to the matins gospel reading. As with the exapostilarion, there are eleven gospel stichera.

Next follows the priest's exclamation, "Glory to thee who hast shown us the light," which signifies the rising of the sun. On Sundays and feast days, the great doxology is sung following this exclamation, while on weekdays it is read. As with the small doxology, it begins with the angelic praise, "Glory to God in the highest, and on earth peace, good will towards men." This is followed by a glorification of God the Father and God the Son, which recalls the beginning of the anaphora from the liturgy of Saint Basil the Great:

> We praise thee, we bless thee, we worship thee. We glorify thee, we give thanks
> to thee for thy great glory. O Lord, heavenly King, God the Father Almighty.
> O Lord, the Only-begotten Son, Jesus Christ, and the Holy Spirit. O Lord,
> Lamb of God, Son of the Father who takest away the sins of the world receive
> our prayer; thou who sittest at the right hand of God the Father, have mercy
> on us. For thou only art holy, thou only art the Lord, O Jesus Christ, in the
> glory of God the Father. Amen.

The next part of the great doxology is overwhelmingly made up of selected verses from the Old Testament (in particular, Ps 144.2; Dan 3.26; Ps 32.22; Ps 118.12; Ps 89.2; Ps 40.5; Ps 142.9–10). The selection of verses concludes with the words, "For with thee is the fountain of life, and in thy light shall we see light. O continue thy mercy unto those who know thee" (Ps 35.10–11). The words "in thy light we shall see light" indicate the rising of the sun, which thematically corresponds with the concluding part of matins. In the Christian tradition, these words received a

---

[33]According to one tradition, the exapostilarion (from the Greek verb *exapostello*—"I send") derives its name from the fact that its text speaks of the apostles being sent out to preach the gospel.

[34]John Cassian, *Institutes* 3.6 (*NPNF*[2] 11:216).

christological interpretation. "Light" is understood to be God the Father, and the other "light" is understood to be God the Son. In accordance with this understanding, Saint Gregory the Theologian wrote, "In your light shall we see light, that is, in the Spirit we shall see the Son."[35] The doxology concludes with the singing of "Holy God."

At resurrectional matins, the resurrectional troparion or the troparion of the feast is sung after the conclusion of the great doxology. After this, at Sunday or festal matins the litany of fervent supplication and the litany of supplication are said, followed by the dismissal. At daily matins, the litany of supplication comes first, followed by the singing of the aposticha, the litany of fervent supplication, and finally the dismissal.

Aside from the hymns and prayers cited above, readings from the works of the holy fathers should be a part of matins, according to the Typikon. In particular, such readings are prescribed between vespers and matins when these services are joined in the all-night vigil. In this case, the readings should follow the first and second kathismata, the polyeleos, and the third and sixth odes of the canon, and they should also precede the first hour. Altogether, the all-night vigil should be interspersed with readings seven times. During matins, the Typikon calls for the reading of Saint John Chrysostom's commentaries on the Gospels according to John and Matthew, his *Commentaries on the Six Days* (his opening homilies on the Book of Genesis), Saint Theophylact of Ochrid's commentary on the Gospel

according to Luke, Bishop Palladius of Helenopolis' book the *Lausiac History*, the works of Saint Ephraim the Syrian, and the works of several other authors. At the divine services of the great feasts, the reading of Saint Gregory the Theologian's homilies dedicated to these feasts is prescribed.

Of all the Orthodox divine services, matins most reveals the discrepancy between the Typikon and Church practice—both in monasteries and in parishes. There are a great number of reasons for this. Primarily, in the form in which it is described in the Typikon, matins—in its composition and content—is mainly a monastic divine service, intended for people whose primary occupation is participation in worship services. To

Saint Gregory the Theologian.
Book Miniature. 12th c.

---

[35]Gregory the Theologian, *Orations* 34.13.5–6 (SC 318:220; *NPNF²* 7:337).

fulfill it according to the Typikon, without any abridgements, could require from four to seven and even more hours (depending on the style of singing). When matins is combined with vespers in the all-night vigil, the service may last nine or ten hours—from sunset to daybreak. Participation in such services is possible for monks but extremely difficult for the laity.

The reading of literature from the holy fathers at matins was necessary because, as a rule, monks in Byzantium did not have personal libraries. Books prepared by hand were too expensive to acquire as personal property.[36] But in our time, anyone can acquire the literature of the holy fathers and read it at home; there is in fact no longer any necessity to listen to long teachings during the divine services. Moreover, a significant part of the texts that are prescribed to be read during the divine services is addressed to monks (for example, *The Ladder of Divine Ascent*).[37] There is no need to offer them as mandatory instruction to the laity.

Finally, the extreme difficulty many have in understanding some of the prayers of matins—in particular the troparia of the canon combined with the biblical odes—led to these parts of the service being universally omitted or significantly abridged.

It should be noted that in Greek parish practice matins underwent an even more radical abridgment than in Russian practice. Primarily, as has been stated, the all-night vigils (consisting of vespers combined with matins) are practically absent in the Greek Church. For the Greeks, vespers is served in the evening and matins in the morning, as it is prescribed in the Typikon. Matins is celebrated before the beginning of the liturgy, the reading of the two psalms is omitted, the reading of the six psalms is often omitted (or significantly abridged), the kathismata are

---

[36]The average price of one book in Byzantium was about half the yearly wage of a civil servant and about one fourth of the yearly income of a high court dignitary. So, for example, in the ninth century a manuscript consisting of 300–400 pages cost 15–20 nomismata. See Nigel G. Wilson, "Books and Readers in Byzantium," in *Byzantine Books and Bookmen: A Dumbarton Oaks Colloquium* (Washington, DC: Dumbarton Oaks, 1975), 3. At about the same time (tenth century), the yearly wage of a civil servant in Byzantium was about 40 nomismata, and a protospatharios earned 72 nomismata per year. (See Cyril Mango, *Byzantium and Its Image: History and Culture of the Byzantine Empire and Its Heritage* (London, Variorum Reprints: 1984), 38–39.)

[37]The *Ladder* contains only one short saying directed to married people "in the world" (*Ladder* 1.20–21), and the rest is directed primarily to monastics. In contrast, the *Lausiac History*—written for Lausus, a high-ranking imperial official—has a broader audience. In the prologue (2–3), Palladius explains the book's purpose and audience to Lausus: "I, lowly though I be, in deference to your greatness' stipulation . . . and being aware of your desire for tales of the [desert] fathers (both male and female) . . . have decided to produce this book for you in narrative form and afresh, that you might have a souvenir, sacred and beneficial to the soul . . . [so] you may make progress in your chosen path of piety with unfading zeal. May you be a guide for yourself, for those with you, for those under your authority and for the most pious emperors[.]" Palladius of Aspuna, *The Lausiac History*, trans. John Wortley (Collegeville, MN: Liturgical Press, 2015), 1–2.—*Ed.*

completely omitted, only one of the eight odes of the canon is read (sung), and the opening exclamation of the divine liturgy takes place right after the great doxology. In this way, matins occupies in Greek parish practice almost the same place that the reading of the third and sixth hours before the beginning of the liturgy occupies in the Russian Church. The reading of the hours is completely omitted in Greek parishes.

The Hours

In the Orthodox Church the divine office of the *Hours* includes the first, third, sixth, and ninth hours. In the ancient Church these services were connected to these particular times of day. In contemporary practice, the first hour is celebrated after matins, the third and sixth hours are celebrated before the liturgy, and the ninth hour is celebrated before vespers. In parishes, as a rule, the ninth hour is omitted.

As we have seen, sources from the second through fourth centuries made many references to the third, sixth, and ninth hours as times established for prayer. Services for the third, sixth, and ninth hours existed in the fourth century both in monasteries and in cathedrals. The first hour had its origins later. There are various hypotheses on the question of the origin of this service. The most probable theory is that it originally was a part of matins and only later separated into an independent service.[38]

All the hours have a similar structure. They include three psalms, the reading of the daily troparion and kontakion, "Lord, have mercy" read forty times, a prayer common to all the hours, and a separate concluding prayer for each hour. The common prayer for all the hours begins with the words, "O thou who at every season and every hour in heaven and on earth art worshipped and glorified, O Christ our God," and includes the words, "accept also our prayers at this hour," which renders it neutral in relation to the time of day. Psalms 5, 89, and 100 are included in the first hour, Psalms 16, 24, and 50 in the third hour, Psalms 53, 54, and 90 in the sixth hour, and Psalms 83, 84, and 85 in the ninth hour.

The so-called "usual beginning" precedes the reading of the psalms in the third and sixth hours. It includes the exclamation, "Blessed is our God, always, now and ever, and unto the ages of ages," the reader's response, "Amen," the prayers "O

---

[38]For a detailed review of the existing opinions regarding the origin of the first hour, see Taft, *The Liturgy of the Hours*, 191–209.

Heavenly King," "Holy God," "O Most Holy Trinity," and "Our Father." (Several other daily services, including matins, use the same beginning.)[39] In its contemporary form, the usual beginning is of a rather late origin, but all the prayers included in it date from the first millennium. Of them, the most ancient prayer is "Our Father," of which Christ is the author.

Following the exclamation "For thine is the kingdom," which concludes the "Our Father," "Lord, have mercy" is said twelve times. The repetitive utterance of "Lord, have mercy" is included in all the basic worship services of the daily cycle. In many cases (for example, in the office of the hours), this brief prayerful appeal is read forty times. In some cases (for example, in the litiya), the Typikon prescribes for it to be read fifty times. "Lord, have mercy" is also often read three times or twelve times. Often, the readings of multiple repetitions of "Lord, have mercy" are done in a hurried manner.[40] But this prayer, like all the prayers, requires distinct and unhurried pronunciation, as it is the most concise expression of the essence of every worship service and prayer.

The content of every hour is most fully revealed in its troparion. (In contemporary practice, the "troparion of the hour" is performed only during Great Lent; on regular days, the troparia for the celebrated saints are read at the hours). The troparion of the first hour points to its connection with matins: "Hearken in the morning to my voice, my King and my God." The troparion of the third hour is dedicated to the descent of the Holy Spirit upon the apostles—an event which took place at the third hour of the day (see Acts 2.15): "O Lord, who didst send down thy most holy Spirit upon thine Apostles at the third hour: take him not from us, O Good One, but renew him in us who pray unto thee." The troparion of the sixth hour speaks of the crucifixion of the Lord Jesus Christ on the cross: "O thou who on the sixth day and hour didst nail to the Cross the sin that Adam dared to commit in Paradise: tear up the record of our trespasses, O Christ our God, and save us." The troparion of the ninth hour is dedicated to the Savior's death on the cross: "O thou who at the ninth hour for our sake didst taste death in the flesh, put to death the pride of our flesh, O Christ our God, and save us."

In certain cases, specifically on the eves of the Nativity and Theophany and also on Great Friday, the hours are performed as an independent service. At each

---

[39]The usual beginning is omitted when the service follows after another service without interruption (for example, when first hour follows matins, or when sixth hour follows third hour).

[40]The original meaning of the Russian verb "*kurolesit*"—"to play pranks"—is "to do something in extreme haste." The verb comes from the custom of quickly and repetitively repeating "*Kyrie eleëson*" (Greek for "Lord, have mercy") during the services.

of the hours an excerpt from the Old Testament, the Book of the Epistles, and Gospel Book are read and the troparion and kontakion are sung. It is customary to call this service the "royal hours" because it was a tradition in Byzantium for the emperor to attend.

3

The Divine Liturgy

T HE DIVINE LITURGY IS THE MOST ANCIENT of the worship services of the Christian Church prescribed by the Typikon. According to the teaching of the Orthodox Church, the celebrant of the liturgy is Christ himself. The bishop or priest is only his image, the conductor of his grace. The first liturgy was the Mystical Supper celebrated by Christ himself, and each liturgy that is subsequently celebrated is not a simple symbolic remembrance of this event, but its continuation and actualization. Although the Eucharist is celebrated in different times and in different places, it remains one, regardless of time or space. It began at the Mystical Supper, but continues today and will continue until the end of the age. It began in the upper room in Zion, but has spread throughout the entire universe. Saint John Chrysostom wrote about this:

> Believe, therefore, that even now it is that supper, at which he himself sat down. For this is in no respect different from that. For neither doth man make this and himself the other; but both this and that is his own work. When therefore thou seest the priest delivering it unto thee, account not that it is the priest that doeth so, but that it is Christ's hand that is stretched out.[1]

> For we always offer the same, not one sheep now and tomorrow another, but always the same thing: so that the sacrifice is one. And yet by this reasoning, since the offering is made in many places, are there many Christs? But Christ is one everywhere, being complete here and complete there also, one body. As then while offered in many places, he is one body and not many bodies; so also [he is] one sacrifice. He is our high priest, who offered the sacrifice that cleanses us. That we offer now also, which was then offered, which cannot be exhausted. This is done in remembrance of what was then done. For (saith he) "do this in remembrance of me" (Lk 22.19). It is not another sacrifice, as the high priest, but we offer always the same. . . .[2]

[1]John Chrysostom, *Homilies on the Matthew* 50.30 (*NPNF*[1] 10:312).
[2]John Chrysostom, *Homilies on Hebrews* 17.3 (*NPNF*[1] 14:449).

The Divine Liturgy in the Monastery of Saint Catherine. Mount Sinai.

Christ is present, and he who set in order that meal of old also sets this one in order now. For it is not a man who causes the elements that are set forth to become the body and blood of Christ, but Christ himself, who was crucified for our sake. Fulfilling the figure, the priest stands and utters the words. But the power and the grace belong to God.[3]

While on the whole it is possible to refer to the Orthodox worship services as a school of theology and contemplation of God, the divine liturgy represents the epitome of this characterization. The liturgy teaches the mysteries of the heavenly kingdom because it is itself an icon of this kingdom, the fullest representation of the heavenly reality in earthly conditions, a revelation of the transcendental through the immanent. In the kingdom of God all symbols fall away, and only realities remain. There the faithful will not commune of the body and blood of Christ in the appearance of bread and wine, but will "more fully"[4] commune of Christ himself—the source of life and immortality. But although the appearance, image, and form of communicating with God will change, its essence will not change: it will always remain man's personal meeting with God—man who is not isolated from others, but who is in community with others. In this sense, the liturgy celebrated

[3]John Chrysostom, *On the Betrayal of Judas* 1.6 (PG 49:380–1).
[4]Cf. "Grant that we may more perfectly partake of thee in the never-ending day of thy kingdom." The priest says these words (taken from the ninth ode of the Paschal Canon, written by Saint John of Damascus) as he deposits the contents of the diskos in the chalice.—*Ed.*

on earth is only a part of the unceasing liturgy that is celebrated by men and angels in the heavenly kingdom.

The liturgy is a worship service that takes place in a church, although in exceptional circumstances or in special missionary conditions it may be celebrated outside of a temple. Cases are well known of liturgies celebrated on ships, in private homes, or in forests. In the period of persecutions against the Church in Russia during the twentieth century, clergymen who were deprived of their liberty celebrated liturgies in prison cells and barracks.

The liturgy serves as a supporting pillar of the existence of the Orthodox Church. In the history of the Church there were periods when churches and monasteries were closed, when icons and holy relics were destroyed, when the Church was deprived of the right to carry out charitable and catechetical activities, and when clergymen were killed by the hundreds and thousands. But even in these periods the celebration of the divine liturgy did not cease—openly or secretly, in churches or in private homes. And it was precisely the liturgy that enabled the preservation of the Church in the midst of the cruelest persecutions, and it was precisely the mystery of the Eucharist that spiritually supported and strengthened Christians who found themselves struggling for survival.

In the ancient Church, the bishop presided over the celebration of the liturgy. Over time, as the number of Church communities grew, bishops began to delegate the serving of the liturgies to presbyters. For this, each presbyter was given a special certificate signed by the bishop.

In the early Christian Church, the liturgy was the divine service of the day of the resurrection (Sunday). This determined the character of the prayers—festal, celebratory, and expressing thanks—that became a part of the liturgy. Church feasts were also marked by the celebration of the liturgy. Later, the faithful began to also celebrate the liturgy on days when martyrs were commemorated. The frequent celebration of the liturgy was typical for the city-dwelling monastics of Constantinople, but there are insufficient grounds for asserting that it was performed daily. In the disciplinary rules of Saint Theodore the Studite, days without liturgy are mentioned together with the days when the liturgy was celebrated.[5] Even in the eleventh century, the daily celebration of the liturgy was not the norm in the monasteries of Byzantium.[6]

---

[5] Theodore the Studite, *Poenae monasteriales* 2.31 (PG 99:1753a).

[6] Emil Herman, "Die häufige und tägliche Kommunion in den byzantinischen Klöstern," in *Mémorial Louis Petit: mélanges d'histoire et d'archéologie byzantines* (Bucharest: Institut français d'études byzantines, 1948), 203–217, at 210.

The contemporary Typikon prescribes the daily celebration of the liturgy except on the weekdays of Great Lent. But in practice the liturgy is celebrated daily only in monasteries and large city parishes. The liturgy is served in small parishes on Sundays and feast days, and also on days commemorating saints who are especially venerated.

The term *leitourgia* (literally: "common work") indicates the communal character of this divine service and the participation of the entire church community in it. The whole structure of the liturgy presupposes the presence of the community, which, on an equal basis with the priest, is the celebrant of the liturgy. This community is not made up of spectators, but participants whose participation in the liturgy is primarily in prayer and the communion of the holy mysteries of Christ. Contemporary practice, by which those who have prepared commune, while the others are satisfied with passive attendance in the church, does not correspond with the original practice of the Church.[7]

The active participation of the laity in the liturgy presupposes the possibility for them to answer the exclamations of the priest and to hear the words of the so-called "secret" prayers—in particular, the prayers of the anaphora. In our time these prayers, as a rule, are read silently by the priest. First, this seems to create an additional barrier between the priest and flock, and second, it deprives the worshippers of the opportunity to enter into the basic content of the liturgy, which passes them by. The faithful hear not the prayers themselves, but only the concluding exclamations of the priest. Moreover, insofar as the "secret" prayers are read chiefly during the singing of the choir, a significant part of the divine service is akin to two parallel services: one celebrated by the priest in the sanctuary and another heard by the parishioners in the church.

The following argument is often given in defense of the practice of the secret reading of the prayers: it is not correct for these prayers to be heard by uninitiated people who have simply entered the church. (Along with this they make reference to the "secret discipline" [*disciplina arcani*] existing in the ancient Church.)[8] But

---

[7]In certain parishes of the Russian, Bulgarian, and Serbian Orthodox Churches the author had the experience of participating in liturgies in which not one of the laity communed. In such cases, the chalice is carried out to the ambon with the words "With the fear of God and faith draw near," after which it is immediately carried back into the sanctuary. There is nothing more sinful and contradictory to the spirit and meaning of the liturgy than depriving all of the attending faithful of communion, no matter what reasons may be given to justify it.

[8]So, for example, Deacon Andrei Kuraev points to two reasons for the appearance of the practice of the secret reading of the liturgical prayers in Byzantium. First, in his opinion, the audible reading of the Eucharistic prayers resulted in the fact that children who were situated most near the sanctuary and heard and saw everything better than everybody else would repeat the mysteries in their games (see John Moschus,

in no way were all of the "secret" prayers originally secret. The celebrant read many prayers, including the prayer of the anaphora, in such a way that it was heard by all. When in the sixth century, breaking with ancient tradition, certain clergymen began to read the eucharistic prayers secretly, Saint Justinian the Emperor issued a separate novella on this subject: "We decree for all bishops and presbyters not to celebrate secretly the divine offering and the prayer at the service of holy baptism, but rather to do so in such a voice as may be well heard by the faithful people so that the souls of those hearing it may enter into greater piety, praise of God, and blessing."[9] Despite the prohibition, the secret reading of the liturgical prayers became rooted in Byzantine Church practice, from which it was transferred to the Balkan countries and to Rus', and remains in the practice of the Russian Church to this day.

Serving the liturgy is a creative act into which the whole fullness of the Church is drawn. The text of the liturgy is always the same, but every liturgy makes it possible for every person to experience anew his encounter with the living God.

Many things in the celebration of the liturgy in the Orthodox Church depend upon the clergy. Often the liturgy is "stolen" from the faithful due to its hasty and inattentive celebration by the priest. No matter whether it is celebrated by a bishop in a cathedral or by a priest in a village church, the service of the liturgy must be unhurried and majestic. All the words of the liturgy must be pronounced with all possible care, distinctly and intelligibly. It is very important for the clergyman to pray together with the community and not to mechanically utter words that have long since lost their novelty and freshness for him. It is not acceptable for the liturgy to become something habitual, or for it to be perceived as something ordinary or commonplace, even when it is celebrated daily.

All theatricality, "acting," and artificiality are unacceptable in the serving of the liturgy. The clergyman, moreover, should not openly express his emotions, feelings, or worries. He should not attract attention to himself in his serving, so that the fundamental attention of the faithful may always be focused not on him

Spiritual Meadow 96 [PG 87/3:2953b–c]). Second, the decline of the overall spiritual condition of Christians, which began when the faith became a state requirement, made a visual reminder of the uncommonness of what transpires in the sanctuary necessary. "The discipline of silence and removal from services served as a reminder of the distance which separates the eating of usual bread from the eating of the eucharistic bread, as well as the responsibilities of the people who participate in the mystery." See Andrei Kuraev, *The legacy of Christ: What was not included in the Gospels?* [in Russian] (Moscow: Fond "Blagovest," 1997), 111.

[9]Justinian, *Novellae Constitutiones* 174.6. (Cited in Nikolai Uspenskii, *The Byzantine liturgy: a historical-liturgical study. The Anaphora: the experience of historical-liturgical analysis*, vol. 2 of *Works on liturgics* [in Russian] (Moscow: Izdatel'stvo Moskovskoi Patriarkhii, 2006), 348.)

but on the true celebrant of the liturgy—Christ. Some clergymen (this especially concerns deacons) turn the divine service into theatre, exploiting all the richness of their voices and theatrical talent for the sake of making a bigger impression upon the public.

The Orthodox liturgy, inherited from Byzantium, is in the form of a dialogue. In its fundamental content the liturgy is a dialogue of the church community with God, and the celebrant is the person delegated by the community to fulfill this service. Almost all the liturgy's prayers are addressed to God the Father.

What is more, an essential role in the liturgy is played by the dialogues between the celebrant—be he a bishop or a priest—and the people. At every exclamation of the celebrant an answer follows from the people. "Peace be unto all" is followed by "And to thy spirit;" "Let us lift up our hearts" is followed by "We lift them up unto the Lord"; "Let us depart in peace" is followed by "in the name of the Lord." In the contemporary practice of the Russian Church, congregational singing is a great rarity. As a rule, the choir represents the people in responding to the celebrant. Nonetheless, there are certain parishes and even entire regions (for example, Carpathian Ruthenia) in which congregational singing is practiced.

Yet another participant in the dialogues during the celebration of the divine liturgy is the deacon. In the practice of many parishes there is no deacon, in which case his function is completely fulfilled by the priest. But the "ideal" liturgy—the one prescribed by the Priest's Service Book—presupposes the participation of a deacon, to whom an important role is given. During the entire service, it is the deacon who calls the community to prayer and invites the worshippers to participate in certain liturgical actions: "In peace let us pray to the Lord," "Wisdom, arise," "Bow your heads unto the Lord," "Let us stand aright, let us stand with fear, let us attend," and so forth.

The Priest's Service Book contains several dialogues between the deacon and the celebrant that take place during the course of the celebration of the liturgy. These dialogues are marked by a spirit of warmth and trust. "Pray for me, holy master," "Remember me, holy master"—the deacon addresses the celebrant with these words several times in the course of the liturgy. The bishop or priest responds, "May the Lord direct thy steps," "May the Lord God remember thee in his kingdom." When receiving a blessing from the bishop or priest, or when passing a certain sacred object to him, the deacon kisses his hand; beginning or concluding a sacred action, he bows to him. All of these actions are not simply the remnant of ancient church protocol. They bear the character of an icon, symbolizing the relationship of absolute trust and love that exists between people in the kingdom of heaven, and which should exist between those who live in God. Moreover, these actions emphasize the hierarchical character of the Church, in which, according to the teaching of Saint Dionysius the Areopagite, the divine "procession" and "bright light" pass from the higher ranks to the lower: from angels to men, from priests to deacons, from clergymen to laity. Finally, the veneration rendered during the divine service to the priest or bishop as to the one celebrating the Eucharist, as if acting for Christ himself, is similar to that which is rendered to the holy images: the honor rendered to the image (i.e. the clergyman) passes to the Archetype (i.e. Christ).

The order of the liturgy does not designate various functions to the concelebrating clergy: the fundamental actors are always the bishop or priest, deacon, and the community (choir). This in part explains the natural desire of every sacred server to celebrate the divine liturgy by himself, and not only to concelebrate with other priests. The thirst for the independent serving of the liturgy is explained by the fact that, during its celebration, special, trustful relations are established between the celebrant (bishop or priest) and God. The essence of this relationship transcends the bounds of the liturgical texts, in which the priest almost never addresses God on behalf of himself (an exception is the prayer "None is worthy" during the singing of the Cherubic Hymn), but rather always on behalf of the community. Nonetheless, many clergymen know the feeling of a special closeness to God that emerges during the celebration of the liturgy. Archimandrite Kyprian (Kern) wrote about this:

Indeed, priesthood consists of the priest independently performing the divine liturgy, without concelebrating with another. . . . Therefore, the priest must build up within himself a thirst for the individual performance of the eucharistic service and not be content with a combined "situation," where he is surrounded by higher official representatives, be it bishops, archimandrites, or archpriests. The priest must possess this insatiable thirst for Eucharistic service, which, of course, in no way belittles his thirst to receive communion from the hand of another, not necessarily older and higher ranking, colleague. But the mystical feeling, not understood by the laity, differs from the feeling of himself performing the sacrifice and creating, by the power of the Holy Spirit, gifts of the body and blood, as opposed to the feeling and experience of receiving communion at a liturgy performed by another. The Eucharistic power given to the priest may be accurately measured by his thirst to serve unassisted.[10]

[10]Kyprian (Kern), *Orthodox Pastoral Service*, ed. William C. Mills and trans. Mary Goddard (Rollinsford, NH: Orthodox Research Institute, 2009), 59, 60–61.

Archimandrite Cyprian called the divine liturgy "the most powerful means of pastoral service." He emphasized that "molebens, panikhidas, akathists [which, by the way, Metropolitan Anthony[11] and Metropolitan of Moscow Philaret of blessed memory viewed disapprovingly] cannot replace the divine liturgy."[12] If molebens and panikhidas are necessary, they ought to be served before, not after, the liturgy. However, the liturgy itself, being the universal and all-embracing service, includes in itself all those things for which molebens and panikhidas are served, including the commemoration of the living and the dead.

The Orthodox liturgy has a "dramatic character" in the sense that it is a remembrance of the life and death of Christ, his burial and resurrection, and also the whole history of salvation from the creation of the world up to the second coming.[13] In connection with this, there is a tradition in the Orthodox Church of the symbolic interpretation of the divine liturgy. This tradition is first found in the teachings of Theodore Mopsuestia (5th c.), who saw in certain moments of the liturgy the symbolic depiction of events from the life of Christ. In particular, the great entrance symbolizes the procession of Christ to his suffering, the placing of the holy gifts on the altar table symbolizes Christ being laid in the tomb, and the consecration of the gifts symbolizes the resurrection of Christ.[14] The same type of interpretation of the liturgy is found in Saint Maximus the Confessor's *Mystagogia* (7th c.), in the essays of Saint Germanus of Constantinople (8th c.), Saint Nicholas Cabasilas (9th c.), Saint Symeon of Thessalonica (14th c.), and other Byzantine authors. In the nineteenth century, Nikolai Gogol examined this interpretation in his *Reflections on the Divine Liturgy*.[15]

Despite the early appearance of the symbolic interpretation, it is in no way an inherent part of the liturgy itself, because it does not derive either from the text of the liturgy or from the ritual actions that accompany the liturgy's celebration. Protopresbyter Alexander Schmemann, along with other contemporary Orthodox liturgists, considered the "symbolization" of the liturgy and separate parts of it (especially as encountered in nineteenth-century authors) to be arbitrary and artificial, reducing liturgical rites to the level of "didactic dramatization." In his opinion, the "piling up of symbolical representations" is "disturbing to (people's) prayer and

---

[11]Metropolitan Anthony (Khrapovitsky).

[12]Kyprian (Kern), *Orthodox Pastoral Service*, 63 (altered).

[13]Andrew Louth, *Greek East and Latin West: The Church, AD 681–1071* (Crestwood, NY: St Vladimir's Seminary Press, 2007).

[14]Theodore of Mopsuestia, *Catechetical Homilies* 15.25–29 (ST 145.501–511).

[15]We spoke of this essay in vol. 1, pp. 223–225.

genuine participation in the liturgy and distracts them from that spiritual reality the direct contact with which is the very essence of prayer."[16]

THE PROSKOMEDIA

The divine liturgy in its contemporary form is the fruit of many centuries of development. It is an order that consists of three parts: the proskomedia, the liturgy of the catechumens, and the liturgy of the faithful.

The proskomedia (Gr. *proskomēdē*—literally "offering") is the name of the part of the liturgy celebrated by the clergy in the sanctuary while the third and sixth hours are being read. The main content of this part of the liturgy is the preparation of the bread and wine needed for the celebration of the Eucharist and the reading of corresponding prayers. The term "proskomedia" indicates the custom in the ancient Church of celebrating the Eucharist using bread and wine brought to the church by members of the community. In our day, the "offering" exists in a less direct form. The faithful bring donations to the church treasury or purchase candles, and with this money the wine is bought and bread is baked for the celebration of the Eucharist.

In the Church's contemporary practice, the clergy normally arrive first at the church and the faithful arrive later, by the beginning of the liturgy or even after the beginning. Things were different in the ancient Church. Members of the community arrived at the church before the beginning of the service and waited for the entrance of the celebrant (bishop or priest), upon whose arrival the service would begin. In our own day this order is seen only in the hierarchical service, in which the hierarch is "greeted" in the temple. When this is the case, the special "entrance prayers," in which the clergy ask God

Commemoration of the Living and the Departed by the Hierarch.

for help in performing the coming service, are not read in front of the iconostasis, but rather in the middle of the church, and the vesting of the hierarch takes place not in the sanctuary, but on the cathedra.

After the vesting of the clergy, the proskomedia begins in the sanctuary with the exclamation, "Blessed is our God, always, now and ever and unto the ages of ages."

[16]Schmemann, *Eucharist*, 31.

This exclamation serves as a signal for the reader to begin reading the third and sixth hours. The priest and deacon stand before the table of oblation, on which the sacred vessels are set: the chalice, diskos (a metal plate on a stand), spear (a knife), star (or "asterisk"—two metal arches joined to form a cross), and covers (small cross-shaped covers). The bread for the Eucharist and a decanter containing wine are also placed on the table of oblation. The bread for the celebration of the Eucharist, in accordance with the centuries-long tradition of the eastern Church, is leavened.[17] Wine ought to be made from pure grapes, without any artificial additives.[18]

The bread for the Eucharist is called "prosphora" (Gr. *prosphora*—also meaning "offering") because originally it was prepared and brought to the church by the parishioners. In the liturgical practice of the Greek Church, a single large prosphora is used, from which the "lamb" is taken—the sacred bread for the Eucharist. From it particles are taken out for the commemoration of saints, the living, and the departed. In the practice of the Russian Church, five prosphoras are used, one of which is called the "lamb prosphora" and has on its top a stamp in the form of a circle, in which a Greek cross with the inscription IC XC NI KA (Greek meaning "Jesus Christ is victorious") is inscribed.

After making three bows, the priest takes into his hands the first prosphora (usually the biggest one) and cuts out the lamb in a four-sided form, uttering the words from the prophecy of Isaiah, "He was led as a sheep to the slaughter and as a blameless lamb before his shearer is dumb, so he opens not his mouth. In his lowliness his judgement was taken away and who shall declare his generation?" (cf. Is 53.7–8) The lamb is placed on the diskos with the words, "Sacrificed is the lamb of God that taketh away the sin of the world for the life and salvation of the world." Then wine with water is poured into the chalice while the priest utters the words from the Gospel, "One of the soldiers with a spear pierced his side and forthwith came there out blood and water" (cf. Jn 19.34). All these actions and words are a remembrance of our Lord and Savior's sacrifice on the cross.

Then the priest takes the second prosphora and takes out a particle "in honor and remembrance of our most blessed lady the Theotokos and ever-virgin Mary." The third prosphora is called the "nine-ranks" because the priest removes nine particles from it in memory of the saints: Saint John the Baptist, the prophets, apostles, holy hierarchs, martyrs, venerable saints, unmercenaries, and also saints

---

[17]Unleavened bread is used in the Latin Church. See vol. 1, pp. 112–115.

[18]Every fruit offered to God should be of a natural, not artificial, origin. The addition of sugar or alcohol into the Eucharistic wine is unacceptable. In this way, *kagor*—often used in the liturgy in Orthodox churches—does not conform to canonical requirements.

held in particular veneration in the given country or city, and saints whose memory is commemorated on the given day. The final particle is taken out for the saint who wrote the liturgy—Saint Basil the Great or Saint John Chrysostom.[19]

After this, the priest removes particles from the two remaining prosphoras for the health of the patriarch, the diocesan hierarch, the civil authorities, and also for all whose names have been given by parishioners on commemoration slips. After the prosphora for the living, particles are removed from the prosphora for the departed. The removed particles are placed on the diskos next to the lamb, and at the end of the liturgy, following communion, they are wiped into the chalice while the priest utters the prayer, "Wash away, O Lord, the sins of those commemorated here by thy precious blood, through the prayers of thy saints."

During the liturgy the names of the living and departed are commemorated more than once. The first commemoration by name takes place during the proskomedia. Then, the patriarch and ruling hierarch are commemorated several times during the course of the liturgy. During the petitions of the litany of fervent supplication the names of the living are sometimes added, and names are read aloud during the litany for the departed. Then the clergyman prays for the living and the departed directly following the consecration of the holy gifts. In some parish churches the reading of commemoration slips, given by the faithful, significantly prolongs the service and distracts worshippers from prayer. It is clear that slips containing names to be commemorated aloud during the liturgy should be limited, while the commemoration of names during the service of the proskomedia may be longer.

The tradition of commemoration by name during the worship service has its roots in pre-Christian antiquity. We find in the Bible quite a few geneologies—lists containing the names of a particular person's ancestors (see Gen 10.1; 11.27; 25.12; 36.1, and others). The entire Book of Numbers consists mostly of lists of names that mean nothing to the contemporary reader but were, undoubtedly, very important to the book's authors. The necessity of including genealogies in the Book of Numbers and other parts of the Bible stemmed from the fact that genealogies were in no way perceived as simply lists of names to assist in identifying a particular person by adding certain information to his name (for example, Jacob the son of Isaac, to distinguish him from another Jacob). Genealogies primarily indicated the inheritance that each person bore in himself; they established a person's name in the

---

[19]The Greek practice of commemorating the saints differs from the Russian practice in that the Greek commemoration begins with the angelic ranks, not Saint John the Baptist.

unbroken chain of names beginning with Abraham, the father of the nation, and through him back to Adam. To be written into the genealogy of a particular tribe of Israel meant being a valuable member of God's chosen people, which signifies being present, in some mystical way, in God's memory. It is no coincidence that the Gospels began with a genealogy of Jesus Christ. By naming the ancestors of Christ, the evangelists desired to emphasize the fact that Christ was the son of his people, a real man whose name is woven into an unbroken chain of human names.

The Christian Church knows itself to be the "new Israel," and every member of the Church has his own genealogy. Coming to the liturgy, the faithful offer prayers not only for themselves but also for their loved ones, living and departed. Reading their names aloud, the Christian reminds God of them, so to speak, and at the same time calls on other members of the community to pray for them. It is fitting to recall here the idea of one theologian of the beginning of the twentieth century who stated that "a name encompasses, in one act of naming, the entire being . . . and qualities and particularities and actions of a person, just as the title of a book encompasses all the qualities of the book itself." Each person is like a book, "and while a person can know only a few excerpted pages from the book of the life of another person, God knows every letter and mark in the book." For this reason, in commemorating the names brought to us by the people at the proskomedia, "it is as if we name the chapters of the books of the lives of these people who are unknown to us but who are known to God in certainty."[20]

Following the commemoration of the living and the departed at the proskomedia, the priest removes a particle for himself. The censer is brought to him, over which he utters the prayer, "We offer Thee incense, O Christ our God, as a sweet spiritual fragrance. Receive it upon Thy heavenly altar, and send down upon us in return the grace of Thine All-holy Spirit." Having censed the covers, the priest covers the chalice and diskos with them. A prayer is then read, in which the priest addresses God with the words, "Remember those who offered it and those for whom it was offered, for Thou art good and lovest mankind, and preserve us blameless in the sacred celebration of Thy divine mysteries."

Then the deacon performs a full censing of the sanctuary and church. The full censing begins in the sanctuary before the altar table. After censing the altar table three times on each of its four sides, the deacon censes the table of oblation and

---

[20]Antonii (Bulatovich), *An apology for faith in the Name of God and the Name of Jesus* [in Russian] (Moscow, 1913), 88–89. [This apology was given to the Court of the Holy Council of the Russian Orthodox Church on August 1, 1918. Hieroschemamonk Antony was an advocate of "name-glorifying" (*imiaslavie*). The author has written extensively on the "name-glorifying" controversy elsewhere.—*Ed.*]

the icons in the sanctuary and then all those present in the sanctuary, beginning with the clergy. Then he exits to the ambon and censes the iconostasis, the kliros, and all the worshippers, after which he processes around the periphery of the entire church, censing the icons and the people present.

At the conclusion of the censing the priest and deacon stand before the altar table and the deacon quietly says, "It is time to act for the Lord." These words are often taken to be a signal to begin the service (i.e., "The time has come to serve the Lord"), but the true meaning of these words is different. The words are taken from a psalm and mean, "It is time for the Lord to act" (see Ps 118.126). That is to say, the time for men's actions has ceased, and the time for God to act has arrived. In this way, the belief is confessed that the one who performs the liturgy is the Lord himself, who acts through his serving clergy.

BEGINNING OF THE LITURGY OF THE CATECHUMENS

After receiving a blessing from the priest, the deacon exits to the ambon and exclaims, "Bless, master." The liturgy of the catechumens begins at this moment. It is named such because in the ancient Church it was permissible for the catechumens (those who were preparing for baptism) to attend this part of the liturgy. The ancient liturgy of the catechumens bore a primarily didactic character. In it, excerpts from holy Scripture were read, a homily was given, and special prayers were offered for the catechumens, after which they left church and returned to their homes. Only the faithful—those who had been received in holy baptism—remained in the church to participate in the Eucharist.

We have already discussed how the liturgy possesses an eschatological dimension[21] that raises the faithful from the reality of earthly existence to the reality of the world on high, the kingdom of God. Herein lies the meaning of the opening exclamation of the liturgy of the catechumens, "Blessed is the kingdom of the Father, and of the Son, and of the Holy Spirit, now and ever and unto the ages of ages."

The theme of the kingdom is a central theme of the Christian gospel. Christ's earthly ministry began with the words, "Repent, for the kingdom of heaven is at hand" (Mt 4.17). The kingdom is the theme of all of Christ's parables. He asks, "What is the kingdom of God like? And to what shall I compare it?" And he

[21]See vol. 2, p. 492.

answers that it is like a mustard seed, a pearl found in a field, a dragnet cast into the sea, leaven in meal. Jesus always acknowledged himself as King. To Pilate's question, "Are you the king of the Jews?" Jesus answered, "It is as you say" (Mt 27.11).

But he added, "My kingdom is not of this world. If my kingdom were of this world, my servants would fight, so that I should not be delivered to the Jews; but now my kingdom is not from hence" (Jn 18.36).

The conflict between Jesus and the Jews revolved around the theme of the kingdom. The Jews wanted to see in the person of Jesus a most powerful king and autocrat, who would deliver them from foreign dominion. Instead of this, Jesus offered them the teaching that "the kingdom of God is within you" (Lk 17.21). To the very end the Jews could not understand what kingdom Christ was speaking of. Even Christ's disciples did not understand it until the moment they saw Jesus crucified on the cross with the inscription, "The king of the Jews." Only then was it revealed to the world what Jesus spoke of in his sermons: the kingdom of God is God's love for man, crucified on the cross.

Christ Before Pilate. Fresco. Church of Saint Nicholas in Prilep. Macedonia. 8th c.

The divine liturgy, which is a remembrance of the Savior's sacrifice on the cross, at the same time reveals the kingdom of God which has come in power (cf. Mk 9.1). For this reason, the theme of the kingdom is the liturgy's leitmotif from its very first exclamation:

> The kingdom of God . . . is the content of the Christian life. According to the unanimous witness of all scripture and tradition, it is the knowledge of God, love for him, unity with him and life in him. The kingdom of God is unity with God, the source of all life, indeed life itself. . . . What does it mean to *bless* the kingdom? It means that we acknowledge and confess it to be our highest and ultimate value. . . . It means that we proclaim it to be the goal of the sacrament—of pilgrimage, ascension, entrance—that now begins. It means that we must focus our attention, our mind, heart and soul, i.e. our whole life, upon that which is truly the "one thing needful" [Lk 10.42]. Finally, it means that now, already in "this world," we confirm the possibility of communion with the kingdom, of entrance into its radiance, truth and joy. Each time that Christians "assemble as the Church" they witness before the whole world that

Christ is King and Lord, that his kingdom has already been revealed and given to man and that a new and immortal life has begun. . . . [22]

Following the opening exclamation, the great litany, also known as the litany of peace, is read by the deacon with the proclamation, "In peace let us pray to the Lord." The next petition, "For the peace from above and for the salvation of our souls," speaks of the eschatological consummation of man's earthly sojourning: the peace from on high and eternal salvation that is the goal of the Christian life. The litany's subsequent petitions focus on man's earthly existence: the faithful are called to pray for "the peace of the whole world, for the welfare of the holy Churches of God," the temple and those who enter with faith and piety, for the patriarch and the local bishop, for the civil authorities, for "travelers by land, by sea, and by air; for the sick and the suffering; for captives," "for seasonable weather, for abundance of the fruits of the earth," and for "peaceful times" and the deliverance from every sorrow. The content of the litany corresponds with the character of the liturgy as a worship service possessing a universal, catholic, and cosmic character that includes the whole fullness of the experience of the Church and every believer. In the final petition of the litany, the most-holy Theotokos and all the saints are commemorated.

The great litany is followed by three antiphons interspersed with little litanies and the prayers of the priest. The alternation of the antiphons with the deacon's litanies and the priest's prayers was characteristic of the Constantinopolitan "sung office." Thus, it is necessary to surmise that this part of the liturgy of the catechumens derives from the sung office (this borrowing took place around the eighth century.) This part of the service is made up of several heterogeneous elements and at one time formed a separate service, whereas the liturgy began with the singing of the trisagion.[23]

The Typikon prescribes the performance of the so-called "daily antiphons" for weekday liturgies,[24] made up of verses from Psalm 91 ("It is good to give thanks to the Lord"), Psalm 92 ("The Lord reigns, he is clothed with majesty"), and Psalm 94 ("O come, let us sing unto the Lord"). Refrains are added to the psalm verses as follows: the refrain "Through the prayers of the Theotokos, O Savior, save us"

---

[22]Schmemann, *Eucharist*, 40–41, 47–48.

[23]In the practice of the contemporary divine service, the liturgy begins with the singing of the trisagion (or "As many as have been baptized into Christ") only when it is preceded by vespers, which occurs on the eves of the Nativity and Theophany, and also on Holy Thursday and Holy Saturday. In this case the service of the three antiphons is omitted and vespers turns into the liturgy.

[24]When there is no afterfeast and the Typikon does not indicate verses on the Beatitudes.

is added to the verses of the first antiphon; "Through the prayers of thy saints, O Savior, save us" is added to the verses of the second antiphon; "O Son of God, who art wondrous in the saints, save us, who sing to thee: Alleluia" is added to the verses of the third antiphon. In the Greek Church, the daily antiphons are sung every day, except on days for which festal antiphons are appointed. In parishes of the Russian Church, in contrast, the daily antiphons are used rather infrequently,[25] and in their place, on both weekdays and Sundays, the typical antiphons are sung: Psalm 102 ("Bless the Lord, O my soul"), Psalm 145 ("Praise the Lord, O my soul"), and the Beatitudes from the Gospel. The first two antiphons have a character of praise and thanksgiving, which corresponds with the liturgy as a festal service. For several feasts, special "festal antiphons," which correspond with the feast in their content, are customary.

The prayers read by the priest during the antiphons appear to be extremely ancient.[26] In the first prayer, the priest addresses God with the words, "Look down on us and on this holy house with pity, O Master, and impart the riches of Thy mercy and Thy compassion to us and to those who pray with us." The second prayer is a fragment of the prayer before the ambon read by the priest before the conclusion of the liturgy. The third prayer recalls the Savior's promise: "Where two or three are gathered together in my name, I am there in the midst of them" (Mt 18.20). The liturgy is the "mystery of the assembly" at which the Savior's promise is realized in all its fullness.

Justinian I with his Retinue. Mosaic. Basilica of San Vitale. Ravenna. 6th c.

To the second antiphon is joined the hymn *Only-begotten Son and immortal Word of God* whose author, as has already been stated, was Emperor Justinian. The content of this hymn, included in the liturgy by imperial decree in the year 534, serves as a brief exposition of Orthodox theology, and it was introduced into the liturgy when christological arguments still continued to vex the Orthodox East. In particular, the words of the hymn "who without change didst become man" were directed against the monophysites.[27] These words

[25]See Mikhail Zheltov, "Daily antiphons" [in Russian], in *Orthodox Encyclopedia*, vol. 9 (Moscow: Tserkovno-nauchnyi tsentr "Pravoslavnaia entsiklopediia," 2005), 559–60.

[26]Juan Mateos supposed that originally these prayers were a part of the liturgy of the faithful (Juan Mateos, "Evolution historique de la liturgie de saint Jean Chrysostome," *Proche-Orient Chrétien* 16 (1966): 34) but this supposition does not have reliable confirmation and in our day is rejected by the majority of liturgicists.

[27]Uspenskii, *Byzantine Liturgy*, 71.

point to the fact that following the incarnation, the divine nature of Christ did not undergo change (Gr. *treptos*, Sl. *prelozhenie*)[28] and did not merge into a new "God-human" nature, but was joined with human nature while preserving all its inherent properties and characteristics.

The singing of the Beatitudes from the Gospel at the liturgy has a profound moral significance. The Beatitudes are the quintessential moral teaching of Christ and contain the "reverse perspective" by which every Christian should live. Those things that seem to be unhappiness and weakness to most people—humility, meekness, poverty in spirit, and other qualities—are enumerated in the "commandments of blessedness" as necessary for the attainment of the kingdom of heaven. The Church reminds the faithful of this in the beginning of the divine liturgy.

THE LITTLE ENTRANCE AND THE THRICE-HOLY

In the ancient liturgy, the entrance of the clergy into the temple was accompanied by the singing of *Only-begotten Son*, which marked the beginning of the liturgy of the catechumens. The clergy, including the bishop, presbyters, and deacons, carried the Gospel Book, which was kept in a separate place and was brought to the church every time that the liturgy was celebrated. Over time, the Gospel Book came to be kept on the altar table in the sanctuary, the service of the three antiphons was joined to the liturgy, and the practice of beginning the liturgy with a festive procession ceased. Nevertheless, the so-called "little entrance" remained a part of the liturgy, at which time the Gospel Book is brought out from the sanctuary into the center of the church.

The entrance is performed during the singing of the Beatitudes. The priest bows before the altar table, takes the Gospel Book and gives it to the deacon. Then, preceded by a candle-bearer, the priest exits the sanctuary through the north doors into the center of the church. When the procession stops in the center of the church, the deacon, turning to the priest, says the words, "Bless, master, the holy entrance." The priest replies, "Blessed is the entrance of Thy saints, always, now and ever and unto the ages of ages." One may understand "saints" to mean the clergy entering into the sanctuary, or it may be understood in the wider sense to include the whole community of the Church, including the angels and saints,

[28]This is one of the four key terms of the Chalcedonian definition, which confesses Christ "in two natures, without confusion, change, division, or separation" (*en dyo physesin asynchytōs, atreptōs, adiaiphetōs, achōristōs*).—*Ed.*

who are invisibly present in the church. But the Greek original—*Evlogēmenē hē eisōdos tōn hagiōn sou*—allows for yet another translation: "Blessed is the entrance into the sanctuary." This is because *tōn hagiōn* in the genitive case can be either the masculine *hoi hagioi* (saints) or the neuter *ta hagia* ("the holies" i.e. sanctuary).

Next, the deacon exclaims, "Wisdom, aright." This exclamation refers to the reading from the Book of Epistles and the Gospel Book soon after the little entrance, and means: "Stand aright, because what follows is wisdom." In other words, it is a call to listen attentively to the readings that will follow. Then, the clergy enters the sanctuary through the royal doors.

On great feasts, following "Wisdom, aright" the deacon pronounces the so-called entrance sticheron, which is a verse from the third festal antiphon. In particular, on the Nativity of Christ the following verse is read: "Out of the womb before the morning star have I begotten thee. The Lord has sworn and will not repent: Thou art a priest forever according to the order of Melchizedek" (Ps 109.3–4); on Theophany: "The sea saw it and fled; Jordan turned back" (Ps 113.3); on Pascha: "Bless God in the churches, the Lord, from the fountain of Israel" (Ps 67.27); on Ascension: "God has gone up with a shout, the Lord with the sound of a trumpet" (Ps 46.6); on Pentecost: "Be thou exalted, O Lord, in thy strength; we will sing and chant of thy mighty acts" (Ps 20.14).

During the little entrance, a prayer is read in which the priest asks that angels should enter the church together with his concelebrants. In the prayer of the entrance, as in many other prayers and hymns of the liturgy, we see the notion that the heavenly hosts participate in the celebration of the liturgy. This view was expressed in the words of Saint John Chrysostom:

> The sacred table is ready, the lamb of God is being slain for you, the priest is giving his all for you, the spiritual fire is blazing forth from the holy table, the cherubim are standing by, the seraphim are hovering, the six-winged spirits have their faces covered, all the spiritual powers are praying for you along with the priest, the spiritual fire is descending, the blood in the chalice is being poured from Christ's immaculate side for your cleansing. . . . [29]

The liturgy is a sacred action of cosmic dimensions, not only because the content of the prayers encompasses all aspects of people's earthly and spiritual lives, but also because the liturgy unites the world below with the world above, and angels

---

[29] John Chrysostom, *Homily IX on Repentance*, trans. Andrew Maguire, accessed December 5, 2016, http://earlychurchtexts.com/public/john_chrysostom_homily_ix_on_repentance.htm.

with men. The liturgy is a window into the world on high that discloses a vision of heavenly glory, where the cherubim and seraphim give praise to God. The divine service is called to be the earthly representation of this sacred heavenly action. From this flows the striving for beauty and splendor reflected in the architecture of Orthodox cathedrals, the mosaics and frescoes, the diversity and refinement of the Church's utensils, and the length of the hymns and the festiveness of the liturgical processions.

The famous liturgist Robert Taft described the beginning of the patriarchal liturgy at Constantinople's Hagia Sophia Cathedral in this way:

> The procession has arrived, the liturgy is about to begin. The patriarch is in the narthex, where he has greeted the emperor; both are awaiting the signal to enter the church. . . . The psalmists intone the *Ho Monogenes* troparion. . . . At this signal, the patriarch goes before the Royal Doors[30] to say the Introit Prayer. . . . To the patriarch—his gaze into the nave framed by the open doors and interior western buttresses, his view encompassing the central axis of ambo, solea, and sanctuary, brilliantly bathed in the rays of the sun as it streamed through the windows in the conch of the apse—the words of the prayer must certainly have seemed fulfilled, evoking the vision of the heavenly sanctuary resplendent to the East, as if before his very eyes: "O Lord and Master, our God, who in heaven has established the orders and armies of angels and archangels to minister unto your majesty, grant that the holy angels may enter with us, and with us serve and glorify your goodness."[31]

Although the majority of contemporary Orthodox churches are far from the majesty of the Hagia Sophia Cathedral, and although the contemporary liturgical ritual is noticeably more modest than the Byzantine ritual, the little entrance is performed today at every liturgy. And the prayer of the entrance is read, just as a thousand years ago, at every liturgy, recalling the reality of the angelic world, invisibly present in the church during the celebration of the Eucharist. It is meaningful that the prayer speaks of angels serving with people, and people serving with angels. This notion was reflected also in the fine arts: on the frescoes of several Byzantine churches, Saint Basil the Great is depicted celebrating the liturgy with angels serving with him.

---

[30]The Royal Doors in Byzantine practice are the name for the entrance to the church building, not the entrance to the sanctuary.

[31]Taft, *The Byzantine Rite*, 37.

During the hierarchical service, the little entrance is the first entrance of the hierarch into the sanctuary, because up to the little entrance the hierarch is present among the people, standing on the cathedra. The hierarch walks into the sanctuary carrying the dikirion and trikirion (candlestands with two and three candles, respectively), which symbolize the light of Christ, who is known in two natures, and the uncreated light of the holy Trinity, respectively. After blessing the people with the dikirion and trikirion, the hierarch gives the trikirion to the deacon who stands opposite him. Entering into the sanctuary with the dikirion in his hand, the hierarch performs the censing of the sanctuary, the clergy, the iconostasis, and all those who are present in the church, after which he gives the dikirion to a subdeacon.

Saint Maximus the Confessor.
Fresco. Monastery of Saint
Dionysius. Mount Athos. 16th c.

According to the interpretation of Saint Maximus the Confessor, the entrance of the hierarch into the church symbolizes the coming of the Lord and Savior into the world:

[T]he first entrance of the bishop into the holy Church for the sacred synaxis is a figure and image of the first appearance in the flesh of Jesus Christ the Son of God and our Savior in this world. By it he freed human nature which had been enslaved by corruption, betrayed through its own fault to death because of sin, tyrannically dominated by the devil. He redeemed all its debt as if he were liable even though he was not liable but sinless, and brought us back again to the original grace of his kingdom by giving himself as a ransom for us. And in exchange for our destructive passions he gives us his life-giving Passion as a salutary cure which saves the whole world. After this appearance, his ascension into heaven and return to the heavenly throne are symbolically figured in the bishop's entrance into the sanctuary and ascent to the priestly throne.[32]

The contemporary little entrance, including the entrance performed during the hierarchical service, preserves the christocentric character of the ancient entrance rite of the bishop and clergy into the church. The chris-

---

[32]Maximus the Confessor, *Mystagogy* 8 (Berthold, CWS).

tocentric character of the contemporary liturgy is expressed in the singing of *Only-begotten Son*, the gospel Beatitudes, the procession of the Gospel Book to the center of the church, and the singing of "Come, let us worship and fall down before Christ. O Son of God, who didst rise from the dead,[33] save us who sing to thee: Alleluia." With this verse the faithful are invited to offer up worship to Christ, who became man for the salvation of the world. The Gospel Book is a visible image and symbol of Christ; it is understood in the Orthodox Church not only as a book for reading, but also as an object of liturgical veneration. The Gospel Book is not only read in church; the faithful also bow down before it, process with it, and kiss it.

Following the little entrance, when the hierarchical liturgy is celebrated, the hierarch takes the censer in his hands and performs the censing of the sanctuary, the iconostasis, and all the faithful in the church during the drawn-out singing of "*Eis polla eti, despota.*"[34] After completing the censing, he reads the prayer of the trisagion. When a priest serves [without a bishop present], the celebrant immediately begins reading the prayer after coming into the sanctuary. During the reading, the choir sings the troparia and kontakia—for the resurrection, the feast, and the saint to whom the church is dedicated. The custom of singing troparia and kontakia after the little entrance is of fairly late origin. It appears to have been introduced in order to fill in the pause that arose because of the silent reading of the prayer of the trisagion by the hierarch or priest. However, it is precisely the prayer's content which should have prepared the faithful to understand the meaning of the hymn of the trisagion:

> O Holy God, who dost rest in the saints; who art hymned by the Seraphim with the thrice-holy cry,[35] and glorified by the Cherubim, and worshiped by every heavenly power . . . who hast vouchsafed to us, Thy humble and unworthy servants, even in this hour to stand before the glory of Thy holy altar, and to offer worship and praise which are due unto Thee: Thyself, O Master, accept even from the mouths of us sinners the thrice-holy hymn,[36] and visit us in Thy goodness. . . .

[33]On days commemorating saints, the phrase "who art wondrous in thy saints" is substituted; on feasts of the Theotokos: "through the prayers of the Theotokos." The insertion "through the prayers of the Theotokos" is not found in the Typikon and is used only in Russian, not Greek, practice.

[34]The Greek words "*Eis polla eti despota*" mean "Many years, master." They are sung many times during the hierarchical service; as a rule, after the blessing of the people by the hierarch, or after the performance of a particular sacred action by the hierarch.

[35]Here "thrice-holy" refers to the angelic doxology "Holy, holy, holy, Lord of Sabaoth" (Is 6.3).—*Ed.*

[36]Here "thrice-holy hymn" signifies the prayer "Holy God, holy Mighty, holy Immortal, have mercy on us."—*Ed.*

The prayer ends with the priest's exclamation, "For holy art thou, our God, and unto thee do we send up glory: to the Father, and to the Son, and to the Holy Spirit." The exclamation is usually completed by the deacon, who turns to the people with orarion raised in his hand, saying "And unto ages of ages." In the contemporary practice of the Russian Church, at the patriarchal service, the exclamation, "For holy art thou," is preceded by the deacon's supplication, "O Lord, save the pious and hear us," divided into two parts and repeated by the choir. After this supplication, the "many years" is sung for all the heads of the local Orthodox Churches. At the usual hierarchical or priest's liturgy, it is customary to insert the supplication, "O Lord, save the pious," into the middle of the exclamation, "For holy art thou, our God," which disrupts the natural flow of the worship service. But another widespread practice is for the recitation of "O Lord, save the pious" to follow the exclamation, "For holy art thou," or to precede it, which is more logical than inserting these words into the middle of the exclamation.

The supplication, "O Lord, save the pious," comes from the Byzantine and Russian imperial ceremony. In Byzantium, following the little entrance at the patriarchal liturgy the *slavlenie* ("praising") of the emperor was exclaimed, which concluded with the words "O Lord, save the king." After the fall of Constantinople, this supplication was changed to "O Lord, save the pious." At first it was inserted into the exclamation "For holy art thou" in the Greek euchologion of 1580, and since then it has been included in all subsequent editions of the euchologion. It first appeared in the Moscow service books during the patriarchate of Patriarch Nikon.[37] After the fall of the monarchy in Russia the supplication, "O Lord, save the pious," was removed from the liturgy by the decision of the liturgical section of the Local Council of 1917–1918. On July 17, 1997, by the decision of the synodal liturgical commission, it was again introduced into the liturgical practice of the Russian Church.

Directly following the deacon's exclamation, "And unto the ages of ages," the choir sings "Amen" and begins the singing of the thrice-holy hymn: "Holy God, holy Mighty, holy Immortal, have mercy on us." In the priest's liturgy this hymn is sung three times, after which the choir sings "Glory . . . now and ever . . . ," "Holy Immortal, have mercy on us," and finally the thrice-holy is sung once again in its entirety. In all, the thrice-holy hymn is sung four and a half times.

---

[37]Valentin Pechatnov, *The Divine Liturgy in Russia and Greece: A comparative study of the contemporary order* [in Russian] (Moscow: Palomnik, 2008), 122–123.

The thrice-holy hymn is yet another prayer which reminds us of the participation of angels in the worship service. According to tradition, this hymn is linked to an earthquake that took place in Constantinople in the middle of the fifth century. Saint John of Damascus speaks of this in his *An Exact Exposition of the Orthodox Faith*:

Those who have compiled the history of the Church[38] relate how once, when Proclus was archbishop [d. 446 or 447], the people of Constantinople were making public entreaty to avert some threat of the divine wrath, and it happened that a child was taken up out of the crowd and by some angelic choirmasters was taught the Thrice-Holy Hymn after the following fashion: "Holy God, holy Mighty, holy Immortal, have mercy on us." When the child came back again and told what he had been taught, the whole crowd sang the hymn and the threat was averted.[39]

Other opinions exist concerning the origin of the thrice-holy hymn. Some liturgists consider that the hymn "Holy God" was composed by Saint Basil the Great during the Arian Controversy.[40] Whatever the case, the first documented sources that mention the thrice-holy hymn date to the middle of the fifth century. In particular, the thrice-holy hymn was solemnly sung by the fathers of the Fourth Ecumenical Council (451) following the deposal of Pope Dioscorus.[41]

On days dedicated to the cross of Christ (the Exaltation of the Cross, the Procession of the Venerable Wood of the Cross, and the Sunday of the Cross), the thrice-holy hymn is replaced by the words, "Before thy cross, we bow down in worship, O Master, and thy holy resurrection we glorify." On the feasts of the Nativity of Christ and Theophany, on Lazarus Saturday and Great Saturday, and on Pascha and Pentecost, in the place of the thrice-holy hymn the words of the

---

[38]John of Damascus refers to the Chronicle of John Malalas compiled during the reign of Emperor Justinian I.

[39]John of Damascus, *An Exact Exposition of the Orthodox Faith* 3.10 (Chase, CUA—altered).

[40]In particular, see Uspenskii, *Byzantine Liturgy*, 60.

[41]The Orthodox tradition looks upon the thrice-holy hymn as a prayer addressed to the three persons of the Holy Trinity: "Holy God" refers to God the Father, "Holy Mighty" to the Son, and "Holy Immortal" to the Holy Spirit. But in the epoch following the Council in Chalcedon, the monophysites made an attempt to change the prayer in such a way that it sounded like an address to Jesus Christ. To this end, Patriarch of Antioch Peter the Fuller added the words "who was crucified for us" after "Holy Immortal." The Orthodox saw in this addition a hidden monophysite understanding of the human nature of Christ being fully swallowed up by the divine nature. Peter the Fuller was deposed and the "blasphemous addition" condemned by several local councils and then by Canon 81 of the Sixth Ecumenical Council. In the services of the non-Chalcedonian churches this addition is used up to the present day.

Apostle Paul, "As many as have been baptized into Christ have put on Christ" (cf. Gal 3.27) are sung. The singing of this verse during the liturgy has been preserved since the time when the great feasts, such as Pascha and Theophany, were days of mass baptisms of catechumens. Baptisms were performed in a special section of the church (a baptistery) from which the newly baptized, wearing white garments, entered into the church for participation in the liturgy in a ceremonial procession with the singing of "As many as have been baptized into Christ." The contemporary little entrance reminds us of this procession that marked the entrance into the Church for early Christians.

During the hierarchical service, the thrice-holy hymn (or "Before thy Cross" or "As many as have been baptized into Christ") is performed not four and a half times, as during the usual priest's liturgy, but seven and a half times. After the third singing of the thrice-holy, the hierarch, holding the cross in his left hand and the dikirion in the right hand, walks out onto the ambon, turns to the faithful, and pronounces the words, "O God, look down from heaven and behold and visit this vineyard which thy right hand has planted and establish it."[42] In Greek practice this exclamation is pronounced not between the third and fourth singing of the thrice-holy, but at the last thrice-holy, and it is pronounced three times: after the words "holy God," then after "holy Mighty," and following "holy Immortal." Also, the trisagion is sung in a special drawn-out and melismatic melody. The hierarch, in Greek practice, holds the trikirion and dikirion in his hands at this moment, not the dikirion and cross.

THE LITURGY OF THE WORD

In the early Christian Church, the liturgy of the catechumens was performed not in the sanctuary, but in the middle of the church. This is where the bishop's cathedra was situated and the readings from holy Scripture were performed. In contemporary practice, the reading from the Book of Epistles takes place on the ambon and the reader stands facing the East. The gospel is read by the deacon, who stands on the cathedra in the middle of the church and also reads while facing towards the East. When no deacon serves, the gospel is read by the priest.[43]

[42]Concerning the origin of this exclamation, see Robert F. Taft, "The Pontifical Liturgy of the Great Church According to a Twelfth-Century Diataxis in Codex British Museum Add. 34060," pt. 1, *Orientalia Christiana Periodica* 45 (1979): 279–307, at 284–288.

[43]In Greek practice, the priest stands at the royal doors and faces the people. In Russian practice, priests often read the gospel while standing at the altar table and facing the East, reading from the Gospel Book

The reading of the Book of Epistles is preceded by the singing of the prokeimenon—a special selected verse from a psalm. At the end of the reading, "Alleluia" is sung three times, alternating with selected verses from the psalms called the "Alleluiaria." A censing is to be performed during the "Alleluia," according to the Typikon. But in practice the censing usually takes place during the reading of the epistle, because the contemporary style of singing "Alleluia" does not allow enough time for the censing. In the ancient Church, the singing of "Alleluia" required a long time because a special, melismatic style of singing was used. (The different types of church singing are discussed in another volume). This style has been preserved in the practice of the Greek Church, but has practically been lost in the Russian Church.[44]

Before the reading of the gospel, the priest reads the prayer, "Illumine our hearts, O Master who lovest mankind, with the pure light of Thy divine knowledge. Open the eyes of our mind to the understanding of Thy Gospel teachings." This prayer, read by the priest on behalf of the entire community, indicates that it is necessary for God to open men's spiritual eyes for the understanding of the gospel's meaning. In other words, the proper understanding of the Scriptures is not possible without assistance from above.

Gospel book. Beginning of 12th c.

The reading of the gospel is preceded by the deacon's exclamation, "Wisdom, aright, let us hear the holy gospel," which indicates the ancient custom of listening to the gospel while standing. In the ancient Church it was customary to sit during the reading of the Old Testament and readings from the apostolic epistles, and also during the homily. But before the beginning of the reading of the gospel, the entire community rose as a sign of respect for the Savior, whose word is the gospel.

The celebrant's exclamation, "Peace be unto all," is said before the reading of the gospel, and is encountered many times in the liturgy and other services. At this exclamation, the people respond, through the choir, "And to thy spirit." This is one of the most ancient Christian greetings. Concerning its meaning and its frequent use in the services, Saint John Chrysostom wrote:

sitting on the altar table. The priest's reading of the gospel while facing the people is more in accordance with the meaning of the gospel, because the word is addressed to the flock, not to God.

[44]This melismatic style of singing is used elsewhere in the services in Greek churches, but the "Alleluia" is even shorter in current Greek practice than it is in Russian practice.—*Ed.*

Everywhere we ask for peace (for there is nothing equal to this); peace, in the churches, in the prayers, in the supplications, in the salutations; and once, and twice, and thrice, and many times, does he that is over the Church give it, "Peace be unto you." Wherefore? Because this is the mother of all good things; this is the foundation of joy. Therefore Christ also commanded the apostles on entering into houses straightway to say this, as being a sort of symbol of the good things; for he saith, "When ye come into houses, say, 'Peace be unto you'"; for where this is wanting, everything is useless. And to His disciples Christ said, "Peace I leave with you, My peace I give unto you" (*Jn 14.27*). This prepareth the way for love. And he that is over the Church, says not, "Peace be unto you," simply, but "Peace be unto all." . . . When he that is over the Church cometh in, he straightway says, "Peace unto all"; when he preacheth, "Peace unto all"; when he blesseth, "Peace unto all"; when he biddeth to salute, "Peace unto all"; when the sacrifice is finished, "Peace unto all": and again, in the middle, "Grace to you and peace." How then is it not monstrous, if, while hearing so many times that we are to have peace, we are in a state of feud with each other; and receiving peace, and giving it back, are at war with him that giveth it to us? Thou sayest, "And to thy spirit." And dost thou traduce him abroad? Woe is me! That the majestic usages of the Church are become forms of things merely, not a truth.[45]

A homily (or even several homilies) followed the reading of the gospel in the liturgical practice of the ancient Church. In our own day, the homily is most often transferred to the very end of the service. This is due to practical considerations—such as the fact that some of the faithful do not arrive by the beginning of the service, but only after the reading of the gospel. Sometimes the homily is given at the time of the communion verse, that is, during the clergy communion (this custom will be discussed in detail later).

The homily, whether delivered directly following the reading of the gospel or at the end of the liturgy, is an integral part of the eucharistic service. It should not be seen as an insertion into the service, nor as an addition to it. We have already discussed how the liturgy ought to be a school of theology and contemplation of God for every Christian. An instructive, didactic, and catechetical aspect of the liturgy is found not only in the reading of holy Scripture, but also in the homily, which should be heard at every liturgy, not only on Sundays and feast days, but at those services performed during the week as well. The priest who turns away from

[45]John Chrysostom, *Homilies on Colossians* 3.4 (PG 62:322–323; *NPNF*[1] 13:273–274).

delivering the homily at the liturgy turns away from the apostolic mission laid upon him at his ordination.

Traditionally, the bishop or priest performs the role of homilist in the Orthodox Church. But in certain churches the homily may be assigned to a subdeacon, reader, or layman. The tradition of the Church forbids a layman from performing a sacramental function assumed by the priest (with the exception of the right to perform the mystery of baptism in extreme circumstances, when a priest is not available and the one who desires baptism is in danger of death). But tradition does not forbid a layman to perform certain instructive functions, such as catechesis and educational activities. Catechists in the ancient Church were often members of the church community who did not possess the priestly rank. And in our own time a layman may give homilies not only in youth groups or church schools but also during divine services. Naturally, the instructive role of the bishop or priest should in no way be diminished. The homily of a layman is possible as an addition to the homily of the bishop or priest, not as a replacement for it.

The litany of fervent supplication follows the homily, if it comes after the reading of the gospel, or right after the gospel reading when the homily is transferred to the end of the service. In ancient liturgies, the service of the three antiphons was not yet connected to the liturgy, and the great litany was heard directly following the reading of the gospel. When the service of the three antiphons was added to the liturgy, the great litany was transferred to the beginning of the service, and the litany of fervent supplication took its place after the gospel reading. The litany of fervent supplication originated in the Constantinopolitan liturgical processions (which is the source of the threefold "Lord, have mercy"). Petitions may be inserted into the litany of fervent supplication that address specific situations in the life of the members of the community: sickness, deliverance from natural disasters, rainfall in times of drought, and other needs. In contemporary parish practice, commemoration slips, which are given by members of the community and contain the names of those for whom a fervent prayer is needed, are read at the litany of fervent supplication.[46]

A litany for the departed, to commemorate those who have fallen asleep in the Lord, may follow the litany of fervent supplication. The litany for the departed

---

[46]In certain municipal parishes of the Russian Orthodox Church, the reading of commemoration slips with names of the living and departed lasts for fifteen to twenty minutes, even up to half an hour. This unwarranted practice creates an artificial "pause" in the divine service, filled with the singing of "Lord, have mercy" over and over. Common sense dictates that the number of names pronounced aloud should not be more than a few dozen.

was not a part of the ancient liturgy, insofar as the liturgy was perceived as a festal service. The litany for the departed is not printed in the order of the liturgy of Saint Basil the Great since this liturgy is performed only on special feast days. According to the Church Typikon, the litany for the departed should not be inserted into the liturgy of Saint John Chrysostom when performed on feast days or Sundays; it may only be pronounced at special liturgies celebrated in commemoration of the departed. This litany does not exist in Greek liturgical practice. In the Russian Church, on the contrary, in those parishes where the liturgy is not performed daily, the litany for the departed is added to the liturgy even on Sundays. This is to give the faithful an opportunity, during the liturgy, to commemorate their loved ones who have passed to the other world.

The liturgy of the catechumens concludes with the litany for the catechumens, which begins with the words, "Pray to the Lord, ye catechumens." In our day this call is not addressed to anyone. Nor are the concluding words of the litany, "Catechumens, depart," addressed to anyone in particular, because, as we have already noted, the catechumenate is practically absent in the contemporary Church. Several people see the litany for the catechumens as an atavism, and in the contemporary Greek service books this litany is either not printed at all, or it is printed in small print.[47] But it is also possible to perceive the presence of the litany for the catechumens in a different way: namely, as a call for the rebirth of the catechumenate. It may be a question not so much of the artificial restoration of an institution that long ago went into disuse, as of a greater acknowledgment by the Orthodox Church of its mission in relation to the unchurched world.

One of the problems that contemporary Orthodoxy faces is the almost complete absence of bridges that would join the Church to the outside world. A great number of barriers stand between the Church and the person "on the outside." These include language, culture, and psychology. When an unchurched person, either knowingly or by chance, enters into an Orthodox church, he finds himself in a cultural environment that is foreign to him, in which sacred actions unknown to him are performed and a speech unfamiliar to him is heard. In the ancient Church, the liturgy of the catechumens was a form of catechesis for future Christians; it served as a bridge between the Church and people who had not yet become her members. The contemporary liturgy has almost completely lost this character

---

[47] In contemporary Greek parish practice, the gospel reading may be followed by the exclamation, "That always being guarded under thy dominion," and the Cherubic Hymn, or the fervent supplication concluding with the exclamation, "That always being guarded under thy dominion." In this way, the litany for the catechumens and two subsequent litanies of the faithful are omitted.

and has become a divine service understood only by the faithful who are familiar with the liturgical language and the rites rooted in the cultural tradition of the Church.

It is no coincidence, then, that in our own day, the transition from the liturgy of the catechumens to the liturgy of the faithful is extremely nominal. But the text of the liturgy, as well as the liturgical Typikon, which have not been changed, suggest that contemporary practice is incompatible with the original order that once existed, and should exist, in the Church. Correcting this situation should not be done by removing those parts of the liturgy that appear to be obsolete, but rather by turning the life of the Church back to its traditional course. Orthodox worship is precious in that it provides the clear standard of Orthodoxy as a mode of thinking and a way of life. And it is necessary to reconcile *our life in the Church* with the liturgical Typikon—not to correct the divine services in accordance with newly emerging realities of church life.

During the litany for the catechumens, the priest reads a prayer that is different in the liturgies of Saint Basil the Great and Saint John Chrysostom.[48] In the first case, the prayer reads as follows:

O Lord our God, who dwellest in the heavens, and lookest down upon all thy works, look down upon thy servants, the catechumens, who have bowed their necks before thee, and grant them the light yoke. Make them honorable members of thy holy Church, and vouchsafe unto them the laver of regeneration, the forgiveness of sins, and the robe of incorruption, unto the knowledge of thee, our true God.

A different prayer is read in Saint John's liturgy. Its theme is similar to the prayer from the liturgy of Saint Basil:

O Lord our God, who dwellest on high and regardest the humble of heart; who hast sent forth as the salvation of the race of men Thine Only-begotten Son and God, our Lord Jesus Christ: look down upon Thy servants, the catechumens, who have bowed their necks before Thee; make them worthy in due time of the laver of regeneration, the remission of sins, and the robe of incorruption. Unite them to Thy Holy, Catholic, and Apostolic Church, and number them with Thy chosen flock

---

[48]This is the first difference between the two liturgies. Before the litany for the catechumens, the two liturgies are identical.—*Ed.*

The Beginning of the Liturgy of the Faithful: The Great Entrance

The liturgy of the faithful begins with the exclamation, "As many as are of the faithful, again and again, in peace let us pray to the Lord." The first two prayers of the faithful (read by the priest while two litanies are said) are different in the liturgies of Saints Basil the Great and John Chrysostom:

> Thou, O Lord, hast revealed to us this great mystery of salvation. Thou hast enabled us, Thy humble servants, to be ministers at Thy holy altar. By the power of Thy Holy Spirit, enable us also to perform this service; so that standing blamelessly before Thy holy glory, we may offer Thee a sacrifice of praise. For Thou alone accomplishest all things in all men. May our sacrifice be acceptable and well-pleasing in Thy sight, O Lord, for our sins and for the errors of all Thy people.[49]

> O God, who in mercy and compassion hast visited our lowliness; who hast set us, Thy humble and sinful and unworthy servants, to serve at Thy holy altar before Thy holy glory: by the power of Thy Holy Spirit, strengthen us for this service, and grant speech to our lips so that we may call down the grace of Thy Holy Spirit upon the Gifts that are about to be offered.[50]

> . . . Receive our supplications, O God; make us worthy to offer unto Thee prayers and supplications and bloodless sacrifices for all Thy people; and enable us . . . to call upon Thee at all times and in every place. . . .[51]

> . . . [G]rant us to stand blameless and without condemnation before Thy holy altar. Grant also to those who pray with us, O God, growth in life and faith and spiritual understanding. Grant them to worship Thee blamelessly with fear and love, and to partake without condemnation of Thy holy Mysteries, and to be accounted worthy of Thy heavenly kingdom.[52]

In all four cases the prayer is recited by the serving clergy on behalf of himself and the church community. God has placed not only the priest but also the entire church community in service to himself; all the worshippers present in the church are servers of the holy oblation; all of them will invoke the grace of the Holy Spirit

---

[49]Liturgy of Saint Basil the Great, First Prayer of the Faithful.—*Ed.*

[50]Liturgy of Saint Basil the Great, Second Prayer of the Faithful.—*Ed.*

[51]Liturgy of Saint John Chrysostom, First Prayer of the Faithful.—*Ed.*

[52]Liturgy of Saint John Chrysostom, Second Prayer of the Faithful.—*Ed.*

on the bread and wine. There is no clear line of demarcation between the clergy and the laity: both are God's servers. (The expression "servers of the holy oblation" refers to the serving clergy but it is also spoken of the laity as "serving" God.)

We have already discussed that in the Christian Church the "royal priesthood" is understood to extend to the entire people of God and not only to the clergy.[53] In the Typikon, the laity does not exist: there are priests, vested in the priestly order, placed in the service of presiding at the services, and priests who are not vested in this order. The Eucharist is the joint action of both. The "royal priesthood" of all the faithful is most fully expressed and realized in the Eucharist: the faithful are called to be servers of the New Covenant, servants of the holy mysteries, "partakers of the divine nature" (2 Pet 1.4).

At the same time, the hierarchical priesthood serves very specific functions in the Church, and the service of presiding at the services is a special calling. The clergyman is a person delegated by the community for service, but he receives holy orders by ordination because of the action of the Holy Spirit. Therefore every clergyman has, besides his participation in the "royal priesthood" of all Christians, his own service, and he is closer to the divine throne (altar) than regular members of the community. This closeness is not only a privilege. It also lays upon the clergyman an individual, personal responsibility before God for himself and for his flock.

The responsibility of the priest is to pray for his parishioners. For this reason in the prayers of the faithful the first person plural "we" may signify not only the entire church community but also the clergy, the assembly of those serving in holy orders. "For our sins" refers to the clergy, but "for the errors of the people" refers to the laity. Speaking of "them that pray with us," the priest understands "us" to be his concelebrants among the clergy and "them that pray" to be the laity who offer prayers simultaneously with the clergy.

In the order of the liturgy a place is found not only for prayers offered by the celebrant on behalf of the community or on behalf of the clergy, but also for a prayer that the celebrant offers for himself personally in the first person singular. The text of the prayer "No one who is bound" appeared no later than the eighth century[54] and is the same in the liturgies of Saint Basil the Great and Saint John Chrysostom. It begins with a confession of the conviction that no carnal man is worthy to draw nigh to God and to serve him because such a service is fearful even for the heavenly hosts. The true hierarch, as it is said later in the prayer, is Christ

---

[53]See vol. 2, pp. 437–438.

[54]It is encountered in the Vatican Codex Barberini Gr. 336, which is found in the Byzantine library and dates to the end of the eighth century.

himself: it is he who gave us the sacred rite of the bloodless sacrifice. The celebrant addresses him with the words:

> Look down on me, a sinner, Thine unprofitable servant, and cleanse my soul and my heart from an evil conscience; and by the power of the Holy Spirit enable me, who am endowed with the grace of the priesthood, to stand before this, Thy holy table, and perform the sacred mystery of Thy holy and pure Body and precious Blood. For I draw near to Thee, and bowing my neck I implore Thee: do not turn Thy face away from me, nor cast me out from among Thy children; but make me, Thy sinful and unworthy servant, worthy to offer gifts to Thee. For Thou art the Offerer and the Offered, the Receiver and the Received, O Christ our God, and to Thee do we send up glory. . . .[55]

A unique feature of this prayer is that it is not only said on behalf of the priest, but also that it is addressed to Jesus Christ, while the majority of other prayers in the liturgy are addressed to God the Father.[56] It is as though the dialogue between the church community and God the Father is interrupted for a few minutes and the celebrant enters into a personal dialogue with Christ, the true celebrant of the liturgy. The personal connection between the priest and Christ, it turns out, is also an intrinsic part of the eucharistic thanksgiving:

> In confessing the priesthood, in the grace of which he is "clothed," to be the priesthood of Christ . . . not only does the priest not separate himself from the gathering, but, on the contrary, he manifests his unity with it as the unity of the head with the body. That is precisely why his *personal* prayer *for himself* is not only appropriate but also necessary and, so to speak, self-evident. . . . The uniqueness of the ministry of the priest consists in that he is called and appointed in the Church, the body of Christ, to be the image of the Head of the body—Christ—and this means to be the one through whom the *personal* ministry of Christ is continued and realized. . . . For Christ's priesthood consists in his personal self-sacrifice to God and to mankind. . . . And this means that the calling to the priesthood itself is directed to the person of the one called and is inseparable from it, and that any difference between "priesthood" and "personality," by which priesthood would prove to be something self-contained

---

[55]Liturgy of Saint Basil the Great and Liturgy of Saint John Chrysostom. Prayer of the Cherubic Hymn.

[56]Only the prayers read at the end of the liturgy, before and after communion, "Attend, O Lord Jesus Christ, our God," and "Thou who thyself art the fulfillment of the law and the prophets," (or "Completed and perfected" in the Liturgy of Saint Basil the Great) are addressed to Jesus Christ.

and having no relation to the personality of the bearer, is false, for it distorts the essence of priesthood as the continuation in the Church of the priesthood of Christ.[57]

The reading of the prayer "No one who is bound" takes place against the backdrop of the choir singing the Cherubic Hymn. After reading the prayer, the priest raises his hands three times and says the Cherubic Hymn, after which he goes to the table of oblation with the deacon. When the liturgy is celebrated by a hierarch, after reading the prayer he exits to the ambon for the washing of hands. Beginning in the tenth century, Byzantine liturgical manuscripts contain the rubric for the washing of hands at the time of the Cherubic Hymn,

The Cherubic Hymn

and in non-liturgical sources the washing of hands before the celebration of the Eucharist is already mentioned in the fourth and fifth centuries.[58] The meaning of this rite is that the hierarch must approach the celebration of the bloodless sacrifice with clean hands.[59] After the washing of hands, the bishop heads to the table of oblation, where he commemorates the living and deceased and covers the holy gifts with covers.[60]

The text of the Cherubic Hymn performed by the choir and read by the priest is as follows:

---

[57] Schmemann, *Eucharist*, 116–117.

[58] Taft, *Great Entrance*, 163–164.

[59] In ancient manuscripts of the *Chinovnik* (Gr. *Archieratikon*, or "Bishop's Service Book"), the washing of hands at the time of the Cherubic Hymn is also prescribed for liturgies served by a priest, but over the course of time this rite was transferred to the beginning of the proskomedia. In the contemporary practice of the Russian Church, the washing of hands is performed three times during the hierarchical service of the liturgy: directly after the vesting, before the singing of "Our Father," and after communion. Washing his hands during the Cherubic Hymn, the bishop reads the prayer for the sanctification of water. In this case, however, it seems to be deprived of its meaning, insofar as the water used is usually poured out afterward. (In the Greek practice, the bishop washes his hands and sprinkles the faithful with the water.) The prayer for the sanctification of water is itself of extremely ancient origin (not later than the 8th century), but it derived from the order of sanctifying a church, in which its presence is justified, since the newly built church is blessed with this water. In the Slavonic *Chinovnik* the prayer appeared extremely late (probably not earlier than the 17th century). See Taft, *Great Entrance*, 172–173.

[60] The "Hierarchical Proskomedia" at the time of the Cherubic Hymn in its current form is a rather late liturgical custom: for the Greeks it appeared in the 16th century, while for the Russians it appeared during the rule of Patriarch Nikon.

Let us who mystically represent the Cherubim, and who sing the thrice-holy hymn to the life-creating Trinity, now lay aside all earthly cares, that we may receive the King of all, who comes invisibly upborne by the angelic hosts.[61]

In this case, the words "thrice-holy hymn" do not signify the prayer "Holy God," but rather, the angelic doxology from the Book of Isaiah, "Holy, holy, holy, Lord of Saboath, heaven and earth are full of thy glory" (cf. Is 6.3).

The history of the Cherubic Hymn is inseparable from the history of the great entrance, of which it is a constituent part. In Russian practice, the great entrance takes place during the singing of the Cherubic Hymn at the words, "Let us now lay aside all earthly cares," while in Greek practice it takes place at the words, "that we may receive the King of all." But the text of the hymn consists of a single phrase and its meaning does not lend itself to being divided at either place.

According to the Byzantine historian George Kedrenos, the Cherubic Hymn was introduced into the liturgy in the ninth year of the reign of Emperor Justin II (565–577); that is, in the year 573 or 574. At that time, "Of thy mystical supper" was introduced into the liturgy of Saint Basil the Great.[62] The contemporary Typikon prescribes the use of the Cherubic Hymn at all full liturgies throughout the year, with the exception of Great Thursday when "Of thy mystical supper" is sung, and on Great Saturday when "Let all mortal flesh keep silent" is sung. Another hymn is sung at the great entrance of the liturgy of the presanctified gifts: "Now the powers of heaven."

Of the four cited hymns, only "Of thy mystical supper" is dedicated to the theme of communion, while the other three hymns are thematically connected to bearing the holy gifts from the table of oblation to the altar table. The leitmotif of these three hymns is the participation of the angels in the sacred ministry of the great entrance. The idea of the angels' participation is expressed with particular power in the hymn sung on Great Saturday:

[61]The literal translation of the Slavonic word "*dorinosima*" (Gr. *doryphoroumenon*) presents difficulties. In Russian literature the widely accepted interpretation of the word connects it to the Roman custom of carrying a victor on folded spears. In this case it signifies "the one guarded by the angelic hosts as if by those bearing spears." In Byzantium, the spear-bearing "*doryphoroi*" was the name given to personal body-guards of the emperor: the emperor went out to the people, surrounded by the *doryphoroi* who bore spears, and in case of danger would point them at the crowd. The verb *doryphoreō* did not mean to "carry someone on spears" but precisely "to be a spear-bearer"—a bodyguard, i.e., simply "to stand guard." Using this interpretation, the meaning of the original phrase "that we may receive the King of all who cometh invisibly upborne by the angelic hosts" leads to the approximate meaning, "that we may receive [in Communion] the King of all, no matter the fact that the spear-bearing angels do not permit us to approach him."

[62]George Kedrenos, *Synopsis: Historiarum compendium* (PG 121:748b).

Let all mortal flesh keep silent, and in fear and trembling stand, pondering nothing earthly-minded. For the King of kings and the Lord of lords comes to be slain, to give Himself as food to the faithful. Before Him go the ranks of angels: all the principalities and powers; the many-eyed cherubim and the six-winged seraphim covering their faces, singing the hymn: Alleluia. Alleluia. Alleluia.

This hymn, whose date of origin is unknown (in manuscripts it appears no earlier than the tenth century),[63] consists of a commentary on the final phrase of the Cherubic Hymn, "invisibly borne by the angelic hosts." The symbolism of the great entrance as a procession in which Christ participates, accompanied by angels, is emphasized in both hymns. It is not clear from the text of the Cherubic Hymn that it speaks of the Savior's sacrifice on the cross, but the text of Great Saturday's hymn clearly indicates that Christ "comes to be slain to give himself as food to the faithful." In this way the eucharistic sacrifice is seen as a remembrance of the Savior's sacrifice on the cross, and the great

The Great Entrance. Fresco. Sretensky Monastery. Moscow. Beginning of 18th c.

entrance symbolizes Christ's procession to his suffering. This symbolism should not be seen literally: the great entrance is not a "dramatization" of the Lord's entrance into Jerusalem or of Christ's procession to Golgotha. It is not a remembrance of a specific event from the life of Christ, but rather of the meaning of his coming into the world—that he became man and offered himself as a sacrifice in order to be the "bread of life" (Jn 6.35, 48) for all those who believe in him.

Historically, the great entrance was a procession during which the serving clergy brought the holy gifts to the altar table. A whole number of ancient liturgical monuments indicate that the bread and wine, prepared by the faithful, were brought into the church and placed in the hands of the deacons. Before the beginning of the eucharistic prayer, the deacons solemnly carried the holy gifts to the altar table, where they were received by the bishop. A priest could participate in the great entrance. The participation of the laity in the great entrance remains a topic of discussion among scholars of liturgics.[64] Sources do not give a clear answer to this question.

[63]See Taft, *Great Entrance*, 76–77.
[64]For details, see Taft, *Great Entrance*, 12–16.

Nor is there full clarity concerning the question of whether the emperor participated in the great entrance, and whether he participated in the service. It is mentioned many times in historical chronicles and liturgical documents that the emperor entered into the sanctuary together with the patriarch.[65] There are also indications that the emperor did not come to the liturgy empty-handed, but bearing gifts for the church. Two examples may be cited. The first is contained in the funeral oration on Saint Basil the Great written by Saint Gregory the Theologian. In this essay, the confrontation between Saint Basil and Emperor Valens is described. The latter was a supporter of Arianism and attempted to compel Saint Basil to accept the heretical teaching; Saint Basil steadfastly refused. On the feast of Theophany, Valens was in Caesarea of Cappadocia and decided to participate in the festal service. The emperor did not arrive by the beginning of the service. When he entered, the church was overflowing and Saint Basil and the other bishops serving with him were standing before the altar table:

> Upon his entrance he was struck by the thundering roll of the psalms, by the sea of heads of the congregation, and by the angelic rather than human order which pervaded the sanctuary and its precincts: while Basil presided over his people, standing erect, as the Scripture says of Samuel (1 Sam 19.20) with body and eyes and mind undisturbed, as if nothing new had happened, but fixed upon God and the sanctuary, as if, so to say, he had been a statue, while his ministers stood around him in fear and reverence. At this sight, and it was indeed a sight unparalleled, overcome by human weakness, his eyes were affected with dimness and giddiness, his mind with dread. This was as yet unnoticed by most people. But when he had to offer the gifts at the table of God, which he must needs do himself, since no one would, as usual, assist him,[66] because it was uncertain whether Basil would admit him, his feelings were revealed. For he was staggering, and had not someone in the sanctuary reached out a hand to steady his tottering steps, he would have sunk to the ground in a lamentable fall.[67]

The second example, similar to the first, is described in *Ecclesiastical History* of Theodoret of Cyrus. This tells of how, during the liturgy, Saint Ambrose did

---

[65]Canon 69 of the Council in Trullo forbids laymen, with the exception of the emperor, from entering into the sanctuary. The exception made for the emperor is stipulated by his special position in the Byzantine state and Byzantine Church due to his role as "greatest pontiff" (*pontifex maximus*).

[66]None of the deacons dared to approach the heretic to receive gifts from his hands.

[67]Gregory the Theologian, *Orations* 43.52.5–22 (SC 384:234–236; *NPNF*[2] 7:412).

not receive the gifts from Emperor Theodosius, whom the saint had banned from communion because he had cruelly put down an uprising in Thessalonica. Eight months after this incident, on the feast of the Nativity of Christ, the emperor, profoundly repenting for his action, had courage to come to the church where Saint Ambrose was serving, in order to participate in the service and receive communion of the holy mysteries of Christ:

> When the time came for him to bring his oblations to the holy table, weeping all the while he stood up and approached the sanctuary. After making his offering, as he was wont, he remained within at the rail, but once more the great Ambrose . . . asked him if he wanted anything; and when the emperor said that he was waiting for participation in the divine mysteries, Ambrose sent word to him by the chief deacon and said, "The inner place, sir, is open only to priests; to all the rest it is inaccessible; go out and stand where others stand; purple can make emperors, but not priests." This instruction too the faithful emperor most gladly received, and intimated in reply that it was not from any audacity that he had remained within the rails, but because he had understood that this was the custom at Constantinople. "I owe thanks," he added, "for being cured too of this error."[68]

In both cases the emperor brought gifts to the sanctuary while the bishop received them. But it is unclear whether the gifts were the eucharistic gifts of bread and wine or something else, such as the gifts that the emperor would customarily give when visiting churches (expensive vessels, money). Also, it is not clear from either the first or second account whether the emperor's offering took place during the great entrance. A certain clarity is given by a later source, the Byzantine *Book of Ceremonies* of Constantine VII Porphyrogenitus (tenth century), which indicates that the emperor's gifts are not the bread and wine, but rather expensive vessels, and that these gifts were made when the emperor entered into the church, not at the time of the great entrance. But this same source describes in detail the participation of the emperor in the great entrance, before which he is vested in a purple mantle, takes hold of a lamp, and walks in the front of the procession of the holy gifts right up to the entrance into the sanctuary, where the patriarch awaited him.[69]

In the church of Hagia Sophia, the building where the holy gifts were prepared for the Eucharist—called the *skeuophylakion* ("vessel depository")—was

---

[68]Theodoret of Cyrus, *Ecclesiastical History* 5.18 (*NPNF*² 3:144).
[69]Taft, *Great Entrance*, 29–30, 195–196.

located separately from the main building; therefore the procession with the holy gifts began outside of the church. In several other Byzantine churches the *skeuophylakion* was an addition to the main building, or a separate wing of the building. Either way, the holy gifts were prepared in one place and carried to another: in this lay the functional meaning of the great entrance. Saint Nicholas Cabasilas wrote:

> The entrance with the gospel takes place out of necessity since it is kept in the vessel depository and it is required to carry it from there into the church to read it. . . . In a similar way, the entrance with the precious gifts takes place out of necessity since they are usually kept in the vessel depository and are carried in with honor, hymns, censing, and candles, as is proper for gifts (offered) to God.[70]

In contemporary Orthodox churches the table of oblation on which the pros-komedia is performed is usually located in the sanctuary on the left side from the altar table; therefore the holy gifts are carried out of the sanctuary (through the north door) and back into the sanctuary (through the royal doors). In this way, the path of the great entrance is identical to the path of the little entrance.[71]

The Great Entrance

In this case, as in the case of the little entrance, the hierarchical liturgy has preserved the functional meaning of the procession to a greater degree than the priest's liturgy. It is indicated in the contemporary hierarchical *Chinovnik* that the bishop does not participate in the procession of the great entrance: he waits for the procession in the royal doors where he receives the diskos from the senior deacon and the chalice from the senior priest. Moreover, the bishop commemorates the patriarch (at the primatial service, all the heads of the local Orthodox Churches are commemorated), clergymen, and all the worshippers in attendance at the church. Receiving the holy gifts from the lower-ranking clergymen, the bishop then places them on the altar table. This symbolizes the dual role of the bishop, which corresponds to the role of Christ as the offered sacrifice and the one who offers it ("for Thou art

---

[70]Nicholas Cabasilas, *A Commentary on the Divine Liturgy* 3–4 (SC 4-bis:370).

[71]We may note that in the Greek Church the procession of the holy gifts exits the sanctuary and moves along the north wall of the church to the exit and then moves down the center of the church and back into the sanctuary. In Russian practice, the procession is limited to the movement along the solea from the north door to the royal doors.

the Offerer and the Offered"). The bishop receives the eucharistic gifts offered by the people from the hands of the lower-ranking clergy and offers them to God on behalf of the clergy and people.

PREPARATION FOR THE EUCHARISTIC OFFERING

After placing the chalice and diskos on the altar table, the hierarch or priest covers them with an aer—a rectangular cloth with the sign of the cross in the center. As he does so, he recites the troparion of Holy Saturday concerning the burial of Christ in the tomb: "The noble Joseph, taking down thy most pure body from the tree, wrapped it in pure linen, anointed it with spices, and laid it in a new tomb." Then, a prayer follows in the liturgy of Saint John Chrysotom that is extremely similar to the first prayer of the faithful, partially cited earlier. But in the liturgy of Saint Basil the Great, the prayer that follows is much richer in theological content:

> O Lord, our God, who hast created us and brought us into this life; who hast shown us the ways to salvation, and bestowed on us the revelation of heavenly mysteries: Thou art the One who has appointed us to this service in the power of Thy Holy Spirit. Therefore, O Lord, enable us to be ministers of Thy New Testament and servants of Thy holy mysteries. . . . Look down on us, O God, and behold this our service. Receive it as thou didst receive the gifts of Abel, the sacrifices of Noah, the whole burnt offerings of Abraham, the priestly offices of Moses and Aaron, and the peace-offerings of Samuel. Even as Thou didst receive from Thy holy apostles this true worship, so now, in Thy goodness, accept these Gifts from the hands of us sinners, O Lord; that having been accounted worthy to serve without offense at Thy holy altar, we may receive the reward of wise and faithful stewards on the awesome day of Thy just retribution.[72]

Service of Moses and Aaron in the Tabernacle. Fresco. Gračanica Monastery. 14th c.

This prayer reveals the meaning of the liturgy as the mystery of the new covenant that unites the whole history of humanity from the creation of the world with the eschatological expectation of the Last Judgment. The prayer establishes the succession from the Old Testament's cult of offering altar sacrifices to the Eucharist

---

[72]Liturgy of Saint Basil the Great. Prayer of the Prothesis, after placing the gifts on the holy table.

of the New Testament, of which these sacrifices were a type. Five subjects are mentioned in the prayer: Abel's offering of sacrifice to God (see Gen 4.4), Noah's offering after the end of the flood (see Gen 8.20–22), Abraham's offering of his son Isaac as a sacrifice (see Gen 22.1–14),[73] and the "peace offerings" made by Samuel (see 1 Sam 11.14–15). In Christian tradition all of these subjects were perceived as types of the Eucharist. These and other eucharistic subjects were reflected in early Christian frescoes, mosaics, and iconographic depictions placed in the sanctuary. For example, in Byzantine mosaics and frescoes, the following appear as types of the Eucharist: Abel offering a sacrifice to God; Abraham receiving the three travelers; Abraham offering Isaac as a sacrifice; Melchizedek bringing forth bread and wine to Abraham;[74] and Moses and Aaron in the tabernacle. Moses and Aaron were depicted on the side doors of Russian iconostases.

For an understanding of the meaning of this prayer and the biblical allusions it contains, it is necessary to recall the Apostle Paul's teaching concerning the priesthood and sacrifices contained in chapters five through ten of his Epistle to the Hebrews. Saint Paul begins by recalling that not a single Old Testament high priest received the priesthood by their own doing, but rather, they were all placed in that service, and in a similar way, Christ became high priest according to the order of Melchizedek and not of his own doing, but because he was placed in that service by the Father (see Heb 5.1–10). Melchizedek, king of Salem, "without father, without mother, without genealogy, having neither beginning of days nor end of life, but made like the Son of God, remains a priest continually" (Heb 7.1–3). He prefigures the true high priest "who has passed through the heavens" (Heb 4.14), dwelling eternally and possessing the unchangeable priesthood (see Heb 7.24). The Old Testament tabernacle consisted of two sections: in the first section the priests always entered for the celebration of the divine service; the high priest entered into the second section only once a year with sacrificed blood that he brought on behalf of himself and for the sins of the people's ignorance (see Heb 9.1–7). Christ "came as high priest of the good things to come, with the greater and more perfect tabernacle not made with hands . . . not with the blood of goats and calves, but with his own blood he entered the most holy place once for all, having obtained

---

[73]The term *holokarpōma* ("all-flesh") is found in the Septuagint (Wis 3.6), from which it entered into numerous Byzantine liturgical texts. The analogous term *holokarpōsis* (see Gen 22.3–14) was used many times in the narrative in Genesis regarding Abraham's offering of sacrifice. In Russian [and English] it is translated as "burnt offering," as is the term *holokautōma* (see Ps 50.18). The use of the term *holokarpōmata* in the eucharistic prayer indicates that it is precisely this sacrifice of Abraham to which the author refers.

[74]These subjects are especially found in the sanctuary mosaics of the Basilica of San Vitale in Ravenna (6th c.).

eternal redemption" (Heb 9.11–12). "For it is not possible that the blood of bulls and goats could take away sins" (Heb 10.4); the Old Testament sacrifices cannot take away sins (Heb 10.11). Christ, "after he had offered one sacrifice for sins forever, sat down at the right hand of God . . . for by one offering he has perfected forever those who are being sanctified" (Heb 10.12, 14).

This elaborate typology is reflected in the text of the divine liturgy. The Eucharist is the single sacrifice that is necessary for salvation, which supersedes all the Old Testament sacrifices and burnt offerings. In celebrating the Eucharist, the church community is "a spiritual home, a holy priesthood, to offer up spiritual sacrifices acceptable to God through Jesus Christ" (1 Pet 2.5). At the same time, in celebrating the Eucharist, the church community continues the work of the apostles ("even as Thou didst receive from Thy holy apostles this true worship"). Hence a direct line of succession is established between the Old Testament worship, the service of the apostolic community, and the Eucharist that is celebrated today.

While the priest reads the prayer, the deacon simultaneously says the litany of supplication. Its content differs from other litanies in that it includes petitions for the personal life of every Christian. In the litany of supplication, worshippers turn to God asking for "an angel of peace, a faithful guide" and "guardian of soul and body." This is the angel of whom Saint John Chrysostom wrote, "Every believer hath an angel; since even from the beginning, every one of those that were approved had his angel, as Jacob says, 'the angel that feedeth me, and delivereth me from my youth'" (see Gen 48.16).[75] In the litany's subsequent petitions, each worshipper turns to God, asking him to grant him to live out the remaining time of his life "in peace and repentance" and to grant him a "painless, blameless, and peaceful" "Christian ending to life" and for a "good defense" at the Last Judgment of Christ.

THE KISS OF PEACE AND THE SYMBOL OF FAITH

Following the end of the litany and the prayer read during it, the deacon exclaims, "Let us love one another, that with one mind we may confess—" and the choir finishes the phrase with the words "Father, Son, and Holy Spirit, the Trinity one in essence and undivided." In the liturgy of the early Church, the deacon's exclamation served as a signal for the kiss of peace, a rite in which the entire community participated. In contemporary practice the kiss of peace is only performed by the clergy in the sanctuary. After kissing the altar table and the holy gifts placed on it,

---

[75]John Chrysostom, *Homilies on Colossians* 3.4 (PG 62:323; *NPNF*[1] 13:273).

"Let all Mortal Flesh Keep Silent." Icon. 1580s–1590s.

the senior priest (or hierarch) stands to the right side of the altar table, and junior clergy approach him for the kiss of peace. The senior cleric greets the junior cleric with the words, "Christ is in our midst." The junior replies, "He is and shall be." Deacons perform the kiss of peace at the high place.

The kiss of peace is one of the liturgy's most ancient rites. In the early Christian community a kiss was the customary means of greeting one another (cf. 1 Pet 5.14; Rom 16.16; 1 Cor 16.20; 2 Cor 13.12; 1 Thess 5.26). It is possible that the eucharistic assembly began with the kiss of peace already in apostolic times. Origen mentions the custom of Christians giving one another a kiss at the end of prayers.[76] The author of *The Apostolic Tradition* says that following prayer, the catechumens were dismissed, and the faithful greeted one another with a kiss—men kissed men and women kissed women.[77] Canon 19 of the Council of Laodicea (*c.* 363) mentions the kiss of peace as a custom that preceded the eucharistic anaphora. Saint John Chrysostom also wrote about the kiss of peace during the eucharistic service; in his time it was accompanied by the bishop's greeting, "Peace be unto all."[78] Interpreting the meaning of this custom, Saint John emphasized:

> "Salute one another with a holy kiss" (2 Cor 13.12). What is "holy?" not hollow, not treacherous, like the kiss which Judas gave to Christ. For therefore is the kiss given, that it may be fuel unto love, that it may kindle the disposition, that we may so love each other, as brothers brothers, as children parents, as parents children; yea, rather even far more. For those things are a disposition implanted by nature, but these by spiritual grace. . . . But about this holy kiss somewhat else may yet be said. To what effect? We are the temple of Christ; we kiss then the porch and entrance of the temple when we kiss each other. See ye not how

[76] Origen, *Commentary on Romans* 10.33 (PG 14:1282c–1283a).

[77] Hippolytus of Rome, *Apostolic Tradition* 18 (Stewart, PPS). [The catechumens did not kiss the faithful (baptized Orthodox Christians), because "their kiss is not yet holy." *Apostolic Tradition* 18.3 (Stewart, PPS). The kiss of peace was seen as an almost sacramental act: "Think not that this kiss ranks with those given in public by common friends. It is not such: this kiss blends souls one with another, and solicits for them entire forgiveness. Therefore this kiss is a sign that our souls are mingled together, and have banished all remembrance of wrong." Cyril of Jerusalem, *Mystagogical Catecheses* 5.3 (Church, PPS)—*Ed.*]

[78] John Chrysostom, *Homilies on Colossians* 3.4 (PG 62:323; *NPNF*[1] 13:273).

many kiss even the porch of this temple, some stooping down, others grasping it with their hand, and putting their hand to their mouth. And through these gates and doors[79] Christ both had entered into us, and doth enter, whensoever we communicate. Ye who partake of the mysteries understand what I say. For it is in no common manner that our lips are honored, when they receive the Lord's body. It is for this reason chiefly that we here kiss.[80]

And so, the kiss of peace is a custom directly linked to the Eucharist. But after the tenth century it gradually began to disappear from use. Saint Nicholas Cabasilas, in the fourteenth century, explaining the order of the celebration of the liturgy, mentions the exclamation, "Let us love one another," but does not mention the kiss of peace following it,[81] because in his time it had gone out of use among the laity. As has been said, the custom was preserved only among the clergy.

The kiss of peace is followed by the deacon's exclamation, "The doors, the doors, in wisdom let us attend." This exclamation was preserved from the time when the custom existed of closing the outside doors of the temple before the celebration of the Eucharist. The doors were closed so that, during the Eucharist, the uninitiated, outsiders, or catechumens would not be present, since only the faithful who were to commune of the holy mysteries of Christ could remain in the temple. Various forms of this exclamation existed; for example, "The doors, the doors, let us attend" (this is the form especially seen in the work of Saint Niketas Stethatos in the eleventh century).[82]

Over time the exclamation "The doors, the doors" was reinterpreted as referring to the royal doors (the central doors of the iconostasis) and the curtain located behind the doors. The royal doors came to be closed right after the great entrance and remained closed during the entire service of the Eucharist, while at the exclamation, "The doors, the doors," the altar curtain was drawn open.

However, the practice of the local Orthodox churches substantially varies on this matter. In many parish churches of the Greek Church there are no royal doors whatsoever, and the curtain is drawn open before the beginning of the liturgy and remains opened until the end of the service. In the Russian Church, the royal doors remain open during the entire liturgy at the hierarchical service, and

[79]That is to say, our mouths. Chrysostom draws a parallel between the custom of kissing a door when entering the temple and the Christian custom of kissing one another on the mouth. We may note that in Orthodox tradition it is customary to kiss the doors upon entering into the altar.

[80]John Chrysostom, *Homilies on 2 Corinthians* 30.2 (PG 61:606–607; *NPNF*[1] 12:418).

[81]Nicholas Cabasilas, *Commentary* 25.2 (SC 4-bis:166–168).

[82]Niketas Stethatos, *Letters* 8.5 (SC 81:286).

also at the priest's service during Bright Week (in this case the royal doors are not closed even at the time of the clergy communion). The right to serve with opened royal doors up to the Cherubic Hymn or until the Lord's Prayer may be bestowed upon the most deserving protopresbyters or archimandrites. Sometimes this right is given to a specific church (the liturgy is normally served in cathedrals with the royal doors opened). As for the usual priest's service, it begins with closed royal doors but with the curtain drawn open. The royal doors are opened at the beginning of the singing of the Beatitudes for the performance of the little entrance, and they are closed after the reading of the gospel and again opened at the beginning of the Cherubic Hymn—prior to performing the great entrance. At the end of the Cherubic Hymn, the royal doors are closed and the curtain is drawn closed. At the exclamation, "The doors, the doors," the curtain is drawn open. The royal doors remain closed during the entire eucharistic canon and the curtain is drawn closed before the exclamation, "The holy things are for the holy." The royal doors are opened before the communion of the laity and are not closed again until the end of the liturgy.

The custom of closing the royal doors during the liturgy is rather ancient. (This custom is mentioned in sources beginning in the eleventh century.)[83] An entire theory concerning why the laity should not see the celebration of the Eucharist appeared in the eleventh century. Niketas Stethatos explained this by the hierarchical structure of the Church: only serving clergy should be in the sanctuary, the space before the sanctuary is reserved for monks and the lower hierarchical orders, and further from the sanctuary should be the laity, for whom it is not permissible to gaze upon the celebration of the mysteries.[84] Being a follower of Saint Dionysius the Areopagite, Niketas Stethatos applied the Areopagite teaching about hierarchy to the liturgical orders. But this kind of contrast between the laity and clergy was completely foreign to the spirit of the eucharistic piety of the ancient Church. Nor is this contrast found in the text of the liturgy itself. On the contrary, as has already been stated, all the members of the community were perceived as a "royal priesthood" and all were called to full participation in the Eucharist.

Niketas Stethatos' theory does not hold up to criticism, because the custom of closing the royal doors did not become universal. The fact that the royal doors remain open during the hierarchical service and on the days of Bright Week is testimony to the fact that no categorical prohibition exists for the laity to look upon

---

[83]Taft, *Great Entrance*, 408–416.
[84]Niketas Stethatos, *Letters* 8.5 (SC 81:286).

the celebration of the mystery of the Eucharist or the communion of the clergy.[85] It seems that, combined with the silent reading of the eucharistic prayers, the custom of serving the Eucharist with closed royal doors only creates an additional barrier between the laity and clergy.[86]

The Russian tradition of serving the liturgy with closed royal doors and opening them only at certain moments has an important symbolic meaning and helps parishioners understand what is taking place in the service, in the opinion of several commentators. In his *Commentary on the Divine Liturgy*, Bishop Bessarion (Nechayev) wrote:

> The liturgy's rite of the little entrance serves as a visual expression of the notion of the relationship between God and man that has changed since the time of redemption. In fact, while the remoteness of the Old Testament's Holy of holies was a sign of the tenuous relationship between God and people, consider what is meant when the sanctuary of the New Testament's holy place—for the most part closed from the view of the people—is opened in the rites of the entrance, and its holy object, the throne of the King of glory, is opened to the sight of all who stand before it. Is it not clear that, by this, the notion of our closest communion with the Heavenly King, mystically present on the holy table of the sanctuary, is momentously expressed?[87]

In the opinion of the same author, the closing of the royal doors and the curtain following the great entrance symbolically depicts the fact that, after the burial of the Savior's body in the tomb, a stone was rolled to the cave and the tomb was sealed. At this time, the priest places the gifts on the altar table as if on the slab in the tomb, and covers them with an aer as if with the winding sheet. "After entering into the sanctuary with the gifts, the royal doors are closed and the curtain is drawn closed as a sign that the clergymen, having entered into the sanctuary, seem to have entered into the dark cave of the Lord's sepulcher."[88] During all of Bright Week the

---

[85] We note that on May 17, 2007, on the Feast of the Ascension of our Lord, when the first joint liturgy of the hierarchs of the Moscow Patriarchate and the Church Abroad was celebrated in Christ the Savior Cathedral, it was decided to leave the royal doors open during the communion of the clergy so that the faithful could see with their own eyes the moment of clergy communion.

[86] Concerning the closing and opening of the Royal Doors in Russian liturgical practice in more detail, see Pechatnov, *The Divine Liturgy*, 181–202.

[87] Bishop Vissarion (Nechaev), *Commentary on the Divine Liturgy* [in Russian] (Moscow: Sviato-Troitskaia Sergieva Lavra, 1996), 121.

[88] Ibid., 190. Regarding this in more detail, see holy martyr Ilarion (Troitskii), "History of the Shroud" [in Russian], in *Works* [in Russian] (Moscow: Sretenskii monastyr', 2004), 3:224–255. [When the priest places the gifts back on the altar table, he recites three troparia about Christ's death, burial, and tomb.—*Ed.*]

open royal doors illustrate the words of the Paschal Canon: "Thou didst rise from the tomb . . . and thou hast opened unto us the gates of paradise."[89]

Bishop Bessarion cites the increasing numbers of visitors to churches, including even the non-Orthodox, as one of the reasons for closing the royal doors during the liturgy:

> At the present time, in [the liturgy of the faithful] it is tolerated even for non-Orthodox Christians and quite grievous sinners to be present, who in antiquity would not be allowed into the temple and would stand outside of it under the open sky. This condescension to those and others is explained by the fact that the sacred ministry of the mystery of the body and blood of Christ is performed in a closed altar, while in antiquity the sanctuaries were open.[90]

After the exclamation "The doors, the doors," the Nicene-Constantinopolitan Symbol of Faith is sung (in the practice of the Greek Church it is read). The *Ecclesiastical History* of Theodorus Lector mentions that Patriarch of Constantinople Timothy I (patriarch from 511–518) ordered that the "Symbol of the 318 Fathers" be read at every eucharistic service.[91] Originally, the Nicene-Constantinopolitan Creed was the baptismal Symbol of Faith, but when heresies spread it was introduced into the liturgy as a ceremonial confession of faith. Since it was the confession of faith for the whole Church, at that time the Creed was also the confession of faith of each individual Christian. Therefore, according to tradition, even when recited during the divine services it begins with the words "I believe" (not "We believe," as one would expect). The reading of the Creed during the divine service is a reminder for each believer—before the beginning of the most holy moment of the Eucharist—of the dogmas of the Christian faith as the pillars on which all Christian piety is built.

The Eucharistic Canon (Anaphora) in the Liturgy of Saint John Chrysostom

Following the singing (or reading) of the Symbol of Faith, the main part of the liturgy—the eucharistic canon or anaphora—begins with the deacon's exclamation, "Let us stand aright, let us stand with fear, let us attend that we may offer the

---

[89]Pentecostarion. Pascha. Matins. Canon. Ode 6.
[90]Bishop Vissarion, *Commentary on the Divine Liturgy*, 175.
[91]Theodorus Lector, *Ecclesiastical History* 2.32 (PG 86/1:201a).

holy oblation in peace," and the choir's response, "A mercy of peace, a sacrifice of praise."[92] Sometimes this part of the liturgy may be called the epiclesis (from the Greek *epiklēsis*—"invocation").[93] It begins with a dialogue between the celebrant (bishop or priest) and the people (choir). The priest utters the formula of blessing taken from Saint Paul's epistle: "The grace of our Lord Jesus Christ, and the love of God the Father, and the communion of the Holy Spirit, be with you all" (cf. 2 Cor 13.13). The people respond, "And with your spirit." Formulae, well-known in literary sources beginning in the third century, follow:

> *Priest:* Let us lift up our hearts.
> *People:* We lift them up unto the Lord.[94]
> *Priest:* Let us give thanks unto the Lord.
> *People:* It is meet and right.[95]

In the liturgies of Saint Basil the Great and Saint John Chrysostom, we have two different texts of the eucharistic canon: the former is significantly longer than the latter, but both texts follow the same semantic structure. The contents of the eucharistic canon may be grouped into the following parts: (1) thanksgiving; (2) remembrance of the Last Supper including the recitation of Christ's "words of institution"; (3) the invocation of the Holy Spirit and the consecration of the holy gifts; (4) commemoration of the saints, the living and the dead, and prayer for the Church.

The eucharistic canon is the part of the liturgy in which one most senses the loss of the service's meaning caused by the custom of reading the prayers silently

[92]The term "eucharistic canon" is of Latin origin. (In the Latin rite it indicates the unchanging part of the mass.) In Orthodox liturgics of the 19th–20th centuries, this term is applied to the anaphora—the eucharistic prayer.

[93]This refers to the invocation of the Holy Spirit upon the Eucharistic Gifts.

[94]One of the earliest mentions of the exclamations "Let us lift up our hearts" and "We lift them up unto the Lord" are contained in the treatise of Saint Cyprian of Carthage (3rd c.), *On the Lord's Prayer (ANF* 5:447–457).

[95]It is spoken in this way in the Greek practice. In Russian practice the choir sings, "It is meet and right to worship the Father, and the Son, and the Holy Spirit: the Trinity, one in essence, and undivided." This hymn appeared in its contemporary form first in the Service Book of 1655. The addition (beginning with the words "to worship . . .") is taken from the baptismal order ("I bow down to the Father, and to the Son, and to the Holy Spirit, the Trinity One in Essence and Undivided.") It first appeared in Greek practice in the sixteenth century and entered into the first printed Greek editions of that time, made in Italy; in the beginning of the seventeenth century it appeared also in the south Russian editions of the Priest's Service Book (first in the Striatinsky edition of 1604), corrected according to the first printed Greek editions; this addition appeared in Moscow editions only in Patriarch Nikon's recension and later was set to a corresponding musical arrangement. In Greece the addition did not receive a musical setting because it did not remain in the Greek editions. In the opinion of Nicholas Ouspensky, the addition of the phrase "worship the Father . . ." was introduced in order to compensate for the pause envisioned by the silent reading of the anaphora. See Uspenskii, *Byzantine Liturgy*, 397.

Saint John Chrysostom Venerates the Holy Gifts. Fresco. Church of the Holy Mother of God in Donja Kamenica. Serbia. 14th c.

and not aloud for all to hear. The text of the anaphora is coherent, integral, logically complete, rich in content, profoundly touching, and inspiring, yet it is practically inaccessible to the worshippers who hear only excerpted, subordinate clauses ("singing the triumphal hymn, shouting, crying aloud, and saying," "thine own of thine own we offer unto thee," etc.). The eucharistic canon is the culmination of the liturgy and its semantic high point: all the preceding order, including the proskomedia, antiphonal hymns, litanies, prayers and readings, lead us to it. When the eucharistic canon begins, the moment arrives at which the worshipper ought to hear at last the most important thing, the reason he came to the service: the words of thanksgiving that embrace the entire universe and the entire history of mankind. Instead of this, he hears the drawn-out singing of the choir (it is especially drawn-out during the liturgy of Saint Basil the Great), and the prayer of thanksgiving is read by the priest in a quiet voice in the sanctuary.[96] Some priests do not even consider it necessary to say this prayer in a quiet voice but rather they skim it with their eyes on the pages of the Priest's Service Book.

Each layman adjusts to this situation in his own way. The most "advanced" in their attitude towards the Church study the order of the liturgy outside of church, and when they come to church, during the reading of the anaphora by the priest, repeat the words to themselves. Others, who only approximately know the content of the anaphora, pray at this time in their own words, under the singing of the choir. The absolute majority of parishioners do not know the meaning of the eucharistic anaphora and even, possibly, do not understand that the texts read by the priest in the Service Book in the sanctuary have anything to do with them, that they are uttered on *their* behalf, and are—or at least ought to be—*their* prayer.[97]

Thanksgiving makes up the main content of the eucharistic prayer. The Greek word "*eucharistia*" means just that: "thanksgiving." In the liturgy of Saint John Chrysostom, the first part of the eucharistic prayer appears as follows:

---

[96]However, thanksgiving to God is distinctly expressed in the priest's exclamations and in the hymns of the choir: "Let us give thanks unto the Lord," "Hosanna in the highest . . . ," "We praise thee, we bless thee, we give thanks unto thee, O Lord . . ." and others.

[97]However, the opinion exists that the eucharistic prayers are precisely the petitions of the celebrant (the clergyman). For example: "Accept also the supplication of us sinners, and bring it to thy holy altar, and enable us to offer unto thee both gifts and spiritual sacrifices for our sins and for the errors of the people . . ." (prayer of the oblation, after placing the holy gifts on the holy table). In this case, as we already indicated on pp. 130–132, a clear distinction is made between the serving clergy and the worshipping congregation.

It is meet and right to hymn Thee, to bless Thee, to give thanks to Thee, and to worship Thee in every place of Thy dominion: for Thou art God ineffable, inconceivable, invisible, incomprehensible, ever-existing and eternally the same, Thou and Thine Only-begotten Son and Thy Holy Spirit. Thou it was who brought us from non-existence into being, and when we had fallen away didst raise us up again, and didst not cease to do all things until Thou hadst brought us up to heaven, and hadst endowed us with Thy kingdom which is to come. For all these things we give thanks to Thee, and to Thine Only-begotten Son, and to Thy Holy Spirit; for all things of which we know and of which we know not, and for all the benefits bestowed upon us, whether manifest or unseen; and we thank Thee for this Liturgy which Thou hast deigned to accept at our hands, though there stand by Thee thousands of archangels and hosts of angels, the cherubim and the seraphim, six-winged, many-eyed, who soar aloft, borne on their pinions. . . .

In this prayer, service to God is presented with the use of five verbs: to hymn, to bless, to praise, to give thanks, and to worship; each of them expresses a particular nuance of religious feeling. God is described by four apophatic elements emphasizing his transcendence: inexpressible, incomprehensible, invisible, unattainable. The prayer is directed to God the Father, but the thanksgiving to the Father is offered together with the Son and the Holy Spirit, so that the prayer acquires a trinitarian character. The thanksgiving of the people is united to the praise of the angels. Four angelic ranks (archangels, angels, cherubim, and seraphim) are mentioned, and they are described with the use of four epithets ("six-winged, many-eyed, who soar aloft,"[98] and "on their pinions").[99]

The reading of the first part of the eucharistic prayer ends with an exclamation that completes the preceding sentence, "singing the triumphant hymn, shouting, crying aloud, and saying." The people (choir), in turn, exclaim the triumphant hymn: "Holy, Holy, Holy, Lord of Sabaoth: heaven and earth are full of thy glory. Hosanna in the highest! Blessed is he that comes in the name of the Lord. Hosanna in the highest!" Both the angelic hymn and the exclamation that precedes it contain a direct allusion to two biblical texts—the prophecy of Isaiah and the Revelation of Saint John the Theologian. In the first case the vision of the Lord sitting on

---

[98]Gr. *Eparsia*—literally, "rising upward."

[99]This draws attention to the author of the prayer's adherence to the series of four names and epithets. I do not think that a certain theological idea is behind this, but rather a certain internal rhythmic character of the prayer that gives it the character of a poetic text.

The Last Supper. Fresco. Church of Saint George in Staro Nagoričane. Macedonia. 14th c.

the throne is described; standing around him, the seraphim sing out: "Holy, Holy, Holy, Lord of Sabaoth! All the earth is full of his glory" (Is 6.1–3). In the second case, the prayer uses the words of the four mysterious animals that glorify God with the exclamation "Holy, Holy, Holy, Lord God Almighty." The word "singing" in the liturgical exclamation refers to the eagle, "shouting" to the calf, "crying aloud" to the lion, and "saying" to the man (see Rev 4.7–8). In the liturgical "triumphant hymn," the words from Saint John's Gospel that sounded from the mouths of the crowds at the entry of our Lord into Jerusalem are added to the angelic doxology: "Hosanna! Blessed is he that comes in the name of the Lord" (Jn 12.13).

In this way, in the mind of the author of the eucharistic prayer, three events were combined: the Old Testament prophet's vision of the Lord in glory, the Israelites' sight of the Lord coming to his "voluntary passion," and the apocalyptic vision of the apostle who beheld the eschatological reality of the eternal kingdom of God. The past, present, and future combine in a united thanksgiving.

We find another testimony to this combination of temporal perspectives in the words: "Thou . . . hadst endowed us with thy kingdom which is come." Thanksgiving is offered for the whole history of mankind from the creation of the world right up to the eschatological kingdom of God, which is perceived not as something expected but as something *already granted*. The worshipper feels himself an integral part of this history, which is revealed as a series of divine benefits both manifest and hidden. The conclusion of history will be and already is the kingdom of God, to which the faithful can be joined through participation in the liturgy. Archimandrite Kyprian (Kern) writes:

> It is characteristic that remembrance extends to all times, not only the past. In the eucharistic remembrance, the boundaries between the past, present, and future are erased. The eucharistic rational and bloodless service is outside of time, and does not submit to the laws of our sensory perception and our logic. In our liturgy, we also remember the future.[100]

The following part of the prayer is dedicated to the remembrance of the Last Supper, celebrated by the Savior together with his disciples:

[100]Kyprian (Kern), *The Eucharist* [in Russian], 2nd ed. (Moscow: Khram svv. bessr. Kosmy i Damiana na Maroseike, 1999), 206.

With these blessed powers, O Master who lovest mankind, we also cry aloud and say: Holy art Thou and all-holy, Thou and Thine Only-begotten Son and Thy Holy Spirit. Holy art Thou and all-holy, and magnificent is Thy glory; who hast so loved Thy world as to give Thine Only-begotten Son, that whoever believes in Him should not perish but have everlasting life; who when He had come and had fulfilled all the dispensation for us, in the night in which He was given up—or rather, gave Himself up for the life of the world—took bread in His holy, pure, and blameless hands; and when He had given thanks and blessed it, and hallowed it, and broken it, He gave it to His holy disciples and apostles saying: Take, eat. This is My Body which is broken for you, for the remission of sins. And likewise, after supper, He took the cup, saying: Drink of it, all of you. This is My Blood of the New Testament, which is shed for you and for many, for the remission of sins.

The prayer begins with the praise of God's sanctity and glory. Describing God, the term "most holy" (*panagios*) is used; in the liturgical texts this term is used to describe the Theotokos. Further, Christ's words from Saint John's Gospel are uttered almost literally: "God so loved the world that he gave his only begotten Son, that whoever believes in him should not perish but have everlasting life" (Jn 3.16). Christ came in order to fulfill the saving providence of God the Father in relation to mankind ("and fulfilled all the dispensation for us"). For this reason he was betrayed, or rather, gave himself up for the life of the world—in order for mankind to receive eternal life.

Christ's words "Take, eat" and "Drink of it, all of you" are a part of the eucharistic prayer. But over the course of many centuries, because people ceased to hear the prayer itself but rather heard only these words in the liturgy, people began to attach to them a meaning of "instituting" and "mystery-performing."[101] Supposedly, Christ established the mystery of the Eucharist precisely with these words and the bread and wine are changed into the body and blood of Christ precisely in the priest's recitation of these words. Then, following the utterance of the words "of institution," the prayer continues:

Priest: Remembering this saving commandment and all those things which have come to pass for us: the Cross, the Tomb, the Resurrection on the third day, the Ascension into heaven, the Sitting at the right hand, and the second

[101]This meaning is assigned to them in the Catholic tradition.

and glorious Coming, Thine own of Thine own, we offer unto Thee, on behalf of all and for all.

People: We praise Thee, we bless Thee, we give thanks unto Thee, O Lord; and we pray unto Thee, O our God.[102]

It is difficult to precisely translate the words "on behalf of all and for all."[103] In the Greek language it is *kata panta kai dia panta.* In both cases *panta* indicates the unspecific quantity of inanimate objects ("all") and, consequently, does not relate to people, but rather to God's benefits enumerated in the prayer of the anaphora. (In this case, the preposition *kata* means "on behalf of" or "in conjunction with", while *dia* means "for" or "thanks to.")

In contemporary liturgical practice, the prayer above is divided between the priest and the choir, and the priest reads a part of it silently (beginning with the words "Remembering this saving commandment") and he reads the other part ("Thine own of Thine own, we offer unto Thee, on behalf of all and for all") in an exclamatory voice, while the choir completes the singing of "We praise Thee." The custom of dividing the text of the anaphora between the priest and the people is extremely ancient: it is present in the earliest copies of the liturgy of Saint John Chrysostom. In them it is emphasized that the prayer is pronounced not only by the priest but by the entire congregation, and that the prayer is addressed to God on behalf of the entire community. Taking up the phrase begun by the priest, the people do not enter into a dialogue with the priest (as usually occurs in the liturgy), but rather they participate together with the priest in a dialogue with God.

Special attention should be given to the words "Thine own of Thine own, we offer unto Thee." The meaning is as follows: we offer unto thee thine own gifts. In the words of Saint Irenaeus of Lyons, "we offer to him his own" (i.e. that which belongs to him).[104] Everything that exists in the world was created by God. Man cannot create anything "out of nothing" or from nothing. He can only take that which is created by God and add to it something of his own and then return it to God in an act of thanksgiving. God created wheat and grapes and from them man prepares bread and wine; in the Eucharist, man returns the bread and wine to God in order that God may turn it into his body and blood. Thanksgiving is given for the

---

[102]Liturgy of Saint John Chrysostom. Prayer of the Anaphora.
[103]See Mikhail Asmus, "'And all mankind' in the anaphora: a clarification of the meaning" [in Russian], in *Annual theological conference PSTBI. Materials for the year 2000* [in Russian] (Moscow, 2000), 65–73; Pechatnov, *The Divine Liturgy*, 212–214.
[104]Irenaeus of Lyons, *Against Heresies* 4.18.5 (PG 7:1028a; *ANF* 1:486).

entire world that is created by God and given into the hands of man. Man is called to "divide up" the world, to be God's partner in the creative process and to return the world to God in the act of thanksgiving. In this sense, the Eucharist is an image of the entire life of man, his calling in life and his destination. The contemporary Orthodox theologian Metropolitan Kallistos (Ware) writes concerning this:

> Our human vocation, briefly expressed, is to be priest of the creation. As logical animals, possessing self-awareness and free choice—and at the same time as eucharistic animals who are being deified—it is our supreme privilege, consciously and gratefully, to offer the created world back to God the Creator. . . . First, we say in the Liturgy, "Thine own from Thine own." That which we offer to God is nothing else than what He Himself has given to us. Unless God had first conferred the world upon us as a free gift, we could make no offering at all. . . . In the Divine Liturgy it is Christ Himself who is the true Offerer, the unique High Priest; we, the ordained ministers and the people present at the Eucharist, can only act as priest by virtue of our unity with Him. He alone is Celebrant in the true sense; we are no more than concelebrants with him. . . . Secondly, in the Divine Liturgy we say not "I offer" but "we offer." Offering the Liturgy . . . we do not act alone but in union with our fellow humans. . . . Thirdly, when we offer, we are ourselves part of that which we offer. As cosmic priests, we stand within nature, not above it. . . . Fourthly, we are offerers rather than rulers or even stewards. . . . This brings us to a fifth point . . . we humans do not offer the world back to God simply in the form in which we received it, but through the work of our hands we transform that which we offer. At the Eucharist we offer to God the fruits of the earth, not in their initial state, but reshaped through our human skills; we bring to the altar not grains of wheat but bread, not bunches of grapes but wine. And so it is throughout all human life.[105]

Finally, the moment in the liturgy arrives when the bread and wine are changed into the body and blood of Christ:

> Again we offer unto Thee this rational and bloodless worship, and ask Thee, and pray Thee, and supplicate Thee: send down Thy Holy Spirit upon us and upon these Gifts here offered, and make this bread the precious Body of Thy Christ, and that which is in this Cup, the precious Blood of Thy Christ, making

[105]Bishop Kallistos (Ware), *Through the Creation to the Creator* (London: Friends of the Centre, 1997), 20–22.

the change by Thy Holy Spirit, that they may be to those who partake for the purification of soul, for the remission of sins, for the communion of Thy Holy Spirit, for the fulfillment of the kingdom of heaven, for boldness towards Thee, and not for judgment or condemnation.[106]

The verb "to change" signifies the action that God performs in relation to the bread and wine at the descent of the Holy Spirit. From this comes the term "change" (Slavonic *prelozhenie*, Greek *metabalōn*), which is used in the Orthodox tradition to signify the qualitative change that takes place with the bread and wine in the Eucharist.

It is significant that in the prayer, the priest makes entreaty for the Holy Spirit to descend "upon us and upon these gifts set forth," that is, on all those participating in the celebration of the Eucharist (clergy and laity) and upon the holy gifts. The moment of the changing of the holy gifts is perceived as an event that relates to the entire community and to each one of its members. The Holy Spirit not only changes the bread and wine into the body and blood of Christ, but also spiritually renews the faithful, making them "partakers of the divine nature" (2 Pet 1.4). The changing of the holy gifts is not an end in itself: it is performed in order for the faithful to be joined, through communion, with the Holy Spirit, and to receive the remission of sins and the kingdom of heaven. A contemporary Athonite monk writes:

Nothing in the liturgy happens mechanically or magically. Nothing is unclear and dark, even though it is beyond reason. Thus nothing remains disincarnate; everything is offered to man as bread which is broken, food to be eaten. Like blood which is poured out, blood which noiselessly pours into the veins of our life and our hope.[107]

The prayer of the anaphora is a united, uninterrupted text comprising a single long sentence. In practice this text is broken up into numerous fragments, between which additional texts are inserted. In particular, in the practice of the Russian Church, the prayer is interrupted after the words, "and upon these gifts set forth," when the troparion of the third hour, "O Lord, who didst send down Thy Most-holy Spirit," is read.[108] This troparion is pronounced three times, alternating with verses from Psalm 50. The troparion is a late addition: it first appeared in the Sla-

[106]Liturgy of Saint John Chrysostom. Prayer of the Anaphora.

[107]Vasileios (Archimandrite of Stavronikita), *Hymn of Entry: Liturgy and Life in the Orthodox Church*, trans. Elizabeth Briere, Contemporary Greek Theologians 1 (Crestwood, NY: St Vladimir's Seminary Press, 1984), 62.

[108]The full text is cited on p. 99.

vonic service books in the fifteenth century, having found its way there from the Greek service books. The universal practice of reading the troparion of the third hour before the change of the holy gifts entered the practice of the Russian Church in the sixteenth century.[109] The reading of this troparion was widespread in the Orthodox East beginning in the middle of the fifteenth century until the middle of the eighteenth century, but at the end of the eighteenth century it was removed from the Greek service books. It has remained in the Slavonic service books used in the Russian Church until the present day.

There is a great deal of literature concerning the reasons for its appearance in the Slavonic service books, and why its presence in the books is inappropriate.[110] First of all, researchers agree that the reading of the troparion interrupts the prayer in mid-sentence and artificially divides it into two parts. Secondly, the toparion of the third hour is addressed to Jesus Christ, while the prayer of the anaphora is addressed to God the Father. When, right after the address to Jesus Christ concerning the descent of the Holy Spirit, the priest pronounces the words, "and make this bread the precious body of thy Christ," there arises an obvious logical discrepancy, since the words "of thy Christ" may only be addressed to the Father and in no way to Christ himself.

It is evident that the exclusion of the troparion of the third hour from the prayer of the anaphora would not damage its meaning; on the contrary, it would help us to perceive the prayer as a coherent text. If the troparion must be preserved, then it ought to be read before the words, "Again we offer unto Thee this rational and bloodless service." In that case, the troparion would not break up the logical flow of the anaphora in such a sharp and obvious way as happens in the existing practice today.

---

[109]Aleksei Dmitrievskii, *Church services in the Russian Church in the 16th century* [in Russian] (Kazan, 1884), 121.

[110]See, for example, Archbishop Vasilii (Krivoshein), "Some liturgical peculiarities of Greeks and Russians and their significance" [in Russian], *Messager de l'Exarchat du Patriarcat russe en Europe occidentale* 89/90 (1975): 71–88; Nikolai Desnov, "A few more words concerning well-known discrepancies between Russians and Greeks in the Liturgies of Saints Basil the Great and John Chrysostom" [in Russian], *Theological Writings* 31 (1992): 86–96; Kyprian (Kern), *The Eucharist*, 252–259. For the most thorough and detailed exposition on this theme, see Pechatnov, *The Divine Liturgy*, 220–229.

The Eucharistic Canon in the
Liturgy of Saint Basil the Great

In the liturgy of Saint Basil the Great, the prayer of the anaphora is considerably longer and richer in content than in the liturgy of Saint John Chrysostom. Consequently, it is important to examine this prayer, since it contains the quintessence of the entire eucharistic theology of the eastern Church. The prayer begins with thanksgiving addressed to God the Father:

> O Existing One, Master, Lord God, Father almighty and adorable: it is truly meet and right and befitting the magnificence of Thy holiness to praise Thee, to sing to Thee, to bless Thee, to worship Thee, to give thanks to Thee, to glorify Thee—the only truly existing God—and to offer to Thee this our reasonable worship with a contrite heart and a spirit of humility, for Thou hast granted us the knowledge of Thy truth. Who can utter Thy mighty acts? Or make all Thy praises known? Or tell of all Thy miracles at all times? O Master of all, Lord of heaven and earth and of all creation, both visible and invisible, who sittest upon the throne of glory and beholdest the depths; without beginning, invisible, incomprehensible, indescribable, changeless, O Father of our Lord Jesus Christ, the great God and Savior, our hope, who is the image of Thy goodness, the seal of Thy very likeness, showing forth in Himself Thee, O Father—the living Word, the true God, the eternal Wisdom, the Life, the Sanctification, the Power, the true Light, through whom the Holy Spirit was revealed—the Spirit of truth, the gift of sonship, the pledge of future inheritance, the first fruits of eternal blessings, the life-creating power, the fountain of sanctification, through whom every creature of reason and understanding worships Thee and always sings to Thee a hymn of glory, for all things are Thy servants.

The prayer is woven from biblical allusions, replete with citations from the psalms, prophetic books, and epistles of Saint Paul. It possesses a trinitarian character and is founded on the enumeration of the divine names related to the three persons of the holy Trinity.

The first part of the prayer focuses on the names of God the Father, who is called the "Existing One," "Master," "almighty," "Lord of heaven and earth and of all creation, both visible and invisible," "the Father of our Lord Jesus Christ." God the Father sits on the throne of glory and looks upon the depths: this poetic image is taken from the song of the three youths in the Babylonian furnace (see Dan 3.54).

God the Father is described in the anaphora in five apophatic terms: without beginning, invisible, incomprehensible, indescribable, changeless. The term "without beginning" was used in the course of polemics against Eunomianism. It possesses a double meaning: it indicates that God the Father is not begotten by anyone and does not proceed (according to this meaning, the Son and Spirit are not "without beginning" [i.e. without cause]); the term also indicates that God abides outside of time, outside of the categories of beginning and end (according to this meaning, the Son and Spirit are also "without beginning" [in time]). God the Father is not visible to man's eyes and cannot be comprehended by the human mind, does not have limits in space, and his nature is not subject to change. All of these confirmations reflect the classic Christian understanding of God's nature and characteristics.

The names of the Son in the anaphora of Saint Basil the Great proceed mainly from Saint Paul's epistles and the writings of Saint John the Theologian: The Son is "the great God and Savior" (see Tit 2.13), "our hope" (see 1 Tim 1.1), "the image of [the Father's] goodness" (see 2 Cor 4.4; Col 1.15; Heb 1.3). The Son is "the seal of equal type" (see Jn 6.27), that is, the image of God the Father, equal to him. The Son in himself shows forth the Father (see Jn 14.9), he is the "living Word" (see 1 Jn 1.1; Heb 4.12), "true God" (see 1 Jn 5.20), "the Wisdom before the ages" (see 1 Cor 2.7), "the Life" (see Jn 14.6; 1.4), "Sanctification" (see 1 Cor 1.30), "Power" (see 1 Cor 1.24), "the true Light" (see Jn 1.9).

The names of the Holy Spirit are taken from these same sources: "the Spirit of truth" (see Jn 14.17), "the Gift of adoption" (see Rom 8.15), "the Pledge of future inheritance" (see Eph 1.14), "the First-fruits [cf. Rom 8.23] of eternal good things", "the life-creating Power" (see Jn 6.63; 2 Cor 3.6), "the Fountain of sanctification" (cf. 1 Cor 3.16–17). The Holy Spirit strengthens all of creation, guiding rational and intelligent creatures (i.e., angels) to offer up to the Father ever-existing (eternal) doxologies.

Further, the names of the nine angelic ranks encountered in the Bible are enumerated (this is the very list of angelic ranks that forms the basis of Saint Dionysius the Areopagite's treatise, *The Celestial Hierarchy*):

Thou art praised by angels, archangels, thrones, dominions, principalities, authorities, powers, and many-eyed cherubim. Round about Thee stand the seraphim, one with six wings and the other with six wings; with two they cover their faces, with two they cover their feet, and with two they fly, crying one to another with unceasing voices and ever-resounding praises. . . .

In the next part of the anaphora, the thanksgiving becomes a remembrance—
the Eucharist in anamnesis (Gr. *anamnēsis*—"remembrance"). Beginning with the
confession of the holiness and goodness of God, the prayer turns to the history of
mankind, which is examined as an unbroken succession of God's benefits:

> With these blessed powers, O Master who lovest mankind, we sinners also cry
> aloud and say: Holy art Thou—truly most holy—and there are no bounds to
> the magnificence of Thy holiness. Thou art gracious in all Thy deeds, for with
> righteousness and true judgment Thou hast ordered all things for us.
>
> When Thou didst create man by taking dust from the earth, and didst
> honor him with Thine own image, O God, Thou didst set him in a paradise of
> delight, promising him eternal life and the enjoyment of everlasting blessings
> in the observance of Thy commandments. But when man disobeyed Thee, the
> true God who had created him, and was deceived by the guile of the serpent,
> becoming subject to death through his own transgressions, Thou, O God, in
> Thy righteous judgment, didst send him forth from paradise into this world,
> returning him to the earth from which he was taken, yet providing for him the
> salvation of regeneration in Thy Christ Himself.
>
> For Thou didst not turn Thyself away forever from Thy creature whom
> Thou hadst made, O Good One, nor didst Thou forget the work of Thy hands.
> Through the tender compassion of Thy mercy, Thou didst visit him in various
> ways: Thou didst send prophets; Thou didst perform mighty works by Thy
> saints, who in every generation were well-pleasing to Thee; Thou didst speak
> to us by the mouth of Thy servants the prophets, foretelling to us the salvation
> which was to come; Thou didst give us the Law as a help; Thou didst appoint
> angels as guardians.

God is "gracious" (i.e., good) in all his works: all that he makes is absolute
good. God is not responsible for evil: allowing the evil that came into the world
through sin, God directs evil to good consequences. All that God sends man is
the result of the justice (truth) of God and "true judgment;" i.e. divine justice.
When man transgressed the commandment in paradise, he was banished from
paradise according to God's just sentence. But a benefit was also contained in this
sentence, since salvation and eternal life were first prepared by God through his
Son. The entire history of the Old Testament was the preparation for the Savior's
coming into the world: God sent prophets to people, performed miracles through
his saints, gave people the law, and assigned every person a guardian angel. The

conclusion of this succession of God's benefits was the coming into the world of the Lord and Savior:

> And when the fullness of time had come, Thou didst speak to us through Thy Son Himself, by whom Thou didst also make the ages; who, being the Radiance of Thy glory and the Image of Thy Person, upholding all things by the word of His power, thought it not robbery to be equal to Thee, the God and Father. He was God before the ages, yet He appeared on earth and lived among men, becoming incarnate of a holy Virgin; He emptied Himself, taking the form of a servant, being likened to the body of our lowliness, that He might liken us to the image of His glory.
>
> For as by man sin entered into the world, and by sin death, so it pleased Thine Only-begotten Son, who was in the bosom of Thee, the God and Father, who was born of a woman, the holy Theotokos and Ever-virgin Mary, who was born under the law, to condemn sin in His flesh, so that those who were dead in Adam might be made alive in Thy Christ Himself.
>
> He lived in this world and gave us commandments of salvation; releasing us from the delusions of idolatry, He brought us to knowledge of Thee, the true God and Father. He obtained us for His own chosen people, a royal priesthood, a holy nation. Having cleansed us in water, and sanctified us with the Holy Spirit, He gave Himself as a ransom to death, in which we were held captive, sold under sin. Descending through the Cross into hell—that He might fill all things with Himself—He loosed the pangs of death. He arose on the third day, having made for all flesh a path to the resurrection from the dead, since it was not possible for the Author of Life to be a victim of corruption. So He became the firstfruits of those who have fallen asleep, the first-born of the dead, that He might be Himself truly the first in all things. Ascending into heaven, He sat down at the right hand of Thy majesty on high, and He will come to render to every man according to his works.

This part of the anaphora contains an exposition of New Testament christology, based mainly on Saint Paul's epistles. According to the anaphora, "when the fullness of time was come" (Gal 4.4), God "spoke to us through his Son . . . through whom also he made the ages" (Heb 1.2). The Son of God, "being the brightness of his glory and the express image of his person, and upholding all things by the word of his power" (Heb 1.3), "did not consider it robbery to be equal with God" the Father (Phil 2.6), but being the eternal God, "appeared on

Saints Basil the Great and John Chrysostom. Fresco. Monastery of Dečani. Kosovo. 14th c.

earth and sojourned among men" (see Bar 3.38). He "emptied himself, taking on the form of a servant" (Phil 2.7), conforming himself to the body of our humility that he might make us conform to the image of his glory" (see Phil 3.21). For as "sin entered the world, and by sin death" (Rom 5.12), "the only-begotten Son who is in the bosom of God" the Father (Jn 1.18), "born of a woman" (see Gal 4.4)—the holy Theotokos and ever-virgin Mary—who submitted herself to the law, "condemned sin in his flesh" (Rom 8.3) so that, having died in Adam, we might be made alive in Christ (see 1 Cor 15.22).

The Son of God, it says later in the prayer, lived for a time in this world and gave us the saving commandments, liberated us from the worship of false gods, brought us to the knowledge of the true God and Father, having made us a chosen people, a royal priesthood, a holy nation (see 1 Pet 2.9; cf. Tit 2.14). Having cleansed us with the water of baptism (see Eph 5.26) and sanctified us with the Holy Spirit (see Rom 15.16), he gave himself in order to deliver us from death (see Tit 2.14), to which we were enslaved through sin (see Rom 7.13–14). Having died on the cross, he descended into hell in order to fill all things with himself (see Eph 4.10), loosed the pains of death (see Acts 2.24), and "rose on the third day" (1 Cor 15.4), having opened to all flesh the way to the resurrection from the dead. It was not possible for death to hold (see Acts 2.24) the "author of life" (see Acts 3.15); therefore he became the first-fruits of those who have fallen asleep (see 1 Cor 15.20), the first-born of the dead, so that he might "be first in all" (Col 1.18). Rising into the heavens, he "sat down at the right hand of the majesty on high" (Eph 1.3), and he will come to render unto everyone according to his works (see Rom 2.6).

In the anaphora of the liturgy of Saint Basil the Great, there are words and expressions that resonate with Saint Basil's literary works in a remarkable manner. Scholars[111] noticed this and saw in the parallels a confirmation of the authorship of Saint Basil the Great. The following is an example:

> What words can fitly treat of the gifts of God? So many are they in number as even to defy enumeration; so great and marvelous are they that a single one of them claims for the Giver all our gratitude. . . . God made man according

[111]Ferdinand Probst, *Liturgie des vierten Jahrhunderts und deren Reform* (Münster, 1893), 136; Ivan Karabinov, "The Anaphora. The Eucharistic prayer. The experience of historical-liturgical analysis" [in Russian], in *Collection of the ancient liturgies of the East and West* [in Russian] (Moscow: Dar, 2007), 912–913.

to His image and likeness, that He deemed him worthy of the knowledge of Himself, that in preference to all the animals He adorned him with rationality, bestowed upon him the opportunity of taking his delight in the unbelievable beauties of paradise, and made him the chief of all the creatures on earth. Then, even after he was seduced by the serpent and fell into sin, and by sin into death and its attendant evils, God did not forsake him. First, He gave to him the Law as an aid, appointed angels to watch over and care for him, sent prophets to refute evil and teach virtue, checked his impulses toward vice by threats, aroused his eagerness for the good by promises, revealed again and again the fate of each of the two classes [the good and the wicked], by making a prejudgment in the case of divers persons so as to warn the rest. In addition to all these and other favors equally great, He did not turn away from man when he persisted in disobedience. We have not been deserted by the Lord's goodness, nor have we impeded His love for us. . . . [W]e have even been recalled from death and restored to life again by our Lord Jesus Christ Himself. Even the manner in which this favor was granted calls for the greatest wonder: "Who, being in the form of God, thought it not robbery to be equal with God; but emptied Himself, taking the form of a servant" [Phil 2.6, 7]. He has, moreover, taken upon Himself our infirmities and carried our sorrows [Is 53.4]. He was crucified for us that we might be healed by His bruises [Is 53.5]. He also redeemed us from the curse, "being made a curse for us" [Gal 3.13], and endured the most ignominious death that He might restore us to the life of glory. Nor was He content with merely bringing back to life those who were dead, but He conferred upon them the dignity of divinity and prepared everlasting rest. . . .[112]

The overall theme of the text cited above is extremely similar to the anaphora of Saint Basil the Great: several expressions are completely identical and the same citations from Saint Paul's epistles are found in both texts.

The prayer of the anaphora transitions from an exposition of the Church's christological teaching into a remembrance of the Last Supper:

And as memorials of His saving Passion, He has left us these things, which we have set forth according to His command. For when He was about to go forth to His voluntary and ever-memorable and life-creating death—in the night in which He gave Himself up for the life of the world—He took bread into His

[112]Basil the Great, *The Long Rules* 2.2, 3–4 (PG 31:912c, 913b–916a; Wagner, CUA).

holy and pure hands; and having shown it to Thee, the God and Father, having given thanks, blessed and hallowed it, and broken it—*He gave it to His holy disciples and apostles, saying: Take, Eat. This is My Body which is broken for you, for the remission of sins.* Likewise He took the cup of the fruit of the vine, and having mingled it and given thanks, blessed and hallowed it—*He gave it to His holy disciples and apostles, saying: Drink of it, all of you. This is My Blood of the New Testament, which is shed for you and for many, for the remission of sins.* Do this in remembrance of Me. For as often as you eat this Bread and drink this Cup, you proclaim My Death, you confess My Resurrection.

Therefore, we also, O Master, remembering His saving Passion and life-creating Cross, His three-day Burial and Resurrection from the dead, His Ascension into heaven and Sitting at the right hand of Thee the God and Father, and His glorious and awesome Second Coming—*Thine own of Thine own, we offer unto Thee, on behalf of all and for all.* We praise Thee, we bless Thee, we give thanks unto Thee, O Lord; and we pray unto Thee, O our God.

In contemporary practice, only the italicized words are exclaimed in a loud voice; the priest pronounces all the other words in the sanctuary quietly or silently, while the choir sings "We praise thee. . . ." It is not fully understood why "He gave it to his holy disciples and apostles, saying" is pronounced as an exclamation in Saint Basil's liturgy while the analogous words in the liturgy of Saint John Chrysostom are read silently. In any event, this short fragment of this sentence is the only phrase that enables parishioners, who do not hear the reading of the anaphora, to know that the anaphora of Saint Basil the Great was read by the priest, not the anaphora of Saint John Chrysostom.

Uttering Christ's words "of institution," the priest continues the prayer, asking God to send down the Holy Spirit on the community of the faithful and on the holy gifts:

Therefore, most holy Master, we also Thy sinful and unworthy servants, whom Thou hast permitted to serve at Thy holy altar not because of our own righteousness (for we have done nothing good upon the earth), but because of Thy mercy and compassions (which thou hast so richly poured out on us), we now dare to approach Thy holy altar and, offering to Thee the antitypes of the holy Body and Blood of Thy Christ, we pray Thee and call upon Thee, O Holy of Holies, that by the favor of Thy goodness Thy Holy Spirit may come upon us and upon the Gifts now offered to bless, to hallow, and to show this Bread to be the precious Body of our Lord and God and Savior Jesus Christ, and this Cup to be the precious Blood of our Lord and God and Savior Jesus Christ, shed for the life of the world.

And unite all of us to one another who become partakers of the one Bread and Cup in the communion of the Holy Spirit. Grant that none of us may partake of the holy Body and Blood of Thy Christ for judgment or condemnation.

The expression "antitypes [Gr. *antitypa*] of the holy body and blood of Christ" is used in Saint Basil's anaphora in relation to the holy gifts. The term "antitypes" is also found to apply to the holy gifts in patristic sources of the third and fourth centuries, especially in the works of Saint Irenaeus of Lyons, Saint Hippolytus the Roman, Saint Cyril of Jerusalem, Saint Gregory the Theologian, and Saint Macarius of Egypt.[113] This term in no way indicates that the change of the holy gifts is illusory or symbolic; on the contrary, it indicates that although the holy gifts keep their appearance—the "image" of bread and wine—they in fact become the body and blood of Christ. This is precisely the way in which Saint Macarius of Egypt understood the term "antitypes": the faithful commune of the visible (*phainomenou*) bread, but spiritually eat the Lord's flesh.[114] In a later period, the term came to be explained as relating to the holy gifts only up to the consecration. Saint John of Damascus, in particular, wrote:

> The bread and wine are not a figure of the body and blood of Christ—God forbid!—but the actual deified body of the Lord, because the Lord himself said: "This is my body"; not "a figure of my body" but "my body," and not "a figure of my blood" but "my blood." . . . Although some may have called the bread and wine antitypes of the body and blood of the Lord, as did the inspired Basil, they did not say this as referring to after the consecration, but to before the consecration.[115]

This explanation was repeated by the Seventh Ecumenical Council[116] and later expressed at the Council of Florence by Saint Mark of Ephesus. In his words, the

---

[113]Irenaeus of Lyons, *Fragments from the Lost Writings of Irenaeus* 37 (*ANF* 1:574); Hippolytus of Rome, *Apostolic Tradition* 38 (Stewart, PPS); Cyril of Jerusalem, *Mystagogical Catecheses* 5.20 (Church, PPS); Gregory the Theologian, *Orations* 8.18 (PG 35:809c; *NPNF*² 7:243); Macarius of Egypt, *Homilies* 27.17 (PG 34:705b).

[114]Macarius of Egypt, *Homilies* 27.17 (PG 34:705b).

[115]John of Damascus, *An Exact Exposition of the Orthodox Faith* 4.13 (Chase, CUA).

[116]*Acts of the Ecumenical Councils* [in Russian] (St Petersburg: Voskresenie, 1996), 4:538–540.

Veneration of the Holy Gifts.
Fresco. Saint Andrew Church on
the Treska River. 14th c.

holy gifts are called "antitypes" up to the consecration because they "are still offered as a certain image and depiction."[117]

The anaphora of the liturgy of Saint Basil the Great, just as the anaphora of the liturgy of Saint John Chrysostom, constitutes a coherent text in which the priest asks God to bless the holy gifts, consecrate them, and show (that is to say, reveal) the bread to be the body of Christ and the wine to be the blood of Christ, shed for the life of the world. In practice, however, the prayer is interrupted at the word "show," after which the troparion of the third hour is read; then the deacon says, "Bless, Master, the holy bread," and the priest pronounces "this bread to be itself the precious body." In this way, the entire sentence is broken up into two incomplete phrases, and the words "this bread" is turned from a part of the prayerful petition into a statement. Once again, it would be more reasonable to read the troparion of the third hour, if it is not possible to remove it altogether, before the words "Because of this, O all-holy Master," in order, at least, to not destroy the meaning of the prayer for the changing of the holy gifts.

In the contemporary Russian Priest's Service Books, the words "making the change by thy Holy Spirit"—taken from the anaphora of Saint John Chrysostom—have been added after "shed for the life of the world." This phrase did not appear in ancient Greek and Russian service books and is not found in contemporary Greek service books. It appeared in the Greek service books for the first time in the twelfth century, but it entered into universal usage in Greece only in the middle of the sixteenth century. In Kiev it first appeared in the printed Kievan Priest's Service Books of 1629 and 1639, and in Moscow during the time of Patriarch Nikon, in the service book of 1655.[118] (Old-Rite believers to the present day preserve the original text.) It is possible that the reason for this addition was the desire to clearly indicate in the anaphora of Saint Basil the Great the moment at which the change of the holy gifts into the body and blood of Christ takes place. Some scholars link the spread of the addition to the debates over the time of the change of the holy gifts (this will be discussed later). But syntactically the words "making the change by thy Holy Spirit" do not fit into the rest of the prayer's text. Saint Nicodemus of the Holy Mountain indicated this in the eighteenth century:

[117]Mark of Ephesus, *Essay on how the Divine Gifts are consecrated*, chapter 4, in Amvrosii (Pogodin), *St Mark of Ephesus*, 298.

[118]Pechatnov, *The Divine Liturgy*, 230–231.

When priests are celebrating the liturgy of St Basil, in the hour of the transubstantiation [*metousiōseōs*] and of the sanctification of the mysteries, they must not repeat the words "changing them by thy Holy Spirit," because this is an addition made by some ignorant and bold person who, being opposed, it would seem, to the Latins, took these words from the liturgy of St John Chrysostom and inserted them in the liturgy of St Basil. Hence the words are not found in the old handwritten liturgies, as we have determined by a search, but neither will such words fit the context there.[119]

The Change of the Holy Gifts: Theological Aspects

The Orthodox Church carefully preserves the belief of the ancient Church that the eucharistic bread and wine do not simply symbolize the body and blood of Christ, but are in truth his body and blood. This belief is based on Christ's words, "My flesh is food indeed, and my blood is drink indeed. He who eats my flesh and drinks my blood abides in me, and I in him" (Jn 6.55–56).

All ancient liturgical orders—both eastern and western, those still in use and those that have fallen out of use—emphasize that following the change of the holy gifts the eucharistic bread and wine are "the most precious body and blood" of our Lord Jesus Christ (liturgy of Saint Basil the Great), "the most pure body and precious blood" of the Son of God (liturgy of the Apostle Mark),[120] "the holy body" and "precious blood" of Christ (liturgy of the Apostle James),[121] "the true body and blood of our Lord and Savior Jesus Christ" (liturgy of Saint Gregory, Enlightener of Armenia),[122] "the most holy body and blood" of the Son of God (Roman liturgy).[123]

Faith in the real body and blood of Christ is found in sources from the writings of the holy fathers and is a leitmotif throughout the works of the Church fathers beginning in the second century:

> . . . the Eucharist is *the flesh of our Saviour Jesus Christ* who suffered for our sins.[124]

---

[119]Nicodemus the Hagiorite, *The Rudder*, cited in Pechatnov, *The Divine Liturgy*, 231. The above English translation is altered from *The Rudder*, trans. Denver Cummings (Chicago, IL: Orthodox Christian Educational Society, 1957), 561.

[120]*Collection of Ancient Liturgies*, 426.

[121]Ibid., 148.

[122]Ibid., 356.

[123]Ibid., 782.

[124]Ignatius of Antioch, *Epistle to the Smyrnaeans* 7 (Lake, LCL).

[This flesh] is nourished by the cup *which is his blood*, and receives increase from the bread *which is his body*.[125]

This food . . . we have been taught . . . *is the flesh and blood of that Jesus who was made flesh*.[126]

Contemplate therefore the bread and wine not as bare elements, for *they are*, according to the Lord's declaration, *the body and blood of Christ*; for though sense suggests this to thee, let faith stablish thee. Judge not the matter from taste, but from faith be fully assured without misgiving, that thou hast been vouchsafed the body and blood of Christ. . . . These things having learnt, and being fully persuaded that what seems bread is not bread, though bread by taste, but the body of Christ; and that what seems wine is not wine, though the taste will have it so, but the blood of Christ. . . .[127]

Because it is man's custom to eat bread and drink water and wine he joined his divinity to these and *made them his body and blood*. . . . The bread and wine are not a figure of the body and blood of Christ—God forbid!—but *the actual deified body of the Lord*.[128]

And so, in accordance with the holy Scriptures and tradition of the Church, the bread and wine of the Eucharist are the true body and true blood of Christ. But in what way are the bread and wine changed into the Savior's body and blood? What happens to them during the Eucharist? Western and eastern traditions do not answer these questions in the same way.

In the Latin tradition, the opinion took hold that the bread and wine "are transubstantiated" into the body and blood of Christ during the Eucharist. The teaching of "transubstantiation" is based on a theory according to which the bread and wine lose their "substance" after the consecration as they change into the body and blood of Christ. Developing this theory, Thomas Aquinas used the Aristotelian distinction between substance (essence) and accidents (characteristics): substance makes a thing what it is and is its ontological basis, while accidents are secondary characteristics, perceived by our senses. At the moment of the change of the holy gifts, their ontological essence is changed, while their characteristics remain as they were before—explaining why they also continue to appear as bread and wine. The

[125]Irenaus of Lyons, *Against Heresies* 5.2.3 (ANF 1:528).

[126]Justin Martyr, *First Apology* 66 (ANF 1:185).

[127]Cyril of Jerusalem, *Mystagogical Catecheses* 4.6, 9 (Church, PPS).

[128]John of Damascus, *An Exact Exposition of the Orthodox Faith* 4.13 (Chase, CUA).

preservation of the characteristics of bread and wine is necessary because, first of all, "people are not accustomed to eating human flesh and drinking human blood," and secondly, "eating the body and blood of our Lord in their invisible presence, we increase the merits of our faith."[129]

This teaching was made dogma by the Fourth Council of the Lateran in 1215. The Council of Trent (1545–1563) decreed: "By the consecration of the bread and wine, a change takes place of the entire substance of the bread into the substance of the body of our Lord Christ, and of the entire substance of the wine into the substance of his blood; the Catholic Church justly and precisely named this change transubstantiation."[130]

In the period of the Reformation and Counter-Reformation, the Catholic teaching on transubstantiation came to be used in polemics against Protestants who denied the reality of the change of the bread and wine into the body and blood of Christ (however, Patriarch Gennadius Scholarius used the teaching in the fifteenth century even before the appearance of Protestantism). In the middle of the seventeenth century, the Latin teaching on transubstantiation was used by Orthodox theologians polemicizing against the teaching of Patriarch Cyril Loukaris who, under the influence of Calvinism, actually denied the reality of the body and blood of Christ in the Eucharist. As a result, the term "transubstantiation" entered into the so-called symbolic books of the Orthodox Church[131] and into seminary courses of dogmatic theology.

Gennadius Scholarius, Patriarch of Constantinople. Mosaic. 20th c.

Beginning in the middle of the nineteenth century, voices were heard in Orthodox circles opposing the Catholic teaching of transubstantiation. The first to criticize this teaching was the Russian slavophile Alexei Khomiakov.[132] Other opponents of the Latin understanding of transubstantiation were V. Bolotov and Archpriest Sergei Bulgakov, as well as other Russian theologians: Paul Evdokimov,

[129]Thomas Aquinas, *Summa Theologiae* 3.75.2–5.

[130]Council of Trent, *Decree Concerning the Holy Eucharist* 4. Cited in *Christian doctrine: Dogmatic texts of the teaching of the Church (3rd c. to 10th c.)* [in Russian], ed. Pierre Dumoulin, trans. Nataliia Sokolova and Iuliia Kurkina (St Petersburg: Izdatel'stvo Sv. Petra, 2002), 403.

[131]Concerning the symbolic books, see vol. 2, pp. 48–49.

[132]See Aleksei Khomiakov, *The complete works of Aleksei Stepanovich Khomiakov* [in Russian], vol. 2, *Theological writings*, 5th ed. (Moscow, 1907), 131–132. Cf. the objections of the priest Pavel Florensky in his article "Near Khomiakov" [in Russian], in *Writings* [in Russian] (Moscow: Mysl', 1996), 2:278–320.

Nicholas Ouspensky, and Protopresbyters John Meyendorff and Alexander Schmemann.[133] These theologians perceived a fundamental difference between East and
West in the debate concerning transubstantiation. In the opinion of the most
extreme opponents of the Latin teaching on transubstantiation, the Orthodox
understanding of the mystery of the Eucharist supposes a belief that the nature of
the bread and wine are preserved following the changing of the holy gifts.

However, in Orthodox circles there are more than a few supporters of the teaching of "transubstantiation." These do not fully accept the Latin conception of the
change of substance while preserving characteristics, but they insist that the substance of the bread and wine is not preserved in the eucharistic gifts following the
change of the bread and wine into the body and blood of Christ. These theologians
essentially accept the teaching on transubstantiation, while the term "transubstantiation" is proclaimed to be an equivalent to the traditional eastern Christian term
"change." In this way, the difference between East and West is no longer a dispute
concerning essence, but merely a debate concerning terminology.[134]

It is hardly possible to fully resolve this issue by using citations from the works
of the eastern Fathers of the Church. The same citations are brought forth by both
supporters and opponents of the teaching on transubstantiation, and the interpretation of the citations is varied and sometimes completely contradictory. The mystical and inexplicable character of the change—not subject to human reason—is the
prime reason for the absence of a clear and definite opinion regarding the question
of whether the nature of the bread and wine following the change is preserved or
not in the eastern Christian patristic tradition. Moreover, the question of what
exactly happens to the bread and wine in the Eucharist was not a subject of debate

[133]See, in particular, Sergii Bulgakov, "The Eucharistic dogma" [in Russian], *The Way* 20 (February
1930): 3–46 and 21 (April 1930): 3–33; see also Uspenskii, *Byzantine Liturgy*, 425–429. Cf. the objections
of Aleksei Georgievskii in his articles "Concerning the resurrection of the dead in connection with the
Eucharist, in light of Holy Scripture" [in Russian], *Theological Writings* 16 (1976): 33–45; and "The most holy
Eucharist in connection with the teaching of the Orthodox Church" [in Russian], *Journal of the Moscow
Patriarchate* no. 6 (1977): 74–75 and 7 (1977): 75–78.

[134]Debates between supporters and opponents of "transubstantiation" in Orthodox circles periodi-
cally resurface. At the beginning of the 21st century, a debate occurred once again. See Aleksei Fokin, "The
Change of the Holy Gifts in the Mystery of the Eucharist" [in Russian], *Alpha and Omega* 2/3 (9/10) (1996):
117–130; Aleksei Zaitsev, "The Eucharistic Change" [in Russian], *Church and Time* 29 (2004): 208–226; Sergii
(Troitskii), "Experience of Exposition of the Teachings of the Holy Fathers Concerning the Holy Eucharist"
[in Russian], in *Patristic christology and anthropology: A collection of articles* [in Russian] (Moscow: Peresvet,
2003), 61–76; Dmitrii Pashkov, "Concerning the Eucharistic Transubstantiation" [in Russian], *Theological
Digest* 13 (2005): 381–391; Mikhail Zheltov, foreword to *The Byzantine liturgy: a historical-liturgical study. The
Anaphora: the experience of historical-liturgical analysis*, by Nikolai Uspenskii, vol. 2 of *Works on liturgics* [in
Russian] (Moscow: Izdatel'stvo Moskovskoi Patriarkhii, 2006).

in the epoch of the Ecumenical Councils, and therefore no particular explanation was ever made dogma in the Orthodox East.

The eastern fathers of the Church unconditionally agree that the nature of the bread and wine at the moment of change becomes the real—not illusory—body of Christ. Protopresbyter John Meyendorff explains that, according to Byzantine theology, the eucharistic bread and wine are not a "type," "symbol," or "image" of the body of Christ; it is the very "flesh of God," which came in order to save the flesh of man. But Byzantine theologians did not venture any further than this eucharistic realism. For them, the Eucharist always remained a mystery whose explanation exceeds the limits of human possibilities.[135] As Saint John of Damascus emphasizes, the change of the holy gifts in the Eucharist undoubtedly takes place, but the means of change are not known to us:

> And now you ask how the bread becomes the body of Christ and the wine and water the blood of Christ. And I tell you that the Holy Spirit comes down and works these things which are beyond description and understanding. . . . The very bread and wine are changed into the body and blood of God. However, should you inquire as to the manner in which this is done, let it suffice for you to hear that it is done through the Holy Spirit, just as it was through the Holy Spirit that the Lord made flesh subsist for himself and in himself from the blessed Mother of God. And more than this we do not know, except that the word of God is true and effective and omnipotent, but the manner in which it is so is impossible to find out. What is more, it is not amiss to say this, that just as bread by being eaten and wine and water by being drunk are naturally changed into the body of the person eating and drinking and yet do not become another body than that which the person had before, so in the same way are the bread of the offertory and the wine and water supernaturally changed into the body and blood of Christ by the invocation and coming down of the Holy Spirit, yet they are not two bodies, but one and the same.[136]

Following the example of Saint Gregory of Nyssa—who affirmed that as "the body, through the indwelling of God the Word, was translated to the dignity of Godhead," so too the eucharistic bread "which is sanctified by the Word of God is transmuted into the body of God the Word"[137]—Saint John of Damascus drew a

---

[135]John Meyendorff, *Byzantine Theology: Historical Trends and Doctrinal Themes* (New York: Fordham University Press, 1979), 202–206.

[136]John of Damascus, *An Exact Exposition of the Orthodox Faith* 4.13 (Chase, CUA).

[137]Gregory of Nyssa, *The Catechetical Oration* 37, in *The Catechetical Oration of St. Gregory of Nyssa*, trans. James Herbert Srawley (London: Society for Promoting Christian Knowledge, 1917), 110–111. We note that

parallel between the two natures of Christ and the Eucharist. He discussed the two natures of the holy gifts following the consecration:

> Isaiah saw the coal [see Is 6.6]. But coal is not plain wood but wood united with fire: in like manner also the bread of the communion is not plain bread but bread united with divinity. But a body which is united with divinity is not one nature, but has one nature belonging to the body and another belonging to the divinity that is united to it, so that the compound is not one nature but two.[138]

What are the two natures in question here? Some theologians consider that the discussion concerns the presence of the physical nature of bread and wine and the body and blood of Christ in the consecrated eucharistic gifts. Others deem that Saint John's discussion concerns the presence of the two natures of Christ—divine and human—in the holy gifts. The general context of chapter thirteen of the fourth book of *An Exact Exposition of the Orthodox Faith*, from which this citation is taken, allows us to say that Saint John had in mind precisely the two natures of Christ. In this case, it is impossible to include Saint John of Damascus among supporters of the notion that the physical properties of bread and wine are preserved following the change.

Yet another difference between the East and West in the teaching on the Eucharist pertains to the time of the change, when the holy gifts become the body and blood of Christ. Polemics were ignited around this question at the Council of Florence.[139] Latin theologians established that the bread and wine become the body

according to the text, ascribed to St John Chrysostom, "the bread, prior to being consecrated, we call bread; when the divine grace consecrates it through the instrument of the priest, it is no longer called bread, but is worthily called the body of the Lord, though the essence of bread remains in it." See John Chrysostom, *Letter to Monk Caesarius* (PG 52:753–760). In *Patrologia Migne* this text is attributed to the category of "spuria," and its authenticity is rejected by contemporary patristic scholarship (see No. 4530 in *Clavis Patrum Graecorum. Volumen II: Ab Athanasio ad Chrysostomum*, ed. Mauritius Geerard [Turnhout: Brepolis, 1974]).

[138]John of Damascus, *An Exact Exposition of the Orthodox Faith* 4.13 (Chase, CUA).

[139]More than two centuries after the Council of Florence, at the end of the 17th century, the controversy concerning the time of the change of the holy gifts ignited in the Russian Church. The Latin opinion was defended by the scholar-monk Sylvester Medvedev while the monk Euthymius and the brothers Ioannikios and Sophronius Likhudy made a stand for the Orthodox teaching. See Grigorii Mirkovich, *Concerning the time of the change of the Holy Gifts. Controversy in Moscow in the second half of the 17th century. Experience of historical research* [in Russian] (Vilnius, 1886); Gerhard Podskalsky, *Griechische Theologie in der Zeit der Tu_rkenherrschaft (1453–1821): die Orthodoxie im Spannungsfeld der nachreformatorischen Konfessionen des Westens* (München: C. H. Beck, 1988), 273–274. One of the results of the controversy was the introduction of the following words into the order of the hierarchical oath during the time of Patriarch Adrian: "And I believe and reason that in the divine liturgy the change of the body and blood of Christ is performed, as the eastern and our Russian teachers teach from antiquity, by the inspiration and action of the Holy Spirit, through the hierarchical or priestly invocation, in the words of prayer to God the Father: 'And make this bread the precious body of thy Christ, and the rest.'" Cited in Viktor Zhivov, *From church history in the time of Peter the Great: Research and materials* [in Russian] (Moscow: Novoe literaturnoe obozrenie, 2004), 191.

and blood of Christ at the moment of the priest's recitation of the words "Take, eat" and "Drink ye all of this." Nominally, this understanding is confirmed by the words of Saint John Chrysostom:

> He said, "This is my body." These words change the offering. And akin to that saying "Be fruitful, and multiply and replenish the earth" [Gen 1.28], though it was uttered once, but in reality bestows upon our nature the power to beget children for all times, so too this utterance, pronounced once, completes the offering at every altar table in the churches from that time to the present, and until his Second Coming.[140]

But Orthodox theologians were not inclined to understand Chrysostom's cited words to mean that the bread and wine are changed into the body and blood of the Savior exclusively because Christ's words are spoken. Moreover, other works by Chrysostom and other eastern fathers clearly speak of the invocation of the Holy Spirit upon the bread and wine:

> Then having sanctified ourselves by these spiritual hymns, we call upon the merciful God *to send forth his Holy Spirit* upon the gifts lying before him; that he may make the bread the body of Christ, and the wine the blood of Christ; for whatsoever the Holy Spirit has touched, is sanctified and changed.[141]

> Have any saints left for us in writing the words to be used in the invocation over the eucharistic bread and the cup of blessing? As everyone knows, we are not content in the liturgy simply to recite the words recorded by St. Paul or the Gospels, but we add other words both before and after, words of great importance for this mystery. We have received these words from unwritten teaching.[142]

> When a priest stands before the altar table with hands outstretched to heaven, *invoking the Holy Spirit* to descend and contact the (gifts) set forth, then there is a great quietness, a great silence.[143]

> The priest stands *bringing down*, not fire, but *the Holy Spirit*. And he offers prayer at length, not that some flame lit from above may consume the offerings, but that grace may fall on the sacrifice through that prayer, [and] set alight the souls of all[.][144]

---

[140]John Chrysostom, *On the Betrayal of Judas* 1.6 (PG 49:380–1).
[141]Cyril of Jerusalem, *Mystagogical Catecheses* 5.7 (Church, PPS).
[142]Basil the Great, *On the Holy Spirit* 66 (PG 32:188b; Hildebrand, PPS).
[143]John Chrysostom, *Homily on the Cemetery and the Cross* 3 (PG 49:397).
[144]John Chrysostom, *On the Priesthood* 3.4 (PG 48:642; Neville, PPS).

On the basis of the teaching of the eastern fathers as well as liturgical texts, the Orthodox at the Council of Florence asserted that the change of the holy gifts takes place after the invocation of the Holy Spirit that comes after the utterance of Christ's words "Take, eat" and "Drink ye all of this." Referring to the order of the liturgies of Saints James, Basil the Great, and John Chrysostom, Saint Mark of Ephesus stated:

> In one accord they all[145] first cite the Lord's words and through these words lead us to a remembrance of those events and invest sanctifying power in the rite being performed. But next they pray and invoke the grace of the Holy Spirit, so that grace, coming, might accordingly make perfect that which is presently uttered and co-make and change the offered gifts into the body and blood of the Lord. . . . It is not that we exclusively assign faith in our prayer or consider those words [of institution] to be without power, but rather we pray for the gifts set forth and in this manner perfect [sanctify] them. We both preserve the characteristic power of those words and reveal the significance of the divine priesthood that perfects all the mysteries by the invocation of the Holy Spirit who acts through it.[146]

In such manner, the bread and wine are changed into the body and blood of Christ, because of the descent of the Holy Spirit upon them by the prayer of the priest. But the exact moment of the change remains concealed and cannot be linked with any specific formula. Up to the point at which the priest begins to read the anaphora, bread and wine—"antitypes" of the body and blood of Christ—remain on the altar table; when the priest completes the reading of the anaphora, the true body and true blood of God made flesh is on the altar table. The recitation of the Savior's words is important—just as is everything else contained in the eucharistic anaphora—but to set these words apart from the prayer of the anaphora as a special "mystery-performing" element is not necessary.

In the middle of the fourteenth century the Byzantine theologian Saint Nicholas Cabasilas examined the question of the manner and time of the change of the holy gifts into the body and blood of Christ in detail in his *Commentary on the Divine Liturgy*:

---

[145] The authors of the liturgies.

[146] Mark of Ephesus, *Essay on how the Divine Gifts are consecrated*, chapter 4, in Amvrosii (Pogodin), *St Mark of Ephesus*, 298–299.

Now that our hearts are filled with such beautiful and holy thoughts, nothing remains but to return thanks to God, the author of all good things; thus the first priest did, who before instituting the sacrament of the holy Eucharist gave thanks to God his Father. So the celebrant, before the great prayer in the course of which he will consecrate the holy offerings, addresses to God this act of thanksgiving: "Let us give thanks to the Lord." The faithful give their consent, saying: "It is meet and right." Then the priest himself gives thanks to God, glorifying him, praising him with the angels, and thanking him for all the gifts which he has bestowed upon us from the beginning of time. Finally he recalls the ineffable and incomprehensible mystery of the incarnation and redemption; then he consecrates the offerings, and the sacrifice is complete.[147]

Cabasilas goes on to ask in what manner the holy gifts are changed into the body and blood of Christ:

The priest recites the story of that august Last Supper, telling how, before he suffered, he gave to the disciples this sacrament, and took the bread and the chalice, and having given thanks said those words which expressed the mystery; repeating those words, the celebrant prostrates himself and prays, while applying to the offerings these words of the Only-Begotten, our Savior, that they may, after having received his most holy and all-powerful Spirit, be transformed—the bread into his holy body, the wine into his precious and sacred blood. When these words have been said, the whole sacred rite is accomplished, the offerings are consecrated, the sacrifice is complete.[148]

In this way, Nicholas Cabasilas "attributes not just one particular phrase to the accomplishing prayer, but the entire anamnesis and the entire epiclesis." Moreover, "he considers the Roman Catholic anaphora to be effective."[149] In Cabasilas' words, the Latins "do not ask explicitly for consecration and the transformation of the elements into the body of the Lord, but use other terms, which, however, have exactly the same meaning."[150] These "other terms" are understood to be the words of the Tridentine Mass:

[147]Nicholas Cabasilas, *Commentary* 27. The above translation is from Nicholas Cabasilas, *A Commentary on the Divine Liturgy*, trans. J. M. Hussey and P. A. McNulty (Crestwood, NY: St Vladimir's Seminary Press, 2002), 69.

[148]Nicholas Cabasilas, *Commentary* 27; see pp. 69–70 in trans. Hussey and McNulty.

[149]Uspenskii, *Byzantine Liturgy*, 432.

[150]Nicholas Cabasilas, *Commentary* 30.1; see p. 76 in trans. Hussey and McNulty.

We humbly beseech thee, almighty God, command these to be carried by the hands of thy holy angel to thine altar on high, in the presence of thy divine majesty, that as many of us as shall, by partaking at this altar, receive the most sacred body and blood of thy Son, may be filled with all heavenly blessing and grace. Through the same Christ our Lord. Amen.[151]

The image of the holy gifts being carried by an angel to God's altar on high is not characteristic for the eastern Christian anaphoras, which speak more of the descent of the Holy Spirit upon the gifts. But the image is found in the litany read following the change of the holy gifts ("That our God, the Lover of mankind, having accepted them upon his holy and most heavenly and noetic altar as an odor of spiritual fragrance, will send down upon us divine grace and the gift of the Holy Spirit"). Cabasilas considers the image used in the Latin Mass to be completely acceptable:

> This prayer can have only one significance—it transforms the offerings into the body and blood of the Lord. . . . The priest then prays that the offerings may be carried up to the heavenly altar—in other words, that they may be consecrated and transformed into the heavenly body of the Lord. . . . Your (Latin) priests, regarding Christ as the victim, pray that the offerings may be placed in him; thus, though in different words, they are asking just what we ask.[152]

Put differently, Cabasilas considers that the divergence of opinion between the East and West regarding the question of the time of the change of the holy gifts is not a principal matter. Rather, it is caused not so much by a theological disagreement as by the details of the liturgical rite in the East and West.

THE PRAYER OF INTERCESSION

In the ancient liturgies, the diptychs—prayerful commemoration of the living and the departed—directly followed the consecration of the holy gifts.[153] Earlier

---

[151]Tridentine Mass, Prayer of the Anaphora. Cited in Uspenskii, *Byzantine Liturgy*, 404–405. The above translation is from Nikolaus Gihr, *The Holy Sacrifice of the Mass*, 6th ed. (Freiburg im Breisgau: B. Herder, 1924), 647.

[152]Nicholas Cabasilas, *Commentary* 30.8–16; see pp. 77–78 in trans. Hussey and McNulty.

[153]The Greek term *diptychos* means "double," "folding in two parts." The term *diptycha* in early Byzantium referred to tablets on which the names of the living and the departed were written for commemoration in churches. Later the term came to be used to denote, in particular, (1) the lists of the local churches and their heads; (2) lists of the region's hierarchs; (3) lists of the living members of the community; (4) lists of the

we discussed the theological meaning of the commemoration of names during the divine liturgy. But the spoken commemoration during the anaphora had another meaning: in the period in which heresies and schisms appeared, it indicated the churches and bishops with which the local church had eucharistic communion.[154] The inclusion of a particular person's name in the diptychs was a witness of his Orthodoxy, while exclusion from the diptychs would have testified to his fall into heresy or schism. Primarily, this pertained to persons vested in high hierarchical rank.

In the contemporary rite of the liturgies of Saints Basil the Great and John Chrysostom, the commemoration of the departed, including the Mother of God and the saints, directly follows the anaphora. In Saint John Chrysostom's liturgy, it has the following form:

Again we offer unto Thee this rational worship for those who have fallen asleep in the faith: ancestors, fathers, patriarchs, prophets, apostles, preachers, evangelists, martyrs, confessors, ascetics, and every righteous spirit made perfect in faith:

Especially for our most holy, most pure, most blessed and glorious Lady Theotokos and Ever-virgin Mary.

. . . for the holy Prophet, Forerunner, and Baptist John; the holy, glorious, and all-laudable apostles; Saint(s) _____ (of the day) whom we commemorate today; and all Thy saints, at whose supplication look down upon us, O God.

Remember all those who have fallen asleep before us in the hope of resurrection to eternal life, especially _____; grant them rest, O God, where the light of Thy countenance shines on them.

Again we entreat Thee: Remember, O Lord, all the Orthodox Episcopate, who rightly teach the word of Thy truth; all the priests, the deacons in Christ, and every order of the clergy.

Again we offer unto Thee this rational worship: for the whole world; for the Holy, Catholic, and Apostolic Church; for those who live in chastity and holiness of life; for all civil authorities; grant them, O Lord, peaceful times, that we, in their tranquility, may lead a calm and peaceful life in all godliness and sanctity.

departed. See Robert F. Taft, *A History of the Liturgy of St. John Chrysostom*, vol. 4, *The Diptychs*, Orientalia Christiana Analecta 238 (Rome: Pontificium Institutum Studiorum Orientalium, 1991), 7–21.

[154]Hugh Wybrew, *The Orthodox Liturgy: The Development of the Eucharistic Service in the Orthodox Rite* (Crestwood, NY: St Vladimir's Seminary Press, 1990), 58.

We see that the most-holy Theotokos is commemorated, albeit "especially," yet nonetheless in the ranks of other departed. The text of the anaphora does not suppose a clear division of the departed saints who do not need the prayers of the Church and sinners in need of prayer. According to contemporary practice, prayer services (molebens) are served to the saints, but saints are not commemorated in services for the departed (panikhidas), which have a character of supplication and petition.[155]

According to Nicholas Cabasilas' explanation, when commemorating the Theotokos and the saints, the priest gives thanks to God for them and does not make a petition for them, while his prayer has a character of petition when said for the other departed. This comment, however, Cabasilas applies only to the liturgy of Saint John Chrysostom, while in the liturgy of Saint Basil the Great, in his opinion, there is no clear division between the prayers of thanksgiving and the prayers of intercession.[156]

"All Creation Rejoices in Thee,
O Full of Grace." Icon.
Beginning of 16th c.

At the time when, following the exclamation "Especially for our most holy . . . ," the priest continues to read the prayer of intercession, the choir in the liturgy of Saint John Chrysostom usually sings the hymn "It is truly meet to bless thee, O Theotokos." On days of great feasts another hymn called the "*zadostoinik*" is sung in the place of "It is truly meet," consisting of the irmos of the ninth ode of the canon dedicated to the feast's celebrated event. In the liturgy of Saint Basil the Great, most often another hymn to the Theotokos is sung— "All of creation rejoices in thee, O full of grace."[157]

Following the commemoration of the Theotokos and saints, the celebrant commemorates the ecclesial authorities. In the practice of the Russian Orthodox Church, His Holiness the Patriarch and the ruling hierarch of the diocese in which the church is located are commemorated. In the practice of some other local churches (in particular, churches of the Patriarchate of Constantinople), the celebrant does not commemorate the local churches but rather the diocesan hierarch

---

[155]"Memory Eternal" is also not sung for the departed saints, with the exception of the order for the Triumph of Orthodoxy performed in cathedrals on the first Sunday of Great Lent.

[156]Nicholas Cabasilas, *Commentary* 33.7–9; see pp. 83–85 in trans. Hussey and McNulty.

[157]The appearance of the hymn to the Theotokos in this part of the liturgy dates to the tenth century, while "It is truly meet" became normative near the last quarter of the 14th century. The system of *zadostoiniki* was definitively formed by the 16th century. See Taft, *Diptychs*, 118–119.

alone is commemorated; the head of the church is commemorated only during hierarchical services. This difference is connected to a difference in emphasis: the Russian practice emphasizes the unity of the local churches consisting of many dioceses, while the Greek practice emphasizes the fullness of the ecclesial reality on the level of a single diocese headed by the local bishop, who is in communion with other bishops.

Following the commemoration of the patriarch and the ruling hierarch, the choir sings "And all mankind" (Sl. *I vsekh, i vsia/*"And all and all"; Gr. *Kai pantōn kai pasōn*). In this case "all" (*pantōn*) refers to all Christian men, while "all" (*pasōn*) refers to all Christian women. But another understanding of this exclamation is also possible: "And all bishops and all dioceses."

Next comes the commemoration of the civil authorities. The prayer for the civil authorities is an ancient tradition of the Church. Saint Paul spoke about the need for such a prayer: "Therefore I exhort first of all that supplications, prayers, intercessions, and giving of thanks be made for all men, for kings and all who are in authority, that we may lead a quiet and peaceable life in all godliness and reverence" (1 Tim 2.1–2). In the contemporary liturgy, the prayer for the civil authorities reproduces Saint Paul's exhortation word for word. In the practice of countries where the monarchy is preserved, the name of the monarch is commemorated in the litanies and in the prayer following the consecration of the holy gifts. Where a democratic or other form of governance exists, as a rule, the "authorities and armed forces" are commemorated, as the two pillars of stability of the state and society that guarantee Christians "a quiet and peaceable life."

The prayer for the civil authorities is not omitted in countries in which the civil authorities take a hostile position vis-à-vis the Church. As it is well known, in the times of Saint Paul, the "kings" for whom he gave exhortation to pray were not Christians by any means: in the first three centuries following the birth of Christ, the Roman emperors were persecutors of Christians. But the Church prayed for them, and apologists of the second and third centuries bear witness to this fact.

In the liturgy of Saint Basil the Great the prayer of intercession is considerably longer than the corresponding prayer in the liturgy of Saint John Chrysostom. It contains separate petitions for the universal Church, the church in which the divine service takes place, the serving clergy, those who labor in the church, and those who are "in the caverns and pits of the earth" (see Heb 11.38)—that is, for the monks and hermits. Following the prayer for the king, "our brethren in the palace" (i.e. in the senate or parliament) and "all the armed forces" are specially commemorated.[158] The prayer is offered not only for those present in the church but also for those who are absent for a good cause. Separate petitions are made to God for married couples, infants, the young, the aged, apostates from the Church, those vexed by unclean spirits, widows, orphans, captives, the sick, those in bondage, and those who are in need. The priest prays for those whom he has forgotten through forgetfulness or the multitude of names:

> Again we entreat Thee: remember, O Lord, Thy Holy, Catholic, and Apostolic Church, which is from end to end of the universe; give peace to her whom Thou hast obtained with the precious Blood of Thy Christ; also preserve this holy house until the end of the world. Remember, O Lord, those who offered Thee these Gifts, and those for whom and through whom they offered them, and their intentions.
>
> Remember, O Lord, those who bring offerings and do good in Thy holy Churches, and those who remember the poor; reward them with Thy rich and heavenly gifts; for their earthly, temporal, and corruptible gifts, do Thou grant them Thy heavenly ones, eternal and incorruptible.
>
> Remember, O Lord, those who are in the deserts, mountains, caverns, and pits of the earth.
>
> Remember, O Lord, those who live in chastity and godliness, in austerity and holiness of life.
>
> Remember, O Lord, this country and all civil authorities; grant them a secure and lasting peace; speak good things into their hearts concerning Thy Church and all Thy people, that we, in their tranquility, may lead a calm and peaceful life in all godliness and sanctity. Remember, O Lord, every principality and authority; our brothers who serve in the government and the armed forces. Preserve the good in goodness, and make the evil be good by Thy goodness.
>
> Remember, O Lord, the people here present and also those who are absent for honorable reasons. Have mercy on them and on us according to the multitude of Thy mercies. Fill their treasuries with every good thing; preserve their marriages in peace and harmony; raise the infants; guide the young; support the aged; encourage the faint-hearted; reunite the separated; lead back those who are in error and join them to Thy Holy, Catholic, and Apostolic Church; free those who are held captive by unclean spirits; sail with those who sail; travel with those who travel by land and by air; defend the widows; protect the

---

[158]Many modern translations alter this, e.g. the OCA priest's service book commemorates: "all civil authorities, and [those who serve in] the armed forces."—*Ed.*

orphans; free the captives; heal the sick. Remember, O God, those who are in courts, in mines, in exile, in harsh labor, and those in any kind of affliction, necessity, or distress.

Remember, O Lord our God, all those who entreat Thy great loving-kindness; those who love us and those who hate us; those who have asked us to pray for them, unworthy though we be; and remember all Thy people O Lord, our God. Pour out Thy rich mercy upon all of them, granting them all the petitions which are for their salvation. And remember, Thyself, O God, all those whom we have not remembered through ignorance, forgetfulness, or the multitude of names; since Thou knowest the name and age of each, even from his mother's womb. For Thou, O Lord, art the Helper of the helpless, the Hope of the hopeless, the Savior of the bestormed, the Haven of the voyager, the Physician of the sick.

Be all things to all men, O Thou who knowest each man and his request, his home and his need.

Deliver this city (*or* village, *or* holy habitation), O Lord, and every city and country, from famine, plague, earthquake, flood, fire, sword, invasion by enemies, and civil war.

In the words of Archimandrite Kyprian (Kern), "the prayers of intercession, especially in the liturgy of Saint Basil the Great, show what significance the Church imparts to all that is being perfected in the life of man and how she enters deeply into the details of people's daily lives. Not a single aspect of the life of man is considered to be a trifle; rather, the entire Church offers care and concern."[159] The prayer of petition in the liturgy of Saint Basil the Great "gathers and unites the entire cosmic, ecclesiological, and eschatological content of the Eucharist."[160]

Next, in the liturgy of Saint Basil the Great the priest offers a petition for the Church, the episcopacy, and priesthood, and adds a special prayer for himself:

Remember, O Lord, all the Orthodox Episcopate, who rightly divide the word of Thy truth.

Remember, O Lord, my unworthiness also, by the multitude of Thy compassions; forgive my every transgression, both voluntary and involuntary. Because of my sins, do not withhold the grace of Thy Holy Spirit from these Gifts here set forth.

---

[159]Kyprian (Kern), *The Eucharist*, 271.
[160]Schmemann, *Eucharist*, 239.

Remember, O Lord, the priesthood, the diaconate in Christ, and every order of the clergy. Let none of us who stand about Thy holy altar be put to confusion. Visit us with Thy loving-kindness, O Lord; manifest Thyself to us through Thy rich compassions. Grant us seasonable and healthful weather; send gentle showers upon the earth so that it may bear fruit; bless the crown of the year with Thy goodness. Prevent schisms among the churches; pacify the ragings of the pagans; quickly destroy the uprisings of heresies by the power of Thy Holy Spirit. Receive us all into Thy Kingdom, showing us to be sons of the light and sons of the day. Grant us Thy peace and Thy love, O Lord our God, for Thou hast given all things to us.

In the liturgy of Saint John Chrysostom, the prayer of intercession concludes with a petition for the city in which the liturgy is celebrated, for other cities and countries and "those who in faith dwell therein," for "those who travel by land, by sea, and by air, the sick, the suffering, captives, and their salvation," and also for those who labor in the Church "who bear fruit and do good works in thy holy churches" and those who are mindful of the poor ("who remember the needy").

Preparation for Communion:
The Lord's Prayer; "Holy Things for the Holy"

Following the conclusion of the prayer of intercession, the part of the liturgy begins that directly prepares the faithful for the mystery of holy communion. The deacon pronounces a litany of supplication, and in the liturgy of Saint John Chrysostom the priest reads the prayer of preparation:

Unto Thee we commend our whole life and our hope, O Master who lovest mankind. We ask Thee, and pray Thee, and supplicate Thee: make us worthy to partake of the heavenly and awesome mysteries of this sacred and spiritual table with a pure conscience: for remission of sins, for forgiveness of transgressions, for the communion of the Holy Spirit, for the inheritance of the kingdom of heaven, for boldness towards Thee, but not for judgment or condemnation.

In the liturgy of Saint Basil the Great a different prayer is read, which is thematically connected to Saint Paul's teaching concerning communion. In this prayer the faithful, through the lips of the priest, ask God to teach them to perfect "holiness in the fear of God" (1 Cor 7.1), that Christ may dwell in their hearts (see Eph 3.17) and that they may become temples of the Holy Spirit (see 1 Cor 6.19). The prayer contains a petition that none of the faithful might be guilty of sinning against the body and blood of the Lord, and that none of the communicants might become infirm or sick through partaking unworthily (see 1 Cor 11.27–30). Rather, the worthy partaking of communion ought to be for Christians a provision for life eternal, and the guarantee of an acceptable defense at the dread judgment seat of Christ, and of those eternal blessings which God has prepared for those who love him (see 1 Cor 2.9).

While the priest says this prayer, the deacon says the litany that begins with the words, "Having called to remembrance all the saints, again and again, in peace let us pray to the Lord." The expression "all the saints" (*pantōn tōn hagiōn*) probably refers to those saints who were commemorated by the priest directly following the consecration of the holy gifts. The Slavonic translator understood the Greek text in this way. But a different understanding is also possible: as in the case of the exclamation "Blessed is the entry of thy saints," "*tōn hagiōn*" may refer to the impersonal "*ta hagia.*" In this case, "*ta hagia*"—"the holy things"—would signify all the holy events and divine benefits that are mentioned during the anaphora.

The litany concludes with the priest's exclamation, "And make us worthy, O Master, that with boldness and without condemnation we may dare to call on Thee, the heavenly God, as Father, and to say." The prayer "Our Father" follows, which in the Greek practice is read by one of the faithful or by the whole congregation together, but in Russian practice it is sung by the choir.

The recitation of the Lord's Prayer during the Eucharist is an extremely ancient tradition, established, in particular, in the description of the Eucharist by Saint Cyril of Jerusalem (around 380).[161] The prayer's inclusion in the liturgy is stipulated not only by the fact that it was given by the Lord himself, but also by the special meaning that the words "Give us this day our daily bread" acquire in the context of the Eucharist. The interpretation of "daily bread"[162] as the eucharistic bread is encountered beginning in the third century both in the East and West. In the third century, the Western church writer Saint Cyprian of Carthage wrote

The Five Loaves and Two Fish. Floor Mosaic. Galilee. 5th c.

---

[161]Cyril of Jerusalem, *Mystagogical Catecheses* 5.11–18 (Church, PPS).

[162]The Greek word *hyperousion* (translated as "daily" in English) can also mean "supersubstantial" (*hyper* + *ousia*).—*Ed.*

concerning the petition "Give us this day our daily bread" in his book *On the Lord's Prayer*:

> For Christ is the bread of life (Jn 6.48), and thus he is not the bread of anybody but ourselves . . . since Christ is the bread of those who participate in his body. Moreover we ask that this bread should be given to us daily lest we who are in Christ, and receive his Eucharist daily as the food of salvation, should be prevented by the interposition of some terrible sin and so be separated from the body of Christ, inhibited from and not receiving the heavenly bread. This he himself taught when he said: "I am the bread of life which came down from heaven. If anyone should eat of my bread he shall live forever. And the bread which I shall give is my flesh for the life of the world" (Jn 6.51). Thus, when he says that anyone who eats of his bread will live forever, so making it clear that those who participate in his body and receive the Eucharist, communicating by right, are those who live. . . .[163]

In the Christian East a similar understanding of "daily bread" is found, in particular, in Saint Cyril of Jerusalem:

> This common bread is not super-substantial bread, but this holy bread is super-substantial, that is, appointed for the substance of the soul. For this bread goeth not into the belly and is cast out into the draught (see Mt 15.17) but is diffused through all thou art, for the benefit of body and soul. But by this day, he means, "each day."[164]

We encounter a similar interpretation in the later church fathers, in particular, in Saint John of Damascus:

> This bread is the first-fruits of the bread to come, which is the supersubstantial bread. For *supersubstantial* either means that which is to come, that is, the bread of the world to come, or it means that which is taken for the sustenance of our substance. So, whether it be the one or the other, the term will be suitably applicable to the body of the Lord, because, since the flesh of the Lord was conceived of the life-giving Spirit, it is itself life-giving spirit—for "that which is born of the Spirit is spirit" (Jn 3.6). I say this not to detract from the nature of the body, but because I wish to show its life-giving and divine character.[165]

[163]Cyprian of Carthage, *On the Lord's Prayer* 18 (Stewart-Sykes, PPS).
[164]Cyril of Jerusalem, *Mystagogical Catecheses* 5.15 (Church, PPS).
[165]John of Damascus, *An Exact Exposition of the Orthodox Faith* 4.13 (Chase, CUA).

The singing of the prayer "Our Father" concludes with the priest's exclamation, "For thine is the kingdom, and the power, and the glory of the Father, and of the Son, and of the Holy Spirit, now and ever, and unto the ages of ages." The choir sings, "Amen." This is the way the Lord's Prayer ends in the Orthodox tradition during divine services performed by a priest. In the absence of a priest (for example, when an individual believer says the "Our Father" at home), the concluding doxology is not pronounced at all. In this, the Orthodox practice of reading the Lord's Prayer differs, in particular, from the Catholic reading, in which it is customary to conclude the prayer with the same doxology contained in the Gospel: "For thine is the kingdom and the power and the glory forever. Amen" (Mt 6.13).

Supposedly this doxology was not present in the original text of the Gospel according to Matthew, and the Lord's Prayer ended with the words "but deliver us from the evil one." The doxology was included in the text of the Lord's Prayer in several Gospel manuscripts under the influence of early Christian liturgical practice[166] (in contemporary critical editions of the New Testament it is absent in the basic text and included only in the critical apparatus). In the Christian East this doxology was already added to the Lord's Prayer at the end of the fourth century, but not universally: it is mentioned by Saint John Chrysostom,[167] but not by Saint Cyril of Jerusalem.[168] Subsequently in the West it preserved its original form, while in the East it acquired a trinitarian character. In the latter form it is encountered in all the known liturgical manuscripts, beginning with the Barberini Euchologion (end of the eighth century). This indicates that in the Orthodox Church the Lord's Prayer, addressed to God the Father, is perceived to pertain also to the two other Persons of the Holy Trinity—the Son and the Holy Spirit.

Following the Lord's Prayer and the concluding doxology, the priest pronounces, "Peace be unto all." The choir responds, "And to your spirit." The deacon exclaims, "Bow your heads unto the Lord" (the exclamation is encountered in this form only in the liturgy, while it takes the form "Let us bow our heads unto the Lord" in the order of vespers and matins). While the faithful stand with bowed heads, the priest reads a prayer whose text is different in the liturgies of Saints Basil the Great and John Chrysostom not only in form, but also in content. In the liturgy of Saint Basil the Great, the prayer bears a character of preparation before the communion of the holy mysteries:

---

[166]The earliest witness of the doxology following the Lord's Prayer is contained in the *Didache* 8.2.
[167]John Chrysostom, *Homilies on Matthew* 19.10 (PG 57:282; *NPNF*¹ 2:136–137).
[168]Cyril of Jerusalem, *Mystagogical Catecheses* 5.15–16 (Church, PPS).

O Master, Lord, Father of compassions and God of every consolation: bless, sanctify, guard, strengthen, and confirm those who have bowed their heads to Thee. Withdraw them from every evil deed; apply them to every good work and make them worthy to partake without condemnation of these, Thy most pure and life-creating mysteries, for remission of sins and for the communion of the Holy Spirit.

In Saint John's liturgy, the prayer bears a character of thanksgiving and intercession; the thematic link with communion is not present in the prayer:

We give thanks unto Thee, O King invisible, who by Thy measureless power didst make all things, and in the greatness of Thy mercy didst bring all things from non-existence into being. Look down from heaven, O Master, upon those who have bowed their heads unto Thee, for they have not bowed down unto flesh and blood, but unto Thee, the awesome God. Do Thou Thyself, O Master, distribute these Gifts here offered unto all of us for good, according to the individual need of each; sail with those who sail, travel with those who travel by land and by air; heal the sick, O Thou who art the physician of our souls and bodies.

In both cases the prayer concludes with the exclamation, "Through the grace and compassions and love for mankind of thine only-begotten Son. . . ." Following the exclamation, the choir sings, "Amen." The deacon exclaims, "Let us attend!" And the priest pronounces one of the most ancient eucharistic formulae: "The holy things are for the holy."[169] This formula is encountered at the end of the fourth century in the works of Saint Cyril of Jerusalem[170] and numerous later sources, including the earliest known liturgical manuscripts.

The meaning of the exclamation "The holy things are for the holy" (*Ta hagia tois hagiois*) is subject to different interpretations, depending on the understanding of the term "holy" in the plural case. In the Acts of the Apostles, members of the community of Christ's disciples in Jerusalem (see Acts 9.13) were called "saints"; in the epistles of Saint Paul this term is applied to the members of other communities (see 1 Cor 16.1; 2 Cor 1.1, 13.12) and to all those who believe in Christ (see Rom 16.2). The word "saints" is used with the same meaning as the word "brethren" (see

---

[169]The Slavonic *Sviataia* is in the dual (number), used in the Slavonic language to denote two objects (in this case the bread and wine). In the Byzantine Greek language the dual number was not present. It is not found in the Russian language with the exception of the words "*dvoye*" and "*oba*"—inherited from the Slavonic language and subject to special rules of declension.

[170]Cyril of Jerusalem, *Mystagogical Catecheses* 5.19 (Church, PPS).

Rom 16.14–15). From this derives the most literal interpretation of the exclamation "The holy things are for the holy"—the communion of the holy mysteries is admissible only for persons who believe in Christ and have received holy baptism; the catechumens or persons not belonging to the Church should not be admitted to communion. Such an understanding of the exclamation is confirmed by the overall character of the liturgy of the faithful as a divine service in which only the baptized members of the ecclesial community participate. Concerning the fact that it is not possible to receive communion for one who does not have faith and who has not been cleansed in the waters of baptism, Saint Justin Martyr wrote: "And this food is called among us Εὐχαριστία [the Eucharist], of which no one is allowed to partake but the man who believes that the things which we teach are true, and who has been washed with the washing that is for the remission of sins, and unto regeneration, and who is so living as Christ has enjoined."[171]

Saint Cyril of Jerusalem sees in the exclamation "The holy things are for the holy" an indication of the holiness communicated to the faithful through the communion of the holy mysteries and through the ascetic way of life:

> After this the priest says, "The holy things are for the holy." Holy are the gifts presented, since they have been visited by the Holy Spirit; holy are you also, having been vouchsafed the Holy Spirit; the holy things therefore correspond to the holy persons. Then ye say, "One is holy, one is Lord, Jesus Christ." For truly One is holy, by nature holy; we, too, are holy, but not by nature, only by participation, and discipline, and prayer.[172]

The exclamation "The holy things are for the holy" may also be interpreted as a call to holiness. In a source from the second century we find an expanded variant of this exclamation: "He who is holy, let him draw near, and he who is not, let him change himself."[173] In the tenth century Saint Symeon the New Theologian interpreted the exclamation "The holy things are for the holy" to indicate that Christians are called to holiness and repentance:

> "The holy things are for the holy!" . . . So, how is this to be understood? He who is not holy is not worthy? Not at all. But he who does not confess daily the secrets of his heart, he who does not show necessary repentance for these secrets . . . he who does not weep constantly . . . is not worthy. But he who

[171]Justin Martyr, *First Apology* 66 (*ANF* 1:185).
[172]Cyril of Jerusalem, *Mystagogical Catecheses* 5.19 (Church, PPS).
[173]*Didache* 10.6 [Cf. Rev 22.11.—*Ed.*].

does all this and leads his life in groanings and tears is fully worthy not only on a feast day, but on every day, although it is bold to say, from the very beginning of his repentance and conversion to be in communion with these divine mysteries.[174]

In the opinion of Saint John Chrysostom, the exclamation "The holy things are for the holy" contains, together with a call to holiness, a prohibition of communion for persons who have not prepared for communion in a worthy manner:

> These things have been given to the holy. This the Deacon also proclaims when he calls on the holy; even by this call searching the faults of all . . . that no person should come to the spiritual fountain carelessly and in a chance way. . . . [L]ike some herald lifting up his hand on high, standing aloft, conspicuous to all, and after that awful silence crying out aloud, he [i.e., the priest] invites some, and some he forbids. . . . For that voice, falling on our ears, just like a hand, thrusts away and casts out some, and introduces and presents others. . . . For when he says, "The holy things are for the holy," he means this: "If any is not holy, let him not draw near." He does not simply say, "free from sins," but, "holy." For it is not merely freedom from sins which makes a man holy, but also the presence of the Spirit, and the wealth of good works.[175]

While exclaiming "The holy things are for the holy," the priest takes the lamb with both hands and lifts it up. The meaning of this gesture, which had spread nearly universally no later than the sixth or seventh century,[176] is to ceremonially show to the faithful the consecrated bread which has become the body of Christ. In the excerpt cited above, Saint John Chrysostom especially notes that the priest should be "seen by all" at the moment of the pronouncement of the exclamation "The holy things are for the holy." In the contemporary practice of the Russian Orthodox Church (with the exception of the week of Pascha), this meaning is lost, since the royal doors are closed and the curtain is drawn closed before the moment of the raising of the lamb. It would be more correct and appropriate to the meaning of this moment in the liturgy to close the royal doors and draw the curtain after the exclamation "The holy things are for the holy," not before it.

---

[174]Symeon the New Theologian, *Catechetical Discourse* 4.604–616 (SC 96).

[175]John Chrysostom, *Homilies on Hebrews* 17.8 (PG 63:132–133; *NPNF*[1] 14:449–450)._

[176]Robert F. Taft, *A History of the Liturgy of St. John Chrysostom*, vol. 5, *The Precommunion Rites*, Orientalia Christiana Analecta 261 (Rome: Pontificium Institutum Studiorum Orientalium, 2000), 209.

After placing the lamb onto the diskos, the priest divides it into four parts. The part with the inscription XC is used for the communion of the clergy, while the parts with the inscription HI and KA are used for the communion of the laity. The priest places the part with the inscription IC into the chalice as he says the words, "The fullness of the Holy Spirit." In this way, the body and blood of Christ are united in one chalice, from which they will later be imparted to the faithful. This action symbolizes the unity of each believer with the risen Christ, which is achieved as a result of communion, by the action of the Holy Spirit.[177]

After this, "warmth"—hot water—is poured into the chalice. The custom of uniting water with wine is of ancient origin: both Jews and Greeks mixed wine with water.[178] The symbolism of this action (and the addition of water into the wine during the proskomedia) is connected with the reference to water pouring out together with blood from the Savior's pierced side (see Jn 19.34). Warm water is used in order to signify that the body of Christ, even following his death on the cross, remained life-bearing: for this reason blood and water flowed from him (which would not have happened if his body had been dead and his blood cold).[179]

At this moment, according to the present practice, priests in large parish churches and cathedrals pour the blood of Christ into several chalices for the subsequent communion of the laity. According to the liturgical practice of the Russian Church in recent years, sometimes in very large cathedrals an enormous chalice containing a volume of three, five, or nine liters may be used. From an aesthetic perspective, the use of such a chalice is laden with a number of practical inconveniences, not to mention the fact that a chalice half the height of a human being does not correspond with the liturgical practice of the church over the span of many centuries, represented in icons and frescoes. At the great entrance two priests must carry the chalice because a single priest does not have sufficient strength to hold it up. To receive communion from such a high and heavy chalice is also extremely awkward. The pouring of the holy blood into a number of chalices increases the risk of spilling it onto the altar table or antimension.

As a rule, eucharistic chalices preserved from the Byzantine period hold no more than one liter (about one quart) of wine. In the ancient Church, several chalices were used when there were a large number of communicants. They were filled with wine at the same time and carried out of the sanctuary at the time of

---

[177] Ibid., 432–434.

[178] The contemporary Greek term for wine—*krasi*—originates from the ancient Greek *krasis,* which means "mixture" (of water and wine).

[179] Taft, *Precommunion Rites,* 485.

the great entrance.[180] Numerous sources bear witness to this, the first of which is Saint Maximus the Confessor (seventh century) who wrote of several loaves and several chalices used in the Eucharist; he noted especially that these should be odd in number.[181] The use of several chalices was not at all perceived as a violation of the unity of the eucharistic chalice: from a theological point of view, the eucharistic chalice still remained one, even if wine was poured into several chalices. In large cathedrals it would be more expedient to return to the ancient practice of using several chalices from the start of the liturgy.

It is also necessary to say something about the holy lamb, which in contemporary practice is usually single, even when the number of communicants may be in the thousands. When the liturgy was performed in the ancient Church, several diskoi with several holy lambs could be used: these diskoi were carried into the sanctuary by deacons during the great entrance. In particular, a fresco dating to 1360–1370 in the Peribleptos Monastery in Mystras (Greece) serves as a confirmation of this. In it, the great entrance is depicted in the form of a procession of angels carrying the diskoi in their hands or on their heads.

COMMUNION

Communion of the Clergy

A special volume dedicated to the sacraments of the Church will describe the significance of the mystery of the Eucharist, the theological and moral meaning of communion, and the question of how often Orthodox Christians should receive communion.[182] At this point our discussion will be limited to describing the order of the communion of clergy and laity during the divine liturgy. We will also make note of several differences in the practice of communion between the Orthodox and Catholics.

In contemporary practice, the sacrament of communion takes place in two receptions. First, the clergy commune in the sanctuary, and then the laity commune

---

[180]See Ivan Karabinov, "The Holy Chalice in the Liturgy of the Presanctified Gifts" [in Russian], *Christian reading* 6 (1915): 746–747.

[181]Maximus the Confessor, *Questions and Doubts* 41 (PG 90:820a).

[182]The fifth and final volume of this series will be dedicated to describing the sacraments of the Church.—*Ed.*

outside of the sanctuary, near the ambon. During the communion of the clergy, the royal doors are closed and the curtain is drawn (except in the week of Pascha). This leads to the perception among the laity that this moment in the liturgy consists of a pause or break. Some people begin to have conversations, while others even leave the church, thinking that the main part of the service is over.

This perception is reinforced by what takes place in the choir at this time. The Typikon prescribes that the choir sing a communion verse—a specially selected psalm verse—at the time of the clergy communion. But since the communion of the clergy takes no less than five minutes, and when there is a large number of clergy it may last considerably longer (fifteen to twenty minutes), there is a pause in the liturgical order after the completion of the singing of the communion verse, which seems to be filled differently in every church. In the Russian Church in the synodal period, the tradition arose of performing a "concert" at this moment—an extensive choral work comprising several parts and written in the Italian style with elements of polyphony, alternating forte and piano, and fast and slow tempos. There is nothing more foreign to the spirit of the Orthodox liturgy than the performance of a "concert" during the communion of the clergy. The concerts of Bortniansky and other ecclesial composers of the nineteenth century ought to be expelled from the confines of the divine services: the most appropriate context for them are concerts of spiritual music in churches at times when divine services are not being served, or in concert halls.

In several churches a homily is given at the time of the communion verse. But it should be acknowledged that this moment—when the clergy is communing in the sanctuary and the laity outside the sanctuary is awaiting the deacon's exit with the eucharistic chalice—is the least appropriate time for a homily to be given. This is because the entire liturgy of the faithful is a preparation for communion, while the homily thematically pertains to the gospel excerpt read during the liturgy of the catechumens. Unless the homily directly relates to the mystery of communion, giving a homily at the communion verse distracts the faithful from prayerful preparation for the mystery, which is the purpose of the liturgy.

When it is necessary to somehow use the pause during clergy communion, the most appropriate way, as is done in many churches, is to fill it with the reading of prayers from the "Order of Preparation for Holy Communion." Although they are not a part of the liturgy, these prayers direct the minds of the faithful to the greatness of the mystery of the Eucharist and help them prepare for a spiritual and bodily union with Christ.

The communion of the clergy is preceded by the senior priest reading the prayers "I believe, O Lord, and I confess . . . ," "Of thy mystical supper . . . ," and "May the communion. . . ." The clergy in the sanctuary first commune of the body of Christ in strict hierarchical order: first the senior priest, then other priests, then deacons. The clergy commune of the blood of Christ in this same order. The priests independently take from the altar table the particles of the body of Christ and drink three times from the chalice. Communion is imparted to the deacons by one of the priests. If the service is performed by a hierarch, he first communes of the body and blood of Christ, and then imparts communion to the priests and deacons.

Having received communion, the clergy leave the area near the altar table and read the "Prayers after Communion." According to tradition, the paschal hymns and troparia "Having beheld the resurrection of Christ," "Shine, shine, O New Jerusalem," and "O great and most holy Pascha" are read.

Following communion, the priest wipes his mouth and hands and then takes the antidoron[183] and *zapivka*—wine mixed with hot water. According to the present tradition, the junior clergy approach the senior clergy and congratulate them on having received the holy mysteries. In cathedrals and during hierarchical services, when there is a large number of clergy serving, this custom lengthens the already extremely long pause that takes place during the communion of the clergy in the sanctuary.

The communion of the laity begins with the opening of the royal doors and the curtain. The deacon emerges from the sanctuary bearing the eucharistic chalice and exclaiming, "In the fear of God, and with faith and love, draw near." The choir sings, "Blessed is he that comes in the name of the Lord. God is the Lord and has revealed himself to us." The priest then reads the prayers, "I believe, O Lord, and I confess," "Of thy mystical supper, O Son of God," and "May the communion." In churches of several local Orthodox churches these prayers are read aloud by the entire congregation; recently this tradition has been seen in churches of the Russian Church as well. During the communion of the laity the choir sings many times, "Receive the body of Christ, taste the fountain of immortality."

When giving communion to a layman, the clergy of the Greek Church pronounce a short formula: "The body and blood of Christ." In the Russian Church the Typikon prescribes the more extensive formula: "The servant of God (name)

---

[183]Antidoron (literally, "in place of the gifts") is the name given to the bread that remains from the prosphora from which the lamb was cut for communion. In the practice of the Greek Church, the antidoron is given to the faithful after the divine liturgy. In the Russian Church, particles of the antidorion are usually given to the faithful who receive communion. Despite what its name suggests, the antidoron in no way replaces communion, because it is not the body of Christ but only blessed bread.

partakes of the most pure body and precious blood of our Lord and God and Savior Jesus Christ unto the remission of his/her sins and unto life everlasting. Amen."[184]

In contemporary Orthodox practice, the clergy commune by receiving a particle of the body of Christ in the right hand and drinking the blood of Christ three times from the eucharistic chalice. In the ancient Church, the laity communed in the exact same way. The words of Saint Basil the Great in particular bear witness to this: "And even in the church, when the priest gives the portion, the recipient takes it with complete power over it, and so lifts it to his lips with his own hand."[185] Saint Cyril of Jerusalem gave detailed instructions to the laity on receiving the body of Christ in their hands:

> Approaching, therefore, come not with thy wrists extended, or thy fingers open; but make thy left hand as if a throne for thy right, which is on the eve of receiving the King. And having hollowed thy palm, receive the body of Christ, saying after it, "Amen." Then after thou hast with carefulness hallowed thine eyes by the touch of the holy body, partake thereof; giving heed lest thou lose any of it. . . . Then after having partaken of the body of Christ, approach also to the cup of his blood; not stretching forth thine hands, but bending and saying in the way of worship and reverence, "Amen," be thou hallowed by partaking also of the blood of Christ. And while the moisture is still upon thy lips, touching it with thine hands, hallow both thine eyes and brow and the other senses. Then wait for the prayer, and give thanks unto God, who hath accounted thee worthy of so great mysteries.[186]

Saint Cyril indicates an interesting custom which no longer exists: to touch one's eyes with the particle of the body of Christ and then to moisten the eyes, face, and other organs of the senses with moisture from the blood of Christ. The saint calls the communicant to be especially careful and cautiously to consider the sanctity of the body and blood of Christ. This warning remains in contemporary practice in the form of the prohibition of making the sign of the cross before receiving communion: the one approaching the eucharistic chalice should not make the sign of the cross or make any other movements, so as to not bump the holy chalice.

---

[184]In practice, when there is a large flow of the faithful, the clergy of the Russian Church do not have time to pronounce the entire prescribed formula and in one way or another shorten it.

[185]Basil the Great, *Letter 93: To Caesaria, Concerning Communion* (PG 32:485a–b; *NPNF*[2] 8:179).

[186]Cyril of Jerusalem, *Mystagogical Catecheses* 5.21–22 (Church, PPS).

Subsequently, the practice of communing the laity changed and the use of a "spoon" (Sl. *lzhitsa*) was introduced to hold a small piece of the body of Christ and a small amount of the blood of Christ.[187] Some authors ascribe the introduction of the spoon in liturgical use to Saint John Chrysostom,[188] but there is no basis for this supposition. Protopresbyter John Meyendorff asserted that the spoon appeared in the seventh century.[189] Other scholars date the appearance of the spoon to the end of the eighth century.[190] Robert Taft notes that the first mention of the use of the spoon in Palestine dates to the seventh century, while Byzantine liturgical sources mention the spoon beginning in the second half of the ninth century, but only by the middle of the eleventh century is undisputed evidence seen of its use during the communion of the faithful. In the middle of the twelfth century, by the account of Patriarch Michael II (1143–1146), several bishops continued to commune the laity using the more ancient method—giving them a particle of the body of Christ in the hand and lifting the chalice to their lips.[191]

In the Orthodox Church all the faithful—not only the clergy—receive communion "in two species," receiving both the body and the blood of Christ. This constitutes a difference of the Byzantine rite from the Latin rite. In the Latin Mass, until the reforms of the Second Vatican Council, it was customary to commune only of the body of Christ. Communion under a single species was the universal practice of the Roman Catholic Church, established in the rules of the Council of Trent: "laymen, and clerics when not consecrating, are not obliged, by any divine precept, to receive the sacrament of the Eucharist under both species; and . . . neither can it by any means be doubted, without injury to faith, that communion under either species is sufficient for them unto salvation."[192] The Council of Trent

---

[187]Communion using a spoon causes apprehension among some parishioners who experience a feeling of squeamishness or fear of being infected with something during communion. In response, it is usually explained that the blood of Christ is of the greatest sanctity, and therefore no infection may be communicated through it. At the same time, in many Orthodox churches in the West, there exists the custom of more "hygienic" communion in which the communicant opens wide his or her mouth, the particle is overturned onto the tongue, the spoon is removed, and only then does the communicant close his or her mouth.

[188]Jacques Goar, *Euchologion sive rituale graecorum* (Venice, 1730; repr. Graz: Akademische Druck- und Verlagsanstalt, 1960), 130, note 179.

[189]See John Meyendorff, *Imperial Unity and Christian Divisions: The Church, 450–680 AD* (Crestwood, NY: St Vladimir's Seminary Press, 1989), 74.

[190]See, for example, Otto Nussbaum, *Die Handkommunion* (Cologne: Bachem, 1969), 28.

[191]Robert F. Taft, "Byzantine Communion Spoons: A Review of the Evidence," *Dumbarton Oaks Papers* 50 (1996): 209–238, at 237–238.

[192]Council of Trent, "Decree on Communion Under Both Species, and the Communion of Infants," Chapter 1, in *The Canons and Decrees of the Sacred and Oecumenical Council of Trent: Celebrated Under the Sovereign Pontiffs, Paul III, Julius III, and Pius IV*, trans. J. Waterworth (London: C. Dolman, 1848), 140–141.

declares anathema on those who doubt the salvific nature of communion under a single species: "If any one denieth, that Christ whole and entire . . . is received under the one species of bread; because that—as some falsely assert—he is not received, according to the institution of Christ himself, under both species; let him be anathema."[193] Following the Second Vatican Council, the practice of communion under one species ceased to be universally accepted, and in some Catholic churches the faithful now commune under two species, but this custom has not become universal.

Orthodox polemical literature, both Byzantine and Russian, is full of accusations against the Latins on account of the exclusion of the laity from the blood of Christ. From the Orthodox perspective, this exclusion has no justification either in holy Scripture or in the tradition of the Church. In the gospel, Christ imparts to his disciples not only his body with the words, "Take, eat . . . ," but also his blood with the words, "Drink of it, all of you. . . ." This is the very divine commandment that prescribes communion under two species. In all the ancient orders of the liturgy, including the Latin Mass, these words are preserved as being addressed to the entire community of the faithful. (Moreover, as has been stated, precisely these words in the Latin tradition are perceived to be the "formula of institution.") This approach, in which communion is perceived as a "duty" and is established as some kind of minimalized ritual form of the mystery that is "sufficient for salvation," is profoundly alien to the Orthodox tradition.

In the Latin rite, the tradition of communing the laity under one species resulted in a situation where communion ceased to be given to infants, as they are unable to eat solid food. This practice also received the approval of the Council of Trent, one of whose decrees proclaims, "little children, who have not attained to the use of reason, are not by any necessity obliged to the sacramental communion of the Eucharist: forasmuch as, having been regenerated by the by the laver of baptism, and being incorporated with Christ, they cannot, at that age, lose the grace which they have already acquired. . . ."[194] In this and other similar decrees, communion is again presented as a "necessity" and "duty"; moreover, the text leads to the notion that communion is necessary only for those who have lost the grace received in baptism.

The Orthodox tradition understands communion in a different way, not so much as the replenishing of lost baptismal grace, but as union with Christ, which

[193]Ibid., Chapter 4, Canon 3, in *Council of Trent*, 143.
[194]Ibid., Chapter 4, in *Council of Trent*, 142–143.

is salvific for each person regardless of age, level of reason, or degree of sinfulness. For this very reason in the ancient Church newly baptized infants were communed together with newly baptized adults. Saint Dionysius the Areopagite, referring to this ancient tradition, wrote that

> infants, despite their inability to understand the divine things, are nevertheless admitted . . . to the sacred symbols of the divine communion. In effect, the hierarch may be seen to teach divine things to those incapable of understanding them, to pass on the sacred traditions to those unable to grasp them. . . . Children raised up in accordance with holy precepts will acquire the habits of holiness. They will avoid all the errors and all the temptations of an unholy life. Understanding the truth of this, our divine leaders decided it was a good thing to admit children, though on condition that the parents of the child would entrust him to some good teacher who is himself initiated in the divine things and who coud provide religious teaching as the child's spiritual father and as the sponsor of salvation.[195]

The opinion that infants should not commune before attaining the age of reason is often based on the perceived need for the communicant to approach the mystery consciously. Some consider that communion without the consent of the one who receives is coercion of his conscience and a violation of his freedom. While this reasoning could be applicable to adults, it cannot apply at all to infants. Communion, according to the Orthodox understanding, is an integral part of Christian upbringing. The body and blood of Christ are the spiritual food necessary for the infant to grow "in spirit and truth." The mother does not require agreement from an infant to breastfeed him. The physical food is given to the infant as a gift, not because he asks for it, but because adults are conscious of the fact that the baby needs it. The same applies with spiritual food. It is given to the infant according to the decision of adults. Once he has reached the age of reason, he may keep this gift or reject it, having attained his freedom.

The communion of infants has remained in the Orthodox East until the present day and is a universally recognized tradition. Infants are communed under one species—the blood of Christ. This is done not because the communion of the blood of Christ is "sufficient for salvation," but for the simple reason that infants are not capable of swallowing solid food. Saint Philaret of Moscow even saw in the

---

[195]Dionysius the Areopagite, *Ecclesiastical Hierarchy* 7.3.11 (PG 3:565d–568b; Luibheid, CWS).

Savior's words, "Drink of it, all of you," an indication that it is not permissible to exclude infants from the communion of the blood of Christ:

> Take heed to yet another of the Lord's words of institutions, specifically concerning the holy cup: "Drink ye all of it" (see Mt 26.27). We must not fail to draw our attention to the little word "all," because light is found in every detail and wisdom in every sound of God's word. The Lord did not say concerning the mystical bread, "Take, eat ye all," and rightly so, since some are not able to "eat"—infants, for example. But concerning the mystical cup he said, "Drink ye all of it," and in this manner he removed all exceptions—it stands to reason, for those who live in the faith and unity of the Church. Notice that those who do not permit infants or youths, not having attained a certain age, to receive the holy mysteries deviate from the precision of the Lord's commandment, while the Orthodox Church, on the contrary, is faithful to the Lord's word when she offers the holy cup to infants, so that all may partake of it, even those who do not have the strength to eat, but are able only to drink.[196]

In the Orthodox Church, both laymen (beginning at seven years of age) and clergymen receive communion on an empty stomach. This is another way in which Orthodox practice differs from Catholic practice. The custom of communing on an empty stomach is linked with the widespread practice of celebrating the liturgy in the morning even when the Typikon prescribes its celebration in the evening: on Wednesdays and Fridays of Great Lent, and also on the eves of Christmas and Theophany, and on Holy Thursday and Holy Saturday.

Moreover, the Orthodox Church observes the ancient tradition of not permitting anyone, including clergymen, to commune more than once in a day. Unlike Catholic priests, who may celebrate several masses in one day, Orthodox clergymen have the right to celebrate the divine liturgy or to participate in its celebration not more than once in a period of twenty-four hours. In Orthodox churches in which two or three liturgies are celebrated in one day, the services are presided over accordingly by two or three different clergymen.

---

[196]Filaret (Drozdov), "Homily on the consecration of the Church of the Transfiguration of the Lord on Ordynka, 1836," in *Sermons and speeches in 5 volumes* [in Russian] (Moscow, 1873–1885), 4:39.

CONCLUSION OF THE LITURGY

Following the communion of the laity, the eucharistic chalice is carried into the altar and the particles that were taken out during proskomedia for the living and the departed are placed into it. The priest says, "Wash away, O Lord, the sins of those commemorated here, by thy precious blood, through the prayers of thy saints."[197] These words indicate that all members of the Church, for whom the liturgical prayer is offered—both the living and the departed—participate in a mystical manner in the Eucharist, even if they are not present in the church.

Then the priest blesses the faithful with the words, "O God, save thy people and bless thine inheritance." The choir sings a prayer which contains a thanksgiving for communion and a request that the Lord preserve the communicants in holiness. Then the priest raises the chalice and traces a cross with it over the antimension, quietly uttering the words, "Blessed is our God," then exclaiming, "Always, now and ever, and unto ages of ages." The choir responds "Amen" and sings:

> We have seen the true Light. We have received the heavenly Spirit. We have found the true Faith, worshiping the undivided Trinity, who has saved us.

The priest blesses the faithful with the chalice, following which it is transferred from the altar table to the table of oblation. The litany "Let us attend. Having partaken . . ." is read, in which the deacon calls the communicants to give thanks to God. At this time the priest reads the prayer of thanksgiving, which ends with the exclamation "For thou art our sanctification. . . ."[198]

This is followed by a proclamation that indicates the imminent conclusion of the liturgy: "Let us depart in peace."[199] The choir responds, "In the name of the Lord." The priest reads aloud the so-called prayer before the ambon,[200] which parallels several other prayers of the liturgy, and also several litanies.

Then, in the sanctuary, the priest reads a prayer addressed to Christ that summarizes the entire content of the liturgy. This is especially true of the prayer in the liturgy of Saint Basil the Great:

---

[197]In Greek practice this is done before the communion of the laity.—*Ed.*

[198]In practice, in parishes of the Russian Orthodox Church this prayer is read by the priest right after he communes; that is, before the communion of the laity.

[199]In contemporary practice this exclamation is made by the priest, or by the bishop in the hierarchical service, but in Byzantium it was made by the deacon.

[200]In the hierarchical or cathedral service this prayer is read by the junior priest, according to tradition [in Russian use, but not in Greek use—*Ed.*].

The mystery of Thy dispensation, O Christ our God, has been accomplished and perfected as far as it was in our power; for we have had the memorial of Thy death; we have seen the type of Thy Resurrection; we have been filled with Thine unending life; we have enjoyed Thine inexhaustible food, which in the world to come be well-pleased to grant to us all. . . .

With this prayer, the bridge is once again extended between the past, the present, and the future. A connection is established between the communion that takes place on earth and the one that the faithful will "more perfectly" partake of in the eschatological kingdom of God.

Illustration of Psalm 33.9: "Taste and see that the Lord is good!" Christ Feeding the Five Thousand with Five Loaves and Two Fishes. Chludov Psalter. Byzantium. c. 840–850.

Following the prayer, "Blessed be the name of the Lord, henceforth and forever more" (Ps 112.2) is sung three times. Following this, the Typikon prescribes the singing of Psalm 33, but in practice it is often omitted. The priest then blesses the people with the words, "The blessing of the Lord be upon you through his grace and love for mankind." The liturgy concludes with the dismissal and the singing of "Many Years" to the patriarch, the ruling hierarch, the rector, and the parishioners of the temple.

The blessing offered by the priest at the end of all divine services (with the exception of the hours) is called the "dismissal." In its contemporary form, the dismissal was formulated approximately in the fifteenth to sixteenth centuries.[201] The briefest form of the dismissal is "May Christ, our true God, through the prayers of his most-pure mother and all the saints, have mercy on us and save us, for he is good and the lover of mankind." But the liturgy never concludes with such a brief dismissal. On Sundays, before "Christ," the words "he who rose from the dead" are added, and on Christmas, the words "he who was born in a cave, and lay in a manger for our salvation" are added. On other feast days, words

Saints Joachim and Anna with the Theotokos. Fresco. Ferapontov Monastery. Beginning of 16th c.

---

[201]Uspenskii, *Orthodox Liturgy*, 317.

may be added at the beginning of the dismissal in accordance with the feast being celebrated.

Moreover, after the words "most-pure mother," it is customary to add the names of saints: on Monday, the heavenly bodiless hosts; on Tuesday, Saint John the Baptist; on Thursday, the holy apostles and Saint Nicholas; on Saturday, the apostles, martyrs, monastic saints, and all the saints. On Wednesday and Friday, before the name of the Theotokos, the words "by the power of the precious and life-giving cross" are added. On all days of the week, with the exception of great feasts, the name of the saint in whose honor the temple was consecrated and also the saints whose memory is celebrated on the given day are commemorated at the dismissal. At the dismissal of the liturgies of Saints Basil the Great and John Chrysostom, the names of these saints are commemorated respectively. Finally, according to the existing practice, the names of the parents of the Most-Holy Theotokos—Saints Joachim and Anna—are commemorated at every dismissal.[202]

In many churches, a homily is given after the dismissal and the singing of "Many Years" (if one was not given earlier after the reading of the gospel or after the communion verse). Then the priest offers the faithful the cross for veneration. At this time, the deacon consumes the remaining holy gifts at the table of oblation and carefully cleans the chalice and wipes it with a dry napkin.

In the practice of many parishes of the Russian Orthodox Church, "private" services are performed following the conclusion of the liturgy: baptisms, weddings, prayer services, akathists, panikhidas. Moreover, in some churches a prayer service is added to the liturgy directly following the dismissal and is even inserted into the liturgy before the dismissal. In this way, it ceases to be a separate private service and becomes a service intended for the entire community and to a considerable extent duplicates the liturgy. In particular, at such prayer services (molebens), the great litany may be pronounced and the gospel may be read. This has the effect of bringing the faithful back to the themes of the liturgy of the catechumens.

The various forms of "private" services will be discussed in a separate section. At this point we will simply pose the question: to what extent is it necessary and justified to serve molebens, akathists, and panikhidas following the liturgy?

---

[202]Up to the seventeenth century, the names of Saints Joachim and Anna were a part of the dismissal on Saturdays, but in the Slavonic Priest's Service Book, published during the rule of Patriarch Job in 1602, the dismissal on Saturday was set forth as an aggregate of the dismissals of the entire week. As a result of this, the names of Saints Joachim and Anna were transferred to the dismissals of all the other days of the week. See Uspenskii, *Orthodox Liturgy*, 318.

The meaning and content of the liturgy do not suppose that other services will be performed following its conclusion. On the contrary, all other divine services prescribed by the Typikon, whether vespers, matins, or the hours, are seen to be a preparation for the liturgy and are performed either in the evening on the eve of the liturgy, or in the morning, before it begins. The liturgy is the conclusion of the entire cycle of divine services of the daily cycle and has such an all-encompassing character that all other additional prayers following its conclusion are out of place. The serving of molebens and panikhidas, and also the reading of akathists, should be performed either outside of the divine services, or at the end of the evening service, or before the liturgy, not afterwards.

Bishop Afanasy (Sakharov), a well-known expert on the Typikon, wrote about this. He commented on the custom of performing panikhidas after the liturgy:

> This custom has no basis in the Typikon. The Typikon does not make provision for the performance of any other services right after the liturgy. The liturgy is the culmination of the daily cycle of services. All other services prepare the faithful for participation in, or presence at, the performance of the mystery of the Eucharist. . . . At the liturgy . . . the joy of the Christian is greater than any festal joy; here is a celebration greater than any festal celebration.[203]

According to the saint, the Church desires that "the faithful return to their homes, thanking God, with a paschal mood" after the liturgy. The celebration of lengthy prayers for the departed following the liturgy does not correspond with the meaning of the liturgy "and indicates that we do not sufficiently understand and appreciate the meaning of this divine service and the great mystery celebrated in it." Bishop Afanasy emphasizes that the Typikon "supposes that all prayers, whatever they may be on a given day, should be completed before the liturgy." The Typikon "allows for the possibility of the celebration of panikhidas either at 'another time,' not connected to the divine service, or only following vespers or matins, but in no way following the liturgy."[204]

---

[203]Bishop Afanasii (Sakharov), *Concerning the commemoration of the departed according to the canons of the Orthodox Church* [in Russian] (St Petersburg: Satis, 1995), 123.

[204]Ibid., 123, 125.

THE LITURGY OF THE PRESANCTIFIED GIFTS

Saint Epiphanius of Salamis.
Fresco. Studenica Monastery.
Serbia. 14th c.

The liturgy of the presanctified gifts is a special, non-eucharistic liturgy that is celebrated in the Orthodox Church only during Great Lent. In the Russian tradition this liturgy is ascribed to Saint Gregory the Dialogist, Pope of Rome, but this attribution is seen only beginning in the sixteenth century. In earlier liturgical manuscripts, the liturgy of the presanctified gifts either had no particular attribution or was ascribed to one of the ancient Byzantine saints—Saint Basil the Great, Saint Ephiphanius of Salamis, or Saint Germanus of Constantinople. In contemporary Greek practice, the attribution of the liturgy of the presanctified gifts to Saint Gregory the Dialogist is rejected, and the text of the liturgy is printed in Euchologia with no mention of his name.[205]

There is insufficient evidence for the claim that the liturgy of the presanctified gifts was transferred to the East from the West. In the Western Church it is celebrated only once during the year—on Good Friday. In the East, on the contrary, it is served considerably more often. In some periods the liturgy of the presanctified gifts was celebrated on Wednesdays and Fridays of the entire year and on all weekdays of Great Lent, on Monday, Tuesday, Wednesday, and Friday of Holy Week, and on the feast of the Exaltation of the Cross of the Lord. In particular, this was the case in Constantinople during the rule of Patriarch Nicephorus (806–815). The Typika of the Great Church of the tenth and eleventh centuries speak of this liturgy being served on all weekdays of Great Lent, and also during Cheesefare Week and Holy Week. In the Jerusalem Typika of the same period it was prescribed to celebrate this liturgy only on Wednesdays and Fridays of Great Lent.[206] After the Jerusalem Typikon supplanted other Typika in the entire Orthodox East in the thirteenth and fourteenth centuries, the liturgy of the presanctified gifts came to be served on Wednesdays and Fridays of Great Lent, on Thursday of the fifth week of Lent, and on Monday, Tuesday, and Wednesday of Holy Week, and also on the day of the finding of the head of Saint John the Baptist (February 24) and the day of commemoration of the forty martyrs (March 9), if these days fall on weekdays of Great Lent.

---

[205]Mikhail Zheltov, "Gregory I the Great. Writings. Liturgical" [in Russian], in *Orthodox Encyclopedia* (Moscow: Tserkovno-nauchnyi tsentr "Pravoslavnaia entsiklopediia," 2006), 12:617–618.

[206]Uspenskii, *Orthodox Liturgy*, 104–106.

Some scholars link the origin and development of the liturgy of the presanctified gifts to the custom that existed in the ancient Church of receiving communion separately from the service of the Eucharist. This custom was described in detail by Saint Basil the Great:

> It is needless to point out that for anyone in times of persecution to be compelled to take the communion in his own hand without the presence of a priest or minister is not a serious offense, as long custom sanctions this practice from the facts themselves. All the solitaries in the desert, where there is no priest, take the communion themselves, keeping communion at home. And at Alexandria and in Egypt, each one of the laity, for

The First and Second Finding of the Head of Saint John the Baptist. Fragment of an Icon. c. 1700.

the most part, keeps the communion, at his own house, and participates in it when he likes. For when once the priest has completed the offering, and given it, the recipient, participating in it each time as entire, is bound to believe that he properly takes and receives it from the giver.[207]

In this way, communion outside of the Eucharist was performed at home. Several people could participate in this kind of communion: John Moschus mentions a woman who "went to her neighbor in order to commune."[208] The reception of communion at home or in a cell was accompanied by the reading of specific prayers. The order for communion in the cell is given in a Palestinian Horologion of the fourth century: it includes the reading of the gospel Beatitudes, the symbol of faith, and the prayer "Our Father," and also several prayers of preparation for communion.[209] The composition of this order is reminiscent of the "typical prayers"—a short service that is performed in the contemporary Orthodox Church during Great Lent between the ninth hour and vespers.

Nonetheless, there is no evidence of a direct connection between the liturgy of the presanctified gifts and partaking of communion at home. Communion at home was performed using a layman's order, while the presanctified liturgy is always celebrated by a priest.

[207]Basil the Great, *Letter 93: To Caesaria, Concerning Communion* (PG 32:485a–b; *NPNF*² 8:179).
[208]John Moschus, *Spiritual Meadow* 29 (PG 87/3:2876c–2877b).
[209]Uspenskii, *Orthodox Liturgy*, 56.

The first certain mentions of the liturgy of the presanctified gifts date to the beginning of the seventh century. The following note, dating to the year 615, is found in the Constantinopolitan Paschal Chronicle:

> In this year when Sergius was Patriarch of Constantinople, beginning at the first week of the fast, of the fourth indiction, people began to sing following "Let my prayer arise," at the time of the transfer of the presanctified gifts from the vessel room to the altar table; after the priest says, "Through the gift of thy Christ," the people right away begin, "Now the powers of heaven with us invisibly do worship. . . ."[210]

The author of the chronicle adds that the hymn "Now the Powers of heaven" is performed "not only during Great Lent at the celebration of the presanctified liturgy, but also on other days, when the liturgy of the presanctified gifts is celebrated."[211] This remark shows that by the beginning of the seventh century the service of the liturgy of the presanctified gifts was a universally accepted custom and that it was celebrated not only during Great Lent.

The order of the liturgy of the presanctified gifts contained in the Barberini Euchologion (end of the eighth century) is extremely similar to the one used at the present time. The order contains the prayer for the catechumens, the prayer for those preparing for holy baptism, two prayers of the faithful, a prayer following the transfer of the gifts to the altar table, the Lord's Prayer, a prayer following communion, and the prayer before the ambon. In the codex this order is not called a liturgy and no name whatsoever is attached to it.[212] The presence of prayers for the catechumens and for those preparing for baptism in this order indirectly reveals its connection with Great Lent—the traditional period of catechetical instruction.

According to the Typikon, the liturgy of the presanctified gifts should be served in the evening in combination with vespers. In the contemporary practice of most of the parishes of the Russian Church, the service is transferred to the morning. The reason for this transfer is the requirement of communing on an empty stomach, which means that, in the case of communion during the evening liturgy, the faithful must abstain from food during the entire day. In those parishes of the Russian Church and other local Orthodox churches in which the liturgy of the presanctified

[210]*Paschal Chronicle* (PG 92:989a–b).
[211]Ibid.
[212]Uspenskii, *Orthodox Liturgy*, 60–61.

gifts is celebrated in the evening, the custom is established of not eating food for several hours before communion.

The liturgy of the presanctified gifts lacks the celebratory, festal mood which characterizes the eucharistic liturgies. Its basic tone is one of repentance and prayerful worship of Christ, who is invisibly present in the already consecrated holy gifts. The eucharistic liturgy is celebrated over bread and wine, which only at the end of the anaphora are changed into the body and blood of Christ. This explains why the bread and wine are not given special veneration during the entire liturgy. Quite the opposite is true of the presanctified liturgy, where the body and blood of Christ are present from the very beginning; therefore this liturgy includes numerous forms of veneration of the holy gifts.

The holy lamb is consecrated for the liturgy of the presanctified gifts at the chronologically nearest preceding complete liturgy. For this purpose, an additional lamb or lambs (between one and three, depending upon the number of upcoming presanctified liturgies) are prepared at the proskomedia of the nearest full liturgy. Following the consecration, the lamb intended for the presanctified liturgy is soaked in the holy blood and placed on a diskos and covered with a special cover, and the diskos remains on the altar table.

Usually the third, sixth, and ninth hours, and the typika prayers are read before the beginning of the liturgy of the presanctified gifts. Vespers begins with the liturgical exclamation "Blessed is the Kingdom. . . ." This is followed by the first part of vespers including the reading of Psalm 103, the great litany, the reading of the kathisma divided into three "glories" with little litanies pronounced after each "glory," the singing of "Lord, I call" with verses, the singing of *O Gladsome Light*, and the vesperal entrance. At the time of the reading of Psalm 103, the priest does not read all seven prayers of light but only four—the fourth through seventh prayer. The first three prayers of light are read during the little litanies. During the reading of the kathisma the priest performs the transfer of the lamb from the altar table to the table of oblation.

The vesperal entrance takes place in the following way, with a censer or the Gospel Book (if the given day calls for a gospel reading). Directly following the singing of *O Gladsome Light* the deacon exclaims, "Wisdom," and the first reading is read, an excerpt from the Old Testament. The reading from the Old Testament at the liturgy of the presanctified gifts bears a catechetical character because the liturgy is performed during Great Lent, when many are preparing to be baptized.

*"The Light of Christ
Illumines All"*

The prokeimenon is recited following the first reading. Then the priest, taking the candle and censer, makes the sign of the cross in the air, saying, "Wisdom, aright." He then walks out to the ambon and, addressing the people and making the sign of the cross over them, exclaims, "The light of Christ illumines all." At this time all those present in the church kneel and bow their heads to the ground. Several scholars recognize in this rite a connection with the ancient rite of carrying a lighted candle. This is mentioned by Tertullian, Hippolytus, Saint Basil the Great, and other ancient authors.[213]

Following the second reading from the Old Testament, the reader and choir sing verses of Psalm 140 in alternating fashion: "Let my prayer arise in thy sight as incense." During the singing of these verses, the priest stands before the altar table and censes; the worshippers kneel. At the singing of the second to last verse, the priest moves to the table of oblation and censes the holy gifts. At the singing of the final verse, he gives up the censer and kneels before the altar table. Then, according to custom, the prayer of Saint Ephraim the Syrian is read.

At this point the service of vespers is concluded and the liturgy of the presanctified gifts begins. Usually it begins with the litany of fervent supplication, but on days that call for a reading from the gospel, the reading precedes the litany. The same prayer is read in the litany as in the liturgies of Saints Basil the Great and John Chrysostom ("O Lord our God, accept this fervent supplication from thy servants").

Next follows the litany for the catechumens, and in the period preceding Pascha (from the Sunday of the Veneration of the Cross until Wednesday of Holy Week) a special litany is called for—for those preparing for illumination (baptism). During the first litany the priest reads a prayer in which he asks God to deliver the catechumens "from their former delusion and from the wiles of the adversary," to call them to life eternal, enlightening their souls and bodies, and numbering them with his "rational flock," which is called by his holy name—that is, with the community of Christians. In the second prayer the priest asks God to reveal his countenance "to those who are preparing for holy illumination and who long to

[213]Ibid., 64.

put away the pollution of sin," to enlighten their minds, instruct them in the faith, confirm them in hope, perfect them in love, and make them precious members of Christ. At the end of the first litany, the deacon says, "As many as are catechumens, depart," and after the second litany he exclaims, "As many as are preparing for holy illumination, depart."

The distinction between catechumens and those preparing for baptism has been preserved in the litugy of the presanctified gifts from the time when catechetical instruction was a lengthy process and could continue for several years. Those who were preparing to be baptized in the coming year (or in the next few years), as well as those whose baptism was planned for the coming Pascha, were permitted to participate in the divine services of Great Lent.

Next, the deacon recites the little litany and the priest reads the first prayer of the faithful:

O God, great and praiseworthy, who by the life-giving death of Thy Christ hast translated us from corruption to incorruption, do Thou free all our senses from deadly passions; set over them as a good guide the understanding that is within us. And let our eyes abstain from every evil sight; our hearing be inaccessible to idle words; and our tongues be purged of unseemly speech. Make clean our lips which praise Thee, O Lord. Make our hands refrain from base deeds, and to work only that which is well-pleasing to Thee, fortifying our members and minds by Thy grace.

The content of the prayer corresponds with Great Lent as a time of spiritual watchfulness, when the faithful are called to keep watch over their feelings and thoughts.

The second prayer of the faithful is different. It is a preparation for the coming great entrance when the holy gifts are transferred from the table of oblation to the altar table:

O Master, holy and exceeding good, we implore Thee, who art rich in mercy: be gracious to us sinners, and make us worthy of the reception of Thine Only-begotten Son and our God, the King of glory. For, behold, His immaculate Body and life-creating Blood, entering at this present hour, are about to be set forth upon this mystical table by multitudes of heavenly hosts invisibly escorted. Grant us to partake of them without condemnation, that through them our mental sight may be illumined and we may become children of the light and of the day.

The prayer ends with the exclamation, "Through the gift of thy Christ, with whom thou art blessed, together with thine all-holy, and good, and life-creating Spirit, now and ever, and unto ages and ages." The choir responds, "Amen," and begins to sing the first part of a special cherubic hymn called for only in the liturgy of the presanctified gifts:

Now the Powers of heaven invisibly with us do serve. Lo, the King of glory enters. Lo, the mystical sacrifice is upborne, fulfilled. Let us draw near in faith and love, and become communicants of life eternal.

During the singing of "Now the powers of heaven," the priest approaches the table of oblation and takes hold of the diskos and chalice. He carries the diskos at the level of his head because the consecrated lamb lies upon it, while the chalice containing wine (not consecrated) is carried at the level of his chest. The priest exits though the north sanctuary door and returns into the sanctuary through the royal doors. The deacon goes before the priest, ceaselessly censing the holy gifts. In the liturgy of the presanctified gifts, the great entrance is executed in complete silence. At this time all the faithful kneel and bow their heads to the ground.

After the priest enters the sanctuary, the choir completes the cherubic hymn with the words, "Let us with faith and longing draw near that we may become partakers of life eternal. Alleluia, alleluia, alleluia." At this time the priest reverently places the holy gifts onto the altar table. Following the singing, three prostrations are made before the altar table and, according to custom, the prayer of Saint Ephraim the Syrian is read. Then the royal doors are closed and the curtain is drawn closed halfway. This action signifies the fact that the presanctified liturgy is not a full liturgy—that is, it does not contain the eucharistic canon.

Next, the litany of supplication is intoned, beginning with the words, "Let us complete our evening prayer unto the Lord." The second petition is, "For the precious gifts set forth and presanctified, let us pray to the Lord." During the recitation of the litany the priest reads the following prayer:

O God of unutterable and unseen mysteries, with whom are the hidden treasures of wisdom and knowledge, who hast revealed the service of this liturgy to us, who hast set us sinners, through Thy great love towards mankind, to offer to Thee gifts and sacrifices for our own sins and for the ignorance of the people: do Thou Thyself, O invisible King, who doest things great and inscrutable, glorious and marvelous, which cannot be numbered, look upon us, Thine unworthy servants who stand at this holy altar as at Thy cherubic throne, upon which resteth Thine Only-begotten Son and our God, in the dread mysteries that are set forth, and having freed us all and all Thy faithful people from uncleanness, sanctify all our souls and bodies with the sanctification which cannot be taken away; that partaking with a clean conscience, with faces unashamed, with hearts illumined, of these divine, sanctified things, and by them being given life, we may be united unto Thy Christ Himself, our true God, who has said: "Whoso eateth My flesh and drinketh My blood abideth in Me and I in him," that by Thy Word, O Lord, dwelling within us and sojourning among us, we may become the temple of Thine all-holy and adorable Spirit, redeemed from every diabolical wile, wrought either by deed or word or thought; and may obtain the good things promised to us with all Thy saints, who in all ages have been well-pleasing unto Thee.

This prayer most fully reveals the meaning of the liturgy of the presanctified gifts and its connection with the full liturgy, in which the change of the bread and wine into the body and blood of Christ took place. It especially underscores that the Only-begotten Son of God himself is present on the altar table in the holy mysteries. The priest asks for communion to be a source of sanctification of soul and body for all the faithful, and that, through communion, all members of the community may be united with Christ and become temples of the Holy Spirit, and that communion may be a pledge of salvation and life eternal. The prayer ends with the exclamation, "And vouchsafe, O Master," followed by the singing of the Lord's Prayer.

Following the Lord's Prayer, the priest blesses the faithful and reads the prayer before holy communion, as is the case during the full liturgy. Also, the prayer "Attend, O Lord Jesus Christ our God," from the full liturgy, is read. But in the place of the exclamation "The holy things are for the holy," the priest exclaims "The presanctified holy things are for the holy." He does not raise up the holy lamb with two hands but only slightly lifts it, without removing the cover from the diskos. Then the cover is removed and the priest breaks the lamb according to the number of communicants. He places the piece with the inscription IC into the chalice without saying anything.

What happens to the wine in the chalice at the moment that the piece of the holy lamb is placed into it? According to the traditional Byzantine understanding, the wine becomes the blood of Christ at this moment because of its union with the body of Christ. In the words of Ivan Karabinov, "the existence of the belief [in the Greek Church] that in the aforementioned liturgy the wine in the chalice changes into the holy blood when a piece of the holy body is placed in it may, according to indisputable, clear, and authoritative accounts, be traced back almost to the tenth century."[214]

In particular, one of these accounts is the *Message to the Emperor* of Patriarch of Constantinople Michael II Kourkouas (1143–1146) concerning the liturgy of the presanctified gifts. The author of the *Message* writes:

> On each Sunday of the venerable days dedicated for the fast . . . loaves are consecrated. . . . A portion of these loaves—perfected, life-creating, and full of divine benefits—is preserved for as long as necessary and for as many circumstances as are required. Not a drop of the divine blood is poured on these loaves, which are acknowledged to be and really are the most life-creating body of our Lord and God and Savior Jesus Christ, and they are reserved without being sprinkled with the holy blood. At each of the days of the fast, when the full liturgy is not celebrated, they are transferred from the place of oblation to the holy table in the sanctuary, and not one of the mysterious and consecrating prayers is uttered over them. . . . At the time of holy communion, a bit earlier before its distribution, the deacons touch the holy chalices on (the holy table) and . . . place the presanctified and earlier perfected holy bread into the mysterious chalice, and the wine contained in the chalice is changed into the holy blood of the Lord. . . .[215]

In this way, the holy lamb, prepared for the liturgy of the presanctified gifts, was not soaked beforehand in the holy blood, as it is now done, but was placed into the chalice before communion. According to the opinion of the author, the change of the wine into the blood of Christ took place precisely because the body of Christ was placed into the chalices containing wine (the author speaks of chalices in the plural).

The tradition emerged of soaking the consecrated lamb with the holy blood no later than in the fifteenth century. Saint Symeon of Thessalonica bears witness to this:

> The presanctified most holy gifts do not receive anything from prayers conjoined to them, because these are consecrated gifts. . . . Wine and water is

---

[214]Karabinov, *Holy Chalice*, 740.
[215]Cited in Karabinov, *Holy Chalice*, 742.

poured into the holy chalice without the reading of any known prayer, so that, after the divine bread is broken and its upper particle, according to the Typikon, is placed into [the wine], that which is in the chalice is consecrated, through the communion [*tē metochē*],[216] and thus the priest, according to the order of the liturgy, can commune both of the bread and of the chalice and offer the communion to those in need: the sacred persons in the sanctuary according to the custom, and the laity, with the spoon. . . . And so, that which is found in the chalice in the presanctified liturgy is consecrated not by invocation and sealing of the Holy Spirit, but by communion and union with the life-creating bread, which truly is the body of Christ, in union with the blood.[217]

In accordance with this understanding, the order of communion of the clergy at the liturgy of the presanctified gifts does not differ from the communion in the liturgies of Saints Basil the Great and John Chrysostom: first they communed of the body of Christ, saturated with the holy blood, and then from the chalice the blood of Christ, consecrated from the union with the body of Christ.

Metropolitan Peter Mogila. Portrait. 19th c.

But in the middle of the seventeenth century, under the influence of Latin theology, a different opinion penetrated into Rus': that the wine in the presanctified liturgy is not changed into the blood of Christ, because the Savior's "words of institution" are not read over it. This opinion was expressed by Metropolitan of Kiev Peter Mogila, who included in the 1646 edition of the Kiev *Book of Needs* the following remark: "When you drink from the chalice or offer it to the deacon, say nothing, for therein is simple wine and not the blood of the Master, which is used only for the sake of ceremonial practice in the place of wiping the mouth."[218] This unexpected turn was due to Metropolitan Peter's overall attitude concerning the change of the holy gifts. In this question he followed Latin scholastic theology precisely, repeating (perhaps unconsciously) the teaching set forth by the Latins at the Council of Florence:

The Lord's words over the bread on the diskos on the altar table are the form or achievement of the body of Christ: "Take, eat . . ." By these words the bread

---

[216]That is, in order for the wine to be consecrated through the union with the presanctified bread.
[217]Symeon of Thessalonica, *Answers to Gabriel of Pentapolis* 57 (PG 155:909b–d).
[218]Cited in Uspenskii, *Orthodox Liturgy*, 184.

is transubstantiated; that is, the substance of the bread is changed truly into the body of Christ, and following the utterance of these words of the Lord, it is no longer the simple bread according to its former substance, but the true body of Christ. The Lord's words over the wine in the chalice, spoken by the priest are the form or achievement of the blood of Christ, namely, "Drink of it, all of you . . ." By these words the substance of the wine is changed into the blood. . . ."[219]

Following this logic, Peter Mogila came to the conviction that insofar as the mystery-performing formula is not uttered in the liturgy of the presanctified gifts, the wine does not become the blood of Christ, but remains normal wine, used "for the sake of ceremonial practice." Under the influence of Peter Mogila, corresponding changes were also introduced into the Moscow Priests' Service Books, which resulted in a change in the very order of communion. Now priests, receiving wine from the chalice, were to consider it not the blood of Christ, but only sanctified wine.[220] From this followed the prohibition of drinking from the chalice for deacons, who at the conclusion of the liturgy of the presanctified gifts must consume the holy gifts. When one priest serves the liturgy without a deacon, the prohibition extends to the priest.

From this also came the practice of not admitting infants to communion during the liturgy of the presanctified gifts. If only particles already soaked with the blood of Christ are the body of Christ, it follows that infants—unable to swallow solid food—cannot receive communion. In this way, under the influence of Latin theology, the ancient Orthodox tradition of communion at the liturgy of the presanctified gifts was deformed: today infants are excluded from receiving this mystery.

In the Russian Orthodox Church to the present day the order of communion at the presanctified liturgy is performed in the form introduced by Metropolitan Peter Mogila. In the Greek Church, however, the ancient view of the consecration of the wine in its union with the particle of the body of Christ is preserved. Therefore, there is no prohibition on the communion of infants at the liturgy of the presanctified gifts in the Greek Church.

---

[219]Peter (Mogila), *Euchologion*, 238–239. Cited in Uspenskii, *Orthodox Liturgy*, 185.

[220]Peter Mogila's words concerning the wine used "in place of wiping the mouth" did not enter into the Moscow Priest's Service Book. It was limited to a more subtle wording of Euthymius Chudovsky: "While the wine is sanctified by the placing of the particle, it does not transubstantiate into the blood of the Master." (Peter Mogila had no word whatsoever for the "sanctification" of the wine at the presanctified liturgy.)

The liturgy of the presanctified gifts is concluded in the same way as the full liturgy, but the prayer before the ambon and the prayer said when the holy gifts are consumed are different. At the prayer before the ambon the priest, recalling the forty-day fast of Moses, asks God to help the faithful to "fight the good fight, to complete the course of the fast, to preserve the faith undivided, to crush the heads of invisible serpents, to be shown to be the conquerers of sins." In the prayer when the holy things are consumed, the priest addresses God with the words, "O Lord our God, who hast led us to these most solemn days, and hast made us communicants of thy dread mysteries, join us to thy reasonable flock, and show us to be heirs of thy kingdom." Both prayers, in this way, are thematically connected with Great Lent as a time of spiritual battle and watchfulness.

At the dismissal of the liturgy of the presanctified gifts, the saints of the church and of the day are commemorated. Also, in the Russian practice, Saint Gregory the Dialogist, the Pope of Rome is commemorated. In contemporary Greek practice the name of Saint Gregory the Dialogist is not mentioned for the reasons cited above.

Saint Gregory the Dialogist, Pope of Rome. Fresco. Varlaam Monastery. Meteora. Greece. 16th c.

PART THREE

The Weekly Cycle of Divine Services

4

The Formation of the Weekly Liturgical Cycle

God Rested from His Works.
Mosaic. Monreale Cathedral. Sicily. 12th c.

T HE ORIGINS OF THE FORMATION of the Christian Church's weekly liturgical cycle may be found in the Old Testament. The fourth Mosaic commandment states: "Remember the sabbath day, to keep it holy. Six days you shall labor and do all your work, but the seventh day is the Sabbath of the Lord your God" (Ex 20.8–10). The Sabbath was primarily understood as a day of rest, a respite from work, in remembrance of the fact that "in six days the Lord made heavens and earth, the sea, and everything in them, and rested on the seventh day." At the same time, the Sabbath is the day that the Lord "blessed . . . and hallowed" (Ex 20.11). "A holy convocation" (Lev 23.3) is called on the Sabbath; on this day burnt offerings and bread offerings (see Lev 24.8) are made as a sacrifice to the Lord (see Num 28.9). In the period following the Babylonian exile, the Sabbath became the week's foremost day of worship: this is the day on which Jews congregate in the synagogue for prayer and the reading of the sacred Scriptures.

In Christianity the Old Testament prescription of observing the Sabbath was radically reexamined. Christ did not rescind this rule and he himself went to the synagogue on the Sabbath (see Lk 4.16), but he allowed himself to break the prescription of Sabbath rest, showing the Jews that the Son of Man is also Lord of the Sabbath (Mk 2.28). After his ascension, Christ's disciples continued to go to the temple on the Sabbath, but the foremost day of Christian worship—the day of the celebration of the Eucharist—was the first day of the week, the "day of the sun." After Christians decisively departed from the temple in Jerusalem and especially after the doors of the Church were opened to the Gentiles, the observance of the Sabbath in the form in which it was prescribed in the Old Testament lost its significance. The resolutions of the Apostolic Council (see Acts 15.6–29) in effect legitimized the revocation of the Old Testament prescription concerning the Sabbath.

Early Christian writers spoke of the Sabbath as of one of the Jewish customs that died out after Christ came into the world. The "keeping of the Sabbath" was exchanged for "the life of the resurrection." The transfer of the center of the worship life from Saturday to the first day of the week—which came to be called "the Lord's day" (Gr. *kyriakē*)—corresponds with this exchange. Often this day was called "the eighth day"—a foreshadowing of eternity:

> Therefore, if those who conducted themselves in accordance with the ancient ways came to a newness of hope, no longer keeping the Sabbath but living in accordance with the Lord's day, on which our life appeared through him and through his death, which some deny, we receive with faith through this mystery, and remain constant in it, so that we may be found to be disciples of Jesus Christ our only teacher, how could we live without regard to him? It is of him that the prophets were disciples in the Spirit, expecting him as a teacher. . . . Therefore put aside the evil yeast, which is aged and soured, and be changed into new yeast, which is Jesus Christ. Be salted in him, so that nothing in you can get corrupted, since you will be convicted by your smell. It is outlandish to speak of Jesus Christ and to Judaize. For Christianity did not put its faith in Judaism but Judaism in Christianity, in which every tongue which believes has been gathered together into God.[1]

Further, also, it is written concerning the Sabbath in the Decalogue which [the Lord] spoke, face to face, to Moses on Mount Sinai, "And sanctify the Sabbath of the Lord with clean hands and a pure heart" (Ex 20.8; Deut 5.12). And he says in another place, "If my sons keep the Sabbath, then will I cause my mercy to rest upon them" (Jer 17.24–25). The Sabbath is mentioned at the beginning of the creation [thus]: "And God made in six days the works of his hands, and made an end on the seventh day, and rested on it, and sanctified

---

[1]Ignatius of Antioch, *Letter to the Magnesians* 9.1–2, 10.2–3 (Stewart, PPS).

it." Attend, my children, to the meaning of this expression, "He finished in six days." This implies that the Lord will finish all things in six thousand years, for a day is with Him a thousand years. And he himself testifies, saying, "Behold, today will be as a thousand years." Therefore, my children, in six days, that is, in six thousand years, all things will be finished. "And he rested on the seventh day." This means: when His Son, coming [again], shall destroy the time of the wicked man, and judge the ungodly, and change the sun, and the moon, and the stars, then shall He truly rest on the seventh day. Moreover, he says, "You shall sanctify it with pure hands and a pure heart." If, therefore, any one can now sanctify the day which God has sanctified, except he is pure in heart in all things, we are deceived. Behold, therefore: certainly then one properly resting sanctifies it, when we ourselves, having received the promise, wickedness no longer existing, and all things having been made new by the Lord, shall be able to work righteousness. Then we shall be able to sanctify it, having been first sanctified ourselves. Further, he says to them, "Your new moons and your Sabbaths I cannot endure" (Is 1.13). You perceive how he speaks: Your present Sabbaths are not acceptable to me, but that is which I have made, [namely this,] when, giving rest to all things, I shall make a beginning of the eighth day, that is, a beginning of another world. Wherefore, also, we keep the eighth day with joyfulness, the day also on which Jesus rose again from the dead. And when he had manifested himself, he ascended into the heavens.[2]

In the middle of the fourth century the contradistinction of Sunday against Saturday was secured in Canon 29 of the Council of Laodicea: "Christians must not Judaize by resting on the Sabbath, but must work on that day, rather honouring the Lord's Day."[3] In the West beginning in the sixth century the understanding became widespread that rest on Sundays completely replaces the Sabbath rest prescribed in the Old Testament.[4] But in the East, Saturday continued to preserve its meaning as a separate liturgical day, especially in those churches which did not decisively sever their connection with the Jewish tradition (in particular, in Ethiopia and in Syria).

---

[2] *Epistle of Barnabas* 15 (*ANF* 1:146–147).

[3] Council of Laodicea, *Canon 29* (*NPNF*[2] 14:148).

[4] As a result, in Catholic catecheses the fourth Mosaic commandment came to be set forth with the word "Sabbath" replaced with "Sunday." See A. A. Tkachenko, "Sunday" [in Russian], in *Orthodox Encyclopedia* (Moscow, 2005), 9:449.

In eastern Christian monasticism, Saturday, together with Sunday, turned into one of the important liturgical days.[5] In the Byzantine liturgical calendar, Saturday became the day of remembrance of Jesus Christ in the tomb and at the same time the day of the remembrance of the departed. This notion is reflected in the divine services of the Octoechos.

The formation of the Octoechos is usually dated to the seventh to eighth centuries, and is connected with the name of Saint John of Damascus. At the same time it is evident that the Octoechos as a book and the very system of the eight tones on which it is built reflect the development of the divine services in the monastic tradition over many centuries and is the fruit of collective work. It has already been mentioned that the eight tones of the Octoechos represent not only eight separate melodies, but also eight full "sets" of liturgical texts for every day of the week. The Octoechos is used during the course of the entire year, with the exception of days on which the Lenten Triodion or Pentecostarion supplants it. The Octoechos' cycle of divine services is repeated every eight weeks.

---

[5]We note that in the Egyptian cenobitic monasteries of Saint Pachomius the liturgy was celebrated twice weekly: on Saturday in the evening and on Sunday before noon. Concerning this, see Veilleux, *La liturgie*, 228–235. But in this case Saturday's liturgy, celebrated in the evening, was already thematically related to the day of resurrection.

5

Sunday Services and Daily Services

THE RESURRECTIONAL DIVINE SERVICES

THE FIRST WORSHIP SERVICE OF THE WEEK is vespers performed in the evening on Saturday and thematically focused on the day of resurrection. The Octoechos contains two resurrectional vespers services for every tone—small and great vespers. The bulk of the texts of these two services is the same. The presence of two vespers services in the Octoechos is linked with the fact that great vespers before Sunday is included as part of the all-night vigil, and therefore the beginning of great vespers is transferred to a time following the setting of the sun. Small vespers, on the other hand, is to be celebrated "before the setting of the sun on the sabbath day."[1]

The first three stichera (verses) of "Lord, I call" make up the earliest stratum of the resurrectional hymns in the Octoechos. They date back to the Jerusalem worship of the pre-iconoclastic period (the fourth through ninth centuries). The majority of the stichera tell of the Savior's death on the cross, his descent into hades, resurrection, and victory over death:

> Come, O people. Let us hymn and fall down before Christ, glorifying his Resurrection from the dead. For he is our God, who has delivered the world from the Enemy's deceit. (Octoechos. Tone 1. Saturday. Great Vespers. Stichera on "Lord, I call.")

> By thy Cross, O Christ our Savior, death's dominion has been shattered; the devil's delusion destroyed. The race of man, being saved by faith, always offers thee a song. (Octoechos. Tone 3. Saturday. Great Vespers. Stichera on "Lord, I call.")

---

[1]In practice, small vespers is not performed at the present time either in parishes or in the majority of monasteries.

All has been enlightened by thy Resurrection, O Lord. Paradise has been opened again. All creation, praising thee, always offers thee a song. (Octoechos. Tone 3. Saturday. Great Vespers. Stichera on "Lord, I call.")

Christ was led as a sheep to the slaughter in order to grant resurrection to the human race. The princes of hell were frightened by this, for the gates of sorrow were lifted. Christ, the King of glory, had entered, saying to those in chains, "Go forth!" and to those in darkness, "Come to the light." (Octoechos. Tone 5. Saturday. Great Vespers. Stichera on "Lord, I call.")

Come, let us rejoice in the Lord who destroyed the dominion of death! Let us sing to him with the bodiless hosts, for he enlightened the race of man. O our Maker and Savior, glory to thee. (Octoechos. Tone 7. Saturday. Great Vespers. Stichera on "Lord, I call.")

Two stichera are connected in content with the time of day, which is evening:

Accept our evening prayers, O holy Lord. Grant us remission of sins, for thou alone hast manifested the Resurrection to the world. (Octoechos. Tone 1. Saturday. Great Vespers. Stichera on "Lord, I call.")

We offer to thee, O Christ, our evening song and reasonable service. For thou didst will to have mercy on us by thy Resurrection. (Octoechos. Tone 8. Saturday. Great Vespers. Stichera on "Lord, I call.")

The other two stichera speak of Zion (Jerusalem) as the place of the Lord's resurrection and "the mother of the Churches." These references confirm that the stichera originated in Jerusalem:

Encircle Zion and surround her, O people. Give glory in her to the one who rose from the dead! For he is our God, who has delivered us from our transgressions. (Octoechos. Tone 1. Saturday. Great Vespers. Stichera on "Lord, I call.")

Rejoice, O Holy Zion, Mother of the churches, the abode of God. For thou wast the first to receive remission of sins by the Resurrection. (Octoechos. Tone 8. Saturday. Great Vespers. Stichera on "Lord, I call.")

"Come, ye people, let us hymn Christ." Mount Athos.

Several stichera have clearly expressed dogmatic content. They speak of the pre-eternal birth of the Son of God the Father, the indivisible power of the three persons of the holy Trinity, and God's omnipresence:

Come, let us worship the Word of God, begotten of the Father before all ages, and incarnate of the Virgin Mary. Having endured the Cross, he was buried as he himself desired! And having risen from the dead, he saved me, an erring man. (Octoechos. Tone 2. Saturday. Great Vespers. Stichera on "Lord, I call.")

With the Archangels let us praise the Resurrection of Christ! He is our Savior, our Redeemer. He is coming with awesome glory and mighty power to judge the world which he made. (Octoechos. Tone 2. Saturday. Great Vespers. Stichera on "Lord, I call.")

I glorify the power of the Father and the Son. I praise the authority of the Holy Spirit. The undivided, uncreated Godhead, the consubstantial Trinity who reigns forever. (Octoechos. Tone 3. Saturday. Great Vespers. Stichera on "Lord, I call.")

O great wonder! The Creator of the invisible suffered in the flesh in his love for man and rose again immortal. Come, O sons of nations, let us worship him. Delivered from error by his compassion, we have learned to sing of one God in three Persons. (Octoechos. Tone 5. Saturday. Great Vespers. Stichera on "Lord, I call.")

Where shall we sinners flee from thee who art in all Creation? In heaven thou dwellest. In hell thou didst trample on death. In the depths of the sea? Even there is thy hand, O Master. To thee we flee, and falling before thee, we pray: "O thou who didst rise from the dead, have mercy on us." (Octoechos. Tone 6. Saturday. Great Vespers. Stichera on "Lord, I call.")

On Saturday evening, following the three stichera at "Lord, I call," four other stichera are called for. These are of a later origin (in the manuscripts they are encountered beginning in the ninth century). In the Greek Octoechos they contain the inscription *anatolika* ("eastern"), which may indicate their origin in Palestine.[2] In content they are similar to the first three stichera and are overwhelmingly dedicated to the glorification of the risen Savior:

We bow down in worship before thy precious Cross, O Christ, and we glorify and praise thy Resurrection, for by thy wounds we have all been healed. (Octoechos. Tone 3. Saturday. Great Vespers. Stichera on "Lord, I call.")

Christ descended to hell proclaiming the glad tidings: "Behold! Now I have triumphed. I am the Resurrection, I will lead you out. For I have shattered the gates of death." (Octoechos. Tone 3. Saturday. Great Vespers. Stichera on "Lord, I call.")

Glory to thy Might, O Lord, for thou didst overthrow the Prince of Death, by thy Cross renewing us, granting us life and incorruption. (Octoechos. Tone 6. Saturday. Great Vespers. Stichera on "Lord, I call.")

The concluding sticheron from the cycle of "Lord, I call" stichera is dedicated to the Theotokos and is called the "dogmatic theotokion." It is thematically connected to the revelation of a christological dogma. The authorship of the dogmatic theotokia is ascribed to Saint John of Damascus. The theological richness of the

---

[2]In the Slavonic Octoechos the term *anatolika* is erroneously translated as "of Anatolius," which would indicate the authorship of one of the three famous hymnographers bearing the name Anatolius: a patriarch of Constantinople (†458), a monk of Stoudion (2nd half of the eighth century), or an archbishop of Thessalonica (end of the ninth century). But in the Greek original, written by one of these Anatolii, the term *Anatoliou* ["of Anatolius"—*Ed.*] is used. See "Anatolian" [in Russian], in *Orthodox Encyclopedia* (Moscow: Tserkovno-nauchnyi tsentr "Pravoslavnaia entsiklopediia," 2005), 9:484.

dogmatic theotokion makes it an important catechetical element of vespers. We may cite as an example the dogmatic theotokion of the eighth tone:

> The King of heaven, because of his love for man, appeared on earth and dwelt with men. He took flesh from the pure Virgin, and after assuming it, he came forth from her. The Son is one; in two Natures, yet one Person. Proclaiming him as perfect God and perfect Man, we confess Christ our God. Entreat him, O unwedded Mother, to have mercy on our souls. (Octoechos. Tone 8. Saturday. Great Vespers. Dogmatic Theotokion.)

This text contains a brief exposition of Orthodox Christology. The Church confesses Christ as the heavenly King, who by his love for mankind became Man and lived among men. He accepted flesh from the most-holy Theotokos, whose virginity was not violated by giving birth to her Son. The Church confesses two natures in Christ, human and divine, but does not divide him into two subjects, "two sons" (an allusion to the heresy of Nestorius). Christ is perfect God and perfect Man: his human nature was not swallowed up by the divine (as Eutyches thought); he possesses perfect, that is, fully-fledged, human nature and not, for example, only a human body (as Apollinaris thought).

Aposticha are a collection of four stichera of which three are dedicated to the resurrection of Christ and the last is dedicated to the Theotokos. The first sticheron, more ancient and brief than the others, stands by itself; the other stichera form an alphabetical acrostic in the Greek original: three letters in each tone for a total of twenty-four stichera, the number of letters in the Greek alphabet.

The final hymns that the Octoechos prescribes for great vespers on Saturdays are the dismissal troparion and the theotokion. But they are performed only when vespers is served separately from matins. If vespers is connected with matins as part of the all-night vigil (as is universally the case in the Russian Orthodox Church), "Rejoice, O Virgin Theotokos" is sung thrice in the place of the troparion and theotokion.

The resurrectional troparion and theotokion are always performed at "God is the Lord" at the beginning of matins (and the troparion is sung twice). In troparia, as in stichera, the resurrection of Christ is glorified as the source of salvation and eternal life:

> Let the heavens rejoice! Let the earth be glad! For the Lord has shown strength with His arm. He has trampled down death by death. He has become the first

born of the dead. He has delivered us from the depths of hell, and has granted to the world great mercy. (Octoechos. Tone 3. Saturday. Great Vespers. Resurrectional Troparion.)

Let us, the faithful, praise and worship the Word, coeternal with the Father and the Spirit, born for our salvation from the Virgin; for He willed to be lifted up on the Cross in the flesh, to endure death, and to raise the dead by His glorious Resurrection. (Octoechos. Tone 5. Saturday. Great Vespers. Resurrectional Troparion.)

Thou didst descend from on high, O Merciful One! Thou didst accept the three-day burial to free us from our sufferings! O Lord, our Life and Resurrection, glory to Thee! (Octoechos. Tone 8. Saturday. Great Vespers. Resurrectional Troparion.)

The resurrectional sedalens are performed after the first and second kathismata at matins. The first two are dedicated to the events connected with the Savior's death on the cross, burial, and resurrection, and the third is dedicated to the Theotokos.

After "Blessed are the blameless in the way . . ." [Ps 118] or the polyeleos [Ps 134–135], the resurrectional troparia "The assembly of the angels" [i.e. the Evlogitaria] follows, whose authorship is attributed to Saint John of Damascus. These troparia, the same for all the tones, are a part of the paschal worship service and are dedicated to the glorification of the risen Christ: they were already found in liturgical manuscripts of the ninth century.[3] They speak of the appearance of an angel to the myrrh-bearing women after the resurrection of Christ:

The angelic host was filled with awe when it saw Thee among the dead. By destroying the power of death, O Savior, Thou didst raise Adam and save all men from Hell.

In the tomb the radiant angel cried to the myrrhbearers: "Why do you women mingle myrrh with your tears? Look at the tomb and understand! The Savior is risen from the dead."

Very early in the morning the myrrhbearers ran with sorrow to Thy tomb. But an angel came to them and said: "The time for sorrow has come to an end. Do not weep, but announce the resurrection to the Apostles."

[3]Skaballanovich, *Typikon* (2004), 647.

The myrrhbearers were sorrowful as they neared Thy tomb, but the angel said to them: "Why do you number the living among the dead? Since He is God, He is risen from the tomb."

We worship the Father, and His Son, and the Holy Spirit, the Holy Trinity, one in essence. We cry with the Seraphim: "Holy, Holy, Holy art Thou, O Lord."

Since you gave birth to the Giver of Life, O Virgin, you delivered Adam from his sin. You gave joy to Eve instead of sadness. The God-man who was born of you has restored to life those who had fallen from it.

> (Octoechos. Tones 1–8. Matins.
> Troparia after "Blessed are the blameless")

Antiphonal hymns, called "songs of ascent" and attributed to Saint Theodore the Studite, are performed before the reading of the resurrectional gospel. Their name comes from the "ascent" psalms (119–132) after which they were modeled. Each verse of the antiphonal hymn corresponds to a certain psalm verse: hymns of the first and fifth tones—Psalms 119–121; hymns of the second and sixth tones—psalms 122–124; hymns of the third and seventh tones—psalms 125–127; hymns of the fourth and eighth tones—psalms 128–132. Each tone has three antiphonal hymns, while the eighth tone has four. Each antiphonal hymn consists of three troparia of which the third is always dedicated to the Holy Spirit. The songs of ascent differ in content from the hymns that glorify the resurrection of Christ. They are inspired by the ascetic, monastic ideal; in them, in particular, the inclination of man's soul to God, love of the temple, and the sweetness of desert-dwelling is expressed:

Divine desire should be neverending for those who are in the desert, beyond this vain world. (Octoechos. Tone 1. Sunday. Matins. Songs of Ascent. Antiphon 1.)

Blessed is the life of those in the desert, who take wing with divine desire. (Octoechos. Tone 5. Sunday. Matins. Songs of Ascent. Antiphon 1.)

For those who said to me, "Let us go up into the courts of the Lord," my spirit has become glad, and my heart shares in rejoicing. (Octoechos. Tone 1. Sunday. Matins. Songs of Ascent. Antiphon 3.)

Just as one has love toward his mother, so we should be all the warmer in our love toward the Lord. (Octoechos. Tone 4. Sunday. Matins. Songs of Ascent. Antiphon 3.)

Full of great joy, I send up supplications for those who have said to me: Let us enter into the courts of the Lord. (Octoechos. Tone 5. Sunday. Matins. Songs of Ascent. Antiphon 3.)

From my youth the enemy tempts me, in order to consume me with pleasures, but when I hope on thee, Lord, I conquer him. (Octoechos. Tone 8. Sunday. Matins. Songs of Ascent. Antiphon 1.)

The songs of ascent precede the reading of an excerpt from the gospel, dedicated to the resurrection of Christ. There are eleven resurrectional gospel readings, and they are read in order regardless of the tone in which the service takes place. Thus the full cycle of resurrectional gospel readings are read over the course of eleven Sundays. The following pericopes are resurrectional gospel readings: (1) Mt 28.16–20; (2) Mk 16.1–8; (3) Mk 16.9–20; (4) Lk 24.1–12; (5) Lk 24.12–35; (6) Lk 24.36–53; (7) Jn 20.1–10; (8) Jn 20.11–18; (9) Jn 20.19–31; (10) Jn 21.1–14; (11) Jn 21.15–25.

In terms of content, the most diverse part of the resurrectional matins is the canon. The resurrectional service of the Octoechos contains three canons: to the resurrection, to the cross and resurrection, and to the Theotokos. Their names indicate that the first canon is always dedicated to the resurrection of Christ; in the second canon the theme of the resurrection is connected with the theme of the Savior's sufferings on the cross;[4] and the third canon is dedicated to the Theotokos. The first of the three resurrectional canons is the more ancient in origin: its authorship is attributed to Saint John of Damascus.

The thematic richness of the canons to the resurrection and to the cross and resurrection may be shown by one example: the canon of the first tone. It speaks of the death and resurrection of Christ, but it also speaks of the creation of man, the incarnation of God, deification, and the Second Coming of Christ. In fact, the entire history of the salvation of mankind comes before the spiritual eyes of those praying the texts of the resurrectional canons:

In the beginning, He whose pure hands formed me from the earth spread out His hands upon the Cross. From the earth He recalled my corruptible body,

---

[4]In content both the first and second canons speak equally of Christ's death on the cross and of his resurrection.

which He had received from the Virgin. (Octoechos. Tone 1. Sunday. Matins. Canon 1. Ode 1.)

Christ crucified exalts me. Christ dead raises me up with Himself. Christ has given me life. Clapping my hands with great joy, I sing to my Lord and Savior a hymn of victory, for as the Conqueror over death, He has been glorified. (Octoechos. Tone 1. Sunday. Matins. Canon 2. Ode 1.)

O Christ, who in thy person art Life, clothing thyself in me who have become corrupt, as the God of compassion, thou didst descend to the dust of death, O Master, and didst rend mortality; and having risen after three days of death, thou hast clothed me in incorruption. (Octoechos. Tone 1. Sunday. Matins. Canon 1. Ode 3.)

Who is this Savior that comes from Edom? He is crowned with thorns and His garments are reddened with blood. Who is this that hangs upon the Tree for our salvation and remaking? He is the Holy One of Israel. (Octoechos. Tone 1. Sunday. Matins. Canon 1. Ode 4.)

Christ, the High Priest of good things to come, is revealed to us. He has scattered our sins in the wind, opening a new path to us by His precious blood. He has entered a better and more perfect tabernacle. He is our forerunner into the holy places. (Octoechos. Tone 1. Sunday. Matins. Canon 2. Ode 4.)

Christ God, the Existing One, unites himself to the flesh for us, and he is crucified and dies; he is buried, and rises again, and radiantly he ascends in the same flesh to the Father, after which he shall come and save those who piously worship him. (Octoechos. Tone 1. Sunday. Matins. Canon 2. Ode 5.)

Following the sixth ode of the canon the resurrectional kontakion and ikos are read. Following the ninth ode of the canon the "matins exapostilarion" is performed, which is thematically connected not with the tone of the week but with the excerpt from the gospel that was read. Accordingly, the number of these exapostilaria in the Octoechos is equal to the number of gospel readings. Each of them is a poetic commentary on the gospel subject. The authorship of the resurrectional exapostilaria is attributed to the Byzantine Emperor Constantine VII Porphyrogenitus (913–959).

The praises are sung before the great doxology. As with the stichera at "Lord, I call" at vespers, the matins stichera at the praises are divided into two groups: four

Descent into Hell. Book Miniature.
Mount Athos. 11th c.

resurrectional stichera and four "eastern" stichera. In content they are similar to the stichera of vespers. The ninth sticheron at the praises is called the "gospel sticheron" and, like the exapostilarion, is related to the resurrectional gospel reading. Emperor Leo the Wise (886–912) is considered the author of the eleven gospel stichera. The concluding sticheron, according to tradition, is addressed to the Theotokos. This sticheron is always the same regardless of the tone of the service:

> You are most blessed, O Virgin Theotokos, for through the God and Man who was born of you, Hell has been captured and Adam recalled, the curse has been annulled and Eve set free; death has been slain, so we are given eternal life: blessed is Christ our God, whose good will it was! Glory to you! (Octoechos. Sunday. Matins. Praises. Theotokion.)

The resurrectional troparion is sung after the great doxology. In the Octoechos there are only two of these: for the first and second tones. The troparion in the first tone is also sung at the services of the third, fifth, and seventh tones, while correspondingly the troparion in the second tone is sung at the services of the fourth, sixth, and eighth tones:

> Today salvation has come to the world; let us sing to him who rose from the tomb, the author of our life. For having destroyed death by death, he has given us the victory and great mercy. (Octoechos. Tones 1, 3, 5, 7. Matins. Resurrectional Troparion.)

> Rising from the tomb, thou didst burst the bonds of hell; and thou didst lift the condemnation of death, O Lord, delivered all from the snares of the enemy. And having shown thyself to thine apostles, thou didst send them forth to preach, and through them thou hast given thy peace to the whole world, O thou only greatly merciful one. (Octoechos. Tones 2, 4, 6, 8. Matins. Resurrectional Troparion.)

These are the basic liturgical texts of the resurrectional service. To them may be added the Beatitude verses: verses which the Typikon prescribes to be inserted into the third antiphonal hymn of the liturgy (in parish practice they are almost universally omitted). Midnight office is also included as part of the resurrectional worship service, in which the *Canon to the Holy and Life-giving Trinity* is read, the work of Metrophanes II, Patriarch of Constantinople (patriarch from 1440–1443). There are eight such canons, according to the number of tones. But midnight office is prescribed only when the all-night vigil is not served. Since on the eve of Sunday the Russian Church always serves the all-night vigil, Sunday midnight office is universally omitted.

The resurrectional service is performed according to the Octoechos during the course of the entire year. Exceptions are the feasts of the Entry of the Lord into Jerusalem, Pascha, Thomas Sunday, and Pentecost, and also the great feasts of the Lord (Nativity, Theophany) when they fall on Sunday. In these cases the Octoechos is not used.

Daily Services

Weekday services have a less solemn aspect than Sunday services. Each day of the week in the Octoechos is dedicated to a particular theme, which is revealed in the material of the stichera, canons, sedalens, troparia, and kontakia.

The services of Monday and Tuesday contain a large number of penitential texts. At Sunday vespers three stichera "of tenderness" are sung at "Lord, I call." Their mood recalls the *Great Canon of Repentance* of Saint Andrew of Crete. The

Six Days (Shestodnev). Icon reflecting the liturgical themes of every day. Workshop of Dionysius. 16th c.

first three stichera at vespers on Tuesday are imbued with the same mood. Many hymns and readings of Monday and Tuesday are called "tender" and "penitential." At matins on both Monday and Tuesday *martyrika*—troparia in honor of the martyrs—are added to the troparia of the canon.

The service to the bodiless powers is added to the penitential texts on Monday. It includes three stichera at "Lord, I call" and a second canon, read at matins—the work of Theophanes Graptus. On Tuesday the service to the Forerunner is added to the basic group of stichera, troparia, and canons. This is also composed of three stichera at "Lord, I call" and a canon.

Wednesday and Friday commemorate the sufferings and death of the Savior on the cross. Fasting is prescribed on these days throughout the entire year with the exception of fast-free weeks. Many hymns on these days, including the canons at matins, are dedicated to the precious and life-giving cross and the most-holy Theotokos. (On Friday the second canon of matins bears the name "of the cross and the Theotokos").

On Thursday the apostles and Saint Nicholas are glorified during the service. At vespers the first three stichera at "Lord, I call" and the aposticha are dedicated to the apostles. At vespers three stichera at "Lord, I call" are dedicated to Saint Nicholas and at matins, the second canon. Troparia to the martyrs are added to the service to the apostles in several places.

Saturday is a day of commemoration of all the saints and departed, connected with the remembrance of the Lord in the tomb and his victory over death. At vespers on the eve of Saturday the first three stichera at "Lord, I call" are dedicated to the memory of the martyrs, enlightener saints (hierarchs), and venerable saints; the next three are stichera "of the martyrs." At the aposticha, the first sticheron is dedicated to the martyrs, while the other two are for the departed. On Saturday at matins two canons are read: the first to the martyrs, enlightener saints, and venerable saints, while the second is dedicated to the departed. At the praises four stichera are dedicated to the martyrs and four others to the departed.

The daily worship cycle of the Octoechos is performed in the period from the Sunday of All Saints (the first Sunday after Pentecost) up to the Sunday of the Publican and the Pharisee (the first Sunday of the Triodion period). On weekdays of this period the service of the Octoechos is combined with the services to the saints according to the Menaion. The order for the combination of the services is regulated by the Typikon. The number of hymns from the Octoechos is reduced in proportion to the increased number of hymns in honor of a saint. When an all-night vigil is served for a saint, the Octoechos is not used at all, and the service is performed solely according to the Menaion. The Octoechos is used only at certain moments of the service on weekdays of Great Lent: in this period it is combined not only with the Menaion, but also with the Lenten Triodion. From Lazarus Saturday until Great Saturday, the Octoechos is not used at all.

PART FOUR

The Yearly Cycle of Worship Services

6

The Formation of the Yearly Cycle of Worship

THE DEVELOPMENT OF THE YEARLY CYCLE OF WORSHIP FROM THE FIRST THROUGH THE NINTH CENTURY

IN THE EARLY CHRISTIAN CHURCH (in the first through third centuries) the yearly cycle of worship services was based on two feasts—Pascha and Pentecost.[1] Both feasts of the Church were inherited from the Jewish tradition, in which Passover was a remembrance of the exodus of the Jewish nation from Egypt, while Pentecost was a remembrance of the covenant made on Mount Sinai between God and the Jewish people (see Ex 19. 1–16). In the Christian Church, from the very beginning Pascha was a celebration of the resurrection of Christ, while Pentecost was a remembrance of the descent of the Holy Spirit upon the apostles (see Acts 2.1–13).

At first, the date of celebrating Pascha was not the same for all Christian churches. At the end of the second century this issue stirred up controversies[2] between the churches of Asia Minor and Pope Victor of Rome (pope from 189–199). Bishop Polycrates of Ephesus participated in the controversy on behalf of the Christians of Asia Minor. He defended the local tradition (supposedly dating back to Apostle John the Theologian) of celebrating Pascha together with the Jews on the fourteenth day of the month Nissan, no matter what day of the week or date it happened to be. Pope Victor, on the contrary, insisted that Pascha ought to be celebrated without fail on the day of resurrection (Sunday): in this he followed the tradition of the churches of Rome, Alexandria, Corinth, and Palestine. The controversy nearly led to mutual excommunications, but Saint Irenaeus of Lyons entered into the controversy and succeeded in reconciling the feuding sides.[3]

---

[1]Hippolytus of Rome, *Apostolic Tradition* 33 (Stewart, PPS); Origen, *Against Celsus* (*ANF* 4:648).

[2]The time of the controversies was AD 190–192. Supposedly the controversies were stirred up because in the year 189 Pascha was celebrated on April 20 in Alexandria, while in the churches of Asia Minor it was celebrated on March 20. See Vasilii Vasil'evich Bolotov, "From the epoch of controversies concerning Pascha at the end of the second century" [in Russian], *Christian reading* no. 1 (1900): 450–454.

[3]Eusebius Pamphilius, *Church History* 5.23–25 (*NPNF²* 1:241–244). [He famously said, "The disagreement in regard to the fast confirms the agreement in the faith." *Church History* 5.24.13 (*NPNF²* 1:243).—*Ed.*]

In the second and third centuries, the celebration of Pascha was preceded by one, two, or several days of fasting. In particular, a two-day fast preceding Pascha is mentioned in the *Apostolic Tradition*.[4] Saint Irenaus of Lyons wrote, "Some think that they should fast one day, others two, yet others more; some, moreover, count their day as consisting of forty hours day and night."[5] A lengthier fast was prescribed for those preparing to receive baptism.[6] The fast preceding Pascha was dedicated to the remembrance of the sufferings and death of Christ on the cross and was called the "pascha of the crucifixion" (*pascha staurosimon*), differing from "pascha of the resurrection" the (*pascha anastasimon*), which was a remembrance of Christ's resurrection.

As with its Jewish prototype, the Christian passover was a nighttime feast: the divine service began on Saturday evening and ended on Sunday morning. The paschal divine worship included readings from the Old Testament, including excerpts from the book of the Prophet Hosea (chapter six) and the Book of Exodus (chapter twelve concerning the exodus from Egypt). Following the readings a homily was given, sometimes in metrical form: a classic example of the paschal homily is the poem by Melito of Sardis, *On Pascha* (*Peri Pascha*).[7] Readings and homilies alternated with the performance of psalms and hymns. In the early morning the baptism of the catechumens was performed, which constituted an integral part of the paschal celebration. The worship service continued with the Eucharist, in which the entire community participated, including the newly baptized Christians.

Pentecost was celebrated fifty days after Pascha and was the conclusion of the paschal cycle. Those who for whatever reason were not ready for baptism on Pascha were baptized on Pentecost.[8] Although the overriding meaning of Christian Pentecost was the remembrance of the descent of the Holy Spirit upon the apostles, this event was understood in light of the Old Testament typology of the feast. In this way, Pentecost became a celebration of the establishment of the new covenant between God and the new Israel—Christians. The gift of the new covenant was foretold in the Old Testament, as was the outpouring of the Holy Spirit (see Jer 31.33; Ezek 36.26–27; Joel 2.28–32), but this was only realized fifty days after Christ's resurrection. For this reason the feast of Pentecost was inseparably linked to Pascha from the very beginning.

[4]Hippolytus of Rome, *Apostolic Tradition* 29.2 (Stewart, PPS).

[5]Irenaeus of Lyons, *Epistle to Victor, Bishop of Rome*, cited in Eusebius Pamphilius, *Church History* 5.24.12 (*NPNF*² 1:243).

[6]Justin Martyr, *First Apology* 61 (*ANF* 1:183).

[7]Concerning this poem, see vol. 2, 246–249 and 303–304.

[8]Dix, *Liturgy*, 341.

The development of the cult of the martyrs and the institution of the days of their commemoration in the local churches date to the second century. The most ancient witness of this veneration is contained in *The Martyrdom of Saint Polycarp of Smyrna*, dating to the middle of the second century (around 156). Here, honoring martyrs is connected to the worship of Christ: "We worship him as the Son of God, while we worthily love the martyrs as disciples and imitators of the Lord for their invincible devotion to their King and Teacher. May God grant us also to be in their company and to be fellow disciples!"[9] After relating the story of the martyr's death, the authors of the narrative write, "Accordingly, we afterwards took up his bones, as being more precious than the most exquisite jewels, and more purified than gold, and deposited them in a fitting place, whither, being gathered together, as opportunity is allowed us, with joy and rejoicing, the Lord shall grant us to celebrate the anniversary of his martyrdom, both in memory of those who have already finished their course, and for the exercising and preparation of those yet to walk in their steps."[10]

In the second and third centuries the veneration of saints was of a local character: every local church had its own list of martyrs. The veneration of each martyr was connected not only with the anniversary of his death but also with the place to which his relics were transferred. The bodies of martyrs were often buried in catacombs where temples were built in their honor and where Christians gathered every year to venerate their memory with prayer and the celebration of the Eucharist.

In this way, the calendar of any given local Church in the second and third centuries consisted of two universal feasts (Pascha and Pentecost) and the days of commemoration of venerated local saints (martyrs). In some places, other dates of commemoration, such as Theophany, were added to this. It is possible that Theophany was celebrated on January 6 in several eastern churches as early as the beginning of the second century. "Theophany" was understood to be an entire series of events linked with the incarnation, including the birth of Jesus from the virgin and his baptism in the waters of the River Jordan. Saint Clement of Alexandria made reference to a separate celebration of the baptism of our Lord Jesus Christ (albeit in connection with the sect of Basilides).[11]

The fasts on Wednesdays and Fridays are an extremely early tradition dating to apostolic times. The *Didache* mentions this tradition as early as the first half of

[9] *The Martyrdom of Saint Polycarp of Smyrna* 18 (*ANF* 1:43).
[10] Ibid.
[11] Clement of Alexandria, *The Stromata* 1.21 (*ANF* 2:324–334).

the second century,[12] and later Tertullian mentions it in the beginning of the third century.[13]

The formation of Great Lent as a forty-day cycle dates to the fourth century. While in the second and third centuries an extended fast before Pascha was prescribed only for catechumens, in the fourth century in various churches the faithful began to join the catechumens. The period of the fast then became a time of repentance and spiritual watchfulness for the faithful. The monastic movement, which had swiftly gained strength in the fourth century, also influenced the formation of this tradition. Moreover, the "forty days" in various churches was calculated in different ways. In Rome the faithful fasted for six weeks. In Jerusalem forty days were assigned over a period of eight weeks preceding Pascha: on Saturdays or Sundays there was no fasting, and the forty days did not include the special fasting during Holy Week before Pascha. In 329, in Alexandria, the faithful observed a fast only for a single week before Pascha, but as early as 336 Saint Athanasius of Alexandria called upon the faithful to observe a forty-day fast. In 339, Saint Athanasius, writing from Rome, wrote to his flock about the necessity of observing a forty-day fast and mentioned that it was done universally.[14]

The fifth-century church historian Socrates Scholasticus wrote about the different lengths of Great Lent in various Churches, and the fact that the abstinence from food itself was interpreted in different ways:

> The fasts before Easter will be found to be differently observed among different people. Those at Rome fast three successive weeks before Easter, excepting Saturdays and Sundays. Those in Illyrica and all over Greece and Alexandria observe a fast of six weeks, which they term "the forty days' fast." Others commencing their fast from the seventh week before Easter, and fasting three five days only, and that at intervals, yet call that time "the forty days' fast." It is indeed surprising to me that thus differing in the number of days, they should both give it one common appellation; but some assign one reason for it, and others another, according to their several fancies. One can see also a disagreement about the manner of abstinence from food, as well as about the number of days. Some wholly abstain from things that have life: others feed on fish only of all living creatures: many together with fish eat fowl also, saying that according to Moses, these were likewise made out of the waters. Some abstain

---

[12]*Didache* 8.
[13]Tertullian, *On Fasting* 2 (*ANF* 4:102–103).
[14]Dix, *Liturgy*, 354–355.

Descent into Hell. Chora Monastery. Constantinople. 14th c.

from eggs, and all kinds of fruits: others partake of dry bread only; still others eat not even this: while others having fasted till the ninth hour, afterwards take any sort of food without distinction.[15]

During the fourth century the liturgical cycle of the Christian churches of the East and West was fundamentally expanded due to the introduction of new feasts, the reinterpretation of old feasts, the addition of the commemoration of new saints, the "exchange of feasts" between local churches, and the increase in the number of fast days. A radical expansion and enrichment of the church calendar was one of the major aspects of the liturgical reform of the fourth century, whose beginning was laid by Emperor Constantine's Edict of Milan, which opened up the possibility for the Church to change from a persecuted religious community into a powerful and elaborate organization on an imperial level.

In the fourth century, the development of the yearly liturgical cycle, as well as the development of the daily liturgical cycle was, as before, linked with the major centers of the Church—Jerusalem, Antioch, Alexandria, and Constantinople, and in the West, Rome.

For the church in Jerusalem, the fourth century was the time of the formation of Holy Week as a pre-paschal liturgical cycle, dedicated to the remembrance of the final days of the earthly life of Christ. This cycle developed out of a more ancient and shorter "Pascha of the Crucifixion." In Jerusalem, which was renewed by the

[15]Socrates Scholasticus, *Church History* 5.22 (*NPNF*[2] 2:131).

order of Emperor Constantine and made into a major church center, the divine services of Holy Week were performed with exceptional solemnity.

We find a similar description of these liturgical services in the writings of Egeria, the pilgrim from Gaul who visited Jerusalem at the end of the fourth century.[16] According to her witness, on the eighth day before Pascha the raising of Lazarus by the Lord was commemorated in Jerusalem: on this day a ceremonial procession set out from Jerusalem to Bethany (the Lazarium), where the major worship service was performed. On the next day, the Entry of the Lord into Jerusalem was celebrated, when the faithful led by the bishop gathered on the Mount of Olives. After celebrating the divine service there, the procession moved into Jerusalem to the singing of antiphonal and other hymns; children from the surrounding villages held palm branches and olive branches in their hands. On Monday, Tuesday, and Wednesday of Holy Week, the divine services were performed in the Church of the Resurrection of Christ according to the order established for the days of Great Lent.

On Great Thursday, matins and the third and sixth hours were performed, as on the previous days, and the service of the ninth hour began at the eighth hour (about two o'clock in the afternoon). This was followed by the divine liturgy. Right after the conclusion of the divine liturgy, the people went to a small chapel behind the life-giving cross of the Lord, where a second liturgy was celebrated. By nightfall, the people gathered on the Mount of Olives, where the vigil of Great Friday began. The people remained there until the fifth hour of night (eleven o'clock in the evening). At about midnight, all went to the place of the Lord's ascension, and while the roosters crowed, the people walked to the place where Jesus prayed on the eve of his sufferings. From there, all went to the Garden of Gethsemane. Here the morning service was celebrated, during which the people heard the gospel reading describing how Jesus Christ was arrested. "And when the passage has been read," noted Egeria, "there is such a moaning and groaning of all the people that no one can help being moved to tears at that hour."[17] Then the procession returned to the main church in Jerusalem. At the end of the all-night vigil the procession moved to the column at which the flogging of Christ took place, after which all departed to their homes.

---

[16]See Egeria, *Pilgrimage* 29–44, in *The Pilgrimage of Etheria*, ed. and trans. M. L. McClure and C. L. Feltoe (London: Society for Promoting Christian Knowledge, 1919).

[17]*The Pilgrimage of Etheria*, ed. and trans. M. L. McClure and C. L. Feltoe (London: Society for Promoting Christian Knowledge, 1919), 69.

During the day, a table was placed on Golgotha on which a piece of the life-giving cross was laid. The people slowly approached to venerate and kiss the cross. At the sixth hour the worship service began in the open air, during which psalms were read, as well as excerpts from the Book of Epistles and Gospel Book, dedicated to the sufferings of Christ. The worship service ended at the ninth hour with a reading concerning the Lord's death on the cross. After this, vespers began right away in the *martyrium* (main basilica), at which the gospel was read concerning the burial of Jesus by Joseph. After vespers many people remained in the church for the entire night, singing hymns and antiphons.

Renewal of the Temple of the Resurrection of Christ. Fragment of an Icon. Rostov the Great. End of 16th–beginning of 17th c.

The liturgy was not celebrated on the morning of Great Saturday. The third and sixth hours were read at the normal time, and around the ninth hour (three o'clock in the afternoon), the paschal vigil began. It included the baptism of the catechumens, who at the end of the mystery were brought into the Church of the Resurrection, from which, together with the bishop, they proceeded into the martyrium. There the first paschal liturgy was celebrated. At its conclusion, a procession again moved to the Church of the Resurrection, where a second paschal liturgy was celebrated in the early morning hours. People returned to their homes at the end of the second liturgy. They congregated again in the evening of the same day on Mount Zion for the celebration of paschal vespers.

The celebration of Pascha continued during the course of the entire week of Pascha. On the next Sunday after Pascha, a service was celebrated at which the gospel concerning the Lord's appearance to Thomas was read.

Jerusalem is where two feasts were born: the Consecration [literally, "Renewal"] of the Church of the Resurrection of Christ and the Exaltation of the Cross of the Lord. The Church of the Resurrection of Christ in Jerusalem was consecrated on September 13 in the year 335, and the feast of the Exaltation of the Cross was established on the next day, September 14. In the fourth century the Exaltation became one of the three major feasts in Jerusalem together with Pascha and Theophany. In the fifth century, according to the account of Sozomen, the feast of the Exaltation was celebrated in Jerusalem over the course of eight days.[18] By the end of the

---

[18]Sozomen, *Church History* 2.26 (*NPNF*² 2:276–277).

fourth century, the celebration of the Exaltation of the Cross was celebrated beyond Jerusalem. The life of Saint John Chrysostom, written by Patriarch George I of Alexandria, indicates that in the time of Chrysostom the feast of the Exaltation was celebrated in Constantinople. The account of the life of Saint Mary of Egypt points to the celebration of this feast in Alexandria at the end of the fifth century.

The celebration of the feast of the Meeting of the Lord began in Jerusalem in the second half of the fourth century. Originally the date of this feast was February 15 (forty days after Theophany) but later, with the establishment of a separate celebration of the Nativity on December 25, the Meeting of the Lord was transferred to February 2 (forty days after Nativity). The Meeting of the Lord was adopted by Constantinople in the sixth century and by Rome no later than the beginning of the eighth century.[19]

Constantinople played an important role in the formation of the Christian calendar. As the capital was founded by Constantine on the site of the insignificant city of Byzantium, where there were no sites for the veneration of martyrs, the relics or parts of relics of martyrs who had suffered in other cities began to be transferred to Constantinople in the fourth and subsequent centuries. It was in this period that the tradition emerged of dividing the relics of the martyrs into numerous parts and exchanging them between local churches. This made the universalization of the veneration of martyrs possible—turning the veneration of martyrs from a local practice to a universal Christian one.[20]

The Roman calendar is the most ancient of the full church calendars to have come down to us and dates to the middle of the fourth century (354). Pascha and Pentecost are not mentioned in it because their celebration was not connected to fixed dates. Generally, twenty-four dates containing feasts are found in the calendar. The only feast of the Lord was Christmas on December 25. All the other dates were days of commemoration of martyrs, including the memory of the apostles Peter and Paul on June 29.[21]

An "exchange of feasts" took place in the fourth century between the two parts of the empire—East and West. The East received from the West the feast of the Nativity, while the West received from the East the feast of the Theophany.

The feast of the Nativity of Christ, celebrated on December 25, emerged in the West no later than in the third century.[22] The beginning of the separate celebration

[19]Dix, *Liturgy*, 358.
[20]Ibid., 351.
[21]Archbishop Sergii (Spasskii), *Complete Menologion of the East* [in Russian] (Vladimir, 1901; repr. Moscow: Pravoslavnyi Palomnik, 1997), 1:40–41.
[22]Dix, *Liturgy*, 357.

of the Nativity of Christ in the East dates to the last quarter of the fourth century. The earliest homily on the Nativity of Christ belongs to Saint Gregory the Theologian and was probably delivered at the end of the year 380. Several scholars consider that it was precisely Saint Gregory the Theologian, the archbishop of Constantinople, who introduced the celebration of the Nativity in the Byzantine capital.[23] It is probable that the feast was established after Emperor Theodosius—who expelled Arians from the capital and restored Orthodoxy—came to power. But it is significant that Saint Gregory calls the celebration of Christmas on December 25 "Theophany," while he calls the feast of the Lord's baptism on January 6 the "Day of Lights."

The feast of the Nativity of Christ arrived in Antioch at about this time. In his *Homily on the Day of the Nativity*, Saint John Chrysostom wrote:

> Although it is not yet the tenth year, from when this day has become clear and well known to us, but nevertheless it has flourished through your zeal, as if delivered to us from the beginning and many years ago. . . . For just as with hardy and good trees (for the latter, as soon as they are put down into the earth, immediately shoot up to a great height and are heavy with fruit), so too this day being well known among those living in the West from the beginning, and now having been brought to us, and not many years ago, thus shot up at once and bore so much fruit, as is possible to see now—our sacred court filled, and the whole church crowded by the multitude of those gathering together.[24]

It is supposed that Chrysostom's homily was delivered between the years 386 and 388 in Antioch. As such, the expression "it is not yet the tenth year" may indicate that the establishment of the feast of the Nativity was in the years 377 to 380.[25] Chrysostom's words indicate that the feast was transferred from the West and quickly became popular over the course of a few years.

But in Jerusalem, on the contrary, the Nativity was celebrated together with Theophany on January 6 for quite a long time—probably until the sixth century. In particular, the Byzantine traveller and historian Cosmas Indicopleustes bears

[23]See Hermann Usener, *Religionsgeschichtliche Untersuchungen* (Bonn, 1911), 260–269; Justin Mossay, *Les fêtes de Noël et d'Épiphanie: d'après les sources littéraires cappadociennes du IVe siècle*, Textes et études liturgiques 3 (Louvain: Abbaye du Mont César, 1965), 34; Jean Bernardi, *La Prédication des pères cappadociens, le prédicateur et son auditoire* (Paris: Presses universitaires de France, 1968), 205.

[24]John Chrysostom, *Homily on the Day of the Nativity* 1. Translation in Beth Elise Dunlop, "Earliest Greek Patristic Orations on the Nativity: A Study Including Translations" (PhD diss., Boston College, 2004), 179–181.

[25]Sergii (Spasskii), *Complete Menologion of the East*, 3:522.

witness to this.[26] Moreover, it was quite late that the feast of the Nativity entered into the calendar of the Alexandrian Church.[27]

The feast of the Ascension of the Lord stood apart from the feast of Pentecost at the end of the fourth century. Homilies for this feast are found in the works of Saint Gregory of Nyssa and Saint John Chrysostom.[28] The *Apostolic Constitutions* contain the words "from the first Lord's day count forty days, from the Lord's day till the fifth day of the week, and celebrate the feast of the Ascension of the Lord, whereon he finished all his dispensation and constitution, and returned to that God and Father that sent him, and sat down at the right hand of power."[29] The first references to the Ascension of the Lord in works of Western authors (Chromatius, Philostorgius) date to the end of the fourth century.[30]

VIEWS OF THE FOURTH-CENTURY FATHERS ON THE CHURCH FEASTS

The works of the Church fathers of the fourth century help us understand the place the feasts held in the life of the Church. Each of the great Eastern fathers left homilies on certain feasts and days commemorating the saints.

In particular, Saint Basil the Great's homilies include "On the Holy Nativity of Christ," and homilies on days commemorating the martyr Julita, the holy martyr Gordius, the holy forty martyrs, and the holy martyr Mamas.

The calendar of Saint Gregory the Theologian—that is, the calendar of the church of Constantinople of the 380s—included Nativity, Theophany, Pascha, New Sunday (the first Sunday after Pascha), and Pentecost. Saint Gregory dedicated a separate homily to each of these feasts. Moreover, Saint Gregory left homilies in memory of the Maccabee martyrs, Saint Cyprian of Carthage, Saint Athanasius of Alexandria, and Saint Basil the Great.

Saint Gregory of Nyssa left homilies on the day of the Savior's Nativity, the Day of Lights, Holy Pascha, the three-day sojourn of our Lord Jesus Christ between

---

[26] Ibid.

[27] Dix, *Liturgy*, 358.

[28] Gregory of Nyssa, *On the Ascension of Christ* (PG 46:689c–693b). John Chrysostom, *On the Ascension* (PG 50:441–452). See also John Chrysostom, *On Holy Pentecost* 1.2 (PG 50:456)—"Ten days ago our essence rose up to the King's throne"; ibid., 2.1 (PG 50:463)—"First we celebrated the cross, suffering, resurrection, and then the rising into the heavens of our Lord Jesus Christ", and others.

[29] *Apostolic Constitutions* 5.19 (*ANF* 7:447–448).

[30] A. A. Lukashevich and A. A. Tkachenko, "The Ascension of the Lord" [in Russian], in *Orthodox Encyclopedia* (Moscow: Tserkovno-nauchnyi tsentr "Pravoslavnaia entsiklopediia," 2005), 9:200.

his death and the resurrection (paschal homily), Holy and Saving Pascha, the Resurrection of Christ, the Ascension of our Lord Jesus Christ, and the Holy Spirit (homily on Pentecost). The works of this saint also include two homilies in memory of the protomartyr Stephen, an oration in praise of the great martyr Theodore, three homilies on the forty martyrs of Sebaste, a homily on the life of Saint Gregory the Wonderworker, an oration in praise of his brother Saint Basil, archbishop of Ceasarea in Cappadocia, and an oration in praise of Saint Ephraim the Syrian (the authenticity of this last homily is disputed).

Saints Gregory the Theologian, John Chrysostom, and Basil the Great. Icon. 14th c.

Among the authentic works of Saint John Chrysostom, we have his homilies on the Nativity, the baptism of the Lord (Theophany), the resurrection of the dead, the Ascension, Pentecost, the Apostle Paul, the martyrs Lucian, Babylas, Juventinus, and Maximinus, Romanus, Julian, Barlaam, the martyr Pelagia, the martyrs Bernike, Prosdoke, and Domnina, the hieromartyr Ignatius the God-bearer, the Maccabee martyrs, the great martyr Drosis, and the hieromartyr Phocas.

Each of the fathers of the fourth century contributed not only to the understanding of a particular feast, but also to the notion of the very phenomenon of the church feast in general. Saint Gregory the Theologian played an exceptional role in this by constructing his festal homilies as a series of theological treatises dedicated to the theme of the feast.

In his homily on the Nativity of Christ, Saint Gregory speaks of the yearly cycle of church feasts and about the fact that during the course of the liturgical year the whole life of Jesus and his entire work of salvation passes before the eyes of each believer:

> So shortly you will also see[31] the purification of Jesus in the Jordan for my purification; or rather he is cleansed for the purification of the waters, for he indeed did not need purification, who takes away the sin of the world. The heavens are parted and he receives a testimony of the Spirit, who is akin to him. He is tempted and conquers the tempter and is served by angels. He heals every sickness and every infirmity, and gives life to the dead. . . . He drives out demons, some by himself and others through his disciples. With a few loaves he feeds

[31]The expression "shortly you will also see" refers to January 6, the Day of Lights.

tens of thousands, and he walks on the sea. He is betrayed and crucified and crucifies my sin with himself. He is offered as a lamb and offers as a priest, he is buried as a human being, raised as God, then also ascends, and he will return with his own glory. How many celebrations there are for me corresponding to each of the mysteries of Christ! Yet they all have one completion, my perfection and refashioning and restoration to the state of the first Adam.[32]

According to Saint Gregory's teaching, every feast of the Church should be for the faithful a new step on the path to perfection and a new insight into the life and redemptive work of the Messiah. We should celebrate feasts "in a godly manner, not in a worldly way but in a manner above the world."[33]

According to Saint Gregory, the feasts of the Church are not a matter of hanging wreaths on the doors of our homes, gathering dancers, decorating streets, feasting one's eyes on spectacles or one's ears on secular music. The feasts are not for putting on soft clothing, dressing up with precious stones and gold, or using cosmetics (as women do); they are not a matter of preparing banquets, feasting on luxurious meals, drinking expensive wines, and surpassing others in lack of restraint. Rather, the feasts of the Church are for believers a matter of coming to church to delight in the word of God and to worship the Word who became flesh.[34]

The main objective of every feast of the Church is to teach Christians to imitate Christ in every stage of one's life. Each person receives a share of sufferings, but Christ's life consisted of suffering and sorrows—beginning with the flight to Egypt right up to his death on the cross. Christ's sufferings and death lead him to resurrection and glory. In the same way, by imitating Christ by doing good deeds and ascetic works, and by being crucified with Christ, the life of every believer becomes a path to glory and deification. So, too, in passing through the stages of the Savior's suffering, Christians rise together with him and are led by him into the kingdom of heaven:

It is good to flee with the persecuted Christ. . . . Travel blamelessly through all the stages of Christ's life and all his powers, as a disciple of Christ. Be purified, be circumcised,[35] that is remove the veil that has surrounded you since birth. After this teach in the temple, drive out the traders in divine things, be stoned if it is necessary that you suffer this. . . . If you are brought before Herod, do

[32]Gregory the Theologian, *Orations* 38.16 (SC 358:140–142; Harrison, PPS).
[33]Ibid. 38.4 (SC 358:110; Harrison, PPS).
[34]Ibid. 38.5 (SC 358:110–112; Harrison, PPS).
[35]Gregory is speaking of spiritual circumcision.

not answer for the most part. He will revere your silence more than the long discourses of others. If you are scourged, seek the other tortures. Taste the gall because of the taste [of the forbidden fruit]. Drink the vinegar, seek the spittings, accept the blows, the beatings; be crowned with thorns through the harshness of a life in accord with God. Put on the scarlet robe, accept the reed, and the worship of those who mock the truth. Finally, be crucified with him, die with him, be buried with him willingly, so as also to be resurrected with him and glorified with him and reign with him, seeing God as far as is possible and being seen by him, who is worshiped and glorified in the Trinity. . . .[36]

In Homily 39, dedicated to the celebration of the baptism of the Lord, a direct continuation of the Nativity homily, Saint Gregory speaks of the feast as a mystery that reveals the meaning of the term "mystery" (Gr. *mystērion*, from *myeō*—to cover, conceal), which from the time of early antiquity signified "initiation." In ancient Greek religion there were various mysteries that accompanied the whole life of a person from birth to death: they were called by the names of the gods to whom they were dedicated (e.g. the mysteries of Mithras), and also by the name of the place in which they were performed (e.g. the Eleusinian Mysteries). In late Neo-platonism mysteries were perceived as separate stages of "*theourgia*"—a person's gradual introduction to personal contact with the world of gods. In the beginning of the 360s, Julian the Apostate attempted to revive the mysteries on the state level and himself took part in several initiations; in the 370s Emperor Valens wanted to suppress the Eleusinian Mysteries, but he had to abandon his intention because paganism in the empire was still strong.[37]

The question of pagan mysteries was most pressing for Saint Gregory's audience at the turn of the 380s, and he deemed it necessary to draw a clear distinction between such mysteries and the Christian feasts. The saint asserted that the two had nothing in common:

Again my Jesus, and again a mystery, a mystery not deceitful or disorderly, nor belonging to the disorder and drunkenness of the [pagan] Greeks—for thus I name their solemnities, as, I think, everyone sensible will—but a mystery exalted and divine and bringing the radiance from above. For the holy day of lights, to which we have come and which we are deemed worthy to celebrate

---

[36]Gregory the Theologian, *Orations* 38.18 (SC 358:146–148; Harrison, PPS).

[37]See Diether Lauenstein, *The Eleusinian Mysteries* [in Russian], trans. N. Fedorova (Moscow: Enigma, 1996), 52.

today, takes its origin from the baptism of my Christ, the true light, which illumines every human being coming into the world, effects my purification, and strengthens the light we received from him from the beginning, which we darkened and blotted out through sin. . . . Is it something like what the Greeks reveal in their initiations? To me all their initiations and mysteries are nonsense, dark inventions of demons and fabrications of a demon-possessed mind. . . . For I am ashamed to grant to the day the initiation of the night and make what is unseemly a mystery. Eleusis knows these things, as do those who see the things that are guarded in silence and are surely deserving of silence.[38]

After emphasizing the demonic character of pagan mysteries, Saint Gregory speaks of the divine and sanctifying character of Christian mysteries and feasts. Christ himself is present in these mysteries and sanctifies and cleanses the person who participates in them. The baptism of each person is performed according to the model of the baptism of Christ, and the feast of the baptism of Christ becomes a holy day for all who are baptized in Christ:

Therefore at his birth we kept festival as was fitting. . . . But now there is another deed of Christ. . . . Christ is illumined, let us flash like lightning with him. Christ is baptized, let us go down with him, that we also come up again with him. . . . Yet as John is baptizing, Jesus approaches, perhaps also to sanc-tify the baptizer, and certainly to bury all the old Adam in the water. . . . Jesus comes up again out of the water. For he carries up with himself the world and "sees the heavens opened" [Mk 1.10] which Adam closed for himself and for those after him. . . .[39]

Saint Gregory says that earthly life is given to man for repentance and purifica-tion. Every feast of the Church serves the objective of man's purification:

But let us honor today the baptism of Christ and celebrate well, not feasting with the stomach but rejoicing spiritually. And how shall we feast? "Wash, become pure." If you are "red" with sin but less than blood-red, become "white as snow" [Is 1.16–18]; but if you are scarlet and complete "men of blood," still, come to be "white as wool." Be entirely purified and be pure, for nothing gives so much joy to God as the correction and salvation of the human being, for whose sake every discourse and every mystery exist. . . .[40]

[38]Gregory the Theologian, *Oration* 39.1, 3–4 (SC 358:150–154; Harrison, PPS).
[39]Ibid. 39.1, 3–4 (SC 358:150–154; Harrison, PPS).
[40]Ibid. 39.20 (SC 358:194; Harrison, PPS).

The Christian temple is a prototype of the kingdom of heaven. The feasts of the Church are a foretaste of the unceasing joy of the faithful in the age to come; the mysteries are a pledge of the mystical union of human souls with Christ. For Christians, the transition to "the life of the age to come" begins here—by participation in the life of the Church, in her mysteries and feasts. Saint Gregory speaks of this, recalling the solemn entry of the newly baptized into the temple for participation in the celebration of the Eucharist, indicating the symbolic meaning of the temple service:

> The position in which you will stand immediately after baptism before the great sanctuary is a foreshadowing of the future glory. The psalmody with which you will be received is a prelude of the hymnody there. The lamps that you will kindle are a symbol[41] of the procession of lights there, with which you will go to meet the Bridegroom with bright and virgin souls, with lamps bright with faith.[42]

Here the feast is the "transition" from one reality to another—from the reality of earthly existence to the reality of the kingdom of heaven. Saint Gregory speaks of this in his Homily 45, *On Holy Pascha*. The homily is built on the juxtaposition of the Old Testament Passover as a remembrance of the Israelites' passing over the Red Sea and the New Testament Pascha as the celebration of the resurrection of Christ. Saint Gregory interprets all the details of the Old Testament Passover as a foreshadowing of the New Testament reality.

Saint Gregory speaks of Pascha as the main event in the Church year, surpassing all other feasts in its significance. As with the baptism of the Lord, Pascha is a feast of light, which is symbolized by the lighting of candles throughout the entire city on the night of Pascha:

> Beautiful indeed yesterday[43] were our splendid array and procession of lights, in which we were united both privately and publicly, almost every sort of people and every rank, lighting up the night with plentiful fires. This is a symbol of the great light, both the heavenly light that makes fire signals from above . . . and equally . . . the Trinity, by which every light has been produced, divided off from the undivided light and honored. Yet today is more beautiful and more

[41]I.e., a mystical type.

[42]Gregory the Theologian, *Orations* 40.46 (SC 358:308; Harrison, PPS).

[43]"Yesterday" means the evening of Great and Holy Saturday. It is evident that Saint Gregory intended to deliver his sermon at the liturgy on the day of Pascha itself.

illustrious, inasmuch as yesterday's light was a forerunner of the great light's rising, and as it were a kind of pre-festal gladness. But today we celebrate the resurrection itself, not as still hoped for but as having already occurred and gathering the whole world to itself.[44]

How are the faithful joined to the paschal celebration? By participation in Christ's sufferings and through empathy with the characters of the gospel story who are mentioned in the narrative of the final days of the earthly life of Jesus:

> If you are a Simeon of Cyrene, take up the cross and follow. If you are crucified with him as a thief, come to know God as kindhearted. . . . Worship the one hanged for you even if you are hanging. . . . And if you are Joseph from Arimathaea, ask for the body from the crucifier; let that which cleanses the world become yours. And if you are Nicodemus, the nocturnal worshipper of God, bury him with scented ointment. And if you are a certain Mary or another Mary or Salome or Joanna, weep at daybreak. Be first to see the stone removed, and perhaps the angels and Jesus himself. . . . Become a Peter or John, hasten to the tomb. . . . And if he descends into Hades, go down with him.[45]

In Homily 41, dedicated to the feast of Pentecost, Saint Gregory says that the prototype of the Christian feast is the Old Testament "jubilee"—a year of remission. According to the mosaic law, every seventh year was considered a year of peace in which it was not permitted to sow the field or gather grapes. Each fiftieth year was proclaimed to be a jubilee—a feast year in which people receieved their possessions back, forgave debtors their debts, and freed slaves (Lev 25). The designation of a year of jubilee, dedicated in a special way to God, consisted not only in giving people rest, but also, as far as possible, in correcting the inequality and injustice existing in human society. The jubilee was a year of reckoning in which people gave an account to God and each other regarding how they lived their lives, and began to live them more in accordance with God's commandments. In this way, the jubilee became a prototype for the life of people in the age to come, in which there is no social inequality, no slaves or lords, no lenders or debtors.

> The children of the Hebrews honor the number seven following the legislation of Moses. . . . Yet this honor is not for these days alone but also extends to years. Thus among days the Sabbath is that which they continually honor. . . .

---

[44]Gregory the Theologian, *Orations* 45.2 (PG 36:624–625; Harrison, PPS).
[45]Ibid. 45.24 (PG 36:656–657; Harrison, PPS).

[A]nd among years the seventh is the year of release. And this concerns not only sevens but sevens of sevens, alike in days and years. Thus the sevens of days generate Pentecost which is called by them a holy day; the sevens of years to what they call Jubilee, which brings all at once release of land, freedom for slaves, and release of property bought. For this people consecrates to God not only the firstfruits of offspring or the firstborn but also the firstfruits of days and years. Thus the honoring of the number seven brought with it the honor of Pentecost. For seven multiplied by itself generates fifty minus one day, and this we have taken from the age to come, which is at once the eighth and the first, or rather one and indissoluble.[46]

In the Christian tradition, Pentecost is the feast of the Holy Spirit—the Comforter, who comes to take the place of Christ, who ascended into heaven. Christ's works on earth are finished, and the Sabbath rest began for Christ—as a man—at the moment of his burial. An era of jubilee has come for Christians after Christ's resurrection—an unending fiftieth year beginning on earth and overflowing into eternity. The era of the jubilee is characterized primarily by the active renewing work of the Holy Spirit. Under the influence of the grace of the Spirit, people are changed in a fundamental way; they are transformed from shepherds into prophets, from fishermen into apostles.[47]

Saint Gregory thinks that Christian feasts should never cease. He speaks of this at the conclusion of his homily on Pentecost:

But now we must dissolve the gathering, for the discourse is sufficient, but never the feast. But it is necessary to celebrate, now indeed in a bodily manner, and a little later in a wholly spiritual manner, where also we will know the reasons for these things more purely and more clearly, in the Word himself, our Lord and God Jesus Christ, in the true feast and joy of the saved.[48]

To Saint Gregory's mind, the Christian's entire life should become an endless feast, an unceasing Pentecost, a year of jubilee that begins at the moment of baptism and has no end. Earthly life may become for Christians a never-ending celebration of communion with God through the Church and her mysteries. The yearly cycle of church feasts, as well as the mysteries of the Church, enables a person's gradual transition from time to eternity, his gradual renunciation of worldly things and

[46]Ibid. 41.2 (SC 358:314–318; Harrison, PPS).
[47]Ibid. 41.5, 14 (SC 358:324, 346; Harrison, PPS).
[48]Ibid. 41.18 (SC 358:352–354; Harrison, PPS).

acquisition of heavenly things. But the real feast and true mystery comes only in that place—beyond the boundary of time—where man encounters God face to face. The true feast is the Lord Jesus Christ himself, whom the faithful contemplate in ceaseless jubilation in the kingdom of God.

THE DEVELOPMENT OF THE YEARLY LITURGICAL CYCLE AFTER THE FOURTH CENTURY

By the fifth century the Christian Church in the East and West arrived at an established calendar that included several major feasts and numerous days of saints' commemoration.

The most ancient menologion known to scholars—the Syrian—dates to the beginning of the fifth century.[49] It is a martyrology entitled "Names of the lords our martyrs and victors and their days on which they received crowns." It is possible that the menologion reflects the theological practice of Arians, since on June 6 the memory of "Arius, priest of Alexandria" is found. The menologion begins on December 26, the first day after the Nativity of Christ. In total, it includes one hundred and sixty-two feast days and one hundred and eighty commemorations of saints. The largest number of commemorations appears for the cities of Alexandria, Nicomedia, and Antioch: eighteen days for Alexandria, twenty-nine days and thirty commemorations for Nicomedia, and twenty-seven commemorations for Antioch.[50] Between December 1 and December 26 there are no commemorations of saints at all. The overwhelming majority of the saints included in the menologia are among the ranks of martyrs.

In this menologion there is not a single feast dedicated to the Theotokos. Information concerning the development of the cycle of feasts of the Theotokos dates to the fifth and subsequent centuries (which does not exclude the existence of individual feasts of the Theotokos in several local churches before this period). Historians attribute the fact that feasts of the Theotokos appear relatively late to the lack of relics or some other visible holy object around which such feasts could arise.[51] It is significant that one of the ancient feasts of the Theotokos (469)—the Placing of the Robe of the Most-Holy Theotokos in Blachernae Church in

---

[49]William Wright, "An Ancient Syrian Martyrology," *Journal of Sacred Literature and Biblical Record* 8, no. 15 (October 1865): 45–56 and no. 16 (January 1866): 423–432.

[50]Sergii (Spasskii), *Complete Menologion of the East*, 1:75–86.

[51]Dix, *Liturgy*, 376.

Constantinople—was established precisely in honor of a holy object linked with the Theotokos.

On the other hand, the appearance of the feasts of the Theotokos in the fifth century in particular could be connected with the christological controversies in the East, including the controversy concerning the name "Theotokos." In the second half of the fifth century, following the Church's decisive victory over the Nestorian heresy, the place of the Theotokos in the Church's calendar became significantly more important. The formation of the cycle of feasts of the Theotokos, parallel to the cycle of feasts of the Lord, began at this time.

The Placing of the Robe of the Most-Holy Theotokos in Blachernae. Icon. Studio of Dionysius. c. 1486.

The celebration of the Annunciation became widespread in the East no later than the fifth century. The Annunciation was celebrated in Jerusalem on January 9 in the fifth century, on the fourth day of Theophany; already in the seventh century, however, another date was established—March 25—which was chosen so Annunciation might be celebrated nine months before the Nativity, according to the duration of pregnancy. Saint Proclus of Constantinople (archbishop from 434 to 446) preached several homilies on the Annunciation.

The feasts of the Nativity and the Dormition of the Theotokos became widespread in this period. Both feasts are mentioned in the sacramentary of Pope Gelasius I (pope from 492 to 496), which testifies to their existence in the West. In the East, a homily on the Nativity of the Theotokos was given by Saint Proclus of Constantinople, while homilies on the Dormition are found in the works of Modestus of Jerusalem (d. 634), Saint Andrew of Crete (d. 712), and Saint John of Damascus (8th c.). The historian Nikephoros Kallistos affirms that the celebration of the Dormition in Constantinople on August 15 was introduced by Emperor Maurice (reigned from 592–602).

The cycle of feasts of the Lord was expanded in the fifth and sixth centuries due to the gradual introduction of the feasts of the Transfiguration and the Circumcision of the Lord in various local churches. The Transfiguration was quite widely celebrated in Byzantium in the fifth century, which is evidenced by

Saint Proclus of Constantinople. Monastery of Saint Bessarion. Meteora. Greece. 16th c.

homilies on this feast by Saint Proclus of Constantinople and Basil of Seleucia (d. 459). The Transfiguration was also celebrated in the West, but it was affirmed as a universal feast of the Roman Catholic Church only in the year 1457. The feast of the Circumcision of the Lord arose primarily as a conclusion to the seven-day feast of the Nativity of Christ, which coincided with the civil New Year and the day of the commemoration of Saint Basil the Great.

The feast of the Entry of the Theotokos into the Temple was of later origin than other feasts of the Theotokos cited above. Two homilies on the Entry into the Temple are ascribed to Saint Germanus, patriarch of Constantinople. The feast became very widespread in the ninth century.[52] The menologia make mention of this feast beginning in the eighth century. A reading for this feast is included in a Sinai Gospel Book at the beginning of the eighth century, given to Saint Catherine's Monastery on Mount Sinai by Emperor Theodosius III (r. 715–717). It contains readings for the following feasts: September 1—the beginning of the indiction and the commemoration of Saint Symeon the Stylite; September 8—the Birth of the Theotokos; September 14—the Exaltation of the Cross; November 21—the Entry of the Theotokos into the Temple; December 24—the Eve of the Nativity of Christ; December 25—the Nativity of Christ; January 1—the Circumcision of the Lord and the commemoration of Saint Basil the Great; January 5—the sanctification of water; January 6—Theophany; February 2—the Meeting of the Lord; February 7—the commemoration of venerable Peter (probably Saint Peter of Galatia); March 9—the commemoration of the forty martyrs of Sebaste; March 25—the Annunciation; April 23—the commemoration of Great Martyr George; May 8—the commemoration of Saint John the Theologian; May 10—the renewal of the monastery of the Mother of God;[53] June 29—the commemoration of the apostles Peter and Paul; August 6—the Transfiguration of the Lord; August 15—the Dormition of the Theotokos; August 29—the Beheading of Saint John the Forerunner.[54]

In the first half of the eighth century John of Euboea named ten church feasts: the Conception of the Theotokos, the Nativity of the Theotokos, the Annunciation, the Nativity of Christ, the Meeting of the Lord, Theophany, Pascha, Ascension, and Pentecost.[55] "Higher than the fullness of the ten feasts," he noted, "we also celebrate the Dormition (of the Theotokos)."[56]

---

[52]Mikhail Skaballanovich, *The Typikon Interpreted: An explanatory presentation of the Typikon with a historical introduction* [in Russian], 1st ed. (Kiev, 1910; Reprint, Moscow: Palomnik, 1995), 110.

[53]Probably one of the monasteries in Constantinople, where the Gospel Book was written.

[54]Sergii (Spasskii), *Complete Menologion of the East*, 1:91.

[55]John of Euboea, *Homily on the Conception of the Theotokos* 10 (PG 96:1473b–1476b).

[56]Ibid., 22 (PG 96:1497b).

The "exchange of feasts" between the East and West continued in the second half of the first millennium. Around the year 700, four eastern feasts of the Theotokos—the Nativity of the Theotokos, the Meeting of the Lord, Annunciation, and Dormition—were adopted in Rome during the reign of Pope Sergius I, a Syrian by birth.[57] The western calendar of the eighth century (from a breviary in the Vatican Library) included eighty-four commemorations of saints and the following feasts: the Nativity of Christ, the Circumcision of the Lord, Annunciation, Pascha, Ascension, Pentecost, the Exaltation of the Cross, the Nativity of the Theotokos, and Dormition.[58]

By the end of the eighth century, almost every day of the church calendar was dedicated either to a feast or to the memory of a saint. In particular, Saint Theodore the Studite testifies to this. In one of his homilies (given on January 28) he said, "Yesterday we highly praised Saint Chrysostom; today we highly praise the ever memorable Saint Ephraim, and tomorrow we will highly praise another saint."[59] He describes life in the monastery as an unceasing transition "from feast from feast."[60]

At the beginning of the second millennium, twelve major feasts were distinguished from the other feasts and given the name "The Twelve" in the Typikon. They include nine fixed feasts (i.e., feasts celebrated every year on the same day) and three movable feasts (feasts whose date varies depending on the lunar calendar). Of the twelve major feasts, the following are fixed feasts:

- September 8—the Nativity of the Most-Holy Theotokos
- September 14—the Exaltation of the Cross of the Lord
- November 21—the Entry into the Temple of the Most-Holy Theotokos
- December 25—the Nativity of Christ
- January 6—the Baptism of the Lord (Theophany)
- February 2—the Meeting of the Lord
- March 25—the Annunciation of the Most-Holy Theotokos
- August 6—the Transfiguration of the Lord
- August 15—the Dormition of the Most-Holy Theotokos

[57] Dix, *Liturgy*, 376–377.

[58] Sergii (Spasskii), *Complete Menologion of the East*, 1:44.

[59] Theodore the Studite, *Small Catechesis* 42, in *Sancti patris nostri et confessoris Theodori Studitis Praepositi Parva catechesis*, ed. Emmanuel Auvray (Paris, 1891). In another place (*Studite Constitutions* 29 [PG 99:1716a]) Theodore especially mentions "days when there is the memory of a saint." But it does not mean that there were days without a commemoration of a saint; rather, it is a question of the so-called "great saints" whose commemoration was considered to be a feast.

[60] Theodore the Studite, *Small Catechesis* 34.

Among the movable feasts whose date depends on the date of Pascha are:

- One week before Pascha—the Entry of the Lord into Jerusalem
- Forty days after Pascha—the Ascension of the Lord
- Fifty days after Pascha—Pentecost

Of the twelve major feasts, the feasts connected with the life of Christ are called feasts of the Lord; those connected with the life of the Theotokos are called feasts of the Theotokos. Pascha is not included in the twelve major feasts since it stands alone in the Church calendar and is perceived as "the feasts of feasts and holy day of holy days." Before several major feasts, "forefeast" days were established, while a number of days following the feast were called the "afterfeast." Some prayers and hymns dedicated to the particular feast are read and sung during the services on the days of the forefeast and afterfeast.

The Typikon continued to be enriched with the commemorations of saints and new feasts at the end of the first and during the entire second millennium. Around the year 930, in commemoration of the appearance of the most-holy Theotokos in the Blachernae Church, the feast of the Protection of the Most-Holy Theotokos was established. The feast became especially popular in Rus', where it was introduced by the righteous prince Andrey Bogolyubsky around 1164.

In the Typikon, saints whose memories are celebrated by the Church are divided into several categories depending on the degree of solemnity of the service dedicated to them. A saint "with a vigil" is a saint whose day of commemoration is celebrated with an all-night vigil. On days of commemoration of saints "with a polyeleos," it is customary at matins to perform the polyeleos and to sing the great doxology, while on days of commemoration for saints "with a doxology," only the doxology is sung, without the polyeleos. For a saint with the designation "on six," six stichera are sung on "Lord, I call." Only three stichera are sung for saints who do not have a festal designation. There are also saints in the church calendar for whom a separate service was not composed at all.

The days of commemoration of saints "with a vigil" are observed with the greatest solemnity. There are few such days in the Church calendar:

- September 26 and May 8—days of commemoration of the Apostle and Evangelist John the Theologian
- November 13—Saint John Chrysostom
- December 5—Venerable Sabba the Sanctified

- December 6—Hierarch Nicholas the Wonderworker
- January 30—Three Hierarchs (Saints Basil the Great, Gregory the Theologian, and John Chrysostom)
- April 23—Great Martyr George
- May 11—Equals-to-the-Apostles Saints Cyril and Methodius
- June 24—Nativity of Saint John the Forerunner
- July 15—Equal-to-the-Apostles Great Prince Vladimir
- June 29—Preeminent Apostles Saints Peter and Paul
- August 29—the Beheading of Saint John the Forerunner

In addition to the above commemorations of saints, there are those for whom the Typikon notes, "If the rector chooses, we serve a vigil." In particular, these are the days of commemoration of the great martyr Demetrius of Thessaloniki (October 26), Archangel Michael and the other Bodiless Heavenly Hosts (November 8), Saint Gregory the Theologian (January 25), and the Prophet Elijah (July 20). The Typikon prescribes a vigil also on days of commemoration of the saint to whom a church is dedicated.

Aside from saints included in the general Orthodox list of saints "with a vigil," each local Orthodox Church has particularly venerated saints in whose memory an all-night vigil is served. In Slavic Churches these include, in particular, the Equals-to-the-Apostles Cyril and Methodius (May 11). In addition to the commemoration of Saint Nicholas the Wonderworker on December 6, another feast, on May 9, became widespread in Rus' in honor of the translation of his relics from Myra in Lycia to the Italian city Bari.[61] In the Russian Orthodox Church the all-night vigil is served also on the days of the commemoration of many Russian saints, including the Equal-of-the-Apostles Saint Vladimir (July 15), Venerable Saint Sergius of Radonezh (July 5 and September 25), Enlighteners of Moscow Peter, Alexis, Jonah, Philip, and Hermogenes (October 5), Venerable Saint Seraphim of Sarov (January 2), and the Holy New Martyrs and Confessors of Russia (on the Sunday following January 25, Old Style).

The church calendar of the Russian Orthodox Church continued to be enriched by the commemoration of saints over the course of the entire second millennium. The process of including the names of saints in the church calendar continues to

[61]This event took place in 1087 and was nothing more than the theft of the saint's relics from Greek monks by merchants from Venice. It stands to reason that in the Greek Church this event was not a reason for a feast, while in Rus' it was seen as the saving of the wonderworking relics of the saint from Turkish captivity.

the present day. In particular, through the process of studying the lives of the new
martyrs and confessors of Russia, canonized in the year 2000, the list of their names
continues to grow. Days of commemoration are being established for each of them
and new liturgical services are being composed.

7

Divine Services from the Beginning of the Church Year to the Entry of the Theotokos into the Temple

ACCORDING TO THE TYPIKON, the ecclesiastical year begins on September 1. On the day of the "Ecclesiastical New Year," the Typikon prescribes the celebration of a divine service with special prayers at the "beginning of the indiction" and the singing of the troparion, "O Fashioner of all creation, who in thine authority hast appointed the times and seasons: bless thou the crown of the year with thy goodness, O Lord, preserving in peace Orthodox Christians and thy city,[1] and save us at the supplications of the Theotokos."[2] But in practice, in the majority of parishes of the Russian Orthodox Church, this feast is not observed because the ecclesiastical new year is observed almost nowhere and the troparion for the "beginning of the indiction" is sung at the New Year moleben performed on December 31 on the civil calendar.[3]

THE NATIVITY OF THE THEOTOKOS

The first great feast of the ecclesiastical year is the Nativity of the Theotokos (September 8). The basis of this feast is the narrative from the New Testament apocryphal book, the *Protoevangelium of James*, which presumably appeared around the middle of the second century. The narrative concerns Joachim and Anna, a righteous Jewish couple living in Nazareth. Once, Joachim brought a sacrifice to the temple in Jerusalem, but it was not accepted, because he did not have any childen.

---

[1]In the Byzantine liturgical books used up to the present day in the Orthodox Church, "city" refers to Constantinople.

[2]Menaion. September 1. Vespers. Troparion.

[3]Russia follows the Old Calendar, and therefore the civil new year falls one week before Christmas (which falls on January 7 on the civil calendar).—*Ed.*

Nativity of the Most-Holy Theotokos. Contemporary Icon.

Deeply sorrowful, he departed into the wilderness where he prayed for forty days and forty nights, asking God for the gift of progeny. The Lord heard the prayer of the righteous man and an angel brought Anna the news that she would give birth to a child. Anna brought the same news to Joachim. He returned home and Anna conceived a child, and after nine months she gave birth to a daughter—the most-blessed Virgin Mary.[4]

This narrative was reflected in *The First Homily of Praise on the Dormition of the Mother of God* of Saint John of Damascus, in which it is said of the most-holy virgin:

Her parents were called Joachim and Anna. Joachim, being the shepherd of a flock, was no less careful of his thoughts than of his sheep, and led them both as well as he could, wherever he wished. For since he had been watched over like a sheep himself by the Lord God, he lacked none of the choicest gifts. . . . And Anna . . . was one with her husband in heart as well as home; yet although she abounded in all good qualities, she was, for some mysterious reason, affected by the complaint of sterility. . . . Then the good God looked down and had pity on the creatures of his own hand; willing to save his creation, he put an end to the sterile period of grace—I mean the sterility of Anna, whose thoughts were turned to God. She bore a child, one such as never before had been, and never again will be. . . . Then the Mother of God came forth, according to the promise. An angel announced the conception of her who was to be born. For in this respect, too, it was right that she who was to be the bearer, in flesh, of the sole and truly perfect God should not be lacking anything, or take second place.[5]

The narrative of the birth of the most-holy virgin from a barren womb is reflected in numerous liturgical texts dedicated to the feast. In them the barrenness of Joachim and Anna is seen as an image of the spiritual barrenness of mankind, and the birth of the most-holy Theotokos is a remission of this barrenness:

Today is the beginning of joy for all the world; today the winds blow that bring tidings of salvation. The barrenness of our nature has been loosed: for the barren woman is revealed as mother of her who, after bearing the Maker, still

[4] *Protoevangelium of James* 1–5 (*ANF* 8:361–362).
[5] John of Damascus, *Homily on the Dormition* 1.5–6 (Daley, PPS).

remained Virgin. From her He who is God by nature takes what is alien to Him and makes it His own; through her Christ works salvation for those gone astray in the flesh, He who loves mankind and is the Deliverer of our souls. (Menaion. Nativity of the Theotokos. Great Vespers. Stichera on "Lord, I call.")

Celebrating the birth of the Theotokos, the Church glorifies the "divine maiden,"[6] the "bridal-chamber of the Light and the book of the Word of life."[7] In the person of the most-holy Virgin Mary, God who rests on the noetic thrones (angels) prepared for himself a holy throne on earth.[8] The Theotokos is the "living temple of God,"[9] the "dwelling-place of Christ our God, the King and Creator of all."[10]

As with all the feasts of the Theotokos, the Nativity of the Theotokos is understood by the Church primarily from a christological perspective. Without this event the incarnation of God would have been impossible, and without the incarnation of God the salvation of mankind would have been impossible. Saint Andrew of Crete in his *Homily on the Nativity of the Most-Holy Theotokos* wrote:

For after the first formation of humankind had been fashioned from pure and undefiled earth, nature concealed [our] intrinsic honor, having been robbed of grace by the lapse of disobedience as a result of which we were cast out of the life-giving place, and nature exchanged the joy in paradise for perishable life, so that this became, as it were, our ancestral heritage, [and] from it came death and hence the corruption of our race. . . . [No one knew] how to correct human nature, and by what means it might be restored quickly and easily to its former noble state. Now the Sovereign Artificer of all things, God, has been well pleased to make manifest one who is like another all-harmonious and newly created universe and at the same time to hold back for a while the misfortune of sin which formerly fell upon [us], through which [came] death. And so [he has been pleased] to point the way towards a free and truly passionless new life for those of us who have, as it were, been reborn by the baptism of divine generation.

And so, how would this benevolence, which is great, most miraculous, and in keeping with divine laws, be introduced on our behalf, unless God appeared

[6]Menaion. Nativity of the Theotokos. Great Vespers. Stichera on "Lord, I call."
[7]Ibid.
[8]Ibid.
[9]Menaion. Nativity of the Theotokos. Great Vespers. Aposticha.
[10]Menaion. Nativity of the Theotokos. Great Vespers. Stichera on "Lord, I call."

to us in the flesh, and came in accordance with the laws of nature, and assented in a new way to dwell, as he knew how, in accordance with our understanding of things? In what manner might this be brought to a conclusion, unless a pure and untouched Virgin first attended to the mystery, bearing in her womb the One who is above being, according to a law which transcended the laws of nature? Who could be thought of as this one except she alone, who was chosen before all generations for the One who engendered all nature? She is the Theotokos Mary, the name called by God, from whose womb the Supremely Divine One came forth with flesh, having made [it] into a temple for himself in a transcendent way. . . .[11]

This theological idea is contained in condensed form in the troparion of the Nativity of the Theotokos:

Thy Nativity, O Virgin, has proclaimed joy to the whole universe! The Sun of Righteousness, Christ our God, has shone from thee, O Theotokos! By annulling the curse, He bestowed a blessing. By destroying death, He has granted us eternal Life. (Menaion. Nativity of the Theotokos. Great Vespers. Troparion.)

The thought of the authors of the liturgical texts constantly turns from the Nativity of the Theotokos to the Nativity of Christ. The first canon, inscribed with the name "Kyr John of Damascus," and the second canon written by the hand of "Kyr Andrew" (Saint Andrew of Crete) speak about the birth of Christ from the virgin:

The Lord, who is a spring of life to all, led forth the Virgin from a barren womb. Into her He deigned to enter, preserving her virginity inviolate after childbirth. (Menaion. Nativity of the Theotokos. Matins. Canon 1. Ode 3.)

O strangest of tidings! God has become the Son of a woman. The birth without seed, the Mother knew not a man, and the Child she bore is God. O dread sight! O strange conceiving by the Virgin! O nativity beyond speech! Indeed all these things are past sight and mind. (Menaion. Nativity of the Theotokos. Matins. Canon 2. Ode 8.)

The theology of "Mary, the new Eve," dating back to Saint Irenaeus of Lyons, was reflected in the liturgical texts of the feast:[12]

---

[11]Andrew of Crete, *Homily on the Nativity of the Theotokos* 1.4–5 (PG 97:812c–813c; Cunningham, PPS).

[12]Concerning this, see vol. 2, p. 474.

Today let Ann, barren and childless, clap her hands with joy. Let all things on earth put on their bright array; let kings dance and priests make glad in hymns of blessing; let the whole world keep feast. For lo, the Queen and spotless Bride of the Father has blossomed from the root of Jesse. No more shall women bear children in sorrow: for joy has put forth its flower, and the Life of men has come to dwell in the world. No more are the gifts of Joachim turned away: for the lament of Ann is changed to joy. "Let all the chosen Israel rejoice with me," she says: "for behold, the Lord has given me the living Pavilion of His divine glory, unto the joy and gladness of us all and the salvation of our souls." (Menaion. Birth of the Theotokos. Great Vespers. Aposticha.)

Some texts of the feast are dedicated to the praise of Saints Joachim and Anna— the parents of the most-holy Theotokos. They are glorified primarily as an example of a pious family. These righteous saints are especially venerated in the Orthodox Church. On September 9, the day following the feast of the Nativity of the The-otokos, the commemoration of Saints Joachim and Anna is performed separately. Moreover, the names of "the holy and righteous ancestors of God Joachim and Anna" are commemorated at the daily dismissals during the entire liturgical year.

THE EXALTATION OF THE CROSS OF THE LORD

The feast of the Exaltation of the Cross of the Lord is established in honor of the finding of the cross by the pious empress Helen (d. 327), the mother of Emperor Constantine, in the year 326. According to the witness of ecclesiastical sources, three crosses were found on Golgotha, and a placard bearing the inscription "Jesus of Nazareth, King of the Jews," written in Hebrew, Greek, and Latin, was found lying separately from them. According to one account, cited by the church histo-rians Rufinus, Socrates, Sozomen, and Thedoret, the Savior's cross was identified through laying it on an extremely sick woman who was lying on her death bed:

The sign was this: a certain woman of the neighborhood, who had been long afflicted with disease, was now just at the point of death; the bishop therefore arranged it so that each of the crosses should be brought to the dying woman, believing that she would be healed on touching the precious cross. Nor was he disappointed in his expectation: for the two crosses having been applied which were not the Lord's, the woman still continued in a dying state; but when the third, which was the true cross, touched her, she was immediately healed, and recovered her former strength. In this manner then was the genuine cross discovered. . . . I have written this from report indeed; but almost all the inhabitants of Constantinople affirm that it is true.[13]

Exaltation of the Cross.
Contemporary Icon.

According to another account, the crosses were laid on a dead man who was raised from the dead after the cross of Christ was laid on him.[14] Learning of the finding of the cross, countless crowds of people streamed to Golgotha in order to venerate it. In order for the cross to be visible to all, Patriarch Macarius began to raise it and the people exclaimed, "Lord, have mercy." Soon after the finding of the cross, the construction of the Church of the Resurrection of Christ began on Golgotha by the decree of Emperor Constantine. Its consecration took place on September 13, 335. On the next day, September 14, the celebration of the Exaltation of the Cross was established.

In the divine services of the feast only a few texts are dedicated to the event in whose honor the feast was established. The major part of the liturgical texts is dedicated to the glorification of the cross as an instrument of death that became an instrument of the salvation of mankind.[15]

In the service texts of the Exaltation much attention is focused on the special Old Testament foreshadowing of the cross. These include, in particular, the blessing of Ephraim and Manasseh by Jacob, in which he laid his hands in a crosswise manner (see Gen 48.14). The rod that Moses raised and then used to divide the waters of the Red Sea (see Ex 14.16) was a foreshadowing of the cross. The tree Moses cast into the bitter water at Marah, which became sweet (see Ex 15.23–25), and Aaron's rod that budded (see Num 17.1–8) are seen as symbols of the cross in Christian tradition. Moses stretching out his hands and defeating Amalek (see Ex 17.8–12) is a symbol of the cross. Christ himself pointed to the bronze serpent, displayed by Moses as a sign, as a foreshadowing of the cross. Joshua stretching

[13]Socrates Scholasticus, *Church History* 1.17 (*NPNF*[2] 2:21). The same version in other sources: Rufinus, *Church History* 1.7–8; Sozomen, *Church History* 2.1; Theodoret of Cyrus, *Ecclesiastical History* 1.18.

[14]Concerning various accounts of this event, see Mikhail Skaballanovich, *The Exaltation of the Precious and Life-Creating Cross of the Lord* [in Russian] (Kiev: Prolog, 2004), 14, 46.

[15]The theology of the cross and its liturgical veneration is discussed in detail in another part of this series: See vol. 2, pp. 315–329.

out his hands in crosswise fashion and stopping the sun also symbolizes the cross (see Joshua 10.12). Jonah, who spent three days and three nights in the belly of the whale, is a foreshadowing of Christ, crucified on the cross and raised on the third day. All of this rich typology of the cross is reflected in the liturgical texts of the feast of the Exaltation:

> Prefiguring Thy Cross, O Christ, Jacob the Patriarch, when he gave the blessing to his descendants, laid his hands crosswise upon their heads. And today as we exalt Thy Cross, O Saviour, we cry: Give victory to Thine Orthodox people as Thou once gavest it to Constantine. (Menaion. Exaltation of the Holy Cross. Great Vespers. Litiya.)

> Inscribing the invincible weapon of the Cross upon the waters, Moses marked a straight line before him with his staff and divided the Red Sea, opening a path for Israel who went over dry-shod. Then he marked a second line across the waters and united them in one, overwhelming the chariots of Pharaoh. Therefore let us sing to Christ our God, for He has been glorified. (Menaion. Exaltation of the Hoy Cross. Canon. Matins. Ode 1. Irmos.)

> The rod of Aaron is an image of this mystery, for when it budded it showed who should be priest. So in the Church, that once was barren, the wood of the Cross has now put forth flower, filling her with strength and steadfastness. (Menaion. Exaltation of the Holy Cross. Matins. Canon. Ode 3. Irmos.)

> Moses prefigured thee, O precious Cross, when he stretched out his hands on high and put Amalek the tyrant to flight. Thou art the boast of the faithful and succour of the persecuted, the glory of the apostles, the champion of the righteous, and the preserver of all the saints. Therefore, beholding thee raised on high, creation rejoices and keeps feast, glorifying Christ, who in His surpassing goodness through thee has joined together that which was divided. (Menaion. Exaltation of the Holy Cross. Vespers. Stichera on "Lord, I call.")

> Moses set upon a wooden pole a cure against the deadly and poisonous bite of the serpents: for crosswise upon the wood—as a symbol of the Cross—he placed a serpent that creeps about the earth, and thereby he triumphed over calamity. Therefore let us sing to Christ our God, for He has been glorified. (Menaion. Exaltation of the Holy Cross. Matins. Canon. Ode 1.)

The rock that was struck and gushed forth water for a hard-hearted and disobedient people, made manifest the mystery of the Church, chosen by God: for the Cross is her strength and steadfastness. (Menaion. Exaltation of the Holy Cross. Matins. Canon. Ode 3.)

In times past Joshua, the son of Nun, stretched out his arms crosswise, O my Saviour, mystically prefiguring the sign of the Cross: and the sun stood still until he had defeated the enemy that resisted Thee, O God. And now this same sun is darkened, seeing Thee upon the Cross destroying the power of death and despoiling hell. (Menaion. Exaltation of the Holy Cross. Matins. Sedalen [or Sessional Hymn].)

Jonah stretched out his hands in the form of a cross within the belly of the sea monster, plainly prefiguring the redeeming Passion. Cast out from thence after three days, he foreshadowed the marvellous Resurrection of Christ our God, who was crucified in the flesh and enlightened the world by His Rising on the third day. (Menaion. Exaltation of the Holy Cross. Matins. Canon. Ode 6. Irmos.)

The order of the all-night vigil at the feast of the Exaltation of the Cross is different from the usual order in several ways. Before the beginning of the liturgy, a wooden cross, decorated with flowers, is carried from the table of oblation to the altar table. The polyeleos is performed before the altar table rather than in the center of the church. At the end of matins, the cross is carried out into the nave. At the end of the great doxology, the rector lifts the cross from the altar table and, carrying it on his head, comes out of the sanctuary to the center of the church. Here the cross is laid on an analogion and all bow down before it three times, singing, "Before thy cross we bow down, O Master, and thy holy resurrection we glorify." Following this, the faithful approach the cross and, according to custom, the rector anoints the faithful with blessed oil. During the veneration of the cross, the stichera dedicated to Christ's sufferings are sung:

Come, ye faithful, and let us venerate the life-giving Wood, on which Christ, the King of Glory, stretched out His hands of His own will. To the ancient blessedness He raised us up, whom the enemy had before despoiled through pleasure, making us exiles far from God. Come, ye faithful, and let us venerate the Wood, through which we have been counted worthy to crush the heads of our invisible enemies. Come, all ye kindred of the nations, and let us honour in hymns the Cross of the Lord. Hail, O Cross, complete redemption of fallen Adam. (Menaion. Exaltation of the Cross. Matins. Stichera at the Veneration of the Cross. [By Emperor Leo the Wise.])

Today the Master of the Creation and the Lord of Glory is nailed to the Cross, and His side is pierced; and He who is the sweetness of the Church, tastes gall and vinegar. A crown of thorns is put upon Him who covers heaven with clouds; He is clothed in a cloak of mockery. He who formed man with His hands, is struck by a hand of clay. He who wrappeth the heaven in clouds, is smitten upon His back. He accepted spitting and scourging, reproach and buffeting; and all these things my Deliverer and God endures for me that am condemned, that in His compassion He may save the world from error. (Menaion. Exaltation of the Cross. Matins. Stichera at the Veneration of the Cross.)

In cathedrals and other churches, when a bishop is serving, the order of exaltation is performed immediately after the cross is carried out.[16] The hierarch stands on the cathedra facing east and holds the cross above his head. The protodeacon exclaims, "Have mercy upon us, O God, according to Thy great mercy; we pray Thee, hear and have mercy." The hierarch blesses the worshippers thrice with the cross and the choir begins to sing "Lord, have mercy" one hundred times. During the singing of the first half of the one hundred, the hierarch slowly bows down to the ground while priests support him with their hands. During the singing of the second half of the one hundred, he slowly raises himself up. Priests pour water with rose oil onto the cross. Then, turning to face west, the hierarch performs the second exaltation. The third exaltation is performed facing south and the fourth is performed facing north. Before each exaltation, the protodeacon exclaims the petitions for the ecclesiastical and secular authorities, "for every Christian soul, afflicted and weary," and for all who serve and have served in the temple in which the service takes place. At the end of the singing of the fifth set of one hundred repetitions of "Lord, have mercy," the hierarch places the cross on the analogion, and the veneration of the cross takes place according to the order described above.

The Typikon prescribes a strict fast on the feast of the Exaltation because this day not only commemorates the finding of the cross, but also is a remembrance of the sufferings and death of Christ.

---

[16]In Greek practice any priest may perform this rite.—*Ed.*

THE PROTECTION OF THE MOST-HOLY THEOTOKOS

The Protection of the Most=Holy Theotokos. Icon.

The feast of the Protection of the Most-Holy Theotokos (October 1) is considered one of the great feasts of the Church, although it is not one of the twelve great feasts. It was established in honor of the appearance of the most-holy Theotokos to Saint Andrew the Fool-for-Christ around the year 930. On Sunday, October 1, when the all-night vigil was being served in the Church of Blachernae in Constantinople and the church was overflowing with worshippers, Saint Andrew, raising his eyes to heaven, saw the most-holy Theotokos, illuminated by light blue light and surrounded by angels and saints. On bent knees, she began to pray with tears for Christians. Then, approaching the altar table, she removed the cover (or omophorion) from her head and stretched it over the worshippers.

The liturgical texts of the feast speak of the Mother of God as the protectress of pious kings and of all Christians, the defender from natural disasters and all evil, the intercessor for Christians before God, the solicitor for the salvation of all the faithful:

> A living palace of Christ, a wall for the faithful, and protection, and dominion [art thou], O Mother of God: thy city is saved by thee, by thine aid the right-believing are crowned, and those who ever boast in thee gain victories against the pagans, for thou coverest [them] with the omophorion of thy mercy. (Menaion. Protection of the Most-Holy Theotokos. Little Vespers. Stichera idiomela.)

> Today the faithful celebrate the feast with joy illumined by thy coming, O Mother of God. Beholding thy pure image we fervently cry to thee: "Encompass us beneath the precious veil of thy protection; deliver us from every form of evil by entreating Christ, thy Son and our God, that He may save our souls." (Menaion. Protection of the Most-Holy Theotokos. Little Vespers. Troparion.)

> Today the Virgin stands in the midst of the Church and with choirs of saints she invisibly prays to God for us. Angels and bishops worship, apostles and

prophets rejoice together, since for our sake she prays to the pre-eternal God. (Menaion. Protection of the Most-Holy Theotokos. Matins. Kontakion.)

The canon of the feast performed at matins is dedicated mainly to interpreting the Old Testament types of the Theotokos. Acording to the author of the canon, the most-holy Theotokos is the "far-famed virgin who was honorably prefigured by the prophets."[17] The holy tabernacle of the covenant (see Ex 26.1–30) and the objects found in the tabernacle are foreshadowings and types of the Theotokos: the ark of the covenant (see Ex 25.10–22), the candlestick (see Ex 25.31–40), the golden pot containing manna (see Ex 16.33–34), and Aaron's rod (see Num 17.1–8). Other types are seen in the fleece of Gideon (see Judg 6.36–40), the mountain mentioned by the Prophet Habbakuk (see Hab 3.3), the mountain from which a stone (i.e., Christ) was cut out without hands (Dan 2.34), and the bed of Solomon (Song 3.7–10). All of these Old Testament types are enumerated and interpreted in the canon's troparia and irmoi:

> Moses named thee "tabernacle" and "rod of Aaron," for thou didst blossom with Christ, the living wood. . . . (Menaion. Protection of the Most-Holy Theotokos. Matins. Canon. Ode 1.)

> David leaps, not as old before the ark, but even more, since now he has assembled choirs that come before thee in the church together with the ranks of the saints, and they worship thee, saying: Pray for the people who honor thee, so that we may celebrate honorably and glorify thy protection. (Menaion. Protection of the Most-Holy Theotokos. Matins. Canon. Ode 1.)

> Gideon depicted thee beforehand as a fleece, for Christ God descended upon thee like the dew. . . . (Menaion. Protection of the Most-Holy Theotokos. Matins. Canon. Ode 3.)

> . . . Rejoice, butter mountain, curdled by the Spirit. Rejoice, lampstand and jar bearing the manna that delights the senses of all the pious. (Menaion. Protection of the Most-Holy Theotokos. Matins. Canon. Ode 4.)

> God sanctified thee wholly, more than the ark of Aaron, O Theotokos, and he commanded the angels to serve thee. . . . (Menaion. Protection of the Most-Holy Theotokos. Matins. Canon. Ode 4.)

---

[17]Menaion. Protection of the Most-Holy Theotokos. Matins. Canon. Ode 3.

Of old Solomon described thee, the bed and couch of the Heavenly King, surrounded by seraphim. . . . (Menaion. Protection of the Most-Holy Theotokos. Matins. Canon. Ode 5.)

Aforetime Daniel described thee as a great mountain, for from thee Christ was born without seed, and he destroyed all demonic deception and filled the whole earth with his faith. . . . (Menaion. Protection of the Most-Holy Theotokos. Matins. Canon. Ode 6.)

O mountain curdled by the Spirit, which Habbakuk saw pouring out a healing sweetness for the faithful, O Virgin Theotokos, heal us. . . . (Menaion. Protection of the Most-Holy Theotokos. Matins. Canon. Ode 7.)

The birthgiving of the Theotokos, which was imaged then but is now enacted, saved the pious children in the furnace. . . . (Menaion. Protection of the Most-Holy Theotokos. Matins. Canon. Ode 8. Irmos.)

The feast of the Protection of the Most-Holy Theotokos did not become widespread in Greece. But in Rus' it became one of the most honored feasts of the Theotokos. Established around 1164 by the righteous prince Andrey Bogolyubsky, it immediately acquired great popularity: the image of the Mother of God covering the people with her omophorion was loved by the Russian people. The first Church of the Protection in Rus'—the Church of the Protection of the Mother of God on the Nerl—was built in 1165. Subsequently, churches in honor of the Protection emerged in many Russian cities. The most famous of them is the Cathedral of the Protection on Red Square (the Church of Saint Basil the Blessed).

THE ENTRY OF THE MOST-HOLY THEOTOKOS INTO THE TEMPLE

The feast of the Entry of the Most-Holy Theotokos on November 21 is related in meaning to the feast Nativity of the Mother of God and is a type of continuation of the latter feast. Its subject is also based on the *Protoevangelium of James*, which describes how, when the Virgin Mary reached the age of three, Joachim and Anna brought her to the temple in Jerusalem. There she was received by the high priest, who said, "The Lord has magnified thy name in all generations. In thee, on the last of the days, the Lord will manifest his redemption to the sons of Israel."[18]

---

[18] *Protoevangelium of James* 7 (*ANF* 8:363).

According to tradition, this high priest was Zacharias, the future father of Saint John the Baptist: meeting the three-year old Mary, he brought her into the holy of holies, into which only the priest was permitted to enter once each year. After this, she was left to be raised in the temple, where she spent her time in prayer and the reading of holy scripture. As Saint John of Damascus said, "She was later consecrated in the holy temple of God and lived there, displaying a better and purer ideal and way of life than others, free from all contact with immoral men and women."[19]

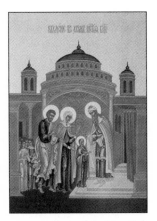

Entry of the Most-Holy Theotokos into the Temple. Contemporary Icon.

In the troparion of the feast, the appearance of the Mother of God in the temple is interpreted as the fulfillment of God's pre-eternal plan, foretelling the coming of Christ the Savior into the world:

> Today is the prelude of the good will of God, of the preaching of the salvation of mankind. The Virgin appears in the temple of God, in anticipation proclaiming Christ to all. Let us rejoice and sing to her: "Rejoice, O fulfillment of the Creator's dispensation." (Menaion. Entry of the Theotokos into the Temple. Great Vespers. Troparion.)

The image of the Mother of God as God's temple occupies the central place in the liturgical texts. Even before conception, the most-pure virgin was dedicated to God, and, having been born on earth, she was brought to him as a gift.[20] She was God's temple from the time of her birth and brought a new grace with her to the temple:

> Today the living Temple of the holy glory of Christ our God, she who alone among women is pure and blessed, is offered in the Temple of the Law, that she may make her dwelling in the sanctuary. Joachim and Ann rejoice with her in spirit, and choirs of virgins sing to the Lord, chanting psalms and honouring His Mother. (Menaion. Entry of the Theotokos into the Temple. Great Vespers. Stichera on "Lord, I call.")

---

[19]John of Damascus, *Homily on the Dormition* 1.6 (Daley, PPS).
[20]Menaion. Entry of the Most-Holy Theotokos into the Temple. Matins. Sedalen.

The most holy Virgin, Temple that is to hold God, is dedicated within the temple of the Lord. . . . (Menaion. Entry of the Theotokos into the Temple. Great Vespers. Aposticha.)

Thou who art honoured, O Most Holy, far above the heavens, thou who art both Temple and Palace, thou art dedicated in the temple of God, to be prepared as a divine dwelling-place for His coming. (Menaion. Entry of the Theotokos into the Temple. Matins. Canon. Ode 1.)

The all-pure Temple of the Saviour, the precious Bridal Chamber and Virgin, the sacred treasure of the glory of God, is led today into the house of the Lord, and with her she brings the grace of the divine Spirit. Of her God's angels sing in praise: "She is indeed the heavenly Tabernacle." (Menaion. Entry of the Theotokos into the Temple. Matins. Kontakion.)

As in the divine services of other feasts of the Theotokos, the major Old Testament types of the Mother of God (discussed earlier in the section on the Protection) are mentioned in the service of the Entry into the Temple. Various details of the celebrated event are also mentioned. In particular, the service tells how Anna, leading the Mother of God into the temple, called other maidens, bearing candles, to go before her.[21] Meeting Mary and her parents on the threshold of the temple, Zacharias entered into a dialogue with Anna, asking whether the temple could hold the one of whom the prophets preached.[22] When the Mother of God was in the temple, the Archangel Gabriel brought her food.[23]

---

[21]Menaion. Entry of the Most-Holy Theotokos into the Temple. Great Vespers. Aposticha.

[22]Menaion. Entry of the Most-Holy Theotokos into the Temple. Matins. Canon 1. Ode 8.

[23]Menaion. Entry of the Most-Holy Theotokos into the Temple. Great Vespers. Stichera at "Lord, I call."

8

The Nativity Cycle

THE NATIVITY FAST

THE PERIOD OF PREPARATION for the Nativity of Christ is called the Nativity Fast and begins on November 15, forty days before the Nativity of Christ. The exact date of the appearance of the Nativity Fast is impossible to establish. In the West, the first mention of a fast preceding Christmas dates to the fifth or sixth centuries. In the East, the forty-day Nativity fast was first mentioned in the ninth century (although its duration was still a point of dispute at that time).[1]

The Three Holy Children in the Fiery Furnace. Early Christian Fresco. Catacomb of Priscilla. 4th c.

One of the particular characteristics of the divine services in the period of the Nativity Fast is that on certain days (November 19, 26, 29, and December 1, 2, 3, 8, 14, 16, 18, 19) the services are to resemble the services of Great Lent by their penitential character. On these days the Typikon calls for the prayer of Saint Ephraim the Syrian to be read with prostrations.[2] Moreover, the period of the Nativity Fast is characterized by an abundance of commemorations of Old Testament righteous saints and prophets, as those who proclaimed the coming of the Savior's birth. The commemorations of the prophets Obadiah, Nahum, Habakkuk, Zephaniah, Haggai, Daniel, and the three holy children—Hananiah, Azariah, and Mishael—are performed during the Nativity Fast.

---

[1]See Mikhail Skaballanovich, *The Nativity of Christ* [in Russian] (Kiev, 1916), 41. We note also that the various eastern Christian sources speak differently of the severity of the Nativity Fast. In the present day, it is a widespread practice to allow fish, with the exception of Wednesdays, Fridays, and Christmas Eve.

[2]But in practice, this prayer is read only during Great Lent.

The theme of the Nativity enters gradually into the liturgical texts. On Sundays and feast days during the fast, beginning with the Entry of the Most-Holy Theotokos into the Temple, the irmoi of the Nativity canon, "Christ is born, give him glory," are sung at matins as katavasia. For the six days preceding Christmas, at vespers after the stichera at "Lord, I call" the sticheron "Make ready, O cave, for the ewe lamb comes, bearing Christ in her womb" is sung. The forefeast of the Nativity begins five days before the feast: on these days the theme of the Nativity begins to dominate in the liturgical texts.

The final two Sundays before Christmas are called the "Sunday of the Holy Forefathers" and the "Sunday of the Holy Fathers." They are dedicated to the remembrance of the Old Testament righteous ones who by their spiritual and moral ascetic efforts prepared the world for the coming of the Savior. On the Sunday of the Holy Fathers, the beginning of the Gospel according to Matthew, containing the genealogy of Jesus Christ, is read during the liturgy.

It is significant that the evangelist Matthew began his narrative of the Nativity of Christ with the enumeration of the ancestors of the Savior. In this way he shows that Jesus Christ was a real and whole person, and a representative of his people. He was flesh of the flesh of the Jewish people and at the same time perfect God. The names of the Old Testament righteous ones are enumerated in the Gospel also because they all lived by faith in the coming Savior. The words of Saint Paul, read on the Sunday of the Holy Fathers, tell of this faith: "By faith Abraham obeyed when he was called to go out to the place which he would receive as an inheritance. . . . By faith he dwelt in the land of promise as in a foreign country, dwelling in tents with Isaac and Jacob, the heirs with him of the same promise. . . . By faith Abraham, when he was tested, offered up Isaac" (Heb 11.8–9; 17). The whole life of the ancestors mentioned in the Gospel was penetrated with faith in God and the expectation of the Savior: precisely here lies the meaning of the reading of the genealogy of Jesus Christ on the Sunday before Christmas.

The list of the ancestors in the liturgical texts begins with the first-formed Adam, whom the Church glorifies as the father of all people:

> Let us honor the first Adam, who was honored by the hand of the Creator, and became the forefather of all, and rests in the heavenly tabernacles with all the elect. (Menaion. Sunday of the Holy Forefathers. Matins. Canon. Ode 1.)

Abel is glorified as the first martyr who suffered at the "murderous hand" of his brother; Noah as the one who preserved the law of God unharmed; Abraham as the "friend of God" who was vouchsafed to behold a vision of the Holy Trinity (insofar as a vision of the Holy Trinity is possible for man); Isaac as the "image of the passion of Christ" (a type of Christ's suffering). It was said concerning Jacob that he "wrestled with the angel" and "perceiving the mind of God was called a god"; concerning Joseph—that he was cast into a pit, "becoming an image of Christ, who was slain and placed in a tomb"; concerning Job—that he was "meek, guileless, righteous, perfect, and blameless." The canon of the Sunday of the Forefathers lists the Old Testament righteous men and pious women who were well pleasing to God, as well as the prophets, "the descendants of Abraham," who proclaimed through the Holy Spirit the Word of God, who came from the lineage of Judah according to the flesh.[3] A special emphasis in the services of the Sunday of the Forefathers and the Sunday of the Holy Fathers is placed on the Prophet Daniel and the three holy children in the Babylonian furnace: they are a foreshadowing of the nativity of Christ, which did not burn "the virgin's womb."

The most-holy Theotokos is glorified in these services as the fruit of all the previous development of the human race, the best of women, and the one whom the prophets foretold:

Through faith thou didst justify the Forefathers, betrothing through them the Church of the gentiles. These saints exult in glory, for from their seed came forth a glorious fruit: she who bore Thee without seed. So by their prayers, O Christ God, have mercy on us. (Menaion. Sunday of the Holy Forefathers. Great Vespers. Troparion.)

The Virgin Theotokos has been prophesied on earth from the age by the prophets in [their] proclamations; her do the wise patriarchs and the assemblies of the righteous announce; and together with them, the beauty of women—Sarah, Rebecca, Rachel, and Hannah, and also the glorious Mariam, [sister] of Moses—exults. The ends of the world rejoice together with them, and all of creation renders honor, for the Creator and God of all comes to be born in the flesh and to grant us great mercy. (Menaion. Sunday of the Holy Fathers. Matins. Praises.)

---

[3]Menaion. Sunday of the Holy Forefathers. Matins. Canon.

THE NATIVITY OF CHRIST

The feast of the Nativity of Christ—the feast of man's meeting with the incarnate God—stands second in importance in the Orthodox ecclesiastical calendar after Pascha. The greatest miracle of the incarnation of God lies in that, having taken place once in history, it is renewed in every person who comes to Christ. The Word of God was made flesh on earth in the profound silence of night; in the same way he is made flesh in the silent depths of the human soul—where reason falls silent, where words are exhausted, where the human mind stands before God. Christ was born unknown and unrecognized on the earth, and only the magi and shepherds together with angels came to meet him. In the same way, Christ is born in the human soul silently and unseen to others, and the soul comes out to meet him because a star leading to the Light flares up within.

Nativity of Christ.
Contemporary Icon.

Twenty centuries ago God decided to enter into the history of humanity in a special way, and by his birth from a virgin he overturned the entire course of history. Since then he again and again is born in the souls of thousands of people, and he changes, transforms, and transfigures their entire lives, making believers of those who were unbelievers, making saints of sinners, and saving those who were perishing.

The duration of the feast reflects the greatness of the event of the Savior's coming into the world: including the five days of the forefeast and the six days of the afterfeast, the Nativity lasts twelve days. Besides the forefeast, the Nativity of Christ also has one day called the eve (or commonly in Russian *sochel'nik*).[4] The Typikon prescribes a strict fast on this day—total abstinence from food until the end of the evening divine service (but in practice, vespers is usually performed in the morning). The divine services on the Eve of the Nativity and the feast itself comprise a unified liturgical cycle spanning two days. A similar structure of services is encountered only two other times in the year: on Theophany, which is also preceded by similar services on its eve, and Pascha, which is preceded by Great Saturday.

---

[4]The Slavonic word "*sochel'nik*" originated from "*sochiva*"—a fasting meal customarily eaten on this day.

On the Eve of the Nativity, the hours are performed separately from the other services: at each hour the Book of Epistles is read as well as the gospel. Vespers is combined with the liturgy of Saint Basil the Great; at vespers eight readings from the Old Testament are read, which contain prophecies concerning the Savior's coming into the world. The all-night vigil before Nativity consists of great compline and matins. On the day of the feast itself, the liturgy of Saint John Chrysostom is celebrated. The order of divine services changes if the Eve falls on a Saturday or Sunday, and when Nativity correspondingly falls on Sunday or Monday. In this case, the hours are performed on Friday, and the liturgy of Saint John Chrysostom is served on the Eve of Nativity, and vespers is performed not before but after the liturgy; the liturgy of Saint Basil the Great is transferred to the day of the feast itself. When the feast of the Nativity of Christ falls on a Sunday, the resurrectional service is completely omitted.

On the Eve of the Nativity of Christ, a candle is brought out into the middle of the church after the end of the divine liturgy. The clergy stand before it and together with the people sing the troparion and kontakion of the feast:

> Thy Nativity, O Christ our God, has shone to the world the Light of wisdom! For by it, those who worshipped the stars, were taught by a Star to adore thee, the Sun of Righteousness, and to know thee, the Orient from on High. O Lord, glory to thee!

> Today the Virgin gives birth to the Transcendent One, and the earth offers a cave to the Unapproachable One! Angels with shepherds glorify Him! The wise men journey with a star! Since for our sake the Eternal God was born as a Little Child!

These hymns then are sung at great compline, matins, and at the liturgy of the Nativity, as well as on subsequent days right up to the leave-taking of the feast.

Part of the Nativity service includes a meditation on the Old Testament types of our Lord and Savior's coming into the world. At vespers eight Old Testament readings are dedicated to this theme. The cycle of Old Testament readings includes:

(1) The biblical narrative of the creation of the world (Gen 1.1–13);

(2) The prophecy of Balaam concerning a Star out of Jacob (Num 24.2–3; 5–9; 17–18);

(3) The prophecy of Micah concerning the birth of an Israelite ruler in Bethlehem (Mic 4.6–7; 5.2–4);

(4) The prophecy of Isaiah concerning the branch from the root of Jesse (Is
11.1–10);

(5) The prophecy of Baruch concerning the Messiah (Bar 3.36–38; 4.1–4);

(6) The interpretation of the vision of Nebuchadnezzar concerning the
statue with feet of clay (Dan 2.31–36; 44–45);

(7) The prophecy of Isaiah concerning the birth of a Child whose name is
Almighty God (Is 9.6–7);

(8) The prophecy of Isaiah concerning the birth of a Son from a virgin (Is
7.10–16; 8.1–4; 8–10).

On the Eve of the Nativity and on the feast of the Nativity of Christ itself,
the liturgical texts speak in detail of the circumstances surrounding our Lord and
Savior's coming into the world. Primarily, the authors of the texts draw attention
to the relationship between the righteous Joseph and the Virgin Mary after it
became known that she would give birth to the Child. A dialogue between Joseph
and Mary, included in the Nativity service, seems to reveal what was transpiring in
Joseph's soul when he learned of the pregnancy of the most-holy virgin.[5]

Another theme expressed in the liturgical texts is the census of the population
that took place in Judea at the command of the Roman Emperor Augustus (see Lk
2.1–5). In the Gospel, only Joseph and the most-holy Theotokos are mentioned,
who came to Bethlehem in connection with the census. But the liturgical texts
speak of Christ's participation in the census—a voluntary participation. Christ
writes his name in the book containing people's names in order for those names
to be written in the Book of Life, and in order to tear up the "handwriting" of
human sins:

> The Master is enrolled with slaves, for he desires to tear to pieces the bill of
> trangressions and to enroll in the book of the living all who have been made
> dead by the serpent's thieivery. . . . (Menaion. Sunday of the Holy Fathers.
> Matins. Praises.)

In one of the Christmas stichera, attributed to the noble poetess Cassia the
Nun, a parallel is drawn between the unification of the Roman Empire under the
dominion of one emperor, which resulted in the political stability of the country,
and the spiritual unification of people that resulted from the incarnation of God:

[5] These dialogues were discussed on pp. 64–65.

When Augustus reigned alone upon earth, the many kingdoms of men came to end: and when Thou wast made man of the pure Virgin, the many gods of idolatry were destroyed. The cities of the world passed under one single rule; and the nations came to believe in one sovereign Godhead. The peoples were enrolled by the decree of Caesar; and we, the faithful, were enrolled in the Name of the Godhead, when Thou, our God, wast made man. . . . (Menaion. Nativity of Christ. Vespers. Stichera on "Lord, I call" [the composition of Cassia the Nun].)

The liturgical texts draw attention to one of the circumstances of the birth of the Savior: there was no place in the inn for Mary and Joseph. This circumstance is interpreted as an indication that Christ revealed himself to the world as a stranger, who from the very moment of his birth had "nowhere to lay his head" (Mt 8.20). For him there was no "dwelling place" in human society; he was a "foreigner"[6] and those who worshipped him were strangers like him:

Mary once, with aged Joseph, went to be taxed in Bethlehem, for they were of the lineage of David; and she bore in her womb the fruit that had not been sown. The time of the birth was at hand and there was no room at the inn; but the cave proved a fair palace for the Queen. Christ is born, that He may raise up again the image that before was fallen. (Menaion. Eve of the Nativity of Christ. Vespers. Troparion.)

. . . Whom do ye seek? For I see that ye have come from a far country. Ye have the appearance, but not the thoughts, of Persians; strange has your journey been, and strange your arrival. Ye have come with zeal to worship Him. . . . (Menaion. Eve of the Nativity of Christ. Vespers. Stichera at "Lord, I call.")

The theme of the murder of the infants by King Herod of Judea occupies an essential place in the liturgical texts of the Nativity. One of the days of the after-feast is specially dedicated to the commemoration of the infants in Bethlehem, who are revered as the first martyrs for Christ. The liturgical texts, dedicated to this theme, speak not only of the innocent infants murdered by Herod, but also of Herod himself. His lack of faith in God is identified as the main source of his crimes. This person's entire life was lived only from an earthly perspective. For him, God did not exist; he did not fear him, and therefore he stopped at nothing to attain his earthly objectives, not even terrible evil. The abolition of the Judean

---

[6]The Greek word *xenos* signifies both "stranger" and "foreigner."

state, its loss of political independence, and its transition to a vassal state are seen as the result of Herod's crimes (although, chronologically, independence was lost by Judea significantly earlier, and the decisive conquest of Jerusalem took place considerably later—in AD 70.)

> O foolish man, lover of darkness, crying out: "There is no God!" Seeking to slay Him who came in the fullness of time, in madness you murdered the blameless infants. The earth groaned in travail at your deed, polluted with innocent blood. (Menaion. December 22. Compline. Canon. Ode 3.)

> When Jesus was born in Bethlehem in Judea, the dominion of the Jews was abolished. Let the infants slaughtered for Christ leap, let Judea lament, for a voice has been heard in Rama: Rachel weeps and laments for her children, as it is written, for the most lawless Herod has murdered the infants, fulfilling the Scripture and satisfying Judea with innocent blood; for the earth is made crimson with the blood of the infants, and the Church from among the nations is mystically cleansed and clothed in beauty. The Truth has come, God is manifest to those sitting in shadow, born of the Virgin in order to save us. (Menaion. December 29. Vespers. Aposticha.)

The liturgical texts indicate that Christ, having just been born, was drawn into the conflict between the kingdom of this world and the kingdom of God. He had not yet done anything, and yet some already wanted to kill him. He had not yet learned how to speak, and yet already he needed to flee to a land of exile. His entire earthly life, too, would be marked by the ceaseless hostility of this world. For all the kindness that he showed for people, this hostility would be given to him in the form of insults, false witnesses, betrayals, and cruel torments, and ultimately it would lead him to the cross.

Although ample attention is given to the circumstances of the birth of the Savior and to other characters of the Nativity story (Joseph, Herod, the magi, shepherds, martyrs), nevertheless the basic theme of the texts is the theological understanding of the event of God's incarnation itself. It is Christ who stands at the center of attention for the authors of the liturgical texts. He is the one Christians are called to come out and meet:

> Christ is born, give ye glory. Christ comes from heaven, meet ye Him. Christ is on earth, be ye exalted. O all the earth, sing unto the Lord, and sing praises in

gladness, O ye people, for He has been glorified. (Menaion. Nativity of Christ. Matins. Canon. Ode 1. Irmos.)

The beginning of Saint Gregory the Theologian's Nativity homily, which the Typikon prescribes to be read at matins on Christmas Day, almost literally reproduces the words of the irmos:[7]

Christ is born, give glory; Christ is from the heavens, go to meet him; Christ is on earth, be lifted up. "Sing to the Lord, all the earth" [Ps 96.1], and, to say both together, "Let the heavens be glad and let the earth rejoice" [Ps 96.11], for the heavenly one is now earthly. Christ is in the flesh, exult with trembling. . . . The fleshless one takes flesh, the Word is made coarse, the invisible one is seen, the impalpable one is touched, the timeless one makes a beginning, the Son of God becomes Son of Man.[8]

Christ is the New Adam come to save the first-formed Adam and, in his person, all of humanity:

In the strength of Thy Godhead Thou hast been joined with mortal men, through a union without confusion, O Saviour, in the likeness of the flesh of Adam; and in thus assuming human nature Thou dost bestow upon it immortality and salvation. (Menaion. Forefeast of the Nativity of Christ. Compline. Canon. Ode 4.)

Adam the prisoner has been set loose and freedom has been given to all the faithful, now that Thou art wrapped in swaddling bands, O Saviour. . . . (Menaion. Forefeast of the Nativity of Christ. Compline. Canon. Ode 8.)

Beholding him that was in God's image and likeness fallen through the transgression, Jesus bowed the heavens and came down, and without changing He took up His dwelling in a Virgin womb: that thereby He might fashion corrupt Adam anew, who cried to Him: "Glory to Thine Epiphany, O my Deliverer and my God." (Menaion. Nativity of Christ. Great Vespers. Stichera at the Litiya.)

The theme of the Mother of God—the second Eve—occupies a no less essential place in the Nativity services. While the first Eve brought death to all the world,

---

[7]Chronologically speaking, the hymns reproduce St Gregory's homily; St John of Damascus similarly echoes and paraphrases St Gregory's homilies on Pascha in his paschal canon.—*Ed.*

[8]Gregory the Theologian, *Orations* 38.1 (SC 358:104–106; Harrison, PPS).

the second Eve frees the human race from the curse, having become the mother of the incarnate God:

> O Theotokos Virgin who hast borne the Saviour, thou hast overthrown the ancient curse of Eve. For thou hast become the Mother of Him in whom the Father was well pleased, and hast carried at thy bosom God the incarnate Word. We cannot fathom this mystery: but by faith alone we all glorify it, crying with thee and saying: O Lord past all interpretation, glory to Thee. (Menaion. Nativity of Christ. Matins. Stichera at the Praises.)

The theme of the divine condescension (we recall that this theme was one of the leitmotifs of the Nativity homily of Saint Gregory the Theologian) occupies an essential place in the liturgical texts:[9]

> The rich becomes poor, enriching those made poor through malice; from a virgin who knows not wedlock, God is made known as a man, without change. . . . (Menaion. Sunday of the Holy Fathers. Matins. Canon of the Forefeast. Ode 1.)

> Thou sawest our affliction and animosity, compassionate Christ, and thou didst not despise us, but didst empty thy very self; while thou didst not leave [thy] Begetter, thou didst come to dwell in the womb of one who knew not wedlock. . . . (Menaion. Sunday of the Holy Fathers. Matins. Canon of the Forefeast. Ode 6.)

> The undefiled Virgin, beholding the pre-eternal God as a child that had taken flesh from her, held Him in her arms and without ceasing she kissed Him. Filled with joy, she said aloud to Him: "O Most High God, O King unseen, how is it that I look upon Thee? I cannot understand the mystery of Thy poverty without measure. For the smallest of caves, a strange dwelling for Thee, finds room for Thee within itself. Thou hast been born without destroying my virginity. . . ." (Menaion. December 24. Vespers. Stichera at "Lord, I call.")

The liturgical texts interpret God's reception of human nature as the beginning of its deification (once again, this recalls Saint Gregory the Theologian):

> The all-perfect one is born, [and] as an infant is wrapped in swaddling clothes; and the one who is without beginning receives a beginning from the Virgin,

[9]See vol. 2, pp. 262–263.

seeking to deify that which is assumed. . . . (Menaion. December 22. Matins. Canon. Ode 7.)

The stichera performed at vespers on the feast of the Nativity of Christ are distinguished by their special depth of theological content. They emphasize that the birth of the divine infant from the Virgin Mary reestablished the connection between God and man that was lost through the Fall. Christ appeared to the world as "Light of Light," in order to restore the image of God in man, which was darkened by sin, and to enlighten the whole world with the radiance of his divinity:

Come, let us greatly rejoice in the Lord as we tell of this present mystery. The middle wall of partition has been destroyed; the flaming sword turns back, the cherubim withdraw from the tree of life, and I partake of the delight of Paradise from which I was cast out through disobedience. For the express Image of the Father, the Imprint of His eternity, takes the form of a servant, and without undergoing change He comes forth from a Mother who knew not wedlock. For what He was, He has remained, true God: and what He was not, He has taken upon Himself, becoming man through love for mankind. Unto Him let us cry aloud: God born of a Virgin, have mercy upon us. (Menaion. Nativity of Christ. Great Vespers. Stichera at "Lord, I call.")

Thy Kingdom, O Christ our God, is a Kingdom of all the ages, and Thy rule is from generation to generation. Made flesh of the Holy Spirit and made man of the ever-Virgin Mary, Thou hast enlightened us by Thy coming. Light of Light, Brightness of the Father, Thou hast made the whole creation shine with joy. All that hath breath praises Thee, the Image of the glory of the Father. O God who art, and who hast ever been, who hast shone forth from a Virgin, have mercy upon us. (Menaion. Nativity of Christ. Great Vespers. Stichera at "Lord, I call.")

The Nativity of Christ is presented as an event of universal significance that unites all of creation. In doxology and thanksgiving to God, angels and men join together and all of creation, together with the magi, bears its gifts to the Infant born in Bethlehem:

What shall we offer Thee, O Christ, who for our sakes hast appeared on earth as man? Every creature made by Thee offers Thee thanks. The angels offer Thee a hymn; the heavens, a star; the Magi, gifts; the shepherds, their wonder; the earth, its cave; the wilderness, the manger; and we offer Thee a Virgin Mother. O pre-eternal God, have mercy upon us. (Menaion. Nativity of Christ. Great Vespers. Stichera at "Lord, I call.")

On the second day of Nativity is the Synaxis of the Most-Holy Theotokos—a meeting, or divine service, in honor of the one who gave birth to the eternal God who granted salvation to the whole world. The Christmas service is almost completely repeated on this day, with special hymns in honor of the Mother of God interspersed throughout.

On the Sunday following the Nativity of Christ, the Church celebrates the memory of Saint Joseph the Betrothed, King David, and James, the brother of the Lord. The Church glorifies Saint Joseph as the man who became the guardian of the virginity of the most-holy Theotokos, accompanied the holy virgin to Egypt, and upon returning to Nazareth took upon himself the cares of raising the Infant Jesus. King David is glorified as one of the ancestors of the Savior, an "ancestor of God"; "from him sprang forth the rod of the virgin, and from her blossomed the Flower, even Christ."[10] James, the brother of the Lord, as he is considered, was the son of Joseph from his first marriage: following the resurrection of the Savior he became the first bishop of Jerusalem and one of the first martyrs for Christ.

THE CIRCUMCISION OF THE LORD

On the eighth day following Christmas, January 1, the Circumcision of the Lord is celebrated. Circumcision was established by God as a sign of his covenant with Abraham and his descendants (see Gen 17.12; Lev 12.2–3). The divine infant born in Bethlehem was circumcised on the eighth day; at the same time he was named by Joseph (see Mt 1.21, 25; Lk 2.21). Saint Paul speaks of circumcision as a foreshadowing of baptism (see Col 2.11–12).

In the liturgical texts of the feast it is emphasized that the incarnate God accepted circumcision out of obedience to the Old Testament law. His acceptance of circumcision was one of the stages of his divine condescension, which began in Bethlehem and ended on Golgotha:

Enthroned on high with the eternal Father and thy divine Spirit, thou didst will to be born on earth, O Jesus, of the unwedded handmaid, thy Mother.

---

[10]Menaion. Sunday following the Nativity of Christ. Great Vespers. Stichera at "Lord, I call."

Circumcision of the Lord. Contemporary Icon.

Therefore thou wast circumcised as an eight-day-old Child. Glory to thy most gracious counsel; glory to thy dispensation; glory to thy condescension, O only Lover of mankind. (Menaion. Circumcision of the Lord. Little Vespers. Troparion.)

The God of all goodness did not disdain to be circumcised. He offered himself as a saving sign and example for us all. He made the Law, and he obeyed his own commands. He fulfilled the words of the prophets concerning himself. . . . (Menaion. Circumcision of the Lord. Great Vespers. Stichera at "Lord, I call.")

Circumcision was necessary as a sign of belonging to the Israel of the Old Testament. But after Christ accepted circumcision out of obedience, it became unnecessary for salvation because the Church became filled with Gentiles:

Circumcision has come to an end, since Christ was circumcised voluntarily, saving a multitude of nations by grace. (Menaion. Circumcision of the Lord. Matins. Canon 1. Ode 4.)

The circumcision of the Lord on the eighth day was an image of the "eighth day," the kingdom of God without evening, which awaits the faithful beyond the threshold of death:

> The eighth of days, which bears an image of the future, is illumined and sanctified by thy voluntary lowliness, O Christ, for on it wast thou circumcised in the flesh in accordance with the law. (Menaion. Circumcision of the Lord. Matins. Canon 1. Ode 1.)

> The [day] on which the Master was circumcised in the flesh makes an image of the neverending life of the future eighth age. (Menaion. Circumcision of the Lord. Matins. Canon 1. Ode 4.)

On the eighth day following birth, when it was required to circumcise the Infant, the naming also took place. The divine infant was given the name Jesus (see Lk 2.21), of which Saint Peter said, "there is no other name under heaven given among men by which we must be saved" (Acts 4.12):

> On the eighth day the Master is circumcised as an infant, and he receives the name Jesus, for he is the Savior and Lord of the world. (Menaion. Circumcision of the Lord. Matins. Canon 1. Ode 8.)

In his homily on the Circumcision of Christ, Saint Dimitry of Rostov spoke about the significance of giving the name "Jesus" to the Savior of the world born in Bethlehem:

> On this day the divine babe also received the name Jesus. When the archangel Gabriel descended from heaven and appeared to the most pure Virgin Mary, he made known that her Son would be called thus. . . . At his circumcision, the name disclosed by the herald before the Virgin conceived was formally given to Christ the Lord to announce the coming of our salvation. Jesus means salvation. . . . The saving name of Jesus was reserved by the pre-eternal counsel of the Holy Trinity for our salvation, and on this day the righteous Joseph brings it forth like a priceless pearl from heaven's treasury, so that it may be used to redeem the whole human race. . . . It shines on the world like the sun. . . . It fills creation with the fragrance of myrrh. . . . The power of Jesus' wondrous name has been revealed, causing angels to marvel, mankind to rejoice, and demons to tremble. . . .[11]

[11]Dimitrii of Rostov, "Homily on the Circumcision of Christ" 8–13, in *The Great Collection of the Lives of the Saints*, trans. Thomas Marretta, vol. 5 (House Springs, MO: Chrysostom Press, 2002), 11–12.

The feast of the Circumcision of the Lord coincides with the day of the commemoration of Saint Basil the Great, one of the most honored fathers of the Church. In the liturgical texts of this day, even more attention is given to Saint Basil than to the Circumcision, and in several texts both holy commemorations are combined in a united prayerful glorification:

> The Lord of all endures circumcision, and as the Good one, he circumcises human trangressions and today grants salvation to the world. And today the hierarch of the Creator, the light-bearing divine initiate of Christ, Basil, rejoices in the highest. (Menaion. Circumcision of the Lord. Matins. Kontakion after Ode 3 of the Canon.)

> An eighth day, the all-glorious memory of the hierarch, has been meetly joined to Christ's Nativity, and honoring it with faith, we hymn the Lord and exalt him unto the ages. (Menaion. Circumcision of the Lord. Matins. Canon 1. Ode 8.)

For the katavasia at matins on the day of the Circumcision of the Lord, irmoi of the canon for Theophany are sung. In this way, the Nativity celebrations flow over without interruption into the celebration of Theophany.

THEOPHANY

Theophany, or the Baptism of the Lord, is celebrated twelve days after Christmas, on January 6. It has already been said that Theophany was originally the feast on which both the birth of Christ from the virgin and his baptism by John in the Jordan were simultaneously remembered. Only at the end of the fourth century did Christians begin celebrating Christmas separately from Theophany in the Christian East. But the original kinship of the two feasts left its mark in Orthodox divine worship. The structure of the divine services of both feasts is identical: both feasts are preceded by an Eve, at which the hours are performed separately, and the liturgy of Saint Basil the Great is celebrated in combination with vespers, at which Old Testament readings

Baptism of the Lord.
Contemporary Icon.

corresponding to the events of the feast are read. When Theophany coincides with
a Sunday or Monday, the liturgical structure changes in exactly the same way as it
would for the Nativity in a similar situation.

Saint Gregory the Theologian spoke concerning the connection between Nativity and Theophany in his homily, which the Typikon prescribes to be read at matins
of the feast of Theophany:

> Therefore at his birth we kept festival as is fitting. . . . But now there is another
> deed of Christ. . . . Christ is illumined, let us flash like lightning with him.
> Christ is baptized, let us go down with him, that we also come up again with
> him. . . . Yet as John is baptizing, Jesus approaches, perhaps also to sanctify the
> baptizer, and certainly to bury all the old Adam in the water. . . . Jesus comes
> up again out of the water. For he carries up with himself the world and "sees
> the heavens opened" [Mk 1.10] which Adam closed for himself and for those
> after him. . . .[12]

The connection between Nativity and Theophany is also seen in numerous
liturgical texts in which the two feasts are compared. A parallel is drawn between
the events at the time of the Savior's birth into the world and the events connected
with his baptism by Saint John:

> There the star revealed Thee to the Magi, but here the Father proclaims Thee
> to the universe. . . . (Menaion. January 2. Forefeast of Theophany. Vespers.
> Aposticha.)

> Much brighter than the sun is the feast of Christ's Nativity, now passed, and the
> coming of his divine manifestation has been shown to be clear and most bright.
> During the one, shepherds with angels sang a doxology, worshipping God
> incarnate; during the other, John, when he touched the Master with his right
> hand, said with trembling: sanctify me and the water, thou who alone hast great
> mercy. (Menaion. January 2. Forefeast of Theophany. Matins. Aposticha.)

In the liturgical texts it is emphasized that while the whole earth was sanctified
thanks to the Nativity of Christ, the nature of water is blessed by the baptism of
the Lord:

> The earth has been sanctified, O Word, by Thy holy birth, and the heavens
> with the stars declared Thy glory: and now the nature of the waters is blessed

---

[12]Gregory the Theologian, *Orations* 39.14–16 (SC 358:178–184; Harrison, PPS).

by Thy baptism in the flesh, and mankind has been restored once more to its former nobility. (Menaion. January 5. Forefeast of Theophany. Compline. Canon. Ode 9.)

The Lord created water as an element of life, but human sin made it a source of death. When the Lord created water, the Spirit of God moved upon the face of the waters (Gen 1.2), filling water with his life-creating energy. But when human sin was multiplied on the earth, the water of life became the water of death and old humanity perished in the waters of the great flood. The biblical flood in Christian tradition is a symbol of renewal—the death of the old man and the birth of the new man.

Before the coming of Christ to earth, Saint John the Forerunner baptized people in the waters of the Jordan. People came down to these waters decrepit and emerged from them new, having been renewed by repentance. Jesus Christ came to the Jordan not in order to be purified of sin, but in order to sanctify the waters of the Jordan, to transfigure them and fill them with life. And the water of death, saturated with human sin, became a source of life, because God himself in his human flesh came down to it and filled it with his divinity.

In the commemoration of the Savior's baptism, a great sanctification of water is performed on the eve of Theophany and again on the day of the feast itself. There will be a discussion concerning the order for this rite in a section dedicated to the sacraments and rites of the Orthodox Church.[13]

In the liturgical texts, the Baptism of the Lord in the Jordan is seen as an integral part of the divine plan for the salvation of mankind. It was incumbent on God not only to take on human flesh but also to descend into the waters of the Jordan in order to bring to the light those sitting in darkness:

Thou who in Bethlehem hast shone forth in the flesh from a Virgin, dost now hasten towards Jordan to wash clean the filth of those born on earth, through holy baptism leading those in darkness to the light. (Menaion. Eve of Theophany. Matins. Canon. Ode 9.)

Wishing to save man gone astray, Thou hast not disdained to clothe Thyself in the form of a servant. For it befitted Thee, as Master and God, to take upon Thyself our nature for our sakes. For Thou, O Deliverer, hast been baptized in the flesh, making us worthy of forgiveness. Therefore we cry unto Thee: O

---

[13]The fifth and final volume of this series will be dedicated to describing the sacraments of the Church.—*Ed.*

Christ our God and Benefactor, glory to Thee. (Menaion. Theophany. Vespers. Stichera on "Lord, I call.")

The Lord, incarnate of the Virgin, having clothed material flesh with the immaterial fire of His divinity, wraps Himself in the waters of the Jordan. . . . (Menaion. Theophany. Matins. Canon 1. Ode 1.)

According to Christian tradition, various events of the Old Testament are types of baptism. Some of them are cited in the selections of the Old Testament readings read at vespers before the beginning of the liturgy of Saint Basil the Great. (Water plays a role in most of the episodes):

1. The account of the creation of the earth (Gen 1.1–13);
2. The narrative of the Hebrews crossing the Red Sea (Ex 14.15–18; 21–23; 27–29);
3. The account of Moses making the bitter waters of Marah sweet (Ex 15.22–25);
4. The account of the parting of the Jordan by the priests who carried the ark of the covenant (Josh 3.7–8, 15–17);
5. The account of Elijah ascending into heaven (2 Kg 2.6–14);
6. The narrative of the cleansing of Naaman (2 Kg 5.9–14);
7. The appeal of Isaiah for spiritual cleansing (Is 1.16–20);
8. The account of how Jacob prepared for his meeting with Esau (Gen 32.1–10);
9. The account of the infant Moses being drawn out of the water (Ex 2.5–10);
10. The account of the dew descending on the fleece of Gideon (Judg 6.36–40);
11. The account of Elijah's burnt sacrifice (1 Kg 18.30–39);
12. The account of Elisha healing the waters of Jericho (2 Kg 2.19–22);
13. The prophecy of Isaiah concerning the new covenant Church (Is 49.8–15).

The very same types are referred to in the liturgical texts, but still others are added to them, in particular the narrative of the great flood (see Gen 7), the history of the salvation of the Hebrews, who anointed the doorposts of their homes with the blood of sacrifice (see Ex 12.21–23), and the account of the appearance of God to Moses in the burning bush (Ex 3.1–5).

We know that in the beginning Thou hast brought upon the world the all-ruining flood, unto the lamentable destruction of all things, O God who revealest wonders most great and strange: And now, O Christ, Thou hast drowned sin in the waters unto the comfort and salvation of mortal men. (Menaion. Theophany. Matins. Canon 2. Ode 7.)

Let us, the faithful, keep ourselves safe through grace and through the seal of baptism. In the past the Hebrews fled destruction by marking the door posts with blood; so also this divine washing unto regeneration shall be our Exodus, and going hence, we shall behold the light of the Trinity that never sets. (Menaion. Theophany. Matins. Canon 1. Ode 9.)

That which was revealed to Moses in the bush we see accomplished here in strange manner. The Virgin bore Fire within her, yet was not consumed, when she gave birth to the Benefactor who brings us light, and the streams of the Jordan suffered no harm when they received Him. (Menaion. Theophany. Matins. Canon 2. Ode 9.)

Several liturgical texts include monologues or dialogues of the protagonists in the account of the baptism of Christ. In particular, the conversation of Saint John the Forerunner with Christ (see Mt 3.13–15) is reproduced in the following texts:

. . . "How shall I stretch forth my hand and touch the head of Him that rules all things? Though Thou art the child of Mary, yet do I know Thee to be the pre-eternal God. Thou whose praises the seraphim sing dost walk upon the earth. And I who am but a servant know not how to baptize the Master." O Lord past all understanding, glory to Thee. (Menaion. Theophany. Matins. Stichera after Psalm 50.)

O Prophet, suffer it to be so now, and baptize me as I wish. . . . (Menaion. Theophany. Matins. Refrains on Ode 9 of the Canon.)

The River Jordan is personified in the liturgical texts, just as it is in frescoes and mosaics depicting the baptism of the Lord. The author of one of the texts enters into a conversation with the Jordan:

O river Jordan, what hast thou seen to be amazed? "I have seen Him naked who cannot be seen, and I trembled," said he. "How should I not tremble before Him and turn back?" The angels, beholding Him, were afraid: heaven was filled with wonder and the earth shook, the sea and all things visible and invisible withdrew. Christ has appeared in the Jordan to sanctify the waters. (Menaion. Theophany. Matins. Sessional Hymn.)

The main attention of the authors of the liturgical texts is devoted to the theological understanding of the baptism of the Lord from the soteriological perspective. It is emphasized that, in contrast to the people who came to the Jordan to be baptized for the cleansing of sins, Christ had no need of such cleansing because he was without sin. He descended into the waters of the Jordan not for purification, but in order to bless the waters, and to cleanse people from the uncleanness of sin through the sacrament of baptism:

The Lord who purges away the filth of men was cleansed in Jordan for their sake, having of His own will made Himself like unto them, while still remaining that which He was; and He enlightens those in darkness, for He has been glorified. (Menaion. Theophany. Matins. Canon 1. Ode 1.)

Immersion in water is a symbol of death, and emerging from the water is a symbol of spiritual renewal and resurrection. The old Adam—personifying all of humanity—descends together with Christ into the waters of Jordan:

O Word without beginning, Thou hast buried man with Thee in the stream: He was corrupted by error, but Thou makest Him new again. And the Father testified to Thee ineffably, saying with mighty voice: "This is My beloved Child, equal to Me by nature." (Menaion. Theophany. Matins. Canon 2. Ode 9.)

Because Christ accepted baptism in the Jordan, baptism "by water and the Spirit" became possible, which opens to the faithful entrance into the Church. The slaughter of the infants in Bethlehem deprived the Old Testament Church of its children, but baptism grants new children to the New Testament Church:

Rejoice today, O Church of Christ, that before wast barren and sadly childless. For through water and the Spirit sons have been born to thee. . . . (Menaion. Theophany. Matins. Canon 1. Ode 3.)

In the ancient Church, Theophany was called "the day of lights," and the sacrament of baptism "enlightenment." Saint Gregory the Theologian devoted his homily on baptism mainly to the theme of the divine light.[14] This theme is also reflected in the liturgical texts:

[14]See citation in vol. 2, pp. 160–161.

Thou hast appeared today to the inhabited earth, and Thy light, O Lord, has been marked upon us, who with knowledge sing Thy praise: Thou hast come, Thou art made manifest, the Light that no man can approach. (Menaion. Theophany. Matins. Kontakion.)

Light from Light, Christ our God has shone upon the world, God made manifest: O ye peoples, let us worship Him. (Menaion. Theophany. Matins. Praises.)

The true Light has appeared and bestows enlightenment on all. Christ who is above all purity is baptized with us; He brings sanctification to the water and it becomes a cleansing for our souls. That which is outward and visible is earthly, that which is inwardly understood is higher than heaven. Salvation comes through washing, and through water the Spirit: by descending into the water we ascend to God. Wonderful are Thy works, O Lord: glory to Thee. (Menaion. Theophany. Matins. Praises.)

The feast of the baptism of the Lord reveals Jesus Christ as the God-man who possesses two natures. As man he comes to be baptized, and as God he makes baptism salvific for the entire human race:

Oh, most-glorious wonder! He who baptizes with the Holy Spirit and with fire comes to be baptized in the Jordan by John. He is neither bare God nor a simple man, but one and the same Only-Begotten Son in two natures, for as a man he seeks baptism from a mortal, but as God he takes away the sin of the world and grants great mercy to all. (Menaion. January 3. Forefeast of Theophany. Vespers. Stichera on "Lord, I call.")

The baptism of Jesus by John in the Jordan was the first event in the history of mankind at which the three persons of the Holy Trinity were revealed: The Lord Jesus was submerged in the water in his flesh, the Holy Spirit descended on Jesus in the form of a dove, and the voice of God the Father said, "This is my beloved Son, in whom I am well pleased" (Mt 3.13–17). The trinitarian aspect of the feast is reflected in the main liturgical texts devoted to this event:

When Thou, O Lord, wast baptized in the Jordan, the worship of the Trinity was made manifest. For the voice of the Father bore witness to Thee, and called Thee His beloved Son. And the Spirit, in the form of a dove, confirmed the truthfulness of His word. O Christ, our God, Thou hast revealed Thyself and hast enlightened the world, glory to Thee! (Menaion. Theophany. Vespers. Troparion.)

The Trinity was made manifest in the Jordan. For, supreme in Godhead, the Father proclaimed, saying, "He who is here baptized is My beloved Son," and the Spirit rested upon His Equal in Godhead. . . . (Menaion. Theophany. Matins. Canon 1. Ode 8.)

Thou hast appeared, O Saviour Christ, in the Jordan and wast baptized by the Forerunner: and testimony was borne to Thee, that Thou art the beloved Son. So wast Thou revealed as coeternal with the Father, and the Holy Spirit descended upon Thee. Enlightened by Thee, we cry: Glory to the God in Trinity. (Menaion. Theophany. Matins. Sessional Hymn.)

In the same way that the synaxis of the most-holy Theotokos follows the feast of the Nativity, the synaxis of Saint John the Forerunner is celebrated on the second day of the feast of Theophany. On this day the Church remembers that Christ himself said, "among those born of women there has not risen one greater than John the Baptist" (Mt 11.11).

THE MEETING OF THE LORD

Meeting of the Lord.
Contemporary Icon.

The final feast of the Nativity cycle is the Meeting of the Lord, celebrated on February 2. If the order of church feasts strictly corresponded with the chronology of the events in the gospel, the Meeting of the Lord would take place after the Circumcision and before Theophany. But the date of the Meeting of the Lord—forty days after the Nativity—was established for the reason that the event commemorated on this day took place forty days following the birth of the Savior. As a result, the Meeting of the Lord is celebrated almost one month after Theophany, returning the minds of the faithful to the continuation of the history of the Nativity.

The feast of the Meeting of the Lord commemorates the event recounted in the Gospel according to Luke (see Lk 2.22–38). The liturgical texts speak of Simeon, who held the Creator of the universe in his hands. The author of the texts places words of pious amazement in the mouth of Simeon, who was in awe of the divine majesty of the Infant Jesus. Simeon speaks of his approaching death and says that when he descends into hades he will proclaim to Adam the birth of the Messiah:

> Simeon, tell us: whom dost thou bear in thine arms, that thou dost rejoice so greatly in the temple? To whom dost thou cry and shout: Now I am set free, for I have seen my Saviour? "This is He who was born of a Virgin: this is He, the Word, God of God, who for our sakes has taken flesh and has saved man." Let us worship Him. (Menaion. Meeting of our Lord. Great Vespers. Stichera at "Lord, I call.")

> The holy Virgin offered in the Holy Place Him who is Holy, giving Him to the minister in holy things. And Simeon with exceeding joy received Him in his outstretched arms, and he cried out: "O Master, now lettest Thou Thy servant depart in peace according to Thy word, O Lord." (Menaion. Meeting of our Lord. Great Vespers. Stichera at the Litiya.)

> "I depart," cried Simeon, "to declare the good tidings to Adam abiding in hell and to Eve"; and with the prophets he sang rejoicing. . . . (Menaion. Meeting of our Lord. Matins. Canon. Ode 7.)

More than once the liturgical texts draw a parallel between Simeon and Moses. The leader of the Israelites could see only the "back parts of God" (see Ex 33.22–23), while the elder Simeon held the incarnate God in his arms and gazed at him with an uncovered face:

> Moses in days of old saw on Mount Sinai the back parts of God and was counted worthy in darkness and a storm of wind faintly to hear the divine voice. But now Simeon has taken in his arms God who for our sakes took flesh without changing; and joyfully has he made haste to depart from hence to the life eternal. . . . (Menaion. Meeting of our Lord. Matins. Sessional Hymn after Ode 3 of Canon.)

It is underscored that the Infant brought to the temple by Joseph and Mary is none other than the one who gave the law to Moses. On the eighth day he received circumcision out of obedience to the law, and now the Lord is brought as an offering to himself in the temple of the Lord, the house of the Father and his own house:

> Today He who once gave the Law to Moses on Sinai submits Himself to the ordinances of the Law, in His compassion becoming for our sakes as we are. Now the God of purity as a holy child has opened a pure womb, and as God

He is brought as an offering to Himself, setting us free from the curse of the Law and granting light to our souls. (Menaion. Meeting of our Lord. Great Vespers. Stichera at the Litiya.)

Unique among the feasts, the Meeting of the Lord is simultaneously a feast of the Lord and of the Theotokos. It is primarily the content of the major liturgical texts, and also several liturgical particularities—in particular the chanting of the entry verse during the liturgy at the little entrance—that witnesses to the fact that it is a feast of the Lord. On the other hand, when the Meeting of the Lord coincides with a Sunday, the resurrectional service is not cancelled, as occurs when there is a feast of the Theotokos. Moreover, although the troparion is addressed to Christ, it begins with an address to the Theotokos:

Rejoice, O Theotokos Virgin full of grace: for from thee has shone forth the Sun of Righteousness, Christ our God, giving light to those in darkness. Be glad also, thou righteous Elder, for thou hast received in thine arms the Deliverer of our souls, who bestows upon us resurrection. (Menaion. Meeting of our Lord. Great Vespers. Troparion.)

The most-holy Theotokos is glorified in the liturgical texts of the Meeting of the Lord as "the portal of heaven," "the throne of the cherubim," and "the cloud of the Light," since she bore in her arms the only-begotten Son of God.[15] In accordance with the accepted tradition, the clergy vests in light blue vestments on the Meeting of the Lord, which emphasizes the understanding that this is a feast of the Theotokos.

The Meeting of the Lord concludes the Nativity cycle of church feasts. The date of the Meeting is fixed, but it often coincides with a particular holy commemoration related to the movable cycle. When Pascha is late, the Meeting falls in the period before the Lenten Triodion is used. If Pascha is early, the Meeting may coincide with one of the preparatory weeks of Great Lent. When the date of the Meeting coincides with one of the days of the Week of Cheesefare, its afterfeast is abbreviated and lasts as long as the number of days remaining until the beginning of Great Lent (the usual length of the afterfeast of the Meeting of the Lord is seven days). When the date of the Meeting of the Lord falls within the Week of Cheesefare, the afterfeast disappears altogether, and when it coincides with Monday of the first week of Great Lent, the feast of the Meeting of the Lord is transferred to the previous day—Cheesefare Sunday (Forgiveness Sunday).

[15]Menaion. Meeting of the Lord. Great Vespers. Aposticha.

9

Divine Services from the
Sunday of the Publican and the Pharisee
until Great Saturday

B EGINNING WITH THE SUNDAY of the Publican and the Pharisee, the Lenten
Triodion is used for the divine services. The services of the period that use
the Lenten Triodion are conceived of as a unified liturgical cycle, which unfolds
over the course of ten weeks. This cycle includes three preparatory Sundays, six
weeks of Great Lent and Holy Week. The prayers and hymns of the Triodion carry
the faithful along the path of repentance during Great Lent, through the "Pascha
of Crucifixion," and to the "Pascha of Resurrection." The period of the Lenten
Triodion is the spiritually richest period of the yearly liturgical cycle. The inten-
sity of the liturgical experience grows with the approach of Pascha and attains its
climax in the days when Christ's suffering, death upon the cross, and resurrection
are commemorated.

PREPARATION FOR GREAT LENT

The Sunday of the Publican and the Pharisee is the first of four Sundays that
precede Great Lent. The major theme of the service on this day is the parable of
the Publican and the Pharisee, which is read during the liturgy (see Lk 18.10–14).
Two types of religiosity are presented to the faithful in this parable. The Pharisee
is a man who fulfills the prescriptions of the law, observes the established fasts,
and offers tithes to the temple. On the other hand, the publican is one who has a
despised profession and does not observe the stipulations of the law, and yet has
humility and repentance. The Pharisee thinks highly of all his good deeds, while
the publican is humbly aware of his unworthiness.

The publican is in no way presented as an ideal for imitation in the parable,
just as the Pharisee is not exclusively a negative character. The parable concludes

with the words, "I tell you, this man went down to his house justified rather[1] than the other; for everyone who exalts himself will be humbled, and he who humbles himself will be exalted" (Lk 18.14). In other words, both the publican and the Pharisee were justified, but the publican was more justified than the Pharisee because of his self-abasement.

In the context of the approaching Great Lent, the parable of the publican and the Pharisee reminds us that the observance of the fast should not become a reason for pride and self-exaltation. Moreover, this parable is a reminder that humility is the basis of all the virtues and that pride is the root of all vices. In the stichera and troparia, the humility and repentance of the publican is juxtaposed with the arrogance and pride of the Pharisee:

> Brethren, let us not pray as the pharisee: for he who exalts himself shall be humbled. Let us humble ourselves before God, and with fasting cry aloud as the publican: God be merciful to us sinners. (Lenten Triodion. Sunday of the Publican and the Pharisee. Vespers. Stichera at "Lord, I call.")

> Through parables leading all mankind to amendment of life, Christ raises up the publican from his abasement and humbles the pharisee in his pride. (Lenten Triodion. Sunday of the Publican and the Pharisee. Matins. Canon. Ode 1.)

> Let us flee from the proud speaking of the pharisee and learn the humility of the publican, and with groaning let us cry unto the Savior: Be merciful to us, for Thou alone art ready to forgive. (Lenten Triodion. Sunday of the Publican and the Pharisee. Matins. Kontakion.)

At matins of the Sunday of the Publican and the Pharisee, the singing of the penitential stichera begins following Psalm 50. These verses will be performed at every Sunday service during all of Great Lent:

> Open to me, O Giver of Life, the gates of repentance: for early in the morning my spirit seeks Thy holy temple, bearing the temple of the body all defiled. But in Thy compassion cleanse it by Thy loving-kindness and Thy mercy.

> Guide me in the paths of salvation, O Theotokos: for I have befouled my soul with shameful sins and have wasted all my life in slothfulness. By thine intercessions deliver me from all uncleanness.

[1] While the Revised Standard Version says that the publican was "justified rather than" the Pharisee, the word "rather" is an interpretive extrapolation which does not appear in the original Greek. It is therefore also an acceptable translation to say that the publican was "justified more than" the Pharisee, which is how it is rendered in the Slavonic, to which the author refers.—*Ed.*

As I ponder in my wretchedness the many evil things that I have done, I tremble for the fearful day of judgment. But trusting in thy merciful compassion, like David do I cry to Thee: Have mercy upon me, O God, in Thy great mercy. (Lenten Triodion. Sunday of the Publican and the Pharisee. Matins. Stichera following Psalm 50.)

The first of these stichera is connected to the theme of the parable of the Publican and the Pharisee; the motif of the parable of the Prodigal Son is heard in the second; the third has a reference to the Last Judgment. In this way, the stichera are thematically linked to the three Sundays preceding Great Lent.

The parable (see Lk 15.11–32) is read during the liturgy on the Sunday of the Prodigal Son, presenting an example of God's unspeakable mercy in relation to

Parable of the Publican and the Pharisee. Mosaic. Basilica of Sant' Appolinare Nuovo. Ravenna. 6th c.

penitent sinners. The parable shows that God loves man regardless of his righteousness or sinfulness and that his love for man does not grow weak even when man abandons God and leaves him to go "to a far country." Man may move far away from God, but God never removes himself from man. The path of repentance is a path of return to God, who is always ready to receive the penitent. Moreover, as with faith itself, repentance is the path upon which God and man move towards one another. The image of the father who goes out to meet his prodigal son is an icon of this notion.

The prodigal son is an image of every person who has lived his life in an improper manner. Each person receives from God and his own ancestors a spiritual inheritance, which is given to him so that he may live by it and pass it on to his children. But often a person, due to youth or recklessness, may squander this inheritance that was accumulated over the centuries by the labor of many generations. Having squandered the wealth, he then comes to the realization of his own poverty and turns to God.

The history of the prodigal son is an example of gradual repentance that takes place in stages. The conversion of the prodigal son began when he "came to himself," that is, when he became conscious of his helplessness and poverty. Then he

The Prodigal Son. N. Losev. 1882.

remembered that he had a father. He arose and went to his father, having resolved to offer him repentance. Meeting his father, he pronounced the formula he had already prepared: "Father, I have sinned against heaven and in your sight, and am no longer worthy to be called your son" (Lk 15.21). In response to his repentance, his father restores him to the dignity of sonship.

In the parable there is another character, the older son, who shows that he is dissatisfied with the reception given to the prodigal son. The older brother, like the Pharisee in the parable of the publican and the Pharisee, is an example of external religiosity, a religiosity based on a feeling of duty and prompted by the expectation of a just reward for good deeds. This type of religiosity does not fit with the notion of an "unjust" God who has mercy on sinners rather than punishing them, who rewards him who comes at the eleventh hour in the same way as the one who labored from the first hour (see Mt 20.1–16).

The theological and moral content of the parable of the prodigal son is revealed in the liturgical texts, which contain an appeal to conversion and repentance:

> Brethren, let us learn the meaning of this mystery. For when the Prodigal Son ran back from sin to his Father's house, his loving Father came out to meet him and kissed him. He restored to the Prodigal the tokens of his proper glory, and mystically He made glad on high, sacrificing the fatted calf. Let our lives, then, be worthy of the loving Father who has offered sacrifice, and of the glorious Victim who is the Savior of our souls. (Lenten Triodion. Sunday of the Publican and the Pharisee. Vespers. Stichera at "Lord, I call.")

> Foolishly have I run away from Thy glory, O Father, wasting in sin the wealth that Thou gavest me. Therefore with the words of the Prodigal I cry unto Thee: I have sinned before Thee, compassionate Father. Accept me in repentance and make me as one of Thy hired servants. (Lenten Triodion. Sunday of the Publican and the Pharisee. Matins. Kontakion.)

On the Sunday of the Prodigal Son and the two following Sundays, Psalm 136, "By the waters of Babylon," is added to the psalms of the polyeleos. This psalm depicts the weeping of the Israelites who find themselves in Babylonian exile and long for their lost homeland. The psalm is understood in eastern Christian exegetical tradition as an ode of repentance in which men mourn the loss of their heavenly homeland as a result of their sinful life. Babylon is interpreted as a symbol of sin; correspondingly, the Babylonian exile is a symbol of living in the captivity of sin. The final verse of the psalm, "Happy shall he be who takes your little ones and dashes them against the rock!" is interpreted allegorically as a call to struggle with sinful thoughts.

On the Saturday before the Sunday of the Last Judgment, which is called in the Typikon "Meatfare Saturday,"[2] the Church performs a commemoration of all the departed throughout the ages. The reason for this commemoration is revealed in the synaxarion for the day. It speaks of the fact that some people meet an unexpected death in the course of their travels, at sea, on impassable mountains, in rapids, or in chasms, and some die from natural disasters, famine, fire, freezing, war, severe frost, and other causes. Many of these, as well as certain poor and sick people, are not granted a proper funeral service. For this reason, the holy fathers—prompted by love for mankind—established a special commemoration of all the departed, so that not one of them would be deprived of the prayer of the Church. It is specially noted in the synaxarion that not all who fall into crevices, perish in

Commemoration of the Departed. Ryazan Synodic. 17th c.

fires, or who die at sea or as a result of natural disasters, suffer according to the command of God: some suffer this by the will of God, while others only with God's allowance.[3]

A significant portion of the liturgical texts of Meatfare Saturday coincide with the texts from the Order of Burial for a Layman.[4] In the canon read during matins, special attention is given to the description of various types of death and an enumeration of various categories of departed:

To those who have been suddenly snatched away, burnt up by lightning, frozen by the cold, or struck down by any other calamity, give rest, O God, when

[2]Meatfare signifies the permission to eat meat.
[3]Lenten Triodion. Meatfare Saturday. Matins. Synaxarion.
[4]The funeral service will be discussed in the fifth and final volume of this series.—*Ed.*

Thou shalt make trial of all things in the fire. (Lenten Triodion. Saturday of the Dead. Matins. Canon. Ode 3.)

Fathers and forefathers, grandfathers and great-grandfathers, those who from the beginning up to these last times have died in holiness of life and in true faith: remember them all, our Saviour. (Lenten Triodion. Saturday of the Dead. Matins. Canon. Ode 4.)

Those who died in faith on the mountainside or the road, in the tombs or the desert, monks and married people, young and old: grant to them all, O Christ, a dwelling with Thy saints. (Lenten Triodion. Saturday of the Dead. Matins. Canon. Ode 4.)

To those destroyed by the cold, killed by falling from their horse, overwhelmed by hail, snow or thunder-storms, crushed by stones or suffocated in the earth, give rest, O Christ our Saviour. (Lenten Triodion. Saturday of the Dead. Matins. Canon. Ode 4.)

The hymns for the departed on Meatfare Saturday recall the hope in the resurrection of all flesh that springs forth from faith in the resurrection of Christ:

Christ is risen, releasing from bondage Adam the first-formed man and destroying the power of hell. Be of good courage, all ye dead, for death is slain and hell despoiled; the crucified and risen Christ is King. He has given incorruption to our flesh; He raises us and grants us resurrection, and He counts worthy of His joy and glory all who, with a faith that wavers not, have trusted fervently in Him. (Lenten Triodion. Saturday of the Dead. Matins. Praises.)

On the Sunday of the Last Judgment, the Church reminds the faithful of the event that will mark the end of human history. We have spoken of the theological and moral meaning of the Last Judgment in a corresponding section of the second volume of this series.[5] The liturgical texts primarily emphasize the universal, general character of the Last Judgment, at which everybody will appear on equal footing:

The day is upon us, the judgment is already at the door. Be vigilant, my soul. Kings and princes, rich and poor are gathering, and each shall receive the due reward for his actions. (Lenten Triodion. Sunday of the Last Judgment. Matins. Canon. Ode 4.)

[5]See vol. 2, pp. 539–547.

Each in his own order, monk and hierarch, old and young, slave and master shall be examined; widow and virgin shall be corrected. And woe to all whose lives are sinful! (Lenten Triodion. Sunday of the Last Judgment. Matins. Canon. Ode 4.)

Reminding us of the Last Judgment, the Church calls Christians to "feed the hungry, give drink to the thirsty, clothe the naked, welcome strangers, visit those in prison and the sick."[6] The central theme of the words of Jesus Christ concerning the Last Judgment, read during the liturgy (see Mt 25.31–46), is a moral appeal to do good deeds. And the presence or absence of good deeds toward our neighbors will be the criterion by which the sheep will be separated from the goats.

The reminder of the Last Judgment is also a call to repentance, necessary as the faithful draw nearer to Great Lent:

Alas, black soul! How long wilt thou continue in evil? How long wilt thou lie in idleness? Why dost thou not think of the fearful hour of death? Why dost thou not tremble at the dread judgement-seat of the Saviour? What defence then wilt thou make, or what wilt thou answer? Thy works will be there to accuse thee; thine actions will reproach thee and condemn thee. O my soul, the time is near at hand; make haste before it is too late, and cry aloud in faith: I have sinned, O Lord, I have sinned against Thee. . . . (Lenten Triodion. Sunday of the Last Judgment. Vespers. Aposticha.)

In the church Typikon the Sunday of the Last Judgment is also called Meatfare Sunday because it is the final day on which the Typikon allows for meat to be eaten. Beginning on the next day is Cheesefare Week, during which one may use eggs and dairy products. The divine services on Wednesday and Friday of Cheesefare Week are performed according to the model of Great Lent, with prostrations and the prayer of Saint Ephraim the Syrian. The liturgy is not celebrated on these two days. On Wednesday of Cheesefare Week a sticheron is sung to proclaim the approach of Great Lent:

The springtime of the fast has dawned, the flower of repentance has begun to open. O brethren, let us cleanse ourselves from all impurity and sing to the Giver of Light: Glory be to Thee who alone lovest mankind. (Lenten Triodion Supplement. Wednesday in Cheese Week. Vespers. Aposticha.)

[6]Lenten Triodion. Meatfare Sunday. Vespers. Stichera at Litiya.

The final Sunday before Great Lent bears the name Cheesefare Sunday; in common parlance it is called "Forgiveness Sunday." On this day the expulsion of Adam and Eve from paradise is remembered during the service: the Church reminds the faithful on the eve of Great Lent that man was created for life in paradise and he fell from the blessedness of paradise because of his disobedience to God. The liturgical texts are written from the perspective of the repentant Christian who identifies with fallen Adam, because the sin of Adam is repeated in the experience of every person:

> In my wretchedness I have cast off the robe woven by God, disobeying Thy divine command, O Lord, at the counsel of the enemy; and I am clothed now in fig leaves and in garments of skin. I am condemned to eat the bread of toil in the sweat of my brow, and the earth has been cursed so that it bears thorns and thistles for me. But, O Lord, who in the last times wast made flesh of a Virgin, call me back again and bring me into paradise. (Lenten Triodion. Sunday of Forgiveness. Vespers. Stichera at "Lord, I call.")

> O precious Paradise, unsurpassed in beauty, tabernacle built by God, unending gladness and delight, glory of the righteous, joy of the prophets, and dwelling of the saints, with the sound of thy leaves pray to the Maker of all: may He open unto me the gates which I closed by my transgression, and may He count me worthy to partake of the Tree of Life and of the joy which was mine when I dwelt in thee before. (Lenten Triodion. Sunday of Forgiveness. Vespers. Stichera at "Lord, I call.")

The path of Great Lent is a path of return to God, of repentance for having violated his commandments. Therefore the remembrance of Adam's expulsion grows into a call to ascetic effort in the fast and to the fulfillment of the gospel's commandments:

> Adam was banished from Paradise through disobedience and cast out from delight, beguiled by the words of a woman. Naked he sat outside the garden, lamenting, "Woe is me!" Therefore let us all make haste to accept the season of the Fast and hearken to the teaching of the Gospel, that we may gain Christ's mercy and receive once more a dwelling-place in paradise. (Lenten Triodion. Sunday of Forgiveness. Vespers. Stichera at "Lord, I call.")

The entrance into Great Lent is marked by vespers, performed on the evening of Cheesefare Sunday. This service already turns its focus to Monday of the first week of the fast. The first part of vespers bears a festal character. The entry with the censer is performed and the great prokeimenon is intoned, "Turn not away thy face from thy child for I am afflicted; hear me speedily, draw near unto my soul, and deliver it." During the prokeimenon all those in the altar change into dark-colored vestments

Tollhouses. Bulgaria. Rila Monastery. 18th c.

and the rest of vespers is already celebrated according to the order of Great Lent. The melodies used during the divine services are changed.

The stichera used at vespers remind the faithful of the meaning of the fast as a spiritual springtime, a time of abstinence not only from meat and dairy foods but also from sinful actions:

> Let us all make haste to humble the flesh by abstinence, as we set out upon the God-given course of the holy Fast; and with prayers and tears let us seek our Lord and Saviour. Laying aside all memories of evil, let us cry aloud: We have sinned against Thee. . . . (Lenten Triodion. Monday of the First Week of the Fast, performed on Sunday. Vespers. Stichera at "Lord, I call.")

> Let us set out with joy upon the season of the Fast, and prepare ourselves for spiritual combat. Let us purify our soul and cleanse our flesh; and as we fast from food, let us abstain also from every passion. Rejoicing in the virtues of the Spirit may we persevere with love, and so be counted worthy to see the solemn Passion of Christ our God, and with great spiritual gladness to behold His holy Passover. (Lenten Triodion. Monday of the First Week of the Fast, performed on Sunday. Vespers. Stichera at "Lord, I call.")

> Thy grace has shone forth, O Lord, it has shone forth and given light to our souls. Behold, now is the accepted time: behold, now is the season of repentance. Let us cast off the works of darkness and put on the armor of light, that having sailed across the great sea of the Fast, we may reach the third-day Resurrection of our Lord Jesus Christ, the Saviour of our souls. (Lenten Triodion. Monday of the First Week of the Fast, performed on Sunday. Vespers. Aposticha.)

The Expulsion from Paradise. Mosaic. Monreale Cathedral. Sicily. 12th c.

Before the dismissal of vespers, the prayer of Great Lent, "O Lord and Master of my life," is pronounced. At the end of the service, according to custom, the rite of forgiveness is conducted. It is performed in the following way. The rector comes out onto the ambon and delivers a homily, after which he asks forgiveness from the clergy and parishioners. The homily ends with the following formula borrowed from the order of the midnight office: "Bless me, holy fathers and brothers,"[7] and "forgive me a sinner, whatever I have sinned this day and in all the days of my life in word, deed, and thought, and in all my senses." Then he makes a prostration before the clergy and the people. All answer him by making a prostration and saying, "May God forgive you, holy father. Forgive us sinners also and bless us." Then each of the members of the clergy approaches the rector and asks his forgiveness. After this, all the parishioners approach the rector, kiss the cross he is holding, and ask forgiveness; the clergy in turn ask forgiveness of the parishioners.

The rite of forgiveness is not mentioned in the Lenten Triodion, but it is an ancient tradition of the Church dating back to the time of early Palestinian monasticism. "The Life of Saint Mary of Egypt," written by Saint Sophronius of Jerusalem (c. 560–638), tells of monks gathering in the church at the beginning of Great Lent, where they asked forgiveness of the hegumen and then left the monastery and went into the wilderness for the entire fast, returning only by Holy Week.

DIVINE SERVICES IN GREAT LENT: THE PRAYER OF SAINT EPHRAIM THE SYRIAN

Great Lent is, for the Orthodox faithful, a time of repentance and fervent prayer. The divine services performed on the days of the fast differ from the normal services in several essential ways. First of all, texts containing a celebratory, festal character are excluded. Dark-colored vestments are used. Many prostrations are made. According to the Typikon, the psalter is read through twice during the course

---

[7]In parish practice it is customary to say "brothers and sisters."

of each week (at other times it is read through once per week). At matins, three odes are read in the place of full canons consisting of eight or nine odes.[8] Vespers contains Old Testament readings from the Book of Genesis and the Wisdom of Solomon (Gen 1.1–46.7 and Wis 1.1–24.5).[9] A considerable part of the Book of Isaiah is read at the sixth hour.[10] The full liturgy is not celebrated on the weekdays of the fast. On Mondays, Tuesdays, and Thursdays there is no liturgy at all, while on Wednesdays and Fridays the liturgy of the presanctified gifts is celebrated. The gospel and Book of Epistles are not read on weekdays of the fast.

The prayer of Saint Ephraim the Syrian is read at every divine service of Great Lent and at certain services it is read several times:

> O Lord and Master of my life, take from me the spirit of sloth, despair, lust of power, and idle talk.
> But give rather the spirit of chastity, humility, patience, and love to Thy servant.
> Yea, O Lord and King, grant me to see mine own transgressions and not to judge my brother, for blessed art Thou unto ages of ages. Amen.

This prayer of repentance is read once in full with three prostrations to the ground made after each part. Then, "O God, cleanse me a sinner" is said twelve times, with twelve bows from the waist. After this, the prayer is read again and a single prostration to the ground is made. The prayer contains a reminder of the spiritual "program" that constitutes the essence of Great Lent, which involves a struggle with the major vices and a striving to acquire the major virtues.

Prostration

Four vices are mentioned in the first part of the prayer: sloth, despair, lust of power, and idle talk. Sloth is nothing other than laziness, passivity, inability to appreciate and control one's time, and the absence of firmness of purpose, self-discipline, and concentration. From sloth springs forth despair—a sin which Saint John of the Ladder characterizes as "paralysis of the

---

[8]The liturgical book called the "Triodion" gets its name from these three-ode canons (Gr. *triōdion*, Sl. *tripesnets*, "three-ode").

[9]The reading of both books takes place on Lazarus Saturday. Genesis 49.33–50.36 and Wisdom 31.8–33 are read.

[10]It is read in its entirety, but with some omissions.

soul" and "enervation of the mind."[11] The demon of despair, in the words of Evagrius, is "the most grievous of all demons."[12] Lust of power is striving to be in command of people, to exalt oneself over them. Lust of power is a type of pride which is a "denial of God" and "the despising of men."[13] As for idle talk, it is a very widespread vice that many do not even consider a sin: it is when a person does not pay attention to the words he says and spends time in conversations that consist of vain and idle subjects.

These four vices are juxtaposed with the four virtues of chastity, humility, patience, and love. The meaning of Christian charity is discussed in detail in another part of this book.[14] Humility, or meekness, in the words of Saint Isaac the Syrian, is "the robe of divinity": in his incarnation the divine Word was clothed in it, and everyone who is clothed in it is made to resemble "him who descended from the height, hiding the radiance of his greatness and covering up his glory by means of his low estate."[15] Patience is necessary for people both in relation to one's neighbors and in relation to life's circumstances, sorrows, and trials; the ascetic effort of the fast also requires patience. Finally, the culmination of all the virtues is love—a gift which is the pinnacle of asceticism.[16]

The concluding part of the prayer reminds us that a Christian ought to see his own sins and not to condemn his neighbor. One of the most widespread spiritual vices, which Christ indicated in the gospel (see Mt 7.3), is the inability or unwillingness to see one's own faults while simultaneously condemning other people for their sins and vices. In the homily *On Not Judging One's Neighbor*, Abba Dorotheus wrote, "There is nothing worse than condemnation." In the words of the ascetic, when the human mind "begins to leave his sins without attention and begins to notice the sins of his neighbor," the person ultimately falls into the same sin for which he condemns the other.[17] Great Lent is a time when Christians are called to concentrate on perfecting themselves, not on correcting the vices of other people.

---

[11]John Climacus, *Ladder* 13.2. English translation in John Climacus, *The Ladder of Divine Ascent* (Boston, MA: Holy Transfiguration Monastery, 2001), 95.

[12]Evagrius Ponticus, *Homily on Spiritual Works* 12 (SC 170; 171).

[13]John Climacus, *Ladder* 23.1. English translation in *The Ladder of Divine Ascent* (2001), 95.

[14]This will be discussed in the fifth and final volume.—Ed.

[15]Isaac the Syrian, *Homily* 53 [82 in Bedjan—*Ed.*]. English translation in Isaac the Syrian, *The Wisdom of Saint Isaac the Syrian*, trans. Sebastian Brock (Oxford: S.L.G. Press, 1997), 12.

[16]Evagrius Ponticus, *Homily on Prayer* 84 (SC 170; 171).

[17]Dorotheus of Gaza, *Teachings* 6 (SC 92:268).

The prayer of Saint Ephraim the Syrian, because of its simplicity and lack of artifice, and also because it is repeated so often during the lenten services, exerts a beneficial effect on the soul of the faithful. In particular, Alexander Pushkin testified to this in a poem that includes a poetic adaptation of the prayer:

The desert-dwelling fathers and the
    blameless women,
To ascend in heart to realms that from
    our eyes are hidden,
To brace themselves in earthly
    tempests, wars malign,
Stored for themselves a wealth of
    prayers most divine.
But not a single prayer of these is so
    endearing
As that one which the priest
    pronounces, persevering,

Hermit Fathers and Immaculate Women.
M. Nestorov. 1934.

Throughout the melancholy days of this Great Lent;
Oft to my lips this prayer rises, as if sent,
To gird me, who am fallen, by a force mysterious:
O Lord of all my days! The spirit of sloth so tedious,
Of lust for power, such a subtle, cunning snake,
Of idle talk—O, grant thou not my soul to take.
But grant to me, O God, to see my own wrongdoing,
So that my brother not fall subject to my ruling;
And let the spirit of meekness, patience, charity,
And chasteness in my heart grow in vitality.[18]

DIVINE SERVICES OF THE FIRST WEEK OF GREAT LENT: THE GREAT CANON OF REPENTANCE

Saint Andrew of Crete's *Canon of Repentance* is read at compline over the course of the first four days of the fast. This canon is called "great" because it contains more than two hundred troparia (a normal canon contains about thirty troparia), and also because of the richness and diversity of its theological content. The main theme

[18]Alexander Pushkin, "Otsy pustynniki i zhëny neporochny, . . ." trans. Brenda Seah for the present work.

of the canon is repentance: this theme is revealed in the context of the Christian teaching on vices and virtues. Numerous examples of repentance, righteousness, and sinful lives, taken from the Old and New Testaments, are projected on the life of the believer, on behalf of whom the canon was written. The believer identifies himself with various characters in sacred history:

> I have rivalled in transgression Adam the first-formed man, and I have found myself stripped naked of God, of the eternal Kingdom and its joy, because of my sins [see Gen 3.6–7]. (Lenten Triodion. Monday in the First Week. Great Compline. Great Canon. Ode 1.)

> Woe, to thee, miserable soul! How like thou art to the first Eve! For thou hast looked in wickedness and wast grievously wounded; thou hast touched the tree and rashly tasted the deceptive food [see Gen 3.6]. (Lenten Triodion. Monday in the First Week. Great Compline. Great Canon. Ode 1.)

> Like David, I have fallen into lust and I am covered with filth; but wash me clean, O Saviour, by my tears [see 2 Sam 11.4]. (Lenten Triodion. Wednesday in the First Week. Great Compline. Great Canon. Ode 2.)

The person at prayer, following the author of the canon, frequently addresses his souls with a call to repentance:

> The end draws near, my soul, the end draws near; yet thou dost not care or make ready. The time grows short, rise up: the Judge is at the door. The days of our life pass swiftly, as a dream, as a flower. Why do we trouble ourselves in vain [see Mt 24.33; Ps 38.7]? (Lenten Triodion. Monday in the First Week. Great Compline. Great Canon. Ode 4.)

> Awake, my soul, consider the actions which thou hast done; set them before thine eyes, and let the drops of thy tears fall. With boldness tell Christ of thy deeds and thoughts, and so be justified. (Lenten Triodion. Monday in the First Week. Great Compline. Great Canon. Ode 4.)

Saint Andrew of Crete, the author of the *Great Canon*, drew the tradition of addressing one's own soul from another hymnographer, Saint Romanos the Melodist, who wrote the kontakion performed after the sixth ode of the canon:

> My soul, O my soul, rise up! Why art thou sleeping? The end draws near and soon thou shalt be troubled. Watch, then, that Christ thy God may spare thee,

for he is everywhere present and fills all things. (Lenten Triodion. Monday in the First Week. Great Compline. Great Canon. Kontakion following Ode 6.)

The *Great Canon* contains many allegorical interpretations of biblical events. The two wives of Jacob, Leah and Rachel, are interpreted respectively as symbols of activity and the life of contemplation.[19] Joseph, sold into slavery, becomes a symbol of the soul which has attached itself to sinful actions.[20] Saul, having slaughtered the asses of his father, but having suddenly acquired the kingdom, becomes a reminder for the soul not to desire animal lusts more than the kingdom of Christ.[21] The entire life of Moses, in accordance with tradition dating back to Origen and Saint Gregory of Nyssa, becomes a series of allegories:

Thou hast heard, my soul, of the basket of Moses: how he was borne on the waves of the river as if in a shrine; and so he avoided the bitter execution of Pharaoh's decree [see Ex 2.3]. (Lenten Triodion. Tuesday in the First Week. Great Compline. Great Canon. Ode 5.)

Thou hast heard, wretched soul, of the midwives who once killed in its infancy the manly action of self-control: like great Moses, then, be suckled on wisdom [see Ex 1.16]. (Lenten Triodion. Tuesday in the First Week. Great Compline. Great Canon. Ode 5.)

O miserable soul, thou hast not struck and killed the Egyptian mind, as did Moses the great. Tell me, then, how wilt thou go to dwell through repentance in the wilderness empty of passions [see Ex 2.12]? (Lenten Triodion. Tuesday in the First Week. Great Compline. Great Canon. Ode 5.)

Moses the great went to dwell in the desert. Come, seek to follow his way of life, my soul, that in contemplation thou mayest attain the vision of God in the bush [see Ex 3.2]. (Lenten Triodion. Tuesday in the First Week. Great Compline. Great Canon. Ode 5.)

Picture to thyself, my soul, the rod of Moses striking the sea and making hard the deep by the sign of the Holy Cross. Through the Cross thou also canst do great things [see Ex 14.21]. (Lenten Triodion. Tuesday in the First Week. Great Compline. Great Canon. Ode 5.)

[19]Lenten Triodion. Monday in the First Week. Compline. Great Canon. Ode 4.
[20]Lenten Triodion. Monday in the First Week. Compline. Great Canon. Ode 5.
[21]Lenten Triodion. Monday in the First Week. Compline. Great Canon. Ode 7.

Modern people encounter various difficulties when they seek to understand the theological and moral meaning of the *Canon of Repentance* and other similar liturgical texts. In the majority of the parishes of the Russian Orthodox Church, the canon is read in the Slavonic translation, reproduced word for word from the original Greek text. The syntax—which in Greek must strictly preserve the rhythmic pattern of the verse—is fully preserved in the Slavonic translation. As a result, to understand the meaning of several troparia, it is necessary to mentally reorder the words. The need for a new edition of the Slavonic translation of the Great Canon has long been felt.

However, even if a new edition were to emerge or if the canon were to be read in Russian,[22] it would only slightly simplify the task of understanding the text by hearing it read aloud. The problem is primarily caused by the fact that in most cases, people nowadays do not know the Bible as well as the Palestinian monks of the seventh century knew it. And moreover, practically every troparion of the canon contains an allusion to a particular biblical event and brings to mind various characters from the Bible, many of which are unknown to the average worshipper even by name (Jannes, Jambres, Uzzah, Ahitophel, Rehoboam, Jeroboam, Ahab, Gehazi, and others). Moreover, the allegorical method of interpretation, on which the canon is built, is foreign and incomprehensible to people today: many allegories, such as the comparison of Leah and Rachel with activity and contemplation, seem artificial. The author of the canon appeals to the consciousness of people who lived thirteen centuries ago in conditions radically different from today's conditions, and who saw the world completely differently from how people today see it.

Sundays of Great Lent

On Sundays in Great Lent the divine services are performed with marked solemnity. On these days the Typikon calls for the celebration of the divine liturgy of Saint Basil the Great, which differs from the liturgy of Saint John Chrysostom in its greater length. In addition to the celebration of the resurrection of Christ, each of these days is marked by the remembrance of some special event or the commemoration of a saint who made a particular contribution to the development of the Orthodox ascetic teaching.

---

[22]Besides the prerevolutionary translation of E. Lovyagin, there are contemporary Russian translations by Metropolitan Nikodim (Rotov) and Archbishop Jonathan (Eletskykh), among others.

The first Sunday of Great Lent is called the Sunday of Orthodoxy or the Sunday of the Triumph of Orthodoxy. This celebration was established by Patriarch Methodius of Constantinople in commemoration of the Church's decisive victory over iconoclasm in the ninth century. The first Sunday of the fast was appointed for the liturgical commemoration of this event because the ceremonial restoration of icon veneration took place in Constantinople on the first Sunday of Great Lent in 842.

The theological meaning of icon veneration has already been discussed in detail.[23] Many liturgical texts of the Sunday of Orthodoxy are dedicated to the theme of the veneration of icons:

> The grace of truth has shone forth upon us; the mysteries darkly prefigured
> in the times of old have now been openly fulfilled. For behold, the Church is
> clothed in a beauty that surpasses all things earthly, through the ikon of the
> incarnate Christ that was foreshadowed by the ark of testimony. This is the
> safeguard of the Orthodox faith; for if we hold fast to the ikon of the Saviour
> whom we worship, we shall not go astray. Let all who do not share this faith
> be covered with shame; but we shall glory in the ikon of the Word made flesh,
> which we venerate but worship not as an idol. . . . (Lenten Triodion. Sunday
> of Orthodoxy. Great Vespers. Stichera at "Lord, I call.")

> Advancing from ungodliness to the true faith, and illumined with the light of
> knowledge, let us clap our hands and sing aloud, offering praise and thanksgiv-
> ing to God; and with due honor let us venerate the holy ikons of Christ, and the
> all-pure Virgin and the saints, whether depicted on walls, on wooden panels or
> on holy vessels, rejecting the impious teaching of the heretics. For, as Basil says,
> the honor shown to the ikon passes to the prototype it represents. . . . (Lenten
> Triodion. Sunday of Orthodoxy. Great Vespers. Aposticha.)

The rite of Orthodoxy is performed in cathedrals on the Sunday of Orthodoxy.[24] This rite includes the ceremonial remembrance of all who over the course of centuries—by their labors and sometimes by the feat of confession and martyrdom—defended the Orthodox faith. This rite is performed, as a rule, following the divine liturgy. Icons of the Savior and the Mother of God are brought to the center of the church; the hierarch stands on the cathedra while priests stand along the two

[23]See vol. 1, pp. 54–58, and also vol. 3, pp. 135–148.
[24]Like the rite of the exaltation of the cross, in Greek practice any priest is able to perform the rite of Orthodoxy in his parish, while in Russian practice only bishops perform the rite.—*Ed.*

Triumph of Orthodoxy.
Constantinople. Icon. 15th c.

sides of the cathedra. The great litany is pronounced, troparia of thanksgiving are sung, and the Book of Epistles (Rom 16.16–20) and the gospel (Mt 18.10–18) are read. The litany of fervent supplication follows, after which the hierarch pronounces a prayer for the heretics and schismatics, asking God to enlighten them with the divine light, to weaken their hard-heartedness, to open their hearing, and to correct their depravity and their life, which is not in accordance with Christian piety.

After this, the protodeacon exclaims three times, "Who is so great a god as our God? Thou art the God who doest wonders." Then he calls the faithful to give thanks to God for the creation of the world, for his providential care for mankind after the fall into sin, the incarnation of the Son of God, and the teaching of the truths of the faith through the prophets and apostles. The Nicene-Constantinopolitan Creed is read, after which the protodeacon pronounces, "Confirm this apostolic faith, this faith of the fathers, this Orthodox faith, this universal faith." After this, the anathemas of heretics are read,[25] "Memory Eternal" is pronounced for the ancient fathers of the Church and pious kings and queens, and "Many Years" is

Saint Gregory of Palamas.
Monastery of Vatopedi.
Mount Athos. 15th c.

sung for the ecclesial and secular authorities. During the singing of the "Many Years," the hierarch blesses the faithful with the icons of the Savior and the Mother of God. At the conclusion of the rite, the hierarch reads the prayer: "Glorify all these, O Holy Trinity, and confirm them in the right faith even to the end; and convert the enemies and those ignorant of the Orthodox faith and Christ's Church, that they may come to know thine eternal truth, through the intercessions of our most holy lady, the Mother of God and ever-virgin Mary, and of all the saints."[26]

In countries where there are Orthodox churches of various jurisdictions (in particular, in Western Europe and America), a pan-Orthodox liturgy or vespers is normally performed on the day of the Triumph of

---

[25]In the contemporary practice of the Russian Church, the anathemas, as a rule, are omitted. In various epochs the composition of the anathemas varied.

[26]From the Service of the Triumph of Orthodoxy.—*Ed.*

Orthodoxy. Such a divine service is a visual witness of the unity of the Orthodox Church in prayer and the Eucharist.

The second Sunday of Great Lent is called the Sunday of the Light-Creating Fasts. The memory of Saint Gregory Palamas is celebrated on this day. The life and teaching of this great enlightener of the fourteenth century has already been discussed several times.[27] The celebration of Saint Gregory's memory is linked to Great Lent because his teaching reminds us of the contemplation of the divine light and deification as the crowning experience of ascetic effort. His disciple Patriarch Philotheus I (fourteenth century) of Constantinople established the service to Saint Gregory, and Patriarch Gennadius Scholarius (fifteenth century) wrote the canon. The liturgical texts call him a "pillar of the faith," a "champion of the Church,"[28] "an instrument of wisdom,"[29] a "torch that shows us the Sun,"[30] "the sun of the light divine and without evening."[31] Saint Gregory Palamas is described as a man who conquered the passions and was united with God:

> Thou hast become a mirror of God, O Gregory, for thou hast kept without stain that which in thyself is according to the divine image; and bravely establishing thy mind as master over the passions of the flesh, thou hast attained that which is according to God's likeness. So thou hast become the glorious dwelling-place of the Holy Trinity. (Lenten Triodion. Second Sunday in Lent. Matins. Canon 2. Ode 9.)

The third Sunday of Great Lent is called the Sunday of the Veneration of the Cross. The liturgical texts of this feast focus on the meaning of the cross of Christ as a weapon of salvation. The Church reminds the faithful of the ascetic effort of the fast as a preparation for Holy Week and an imitation of the cross-bearing of the Lord Jesus Christ. A hymn written by Saint Romanos the Melodist that describes Christ's descent into hades is performed at matins:

> Pilate set up three crosses in the place of the Skull, two for the thieves and one for the Giver of Life. Seeing Him, hell cried to those below: "O my ministers and powers! Who is this that has fixed a nail in my heart? A wooden spear has pierced me suddenly, and I am torn apart. Inwardly I suffer; anguish has seized

[27] See vol. 1, pp. 127–132, and vol. 2, pp. 153–157.
[28] Lenten Triodion. Second Sunday in Great Lent. Matins. Canon 2. Ode 1.
[29] Ibid. Kontakion.
[30] Ibid. Ikos.
[31] Ibid. Synaxarion.

my belly and my senses. My spirit trembles, and I am constrained to cast out Adam and his posterity. A tree brought them to my realm, but now the Tree of the Cross brings them back again to Paradise. (Lenten Triodion. Sunday of the Cross. Matins. Ikos.)

At the end of matins the cross is brought out into the center of the church according to the order prescribed for the feast of the Exaltation of the Cross of the Lord.[32]

Vision of Saint John of the Ladder. Icon. Russia. 16th c.

On the Fourth Sunday of Great Lent the Church celebrates the memory of Saint John of the Ladder.[33] This saint is presented as an example worthy of imitation and his teaching as a guide to the spiritual life, which is especially useful for reading in the period of Great Lent. In the liturgical texts Saint John is called a "ladder of virtues" and a man who rose up to the height of the vision of God.[34]

The Fifth Sunday of Great Lent commemorates Saint Mary of Egypt, an ascetic saint whose life was written in the seventh century and acquired great popularity in Byzantium. This life, according to the Typikon, should be read in the church in its entirety at matins on Thursday of the fifth week of the fast, at which the *Great Canon* of Saint Andrew of Crete is also read in its entirety (in Russian this service is usually called "*Mariino stoyanie*"/"Saint Mary's Standing"). According to the account of her life, Saint Mary was a sinful woman in her youth and over the course of many years led a life of vice. Once she departed for Jerusalem for the feast of the Exaltation of the Cross. In Jerusalem she desired to visit the Church of the Lord's Sepulchre, but some mysterious force held her back and did not permit her to enter the church. When she became conscious of her sinfulness, Mary immediately left the world and departed into the desert, where she spent forty-seven years in the strictest abstinence and ceaseless prayer. The only person to meet with her after this was the monk Zosimas, who told the world about her ascetic feats. Near the end of her life, Saint Mary acquired such a high level of holiness that during prayer she rose into the air, crossed the

[32]See pp. 261–265.
[33]Concerning this saint, see vol. 1, pp. 89–90.
[34]Lenten Triodion. Fourth Sunday in Lent. Matins. Sedalen after Ode 3 of the canon.

Jordan river by walking on water, and cited sacred Scripture that she had never read. The life of Saint Mary of Egypt is read during Great Lent and the memory of this ascetic saint is observed on the fifth Sunday of the fast in order to remind the faithful that repentance can help people escape the abyss of sin and lift them up to the pinnacle of holiness.

The Annunciation of the Most-Holy Theotokos

The feast of the Annunciation of the Most-Holy Theotokos is celebrated on March 25, nine months before Christmas.[35] In the majority of instances this feast falls within the period of Great Lent. The Annunciation may coincide also with Lazarus Saturday, the feast of the Entry of the Lord into Jerusalem, one of the days of Holy Week, Pascha, or one of the three first days of Bright Week. The guidelines for uniting the service of the Annunciation with various divine services of the Lenten Triodion is rather complicated: a large section of the Typikon is called the "Annunciation Chapters," which provide rules for the celebration of the Annunciation depending on the day of the yearly movable cycle with which this feast coincides.

The Annunciation of the Most-Holy Theotokos. Contemporary Icon.

The Annunciation is described in the Gospel according to Saint Luke (see Lk 1.26–38). The history of the incarnation of God began with this event. The appearance of the Archangel Gabriel to the most-holy virgin and her humble consent to become the Mother of God was the starting point of this history. The incarnation of the Son of God took place according to the will of God the Father, but humanity's consent was also necessary. It was given through the lips of the most-holy Theotokos when she pronounced, "Let it be to me according to your word" (Lk 1.38). For this reason, this event is called the "beginning of our salvation" in the troparion of the feast:

---

[35]Regarding the significance of this date, see S. A. Vaniukov, M. S. Zheltov, and K. Kh. Fel'mi, "The Annunciation of the Most-Holy Theotokos" [in Russian], in *Orthodox Encyclopedia* (Moscow: Tserkovno-nauchnyi tsentr "Pravoslavnaia entsiklopediia," 2002), 5:255.

Today is the beginning of our salvation, the revelation of the eternal mystery. The Son of God becomes the Son of the Virgin as Gabriel announces the coming of Grace. Together with him let us cry to the Theotokos: "Rejoice, O Full of Grace, the Lord is with thee."

The divine service of the feast of the Annunciation of the Most-Holy Theotokos is marked by its singularly poetic character. The canon, read during matins, is written in the form of a dialogue between the Theotokos and the Archangel Gabriel.[36] Similar dialogues are found in the hymns of Saint Ephraim the Syrian and Saint Romanos the Melodist, as well as in the homilies of Saint John of Damascus. In one of the latter, the following is said:

"When the fullness of time came," as the divine Apostle says (Gal 4.4), the angel Gabriel was sent by God to this woman who was truly a child of God; he said to her, "Hail, full of grace, the Lord is with you!" (Lk 1.28) The word of the angel, to her who is higher than an angel, is lovely: it brings joy to the whole world. But "she was troubled by his word" (Lk 1.29), having no experience of contact with men—she had chosen rather to keep her virginity intact. So "she wondered within herself what this greeting might mean" (Lk 1.30). She had truly found grace, who had labored much in the field of grace and had reaped grace's abundant harvest. She had found the depths of grace, who had kept safe the vessel of a twofold virginity—for she preserved the virginity of her soul no less than that of her body, and thus her bodily virginity was also preserved. "And you shall bear a son," he said, "and shall call his name Jesus" (Lk 1.31). . . . What did the treasury of true wisdom reply to this? She did not imitate Eve, her mother, but rather made good Eve's lack of caution, using nature as her protection; so she spoke out thus in response to the angel's word: "How shall this happen to me, since I do not know a man?" (Lk 1.34) "You are speaking of the impossible," she tells him. "Your words break the boundaries of nature, which he who formed nature established. I will not let myself act as a second Eve and overturn the will of the Creator. If you are not speaking godless things, tell me the manner of this conception, and put an end to my difficulty." And the messenger of truth replied, "The Holy Spirit will come upon you, and the power of the Most High will overshadow you. Therefore the holy one to be born of you shall be called Son of God (Lk 1.35). What is now being achieved

---

[36]See pp. 63–64.

is not subject to the laws of nature, for the Creator is also lord of nature, and it is in his power to change nature's boundaries."[37]

Several stichera, also in poetic form, reproduce the speech of the archangel who addresses the most-holy virgin:

Revealing to thee the pre-eternal counsel, Gabriel came and stood before thee, O Maid; and greeting thee, he said: "Hail, thou earth that has not been sown; hail, thou burning bush that remains unconsumed; hail, thou unsearchable depth; hail, thou bridge that leads to heaven, and ladder raised on high that Jacob saw; hail, thou divine jar of manna; hail, thou deliverance from the curse; hail, thou restoration of Adam, the Lord is with thee." (Menaion. Annunciation of the Most-holy Theotokos. Great Vespers. Stichera at "Lord, I call.")

In this sticheron all the major Old Testament types of the Mother of God are mentioned. Saint John of Damascus speaks of them, addressing the Mother of God:

The burning bush was a portrait of you in advance (cf. Ex 3.2); the tablets written by God described you (cf. Ex 32.1f.); the ark of the law told your story (cf. Ex 25.10); the golden urn (cf. Ex 16.33) and candelabrum and table (cf. Ex 25.23, 31), the rod of Aaron that had blossomed (cf. Num 17.23)—all clearly were foreshadowings [of you]. For from you issued the flame of divinity, the self-definition and Word of the Father, the sweet heavenly manna, the nameless "name that is above every name" (Phil 2.9), the eternal and inaccessible light, the heavenly "bread of life" (Jn 6.48), the uncultivated fruit that grew bodily to maturity from you. Did not the furnace point to you, whose fire was at once dew and flame (cf. Dan 3.49f.), a type of the divine fire that dwelt within you? . . . And I almost forgot Jacob's ladder (cf. Gen 28.12). . . . Just as [Jacob] saw that ladder joining heaven and earth by its [two] ends, so that angels could go up and down on it, and just as he saw the strong and unconquerable one symbolically struggling with him, so you, too, are an intermediary; you have joined distant extremes together, and have become the ladder for God's descent to us—the God who has taken up our weak material and has woven it into a unity with himself, making the human person a mind that sees God (cf. Gen 32.31). Therefore angels came down to [Christ], worshipping their God and

---

[37]John of Damascus, *Homily on the Dormition* 1.8 (Daley, PPS).

master; and human beings have taken on the angelic way of life, in order to lay hold of heaven.[38]

In the excerpt above, the prefigurations of the Mother of God are built around the theme of the incarnation of God. This theme also appears in the liturgical texts of the feast:

> Today is revealed the mystery that is from all eternity. The Son of God becomes the Son of man, that, sharing in what is worse, He may make me share in what is better. In times of old Adam was once deceived: he sought to become a god, but received not his desire. Now God becomes man, that He may make Adam a god. . . . (Menaion. Annunciation of the Most-Holy Theotokos. Matins. Praises.)

In this way, the Annunciation is understood to be the beginning of the deification of man, perfected by Christ. Moreover, the Annunciation opens the way to the renewal and transformation of the whole creation:

> The captain of the angelic hosts was sent by God Almighty to the pure Virgin, to announce the good tidings of a strange and secret wonder: that, as man, God would be born a babe of her without seed, fashioning again the whole race of man. O ye people, announce the good tidings of the refashioning of the world. (Menaion. Annunciation of the Most-Holy Theotokos. Matins. Exapostilarion.)

LAZARUS SATURDAY AND THE ENTRY OF THE LORD INTO JERUSALEM

Two feasts are served in the transition from Great Lent to Holy Week: Lazarus Saturday and the Entry of the Lord into Jerusalem. The great forty-day fast concludes on the eve of Lazarus Saturday and, although the faithful continue to fast up to and on Holy Saturday, the meaning of the fast changes: it is no longer a penitential fast, but a fast in remembrance of Christ's sufferings. Beginning with Lazarus Saturday, the Orthodox Church remembers the final days and hours of the Lord Jesus Christ, day by day and hour by hour.

On Lazarus Saturday the event described in detail in the Gospel (see Jn 11.1–44), which directly preceded the Entry of the Lord into Jerusalem, is commemorated.

[38]Ibid.

In the liturgical texts this event is primarily interpreted as a proclamation of the universal resurrection, which awaits all people at the end of history:

> By raising Lazarus from the dead before Thy passion, Thou didst confirm the universal resurrection, O Christ God. Like the children with the branches of victory, we cry out to Thee, O Vanquisher of Death: Hosanna in the highest. Blessed is he that comes in the name of the Lord. (Lenten Triodion. Saturday of Lazarus. Vespers. Troparion.)

The troparion and other liturgical texts speak not only of the raising of Lazarus from the dead but also of the entry of the Lord into Jerusalem. The raising of Lazarus is mentioned many times in the divine services of Palm Sunday. In this way, both events are interpreted by the authors of the liturgical texts as inseparably linked, and the two feasts become a united two-day feast. A particularity of Lazarus Saturday is that hymns are sung at the service that glorify the resurrection of Christ, in particular the resurrectional troparia "The angelic host was filled with awe" [i.e. the Evlogitaria]. Conversely, on the day of the Entry of the Lord into Jerusalem, which takes place on Sunday, all the resurrectional troparia are omitted.

The Raising of Lazarus from the Dead. Icon. Monastery of Saint Catherine. Mount Sinai. 12th c.

The liturgical texts speak of the raising of Lazarus from the dead as an event that precedes Christ's descent into hades. The thematic connection between Lazarus Saturday and Great and Holy Saturday is apparent in the canon and stichera performed at matins:

> O Saviour, Thy voice destroyed all the power of death, and the foundations of hell were shaken by Thy divine might. (Lenten Triodion. Saturday of Lazarus. Matins. Canon. Ode 4.)

> At Thy word, O Word of God, Lazarus now leaps up, returning back to life; the people honour Thee with palms, O mighty Lord, for by Thy death Thou shalt destroy hell utterly. (Lenten Triodion. Saturday of Lazarus. Matins. Exapostilarion.)

Through Lazarus, O death, Christ has already despoiled thee. O hell, where is thy triumph? . . . (Lenten Triodion. Saturday of Lazarus. Matins. Another exapostilarion.)

Before Thine own death, O Christ, Thou hast raised from hell Lazarus that was four days dead, and hast shaken the dominion of death. Through this one man whom Thou hast loved, thou hast foretold the deliverance of all men from corruption. . . . (Lenten Triodion. Saturday of Lazarus. Matins. Praises.)

The Entry of the Lord into Jerusalem. Greece. End of 18th c.

The Entry of the Lord into Jerusalem is one of the most joyful feasts of the ecclesial year. In the liturgical books it is called the Sunday of Flower-Bearing or the Sunday of Palms; in the Russian tradition it was given the name of the Sunday of Pussy Willows (*Verbnoye Voskreseniye*) because palm branches are substituted with pussy willows. During the liturgy on this day the words of the Apostle Paul are read: "Rejoice in the Lord always. Again I will say, rejoice!" (Phil 4.4) The Hebrew word "Hosanna" (praise)—which was spoken from the lips of the Hebrew people when Jesus, sitting on a young ass, passed through the city gates—is repeated many times in the liturgical texts. The texts speak of the children's participation in meeting Christ:

Rejoice and be glad, O city of Zion; exult and be exceeding joyful, O Church of God. For behold, thy King has come in righteousness, seated on a foal, and the children sing His praises: Hosanna in the highest! Blessed art Thou who showest great compassion: have mercy upon us. (Lenten Triodion. Palm Sunday. Great Vespers. Aposticha.)

Seated in heaven upon Thy throne and on earth upon a foal, O Christ our God, Thou hast accepted the praise of the angels and the songs of the children who cried out to Thee: Blessed art Thou that comest to call back Adam. (Lenten Triodion. Palm Sunday. Matins. Kontakion.)

The theme of suffering is also found in all the liturgical texts of the feast. The authors of the liturgical texts remind us that Christ entered into Jerusalem not for the people to glorify him, but in order to suffer and die on the cross for the salvation of "young and old":

O immortal Lord, Thou hast bound hell, slain death, and raised the world: therefore the children, carrying palms, sing praise to Thee as Victor, O Christ, and they cry aloud to Thee this day: "Hosanna to the Son of David! For no more," say they, "shall the little children be slain because of Mary's Child; but Thou alone art crucified for all, both young and old. No more shall the sword be drawn against us, for Thy side is pierced by a spear. With great rejoicing, then, we cry: 'Blessed art Thou that comest to call back Adam.'" (Lenten Triodion. Palm Sunday. Matins. Ikos.)

Give praise with one accord, O peoples and nations: for the King of the angels rides now upon a foal, and He comes to smite His enemies with the Cross in his almighty power. Therefore the children sing to Him with palms in their hands: "Glory be to Thee who hast come as Conqueror; glory be to Thee, O Christ the Savior; glory be to Thee, our God, for Thou alone art blessed." (Lenten Triodion. Palm Sunday. Matins. Sessional Hymn.)

The theme of the kingdom is the leitmotif of the liturgical texts of the Entry of the Lord into Jerusalem: Christ is glorified as a meek King who came to save the new Israel—the Church of God. The theme of the kingdom brings together this feast and the feast of the Annunication of the Most-Holy Theotokos. In Nazareth the angel spoke to the Virgin about Jesus: "He will be great, and will be called the Son of the Highest; and the Lord God will give him the throne of his father David. And he will reign over the house of Jacob forever, and of his kingdom there will be no end" (Lk 1.32–33). And in Jerusalem the people welcomed Jesus with the words, "Hosanna! Blessed is he that comes in the name of the Lord, the King of Israel!" (Jn 12.13) Both cases concern a king and a kingdom. But while the angel proclaimed the eternal kingdom of God over all mankind, the Jews were longing for the earthly kingdom of David over Israel. They saw in Jesus a prophet who heals people and performs miracles: he had just raised Lazarus who had been dead for four days. And they were hopeful that this man could become a worthy king, and for this reason they went out to meet him with palm branches.

During the course of his entire life Jesus was a poor, wandering preacher who had "nowhere to lay his head" (Mt 8.20). At the same time he always knew himself to be a king. Even at the trial before Pilate, slandered and reviled, betrayed by his people, he answered in the affirmative to the prosecutor's question, "Are you the King of the Jews?"(Mt 27.11) At the same time he said, "My kingdom is not of this world. If my kingdom were of this world, my servants would fight, so that I should not be delivered to the Jews; but now my kingdom is not from here" (Jn 18.36). In the kingdom of Christ there are no servants who could help him, for example, by applying military force; there are only his friends, just as meek and humble as he himself, ready to follow him to Golgotha.

The tragic character of the feast of the Entry of the Lord into Jerusalem lies in the fact that Christ was received as the king who sits on the throne of David, as a political hero who came to liberate Judea from the hateful Roman occupiers; people hoped that he would reestablish the lost statehood and crown—ideals that were quite dear to many of them, who valued the earthly much more highly than the heavenly. But he did not fulfill these hopes. And for this reason, several days later, the very same crowd that today greets Christ with great celebration will be shouting, "Crucify, crucify him!" And those who now proclaim, "Blessed is the King of Israel," will exclaim with evil irony: "If he is the King of Israel, let him now come down from the cross, and we will believe him" (Mt 27.42). Soldiers will strike Jesus on the head with a reed and spit on him, saying, "Hail, King of the Jews." The Jews' disappointment will be so great that when Pilate writes on Christ's cross: "Jesus of Nazareth, the King of the Jews," they will say to him: "Do not write, 'the King of the Jews,' but 'he said, "I am the King of the Jews"'" (Jn 19.19, 21).

The liturgical texts speak of how quickly the crowd's mood changes. Today the crowd glorifies Christ as a miracle worker, but tomorrow it will call for his crucifixion:

> First they sang the praise of Christ our God with branches, but then the ungrateful Jews seized Him and crucified Him on the Cross. . . . (Lenten Triodion. Palm Sunday. Matin. Hypakoe.)

The Jews awaited a messiah, a powerful monarch, an autocrat before whom they could bow down as slaves. As the Creator of the universe, it would have required nothing of him should he have desired not only to become the ruler of the Jews but also to subdue the entire Roman Empire. But what is great in the eyes of men is nothing before God. Jesus rejected the temptation of earthly domination at the very beginning of his ministry, when the devil tempted him in the desert, offering him all the kingdoms of the world (see Mt 4.8–10). Instead of earthly kingdoms, Jesus sought one thing: the human heart, which he subdued not with strength and might, but with meekness and humility. Jesus does not need slaves, but rather free sons who choose him as their king because they love him, and not because he is able to subdue them with his power. The Son of God became the Son of Man in order for the sons of men to become sons of God—free and God-like. The greatest mystery of the incarnation of God lies in this: God's adoption of men and his calling to imitate God and be deified.

The Jews did not recognize their Messiah: they did not accept the good news of the kingdom, of the Jerusalem on high, of the heavenly throne of the heavenly king, which is contained within the human heart. He taught them in parables of the kingdom of God, and they tried to determine when and where they would behold the kingdom promised to them. But he answered them, "The kingdom of God does not come with observation; nor will they say, 'See here!' or 'See there!' For indeed, the kingdom of God is within you" (Lk 17.20–21). The kingdom of God does not come "with observation" (i.e. in a "perceptible way"), but mystically and quietly, and it fills the human heart with itself. Christ comes to each Christian with the same meekness and humility that he had in coming to Jerusalem. He subdues people not with strength and might, but with humility and love, and people come out to meet him with lighted candles and willow branches, symbolizing palm branches. And the greatest victory ever achieved is found in this meeting of people with the Lord.

HOLY WEEK

Holy Week is a special period in the liturgical life of the Orthodox Church. Each day of this week is called "great and holy" in the Lenten Triodion. There are no commemorations of saints on the days of Holy Week, and the commemoration of the departed does not take place. The full attention of the faithful is focused on sharing the emotional experience of the suffering Savior.

Over the course of the first three days of Holy Week, the divine service is performed according to the order of Great Lent, with prostrations and the prayer of Saint Ephraim the Syrian. The liturgy of the presanctified gifts, preceded by vespers, is celebrated on all three days. The Typikon calls for the reading of the gospel at the hours: Monday prescribes that the Gospel according to Matthew be read in full along with half of the Gospel according to Mark, on Tuesday the other half of the Gospel according to Mark and two thirds of the Gospel according to Luke are read, and on Wednesday the last third of the Gospel according to Luke and the Gospel according to John up to the middle of the twelfth chapter are read. Because of the large volume of readings, in the practice of several parishes they are appointed to be read during the days of the preceding weeks (the fifth and sixth weeks of the fast). In this way it is possible to begin the reading of the Gospel according to John during Holy Week.

On Great Monday, Tuesday, and Wednesday, at matins, after the reading of the six psalms and the kathismata, a troparion is sung that is thematically linked to the parable of the ten virgins (see Mt 25.1–13):

> Behold the Bridegroom comes at midnight, and blessed is the servant whom He shall find watching, and again unworthy is the servant whom He shall find heedless. Beware, therefore, O my soul, do not be weighed down with sleep, lest you be given up to death and lest you be shut out of the Kingdom. But rouse yourself crying: Holy, Holy, Holy, art Thou, O our God. Through the Theotokos have mercy on us. (Lenten Triodion. Great and Holy Monday. Matins. Troparion.)

This troparion is a call to spiritual vigilance and watchfulness. Also, in the general context of the divine services of Holy Week, it reminds us of the coming hour of the Savior's death on the cross, which the faithful should be spiritually prepared to encounter. In view of the special significance of the troparion "Behold the Bridegroom," the Typikon calls for it to be performed three times "slowly, solemnly, with sweet singing."

On the first four days of Holy Week an exapostilarion is sung at the end of matins that is thematically connected to the parable of those invited to the wedding feast (see Mt 22.2–14):

> I see Thy bridal chamber adorned, O my Savior, and I have no wedding gar-ment that I may enter there. Make the robe of my soul to shine, O Giver of Light, and save me.

The Typikon calls for this exapostilarion to be sung three times "slowly and with sweet singing," and specifies: "It is chanted in the middle of the church by the singer and alternately is sung by us." In accordance with this indication the hymn should first be performed by one singer, who comes to the middle of the church for this, and later be repeated by the faithful (the choir).

The liturgical texts of *Great Monday* remember the Old Testament patriarch Joseph, sold by his brothers into slavery in Egypt (see Gen 37.26–28). His sufferings are interpreted as a type of Christ's sufferings. The gospel narrative concerning the cursing of the fig tree by Christ (see Mt 21.18–22) is read during the liturgy of the presanctified gifts. The interpretation of this event is contained in the synaxarion for Great Monday:

> The fig tree, then, is the Jewish synagogue, in which the Savior did not find the necessary fruits of obedience to God and faith in him, but only the leafy shade of the law; he took away even this, leaving it completely bare. (Lenten Triodion. Great and Holy Monday. Matins. Synaxarion.)

At the same time the fig tree is a symbol of the soul of a Christian not living according to the commandments of Christ and not bearing fruits of repentance:

> O brethren, let us fear the punishment of the fig tree, withered because it was unfruitful; and let us bring worthy fruits of repentance unto Christ, who grants us His great mercy. (Lenten Triodion. Great and Holy Monday. Matins. Aposticha.)

On *Great Tuesday* Christ's parable of the ten virgins is remembered, as well as other parables and instructions that the Lord proclaimed in the temple in Jerusalem: on rendering unto Caesar, the Second Coming, the dread judgment, the resurrection of the dead, and the talents (see Mt 22–25). Commentaries on these parables and instructions are given in the liturgical texts:

Parable of the Ten Virgins. Miniature. France. 12th c.

> O my soul, thou hast heard the condemnation of him who hid his talent: hide not the word of God. Proclaim His wonders, increase the gifts of grace entrusted to thee, and thou shall enter into the joy of thy Lord. (Lenten Triodion. Great and Holy Tuesday. Matins. Praises.)

> Behold, my soul, the Master entrusts thee with a talent. Receive his gift with fear; make it gain interest for him; distribute to the needy, and make the Lord thy friend. So shalt thou stand on his right hand when He comes in glory, and thou shalt hear His blessed words: "Enter, servant, into the joy of thy Lord." (Lenten Triodion. Great and Holy Tuesday. Matins. Aposticha.)

On *Great Wednesday* the Church remembers the supper in Bethany at which the sinful woman washed the Savior's feet with her tears. The major liturgical texts of this day, including the stichera and a canon, are dedicated to this event. One of the stichera, written by the Byzantine poet and nun Cassia, reveals the power of the repentance of the sinful woman, who came to know the depth of her sinfulness by her meeting with Christ:

> The woman who had fallen into many sins, perceiving Thy divinity, O Lord, fulfilled the part of a myrrh-bearer; and with lamentations she brought sweet-smelling oil of myrrh to Thee before Thy burial. "Woe is me," she said, "for night surrounds me, dark and moonless, and stings my lustful passion with the love of sin. Accept the fountain of my tears, O Thou who drawest down from the clouds the waters of the sea. Incline to the groanings of my heart, O Thou who in Thine ineffable self-emptying hast bowed down the heavens. I shall kiss Thy most pure feet and wipe them with the hairs of my head, those feet whose sound Eve heard at dusk in paradise, and hid herself for fear. Who can search out the multitude of my sins and the abyss of Thy judgments, O Savior of my soul? Despise me not, Thine handmaiden, for Thou hast mercy without measure." (Lenten Triodion. Great and Holy Wednesday. Matins. Aposticha.)

The prayer of Saint Ephraim the Syrian is read for the last time at the end of the liturgy of the presanctified gifts. After this, prostrations cease until vespers on the feast of Pentecost, with the exception of prostrations made before the holy shroud on Great Friday.

Great Thursday is the day dedicated to the remembrance of the Mystical Supper. The liturgical texts for this day speak of the meaning of the mystery of the Eucharist, the washing of the feet as an example of divine humility, Judas' betrayal, and the Savior's prayer in the Garden of Gethsemane. At matins a troparion is sung in which the "greedy soul" of Judas the Betrayer is described while the goodness of the Lord and Savior is glorified:

> When the glorious disciples were enlightened at the washing of their feet before the supper, then the impious Judas was darkened, ailing with avarice and to the lawless judges he betrays Thee, the righteous Judge. Behold, O lover of money, this man who because of money hanged himself. Flee from the greedy soul which dared such things against the Master. O Lord, who art good towards

all men, glory to Thee. (Lenten Triodion. Great and Holy Thursday. Matins. Troparion.)

The canon read at matins is dedicated to understanding the mystery of the Eucharist. In the Old Testament, Wisdom is a type of Christ and his Mystical Supper. Wisdom built a house for herself and supported it with seven pillars, prepared a meal, and sent servants to proclaim, "Come, eat my bread and drink the wine I mixed for you" (Prov 9.1–5). This image primarily reminds us of God's incarnation and of her who became the first communicant of God, having received in herself the incarnate Word of God:

> Cause of all and Bestower of life, the infinite Wisdom of God has built His house, from a pure Mother who has not known man. For, clothing Himself in a bodily temple, Christ our God is greatly glorified. (Lenten Triodion. Great and Holy Thursday. Matins. Canon. Ode 1.)

God's incarnation was the beginning of the path of divine condescension, and the Savior's death on the cross—when the Lord offered himself as a sacrifice for the salvation of all mankind—was the end. The Eucharist, which Christ himself celebrates, offering his body and blood to his disciples, is a reminder of Christ's sacrifice on the cross:

> O God the Lord and Creator of all, Thou art become poor, uniting a created nature to Thyself, while remaining free from passion. Since Thou art the Passover, Thou hast offered Thyself to those for whose sake Thou wast soon to die; and Thou hast cried: "Eat my Body, and ye shall be firmly established in the faith." (Lenten Triodion. Great and Holy Thursday. Matins. Canon. Ode 3.)

> Filling Thy cup of salvation with joy, O loving Lord, Thou hast made Thy disciples drink from it. For Thou offerest Thyself in sacrifice, crying: "Drink My blood, and ye shall be firmly established in the faith." (Lenten Triodion. Great and Holy Thursday. Matins. Canon 3.)

The communion of the holy mysteries of Christ is a pledge of the deification that awaits Christians in the eschatological kingdom of God:

> "In my kingdom," Thou hast said, O Christ, to Thy friends, "I shall drink a new drink beyond your understanding; I shall be with you as God among gods. For

the Father has sent Me, His only-begotten Son, to cleanse the world from sin."
(Lenten Triodion. Great and Holy Thursday. Matins. Canon 4.)

Matins concludes with stichera that tell of Judas' betrayal. Vespers begins with
these stichera and later transitions into the liturgy of Saint Basil the Great. According to the Typikon this service should be performed at the eighth hour of the day;
that is, around two o'clock in the afternoon, but in practice it begins in the morning. In view of its special meaning, tradition holds that all Orthodox Christians
receive communion at the liturgy of Great Thursday, including those who rarely
come forth to partake. The troparion dedicated to the mystery of the Eucharist is
sung many times—in the place of the cherubic hymn, in place of the communion
verse, and during communion. (According to the tradition of the Russian Orthodox Church, this troparion is read before communion at every divine liturgy):

> Of Thy mystical supper, O Son of God, accept me today as a communicant; for
> I will not speak of Thy mystery to Thine enemies, neither like Judas will I give
> Thee a kiss; but like the thief will I confess Thee: Remember me, O Lord, in
> Thy kingdom. (Lenten Triodion. Great and Holy Thursday. Liturgy. Troparion
> instead of the Cherubic Hymn.)

The rite of the washing of the feet is performed in several cathedrals at the end
of the liturgy on Great Thursday. This rite, contained in the contemporary Hierarchical Service Book, dates back to the Great Typikon of the Church, which reflects
the liturgical practice of the church of Hagia Sophia in Constantinople in the ninth
through twelfth centuries. In Constantinople the rite was performed between vespers and the liturgy, which corresponds more closely to its meaning (according to
the gospel, Christ first washed the feet of his disciples, and only then celebrated
the paschal meal and the breaking of bread). According to the Constantinopolitan
practice, the patriarch washed the feet of three subdeacons, three deacons, three
priests, two metropolitans, and one archbishop.[39] In contemporary practice, the
hierarch washes the feet of twelve priests.

The rite is performed in the following manner. The hierarch comes out from the
sanctuary fully vested, without the staff: before him go deacons bearing the Gospel
Book and two subdeacons carrying a tray with a pitcher of water. The hierarch
ascends the cathedra, the deacons stand behind the cathedra by the analogion on
which the Gospel book is placed, and the vessel with water is placed before the

[39]Mikhail Zheltov, A. A. Lukashevich, and A. A. Tkachenko, "Great Thursday" [in Russian], in *Orthodox Encyclopedia* (Moscow: Tserkovno-nauchnyi tsentr "Pravoslavnaia entsiklopediia," 2004), 7:466.

Jerusalem. The Upper Room in Zion—the Place of the Mystical Supper.

hierarch. Then from the sanctuary the priests exit in pairs and sit in two rows before the hierarch. At this time the fifth ode of the canon of Great Thursday and the stichera for the "washing of the feet" are sung. At the end of the singing the deacon says the litany with petitions "that the washing of his feet may be blessed and sanctified with the power, action, and activity of the Holy Spirit" and "that it may be for the cleansing of the impurity of our sins." Then the hierarch, standing, reads the prayer in which he asks God to cleanse all the participants of the rite from all impurity of the flesh and spiritual uncleanness. During the reading of the prayer the priests continue to sit. Then one more prayer is read, for the granting of humility, followed by the reading from the Gospel according to John (chapter thirteen). At the beginning of the reading all the clergy sit. The protodeacon begins the reading: "At that time, Jesus, knowing that the Father had given all things into his hands, and that he had come from God and was going to God, rose from supper" (at this moment the hierarch rises) "and laid aside his garments" (the hierarch removes his mitre, omophorion, cross, panagia, and sakkos without the assistance of subdeacons), "took a towel and girded himself" (the hierarch fixes a towel around himself). "After that, he poured water into a basin" (the hierarch pours water into a dish) "and began to wash the disciples' feet, and to wipe them with the towel with which he was girded" (the hierarch washes the feet of the presbyters, beginning with the youngest, and wipes them with the towel) (Jn 13.3–6). The gospel verses are repeated if necessary. When the hierarch has washed the feet of eleven priests, he approaches the senior priest; at this moment the protodeacon reads, "Then he came to Simon Peter. And Peter said to him . . ." Then the dialogue between Peter and Jesus is completely reproduced by the senior presbyter and the hierarch (Jn 13.7–10). At the end of the washing of feet the hierarch again ascends the cathedra and the protodeacon finishes the reading of the Gospel up to the words, "You are not all clean" (Jn 13.11).

Then follows the second reading of the gospel (Jn 13.12–17). At the words "taken his garments" the hierarch vests without assistance, at the words "and sat down again" he sits at his place, and after the words "he said to them" he finishes the reading of the Gospel from the words "Do you know what I have done to you?" to the words "If you know these things, blessed are you if you do them." While the hierarch reads the Gospel sitting, the priests stand while listening to the reading. When the Gospel has been read, the hierarch stands and says the final prayer, in which he again asks the Lord to cleanse every impurity of flesh and uncleanness of soul.

The sanctification of myrrh is performed in the patriarchal cathedral during the divine liturgy on Great Thursday. This rite will be described separately.[40]

On *Great Friday* the Church remembers the crucifixion and death of the Savior.[41] The gospel readings heard on this day in the Church, as well as the liturgical texts, tell that on the final days of his earthly life, Jesus Christ was left alone in the face of all those who hated him, in the face of sufferings and death. He drank to the dregs the cup that was prepared for him and experienced the most frightful thing that can befall a person—loneliness and Godforsakenness.

He was alone in Gethsemane because his disciples fell into a deep slumber. He was alone at the trial before the high priests, at the interrogation before Herod, and at the trial before Pilate, because his disciples dispersed in fear. He was alone when he walked to Golgotha: a random bystander, not one of his beloved disciples, helped him to carry the cross. He was alone on the cross; he died alone, forsaken by all. On the cross Jesus called to his Father, "My God, my God, why hast thou forsaken me?" (Mt 27.46) This cry contained the pain of all mankind and every person—the pain of everyone who feels that he is alone and forsaken by God.

The liturgical texts of Great Friday also speak of Judas' betrayal, Jesus' trial before the high priests Annas and Caiaphas, the trial before Pilate, the hatred shown towards Jesus by the Jewish people, who demanded that he be crucified, and the crucifixion itself. At the same time it is emphasized that Christ died not because

---

[40]This will be discussed in the fifth and final volume.—*Ed.*

[41]Concerning the theological and christological meaning of the services of Great Friday, see vol. 2, pp. 301–313.

he was betrayed by Judas and condemned to death by Pilate, not because the Jews demanded his death, but because it was the will of God the Father. Had God the Father wanted it to happen differently, this death would not have taken place. And no human anger, no betrayal or perfidy would have been capable of bringing death to the Messiah who came in order to save the world.

The liturgical texts tell that the Lord willingly went to his death. He was born in order to die on the cross; he became incarnate in order to become a sacrifice for mankind. And he achieved this feat in obedience to his heavenly Father. There is no stronger testimony of God's love for mankind than the cross on which the incarnate God was crucified, or the silence that issues forth from the tomb of the only-begotten Son of God. And there is no greater sacrifice that God could have offered for mankind than the one he offered. Saint Isaac the Syrian said that if God the Father had had something more precious and more beloved than his only-begotten Son, he would have given it for the salvation of every person.[42]

In memory of the Savior's sufferings and death on the cross, it is necessary to observe a strict fast on Great Friday. The divine liturgy is not celebrated, and the worship services differ considerably in structure from the usual services.

The main worship service of Great Friday is matins with the reading of the twelve Passion Gospels. In the Lenten Triodion this service bears the name "Order for the Holy and Saving Passions [or 'Sufferings'] of our Lord Jesus Christ." According to the Typikon, it is performed "at the second hour of the night" (around eight o'clock in the evening). A similar service, which included the eleven gospel pericopes, was performed in Jerusalem and Constantinople already at the end of the first millennium. The gospel pericopes are selected to form a connected narrative, in which all the events of the final hours of the Savior's earthly life are reflected, right up to his death on the cross and his burial. The readings from the gospel alternate with antiphons, troparia, and stichera—poetic commentaries on the pericopes. These texts, amazing in beauty, depth, and content, represent a true masterpiece of Christian hymnography. As a whole, the "Order of the Sufferings of Christ" is one of the most grand divine services of the entire church year.

The first gospel reading (Jn 13.31–18.1) is the longest and contains Jesus' final conversation with his disciples. The following four gospel readings (Jn 18.1–28; Mt 26.56–75; Jn 18.28–19.16; Mt 27.3–32) contain the narrative of Judas' betrayal, the arrest of Jesus, the trial of Jesus before the high priests Annas and Caiaphas,

---

[42]Isaac the Syrian, "Homily 48," in *The Ascetical Homilies of Saint Isaac the Syrian*, trans. Holy Transfiguration Monastery, 2nd ed. (Boston, MA: Holy Transfiguration Monastery, 2011), 363–373.

the trial before Pilate, and the pronouncement of the death sentence upon Jesus. Each reading is followed by three antiphons, a little litany, and a sessional hymn. The events that the gospels relate are recounted and prayerfully interpreted in the antiphons and sessional hymns:

> Judas ran to the lawless scribes and said: "What will ye give me, and I shall deliver Him to you?" And while they conspired together, Thou against whom they were conspiring, wast Thyself standing invisibly in their midst. O Thou who knowest the hearts of men, spare our souls. (Lenten Triodion. Great and Holy Friday. Matins. Antiphon 2.)

> Today the Creator of heaven and earth said to His disciples: "The hour is at hand, and Judas who betrays Me has drawn near. Let none of you deny Me when ye see Me on the Cross between two thieves. For as man I suffer, but as the Lover of mankind I save those who believe in Me." (Lenten Triodion. Great and Holy Friday. Matins. Antiphon 5.)

> What reason led thee, Judas, to betray the Savior? Did He expel thee from the company of the apostles? Did He deprive thee of the gift of healing? When thou wast at supper with the others, did He drive thee from the table? When He washed the others' feet, did He pass thee by? How many are the blessings that thou hast forgotten! Thou art condemned for thine ingratitude, but His measureless longsuffering and great mercy are proclaimed to all. (Lenten Triodion. Great and Holy Friday. Matins. Sessional Hymn after Antiphon 6.)

> Peter denied Thee three times, and straightway he understood Thy words; but he offered Thee tears of repentance, O God, be merciful to me and save me. (Lenten Triodion. Great and Holy Friday. Matins. Antiphon 7.)

> When Thou the Judge, O God, wast standing before Caiaphas and wast delivered unto Pilate, then the powers of heaven quaked with fear. Thou wast raised upon the Cross between two thieves, and though sinless Thou wast numbered with transgressors, for the salvation of mankind. O longsuffering Lord, glory to Thee. (Lenten Triodion. Great and Holy Friday. Matins. Sessional Hymn after Antiphon 12.)

A sessional hymn is performed at the end of the antiphons, which speaks of the redemptive meaning of the Savior's death on the cross. (This text is heard again at the very end of the service):

O Lord, this very day hast Thou vouchsafed the Good Thief paradise. By the Wood of the Cross do Thou enlighten me also and save me. (Lenten Triodion. Great and Holy Friday. Matins. Exapostilarion after the Ninth Ode.)

The antiphons are followed by the sixth gospel reading (see Mk 15.16–32), which is dedicated to the crucifixion of Christ, and the Beatitudes, interspersed with verses on the theme of the crucifixion. Then the deacon intones the prokeimenon "They divided my garments among them, and for my raiment they cast lots" with the verse "My God, my God, look upon me! Why hast thou forsaken me?" These verses from Psalm 21 lead into the seventh and eighth gospel readings (Mt 27.33–54 and Lk 23.32–49), which tell of the Savior's death. These two gospel readings are separated by the reading of Psalm 50. Right after the eighth gospel reading, a three-ode canon follows in which all the major events of the last two days of Christ's life are remembered, beginning with the washing of the feet. At the end of the three-ode canon, the exapostilarion is performed three times:

O Lord, this very day hast Thou vouchsafed the Good Thief paradise. By the Wood of the Cross do Thou enlighten me also and save me. (Lenten Triodion. Great and Holy Friday. Matins. Exapostilarion.)

The final four gospel readings (Jn 19.25–37; Mk 15.43–47; Jn 19.38–42; Mt 27.62–66) are interspersed with the praises, stichera, and the final prayers of matins.

The leitmotif running through the entire divine service of Great Friday is the theme of the Mother standing at the cross of her Son. The gospel narratives make only a cursory mention of the Mother of God's presence on Golgotha. Conversely, the liturgical texts pay great attention to this theme, attributing to the Theotokos touching monologues addressed to her Son, crucified and dying on the cross:

Seeing Thee crucified, O Christ, the whole creation trembled. The foundations of the earth shook with fear at Thy power. For when Thou wast raised up today, the people of the Hebrews was destroyed. The veil of the temple was rent in twain, the graves were opened, and the dead rose from the tombs. When the centurion saw the wonder, he was filled with dread. And Thy mother, standing by Thee, cried with a mother's sorrow: "How shall I not lament and strike my breast, seeing Thee stripped naked and hung upon the wood as one condemned?" Thou wast crucified and buried, and Thou hast risen from the dead: O Lord, glory to Thee. (Lenten Triodion. Great and Holy Friday. Matins. Praises.)

Seeing Thee hanging on the Cross, O Christ the Creator and God of all, bitterly Thy Virgin Mother cried: "O my Son, where is the beauty of Thy form? I cannot bear to look upon Thee crucified unjustly. Maste haste, then, to arise, that I too may see Thy Resurrection on the third day from the dead." (Lenten Triodion. Great and Holy Friday. Matins. Aposticha.)

Yet another leitmotif of the service on Great Friday is the theme of the spiritual death of the Jewish people who crucified Christ. The authors of the liturgical texts address the Jews with accusation on behalf of God:

Thus says the Lord to the Jews: "O My people, what have I done unto thee? Or wherein have I wearied thee? I gave light to thy blind and cleansed thy lepers, I raised up the man who lay upon his bed. O My people, what have I done unto thee, and how hast thou repaid Me? Instead of manna thou hast given Me gall, instead of water vinegar; instead of loving Me, thou hast nailed Me to the Cross. I can endure no more. I shall call My Gentiles and they shall glorify Me with the Father and the Spirit; and I shall bestow on them eternal life." (Lenten Triodion. Great and Holy Friday. Matins. Antiphon 12.)

Israel, My first-born Son, has committed two evils: he has forsaken Me, the fountain of the water of life, and dug for himself a broken cistern. Upon the Cross has he crucified Me, but asked for Barabbas and let him go. Heaven at this was amazed and the sun hid its rays; yet thou, O Israel, wast not ashamed, but hast delivered Me to death. Forgive them, Holy Father, for they do not know what they have done. (Lenten Triodion. Great and Holy Friday. Matins. Praises.)

Similar texts were maintained in the Latin service until recently, but Pope John Paul II decided to eliminate them from the service because of their clearly expressed anti-Jewish tone. Independent voices are also heard in the Orthodox Church calling for the extraction of so-called antisemitic texts from the services of Holy Week.[43]

[43]In particular, Archpriest Sergei Hackel proposed eliminating all texts from the divine services of Holy Week that speak of the guilt of the Jews for the betrayal and death of the Savior (see his article "The Relevance of Western Post-Holocaust Theology to the Thought and Practice of the Russian Orthodox Church" in the collection "Theology after Auschwitz"). Archpriest Hackel calls the twelfth antiphon of Great Friday a "shameless invention" which needs to be removed from the service. In his parish to the south of London the

In response to such propositions it is necessary, first of all, to say that the texts in question do not bear an antisemitic character in any way. They only contain a moral appraisal of how the Jewish people acted towards the Savior. The texts are a warning for every nation that treads the path of struggle with God. After all, in the history of humanity there have been quite a few nations who considered themselves to be the chosen people of God, but who, like Israel, forsook the source of living water and dug broken cisterns for themselves.

Secondly, the very notion of revising the liturgical texts in order to bring them into greater correspondence with contemporary standards and the rules of political correctness is not acceptable. It would be extremely difficult to stop on this path after embarking upon it. The Orthodox divine services are precious in that they give a clear criterion of theological truth, and it is theology that must be aligned with divine worship; worship need not be corrected for the sake of one or another theological premise. *Lex credendi* emerges from *lex orandi*: the truths of the teaching of the faith and the moral directives of Christianity were born in the experience of prayer, and worship led to the opening of churches. For this reason, if, in the understanding of a particular theological or moral question, a disparity is observed between contemporary standards on the one hand and the liturgical texts on the other, the preference should be given to the latter.

---

archpriest conducted what he called a "surgical intervention" and "eliminated anti-Judaism from the ambon." Not limiting himself to an appeal to revision of the liturgical tradition, Archpriest Hackel questions all the early Christian texts which speak of the guilt of the Jews for the betrayal of Christ, including those contained in the Gospels, the Acts of the Apostles, and the works of the Fathers of the Church. The archpriest notes that in the Gospel according to John, the word "Jew" is encountered seventy times, and in half of the cases it bears a negative tone. And the Acts of the Apostles state numerous times that the Jews crucified Christ (see Acts 2.23; 3.13–15; 4.10; 10.39). A "superficial and selective" reading of Scripture brings the reader "to the conclusion that the Jews crucified Christ. In this, the important role played by Pontius Pilate and the Roman administration in the matter of condemning Jesus is removed. As far as that goes, the responsibility for the sentencing and crucifixion of a particular prisoner, as, incidentally, for all other prisoners, lay precisely on them." In the opinion of Archpriest Hackel, every place in the New Testament which speaks of the guilt of the Jews for the death of Jesus was the result of "that influence exerted on the composition and editing of sacred texts by the polemics and divisions in the society of the first century." In this way, the matter is not only about the revision of liturgical tradition, but also of the re-examination of all Christian history, the reconsideration of the teaching of the tradition of faith. The major plot line of all the four Gospels is the conflict between Christ and the Jews who ultimately require the death penalty for Christ. Pilate said regarding Christ, "I find no fault in him" (Jn 19.4) and washed his hands as a sign of his disagreement with the accusations leveled against Jesus, while the Jews cried, "His blood be on us and on our children" (Mt 27.25). There was no conflict between Christ and the Roman administration. The administration was only involved because the Jews did not have the right to carry out a death sentence. All of this is so obvious, it would seem, that no commentary is necessary. The ancient Church understood the gospel story precisely in this way and this is precisely the understanding reflected in the liturgical texts.

The service of the hours on Great Friday is performed according to a special rite: first hour, third hour, sixth hour, and ninth hour are read in order, and an excerpt from the Old Testament, Book of Epistles, and Gospel Book is read at each hour.

The vespers of Great Friday is performed, according to the Typikon, "at the tenth hour of the day" (around four o'clock in the afternoon). The entry with the Gospel Book is performed at this service, as is the prokeimenon "They divided my garments among them, and for my raiment they cast lots." Excerpts from the Old Testament (Ex 33.11–23; Job 42.12–17; Ex 52.13–54.1) and the Book of Epistles (1 Cor 1.18–2.2) are read. The gospel reading is composed of several fragments and reproduces the entire story of Christ's sufferings (Mt 27.1–38; Lk 23.39–43; Mt 27.39–54; Jn 19.31–37; Mt 27.55–61). These readings are followed by stichera in which the theme of Christ's victory over hell and death is heard:

> When Thou, the Redeemer of all, wast laid for the sake of all in a new tomb, hell was brought to scorn and, seeing Thee, drew back in fear. The bars were broken and the gates were shattered, the tombs were opened and the dead arose. Then Adam in thanksgiving and rejoicing cried to Thee: "Glory to Thy self-abasement, O Thou who lovest mankind." (Lenten Triodion. Great Friday. Vespers. Aposticha.)

> In the flesh Thou wast of Thine own will enclosed within the tomb, yet in Thy divine nature Thou dost remain uncircumscribed and limitless. Thou hast shut up the treasury of hell, O Christ, and emptied all his palaces. . . . (Lenten Triodion. Great Friday. Vespers. Aposticha.)

> When Thou didst descend to death, O Life immortal, Thou didst slay hell with the splendor of Thy Godhead. And when from the depths Thou didst raise the dead, all the powers of heaven cried out: "O Giver of life, Christ our God, glory to Thee!" (Lenten Triodion. Great Saturday. Matins. Troparion following "God is the Lord.")

The final sticheron is performed with special solemnity. During the singing of this sticheron the priest performs a censing of the winding sheet that lies on the altar table bearing the image of the dead Savior:

> Joseph with Nicodemus took Thee down from the Tree, who deckest Thyself with light as with a garment; and looking upon Thee dead, stripped, and without burial, in his grief and tender compassion he lamented, saying: "Woe is

Golgotha

me, my sweetest Jesus! When but a little while ago the sun saw Thee hanging on the cross, it wrapped itself in darkness: the earth quaked with fear and the veil of the temple was rent in twain. And now I see Thee for my sake submitting of Thine own will to death. How shall I bury Thee, my God? How shall I wrap Thee in a winding sheet? How shall I touch Thy most pure body with my hands? What song at Thy departure shall I sing of Thee, O compassionate Savior? I magnify Thy sufferings; I sing praises of Thy burial and Thy resurrection, crying: O Lord, glory to Thee." (Lenten Triodion. Great and Holy Friday. Vespers. Aposticha.)

After this, the winding sheet is solemnly carried out and placed in the middle of the church. In cathedral services, four priests lift the winding sheet by holding specially placed poles while the main celebrant (the hierarch or senior priest) carries the Gospel Book and stands underneath the winding sheet. The procession exits the sanctuary though the north doors and approaches the royal doors where the main celebrant proclaims, "Wisdom, stand upright." Then the procession moves to the center of the church, where the winding sheet is placed on a specially prepared raised platform. The winding sheet is censed three times on each side. The troparia are sung at this time, the first of which is dedicated to the burial of Christ, and the second to his resurrection:

Noble Joseph, taking down Thy most pure body from the Tree, wrapped it in clean linen with sweet spices, and he laid it in a new tomb. The angel stood by the tomb, and to the women bearing spices he cried aloud: "Myrrh is fitting for the dead, but Christ has shown himself a stranger to corruption." (Lenten Triodion. Great and Holy Friday. Vespers. Troparion following Saint Symeon's Prayer.)

As a rule, right after bringing the winding sheet out to the center of the church, the clergy reads the *Canon of the Lament of the Most-Holy Theotokos* (The Typikon calls for it to be read in cells during small compline). The authorship of the canon is ascribed to the tenth-century Byzantine poet Saint Symeon Metaphrastes; many troparia are written from the perspective of the Theotokos, who addresses her beloved Son with mournful and bewildered petitions:

"See, my sweet Light, my Hope and Life, my Son and God, has been quenched upon the Cross, and because of Him I burn," said the Virgin shedding tears. (Lenten Triodion. Great Friday. Compline. Canon. Ode 3.)

"My Son, my Lord and God, Thou wast the only hope of Thine handmaiden, my life and the light of mine eyes; and now, alas, I have lost Thee, my sweet and most beloved Child." (Lenten Triodion. Great Friday. Compline. Canon. Ode 5.)

"In my arms I hold Thee as a corpse, O loving Lord, who hast brought the dead to life; grievously is my heart wounded and I long to die with Thee," said the All-Pure, "for I cannot bear to look upon Thee lifeless and without breath." (Lenten Triodion. Great Friday. Compline. Canon. Ode 6.)

The services of *Great Saturday* are dedicated to the glorification of the Savior of the world who died on the cross and was buried. A unique feature of this service is that the faithful continue to stand before the Lord's tomb but already begin to celebrate the resurrection of Christ.

One of the stichera speaks of the meaning of the celebration on Great Saturday: "This is the blessed Sabbath, this is the day of rest, on which the only-begotten Son of God rested from all His works."[44] The Lord's Sabbath rest in the tomb after his torments and death on the cross is compared to the end of the creation of the world:

---

[44]Lenten Triodion, Great and Holy Saturday. Vespers. Stichera at "Lord, I call."

Moses the great mystically prefigured this present day, saying: "And God blessed the seventh day." For this is the blessed Sabbath, this is the day of rest, on which the Only-begotten Son of God rested from all His works. (Lenten Triodion. Great and Holy Saturday. Matins. Praises.)

The main and longest part of matins on Great Saturday is the singing of Psalm 118, divided into three parts ("stases"). From deep antiquity this psalm was used by Christians at burials. In this case, to each verse of the psalm is added a short "praise" whose author was an unknown poet living not later than the fourteenth century.[45] The "praises" tell us that the Son of God suffered and died while fulfilling the will of the Father, who glorified him for the salvation of the world; at the same time his death is called "voluntary" many times.[46] The "praises" speak in a special way of the Mother of God, who stood at the cross and lamented her Son. Several of the "praises" are addressed to the Mother of God and Joseph of Arimathea; several are written from the perspective of the Mother of God and are addressed to Jesus. In words addressed to Judas, the author convicts him of betrayal. The text of the "praises" also contain accusations against the Hebrews for not accepting their Savior and for betraying him to a shameful death.

Holy Shroud. Detail. Embroidery. Russia. 15th c.

The central theme of the "praises" and other liturgical texts of Great Saturday is the descent of Christ into hades.[47] The "praises" speak of the redemption and salvation of mankind by Christ's descent into hades: going to seek fallen Adam, but not finding him on earth, the incarnate God descended into the depths of hell in order to redeem him (this image cannot fail to recall the gospel parables of the lost sheep and the lost coin). As in many hymns of the Octoechos, the emphasis is on the universal character of the redemption that Christ completed not for a

---

[45]The "praises" are first encountered in manuscripts dating to the fourteenth or fifteenth centuries. See Kallistos (Ware), "The Meaning of the Great Fast" in *The Lenten Triodion*, 42. Protopresbyter John Meyendorff dates the "praises" to the fifteenth to the sixteenth centuries, but this dating should be considered inaccurate. John Meyendorff, "The time of Great Saturday" [in Russian], *Journal of the Moscow Patriarchate* no. 4 (1992): 35.

[46]This understanding is based on the traditional eastern Christian teaching expressed, in particular, by Saint Maximus the Confessor, concerning the will of the Son of God, which—although not identical to the will of the Father—is nevertheless in full unity with the Father's will.

[47]This theme and its place in Orthodox Christology was discussed in vol. 2, pp. 331–356. [See also Abp Hilarion (Alfeyev), *Christ the Conqueror of Hell: The Descent into Hades from an Orthodox Perspective* (Crestwood, NY: St Vladimir's Seminary Press, 2009).—*Ed.*]

particular category of people but for all of mankind and for every person. The texts also tell of Christ's raising of the dead, which is described as the "destruction" of hell by the risen Christ:

> O life, how canst thou die? How canst thou dwell in the tomb? Yet thou dost destroy death's kingdom and raise the dead from hell.
>
> O Jesus, my Christ and king of all, why hast Thou come to those in hell? Is it to set free the race of mortal men?
>
> How could hell endure Thy coming, O Savior? Was it not shattered and struck blind by the dazzling radiance of Thy light?
>
> When Thou wast laid in a tomb, O Christ the Creator, the foundations of hell were shaken and the graves of mortal men were opened.
>
> O Savior, my life, dying Thou hast gone to dwell among the dead: yet Thou hast shattered the bars of hell and arisen from corruption.
>
> To earth hast Thou come down, O Master, to save Adam: and not finding him on earth, Thou hast descended into hell, seeking him there.
>
> Buried in the earth like a grain of wheat, Thou hast yielded a rich harvest, raising to life the mortal sons of Adam.
>
> Of Thine own will descending as one dead beneath the earth, O Jesus, Thou leadest up the fallen from earth to heaven.
>
> Through Thy burial, O Christ, Thou dost destroy the palaces of hell: by Thy death Thou slayest death, and dost deliver from corruption the children of the earth.
>
> In obedience to Thine own Father, O Word, Thou hast descended to dread hell and raised up the race of mortal men.
>
> Adam was afraid when God walked in paradise, but now he rejoices when God descends to hell. Then he fell, but now he is raised up.
>
> Hell trembled, O Savior, when he saw Thee, the Giver of life, despoiling him of his wealth and raising up the dead from every age.
>
> (Lenten Triodion. Great and Holy Saturday. Matins. Praises.)

Directly following the end of the "praises" the resurrectional troparia of the Octoechos are sung, one of which is dedicated to Christ's descent into hades ("The angelic choir was filled with awe" [i.e. the Evlogitaria]). Similar troparia are dedicated to Christ's resurrection: their performance at the matins of Great Saturday signals a gradual transition from the mood of Christ's burial to the "paschal mood." In essence, the celebration of Christ's resurrection begins not on the night of Pascha, but on Great Saturday: the resurrectional hymns are sung at matins, and at the liturgy a gospel dedicated to the resurrection (Mt 28.1–20) is read, and the clergy take off their dark vestments and revest in bright vestments.[48]

Yet another major text of the matins of Great Saturday, more ancient than the "praises," is the canon. Its authorship is attributed to three individuals—the irmoi to Cassius (ninth century), the final four odes to Cosmas of Maiuma (eighth century), and the first four odes to Mark, Bishop of Hydruntum (ninth to tenth centuries).[49] The troparia of the canon, addressed to the burial and resurrection of the Son of God, express with great power the idea of the death of hell because of Christ's descent into it, and of the end of hell's power over men:

> O Lord my God, I will sing to Thee a funeral hymn, a song at Thy burial: for by Thy burial Thou hast opened for me the gates of life, and by Thy death Thou hast slain death and hell. (Lenten Triodion. Great and Holy Saturday. Matins. Canon. Ode 1.)

> Hell is king over mortal men, but not forever. Laid in the sepulcher, mighty Lord, with Thy life-giving hand Thou hast burst asunder the bars of death. To those from every age who slept in the tombs, Thou hast proclaimed true deliverance, O Saviour, who art become the firstborn from the dead. (Lenten Triodion. Great and Holy Saturday. Matins. Canon. Ode 6.)

> Hell was wounded in the heart when it received Him whose side was pierced by the spear; consumed by divine fire it groaned aloud at our salvation who sing: O God our deliverer, blessed art Thou. (Lenten Triodion. Great and Holy Saturday. Matins. Canon. Ode 7.)

How are we to understand these words, which state that the dominion of hell over men is not eternal? Is it possible to perceive in these words an echo of the opinion of Saint Gregory of Nyssa in the fourth century, that hell's torments might come to an end? Or is it a matter of hell not being eternal as God is eternal, since hell appeared as something "introduced" and alien to God, and therefore subject to defeat? There is no definitive answer to these questions. The services of Great

---

[48]In contemporary practice, the revesting takes place after the reading from the Book of the Epistles. According to the ancient Jerusalem Typikon, the clergy vested in bright vestments before the start of vespers of Great Saturday. This was connected with the fact that during the reading of the Old Testament, the baptism of the catechumens took place. See Ivan Mansvetov, *The Typikon, its formation and fate in the Greek and Russian Church* [in Russian] (Moscow, 1885), 215.

[49]Concerning Mark of Hydruntum [present-day Otranto—*Ed.*], see, in particular, Mansvetov, *Typikon*, 216–217.

Saturday open slightly the curtain of a mystery that is not subject to discussion: the mystery will be revealed only in the eschatological kingdom, in which God will be "all in all" (1 Cor 15.28). At this time it is only possible to say that the Savior's death and resurrection put an end to hell's power over the human race. If the torments of hell are eternal, then it may be so only for those who eternally oppose God's will concerning the salvation of the entire world. But hell's attempt to *eternally* wage war with God and keep a separate, autonomous kingdom with gates locked and shackled, to lock itself up and to lock people inside as captives, has met with failure. Hell continues to reign over the human race as long as even one person answers "no" to God. Hell continues to reign, but does not *reign eternally,* since its power is forever shaken by Christ, who by his death signed hell's death sentence. Hell reigns, but does not *reign eternally,* because its very existence henceforth depends on the will of man; it does not depend on its own will or the will of the devil.

At the end of the matins of Great Saturday, stichera are performed that speak of the Lord's "keeping Sabbath" in the tomb. The stichera draw a parallel between the burial of the Savior—who by his death fulfilled the human race's "economy of salvation"—and the Sabbath rest that completed the creation of the world:

> Today a tomb holds Him who holds the creation in the hollow of His hand; a stone covers Him who covered the heavens with glory. Life sleeps and hell trembles, and Adam is set free from His bonds. Glory to Thy dispensation, whereby Thou hast accomplished all things, granting us an eternal Sabbath, Thy most holy resurrection from the dead. (Lenten Triodion. Great and Holy Saturday. Matins. Stichera at the Praises.)

> What is this sight that we behold? What is this present rest? The King of the ages, having through his passion fulfilled the plan of salvation, keeps Sabbath in the tomb, granting us a new Sabbath. (Lenten Triodion. Great and Holy Saturday. Matins. Stichera at the Praises.)

The great doxology is sung after the stichera, after which a cross procession is performed in which the holy winding sheet is carried around the church. At the hierarchical service a reader with candle (or lamp) walks at the front of the cross procession, followed by subdeacons carrying the staff, dikirion, trikirion, and fans. The clergy follow, carrying the winding sheet: four priests hold the winding sheet on four poles while the hierarch walks under the winding sheet, carrying the Gospel Book. The parishioners follow the clergy. The procession exits the temple through the west doors and moves around the church in a counterclockwise direction. After walking around the church, the procession enters into the church through the west doors, and the winding sheet is placed in the middle of the church.

At this point the prophecy of Ezekiel is read concerning the field filled with dead bones (Ezek 37.1–14), as is the Book of Epistles (1 Cor 5.6–8; Gal 3.13–14), and the gospel (Mt 27.62–66). The readings are interspersed with psalm verses: "Arise, Lord, and help us: and deliver us for thy name's sake"; "Arise, O Lord my God, lift up thine hand: forget not thy poor forever"; "Let God arise, and let his enemies be scattered. As smoke vanishes, so let them vanish: as wax melts before the fire." These verses, together with Ezekiel's prophecy concerning the universal resurrection, relate not so much to the Savior's burial as to his resurrection.

The reading of the prophecy of Ezekiel about the bones is the semantic core of the service of Great Saturday. This prophecy, like the entire service of Great Saturday, speaks of death and resurrection. Death was brought into this world by human sin, and through people's fault death reigns over the human race. Mankind has been comparable to a field strewn with dead men's bones at many times in the course of history. All of human history is replete with wars and battles in which one side was victorious while the other side suffered defeat; often the earthly fates of entire nations were decided in a single battle. But the main result of all the military conflicts has always been the same: a field strewn with dead bodies.

Meditating on the fates of men and the millions of innocent people killed in wars, epidemics, and natural disasters, one may ask, "Where is God? Where was he looking? Where is the justice of God? Where is his love for mankind, if he so mercilessly brings death to thousands and millions of people?" But people see only one side, that which takes place on earth; people do not see the miracle that takes place with every person after death—the miracle of resurrection. No matter how many people have died, no matter what kind of death they suffered, they will all be resurrected because of the death and resurrection of the Lord. For this reason the Lord became a man; for this reason he underwent sufferings and death—for mankind to be resurrected.

The service of Great Saturday is a testimony that the fate of mankind is decided not on the field of battle, but in that life-giving tomb that became the source of the salvation of the entire world. The winding sheet of the Savior, placed in the center of the church, symbolizes this tomb. The veneration of the winding sheet takes place right after the end of the matins of Great Saturday: the clergy, followed by the laity, approach the winding sheet with piety, make three prostrations to the ground, and kiss it. During the veneration a sticheron is sung that speaks of Christ as a sojourner who had no place to lay his head (we recall that the theme of Christ's sojourning was one of the leitmotifs of the Nativity service):[50]

> Come and let us bless Joseph of everlasting memory, who came to Pilate by night and begged for the Life of all: "Give me this stranger, who has no place to lay His head. Give me this stranger, whom His evil disciple delivered to death. Give me this stranger, whom his mother saw hanging on the cross, and with a mother's sorrow she cried weeping: "Woe is me, my Child! Woe is me, light of mine eyes and beloved fruit of my womb! For what Simeon foretold in the temple is come to pass today: a sword pierces my heart, but do Thou change my grief to gladness by Thy Resurrection." We venerate Thy Passion, O Christ. We venerate Thy Passion, O Christ. We venerate Thy Passion, O Christ, and Thy Holy Resurrection. (Lenten Triodion. Great and Holy Saturday. Matins. Veneration of the Epitaphion.)

The liturgy of Great Saturday begins with vespers, which the Typikon prescribes to be performed "at the tenth hour" (around four o'clock in the afternoon) but in contemporary practice is performed in the morning. Vespers includes the singing of stichera dedicated to the victory of Christ over hell. Hell is personified in these stichera, as in the monuments of early Christian literature dedicated to the theme of Christ's descent into hades (especially the "Gospel of Nicodemus," as well as the hymns of Saint Ephraim the Syrian and the kontakia of Saint Romanos the Melodist):

> Today hell groans and cries aloud: "It had been better for me, had I not accepted Mary's Son, for He has come to me and destroyed my power; He has shattered the gates of brass, and as God He has raised up the souls that once I held. . . ."

> Today hell groans and cries aloud: "My power has been destroyed. I accepted a mortal man as one of the dead; yet I cannot keep Him prisoner, and with Him I shall lose all those over whom I ruled. I held in my power the dead from all the ages; but see, He is raising them all. . . ."

> Today hell groans and cries aloud: "My dominion has been swallowed up; the Shepherd has been crucified and He has raised Adam. I am deprived of those whom once I ruled; in my strength I devoured them, but now I have cast them

[50]Concerning this, see above, pp. 274–282.

forth. He who was crucified has emptied the tombs; the power of death has no more strength. . . ."

(Lenten Triodion. Great and Holy Saturday. Vespers. Stichera on "Lord, I call.")

The notion is confirmed with renewed strength that hell has become barren, devastated, and deprived of all its denizens after Christ descended into it. The "Pascha of the Crucifixion"—the liturgical remembrance of the death and burial of Christ—concludes on this victorious note. After the readings from the Old Testament, the service decisively acquires the character of the "Pascha of the Resurrection." The path on which the Lenten Triodion guided the faithful over the course of ten weeks comes to an end: that which went from the repentance of the services of Great Lent to the remembrance of Christ's Passion and the Savior's death and burial, and through this remembrance to the celebration of Christ's resurrection.

The Vision of the Prophet Ezekiel. Fragment of a Fresco. Yaroslavl. 18th c.

The little entrance is performed at the end of the singing of the stichera, after which the reading of fifteen texts from the Old Testament begins, texts that the early Church saw as foreshadowings of the death and resurrection of Christ. The earliest accounts of the reading of twelve pericopes from the Old Testament at the liturgy of Great Saturday date to the fifth century. The number of Old Testament readings subsequently increased to fifteen, but their contents did not undergo significant change. At the present time, the Old Testament readings are as follows:

1. The biblical narrative of the creation of the world (Gen 1.1–13);
2. The prophecy of the glory of Jerusalem (Is 60.1–16);
3. The narrative from the Book of Exodus regarding the establishment of Passover (Ex 12.1–11);
4. The Book of the Prophet Jonah (read in its entirety);
5. The narrative of Joshua's celebration of Passover (Josh 5.10–15);
6. The account of the Hebrews crossing the Red Sea (Ex 13.20–14.31), concluding with the refrain "For gloriously has he been glorified";

7. The prophecy of Zephaniah about the call of the nations to the Church
   (Zeph 3.8–15);
8. The narrative of the raising of the youth by the Prophet Elijah
   (1 Kg 17.8–23);
9. The prophecy of Isaiah concerning the New Testament Church
   (Is 61.10–62.5);
10. The account of Abraham's offering of Isaac as a sacrifice (Gen 22.1–18);
11. The prophecy concerning the Messiah (Is 61.1–9);
12. The narrative of the raising of the youth by the Prophet Elisha
    (2 Kg 4.8–37);
13. The prayer of the people of Israel (Is 63.11–64.5);
14. The prophecy concerning the New Testament (Jer 31.31–34);
15. The narrative of the three young men in the Babylonian furnace
    (Dan 3.1–51), which concludes with the refrain, "Praise the Lord, sing
    and exalt him throughout all the ages."

As a whole, the fifteen Old Testament readings are a grand compendium of the entire Old Testament: the most significant events of pre-Christian sacred history pass before the spiritual view of the faithful. Directly after the Old Testament readings, "As many as have been baptized into Christ have put on Christ" (Gal 3.27) is sung, and there is a reading from the Book of Epistles (Rom 6.3–11). After the epistle reading, in place of the usual "Alleluia," the choir sings the verse "Arise, O God, judge the earth: for to thee belong all the nations" many times, with the addition of other verses from Psalm 81. During the singing, "the clergy change from dark to white vestments."

In the contemporary liturgical practice of the Orthodox Church the revesting in white vestments during the singing of Psalm 81 is seen as the transition from Holy Week to the celebration of the resurrection of Christ, even more so considering that the revesting of the clergy is followed by a gospel reading that gives an account of the resurrection (Mt 28.1–20). But, historically, the white vestments of the clergy were linked less with the celebration of Pascha than with the baptism of the catechumens that took place on Great Saturday. While the clergy was busy with the celebration of the mystery of baptism, the parishioners congregated in the church and listened to the Old Testament readings. At the end of the readings the newly baptized, dressed in light garments, entered into the church accompanied by the singing of "As many as have been baptized into Christ," after which the entire community participated in the Eucharist.

The liturgy of Saint Basil follows the reading of the gospel. The following troparion is sung in the place of the cherubic hymn:

> Let all mortal flesh keep silent, and in fear and trembling stand, pondering nothing earthly-minded. For the King of kings and the Lord of lords comes to be slain, to give Himself as food to the faithful. Before Him go the ranks of angels: all the principalities and powers; the many-eyed cherubim and the six-winged seraphim covering their faces, singing the hymn: Alleluia. Alleluia. Alleluia.

With utmost fullness and expressiveness this troparion conveys the mood of Great Saturday as the day when the entire cosmos, including all human flesh and the angelic world, freezes in silence while standing before the Lord who offered himself as a sacrifice and became food for the faithful. The worship of Christ, who died on the cross, grows into anxious anticipation of Christ's resurrection, and both moods—of the passion and of the resurrection—are united in eucharistic thanksgiving.

The Typikon calls for the faithful not to leave the church at the end of the liturgy of Great Saturday, but to remain in place to listen to the reading of the Acts of the Holy Apostles, after which the paschal service begins. But in view of the fact that in our present day the liturgy of Great Saturday is celebrated in the morning and not in the evening, the parishioners disperse to their homes and congregate later in the church for the nighttime service. According to tradition, after the liturgy on Great Saturday the loaves of Easter bread (*kulichi*), colored eggs, and other foods for the paschal table are blessed.

10

The Paschal Cycle

T HE USE OF THE LENTEN TRIODION ends on Great Saturday and the
Pentecostarion comes into use. This book contains the divine services of
the paschal cycle—from Pascha to the first Sunday after Pentecost. The basic theme
of the liturgical texts in the Pentecostarion is the glorification of the risen Savior
of the world.

THE RESURRECTION OF CHRIST: PASCHA

The celebration of the resurrection of Christ begins with the paschal midnight
office, which is performed by priests wearing white vestments. The canon of Great
Saturday is read at midnight office. At the ninth ode, the holy winding sheet is
brought into the sanctuary.

Directly following or a few minutes after the conclusion of midnight office,
paschal matins begins. This is the most solemn, festal, and joyful worship service
of the entire Church year. The service is ushered in with the singing of the paschal
sticheron:

> Thy resurrection, O Christ our Savior, the angels in heaven sing; enable us
> on earth to glorify thee in purity of heart. (Pentecostarion. Sunday of Pascha.
> Matins. Sticheron at the Procession.)

This sticheron is first sung by the clergy in the sanctuary, and then the choir
joins in. The paschal cross procession begins, led by the candle-bearer followed by
the choir, clergy, and parishioners. The hierarch or senior priest carries the three-
branched candlestick and hand cross in his left hand and the censer in his right
hand; other clergymen carry the Gospel Book and the icon of the resurrection
of Christ. The procession exits from the temple through the west doors and goes
around the church in a counterclockwise direction. The singing of the sticheron
"Thy resurrection, O Christ our Savior" continues during the cross procession

and the *trezvon* (triple-peal) is performed on the bells ("strike all the bells and the large bells and ring vigorously"). The doors of the church are closed after all the parishioners have exited the church. After walking around the church, the procession returns to the entrance, and the rector stands before the closed doors and pronounces the opening exclamation of matins: "Glory to the holy, consubstantial, life-creating, and undivided Trinity." The choir responds "Amen," and the clergy sing the troparion of Pascha three times:

> Christ is risen from the dead, trampling down death by death, and upon those in the tombs bestowing life. (Pentecostarion. Sunday of Pascha. Matins. Troparion.)

Pascha. Y. Kuzankova. 2002.

Next, the choir sings the troparion three times, after which the rector exclaims verses from Psalm 67: "Let God arise and let his enemies be scattered. Let those who hate him flee from before his face"; "As smoke vanishes so let them vanish, as wax melts before the fire"; "So the sinners perish before the face of God, but let the righteous be glad"; "This is the day which the Lord has made, let us rejoice and be glad in it." At each verse of the psalm the choir answers with the singing of the troparion "Christ is risen from the dead." After the troparion is sung many times, the doors of the temple are opened and the clergy, followed by all the people, enter into the temple, which is overflowing with light (the Typikon prescribes for all the "candles and lampadas" to be lit before the beginning of the paschal service). The priest greets all with the exclamation, "Christ is risen!" The people respond, "Indeed he is risen!" This exclamation and the people's response are often interjected into the course of the service, giving it a special festal quality.

Following the great litany, the Paschal Canon of Saint John of Damascus is sung. It reflects the main substance of the celebration of Christ's resurrection as a passing from death to life, from earth to heaven:

> This is the day of the resurrection. Let us be illumined, O people. Pascha, the Pascha of the Lord. For from death to life and from earth to heaven has Christ

our God led us, as we sing the song of victory. (Pentecostarion. Sunday of Pascha. Matins. Canon. Ode 1. Irmos.)

The inspired prophet Habakkuk now stands with us in holy vigil. He is like a shining angel who cries with a piercing voice: Today salvation has come to the world, for Christ is risen as all-powerful. (Pentecostarion. Sunday of Pascha. Matins. Canon. Ode 4. Irmos.)

This is the chosen and holy day, first of Sabbaths, king and lord of days, the feast of feasts, holy day of holy days. On this day we bless Christ forevermore. (Pentecostarion. Sunday of Pascha. Matins. Canon. Ode 8. Irmos.)

Now all is filled with light: heaven and earth and the lower regions. Let all creation celebrate the rising of Christ. In Him we are established. (Pentecostarion. Sunday of Pascha. Matins. Canon. Ode 3.)

The irmoi above almost literally reproduce the beginning of Saint Gregory the Theologian's Homily 45, "On Holy Pascha," which the Typikon prescribes to be read after the third ode of the canon (in practice this reading is universally omitted).[1] The troparia of the canon are inspired by the content of Saint Gregory's paschal homily. They contain calls for joy in the resurrection of Christ and glorify Christ as the Victor over hell and death:

Let the heavens be glad, and let the earth rejoice. Let the whole world, visible and invisible, keep the feast. For Christ is risen, our eternal joy. (Pentecostarion. Sunday of Pascha. Matins. Canon. Ode 1.)

The souls bound in the chains of hell, O Christ, seeing Thy compassion without measure, pressed onward to the light with joyful steps, praising the eternal Pascha. (Pentecostarion. Sunday of Pascha. Matins. Canon. Ode 5.)

O my Savior, as God Thou didst bring Thyself freely to the Father, a victim living and unsacrificed, resurrecting Adam, the father of us all, when Thou didst arise from the grave. (Pentecostarion. Sunday of Pascha. Matins. Canon. Ode 6.)

We celebrate the death of death, and the overthrow of hell, the beginning of another life which is eternal. . . . (Pentecostarion. Sunday of Pascha. Matins. Canon. Ode 7.)

---

[1] See citation from this homily in vol. 2, p. 339.

Christ is risen, trampling down death and raising the dead. Rejoice, all ye people. (Pentecostarion. Sunday of Pascha. Matins. Canon. Refrain at Ode 9.)

Christ, the new Pascha, the living sacrifice, the lamb of God who takes away the sins of the world. (Pentecostarion. Sunday of Pascha. Matins. Canon. Refrain at Ode 9.)

Today all creation rejoices and makes glad, for Christ is risen and hell has been despoiled. (Pentecostarion. Sunday of Pascha. Matins. Canon. Refrain at Ode 9.)

Today the Master has despoiled hell and raised the prisoners whom it had held from the ages in harsh captivity. (Pentecostarion. Sunday of Pascha. Matins. Canon. Refrain at Ode 9.)

The Myrrhbearing Women at the Tomb of the Lord. Duccio di Buoninsegna. 13th c.

The resurrection of Christ is experienced as an event of cosmic proportions that is relevant not only for all people but also for all of creation. According to the teaching of the apostle Paul, accepted by the eastern Christian tradition, creation together with men "groans and labors with birth pangs together until now," awaiting liberation "from the bondage of corruption into the glorious liberty of the children of God" (Rom 8.19–22). Interpreting these words of the apostle, Saint John Chrysostom says, "what is the meaning of, 'the creation was made subject to vanity?' Why, that it became corruptible. For what cause, and on what account? On account of thee, O man. For since thou hast taken a body mortal and liable to suffering, the earth too has received a curse. . . . It shall be freed from the bondage of corruption, that is, it shall no longer be corruptible, but shall go along with the beauty given to thy body."[2] In other words, creation will become incorrupt when man becomes incorrupt. And man's hope for incorruption is built upon Christ, who died and was buried but was not subject to corruption, having opened the path to incorruption for the entire

[2]John Chrysostom, *Homilies on Romans* 14.5 (*NPNF*[1] 11:444–445).

human race, and consequently for all of creation. In this way, the redemption of man accomplished by Christ is directly related to the fate of the created world.

The author of the Paschal Canon calls not only the material world ("visible") but also the world of spirits ("invisible") to rejoice. From the moment of the fall of the devil and the demons from God, the invisible world was divided into the domain of God and the domain of the power of the devil, which had real—albeit incomplete, relative, and limited—power over people's souls. After Christ descended into hell, hell's fate reached a turning point: Christ filled it with his presence—salvific for those who have believed in him and damning for those who have opposed him, the foremost among the latter being the devil and demons. From now on, hell is no longer a place of oblivion and Godforsakenness, but a place where God is also present with his love, as in heaven.

After the sixth ode of the canon the kontakion and the ikos are sung, which constitute the opening strophes of Saint Romanos the Melodist's fortieth canon. These speak of the myrrh-bearing women who came early to the Savior's tomb; their coming is compared to the magi's worship of the Infant in Bethlehem:

> Thou didst descend into the tomb, O Immortal, Thou didst destroy the power of death. In victory didst Thou arise, O Christ God, proclaiming "Rejoice" to the myrrhbearing women, granting peace to Thine apostles, and bestowing resurrection on the fallen. (Pentecostarion. Sunday of Pascha. Matins. Kontakion.)

> Before the dawn, the myrrhbearing women sought, as those who seek the day, their sun, who was before the sun yet had descended to the grave, and they cried to each other: O friends, come let us anoint with spices His life-bearing yet buried body, the flesh which raised fallen Adam and now lies in the tomb. Let us assemble and, like the magi, let us hasten and let us worship. Let us bring myrrh as a gift to Him who is wrapped now, not in swaddling clothes, but in a winding-sheet. Let us lament and cry: Arise, O Master, and bestow resurrection on the fallen. (Pentecostarion. Sunday of Pascha. Matins. Ikos.)

Next the Typikon calls for the reading of the synaxarion, which tells of Christ's descent into hades and of the appearance of the risen Christ to the myrrh-bearing women (in practice this reading is omitted).[3] Then the hymn "Having beheld the resurrection of Christ," composed in early antiquity (it is in the most ancient copies

---

[3]The paschal synaxarion was discussed in vol. 2, p. 369.

of the Jerusalem and Studite Typika), is sung three times. In this hymn, the joy of Christ's resurrection is united with the remembrance of the Savior's crucifixion and death on the cross:

> Having beheld the resurrection of Christ, let us worship the holy Lord Jesus, the only sinless One. We venerate Thy Cross, O Christ, and we praise and glorify Thy holy resurrection; for Thou art our God, and we know no other than Thee; we call on Thy name. Come, all you faithful, let us venerate Christ's holy resurrection. For, behold, through the Cross joy has come into all the world. Let us ever bless the Lord, praising His resurrection, for by enduring the Cross for us, He has destroyed death by death. (Pentecostarion. Sunday of Pascha. Matins. Hymn.)

After the Paschal Canon, the exapostilarion dedicated to Christ's death and burial is performed three times:

> In the flesh Thou didst fall asleep as a mortal man, O King and Lord. Thou didst rise on the third day, raising Adam from corruption and destroying death: O Pascha of incorruption, the salvation of the world. (Pentecostarion. Sunday of Pascha. Matins. Exapostilarion.)

The psalms of praise are sung at the end of matins, to which the paschal stichera, alternating with verses from Psalm 67, are added. In these stichera Pascha is glorified as the feast of Christ's resurrection. In addition, the stichera speak of the appearance of the angel to the myrrh-bearing women and contain an appeal to brotherly love between Christians:

> Today, a sacred Pascha is revealed to us, a new and holy Pascha, a mystical Pascha, a Pascha worthy of veneration, a Pascha which is Christ the Redeemer, a blameless Pascha, a great Pascha, a Pascha of the faithful, a Pascha which has opened for us the gates of Paradise, a Pascha which sanctifies all the faithful.

> The myrrhbearing women, at the break of dawn, drew near to the tomb of the Life-giver. There they found an angel sitting upon the stone. He greeted them with these words: Why do you seek the living among the dead? Why do you mourn the incorrupt amid corruption? Go, proclaim the glad tidings to His disciples.

This is the day of resurrection. Let us be illumined by the feast. Let us embrace each other. Let us call "brothers" even those that hate us, and forgive all by the resurrection, and so let us cry: Christ is risen from the dead, trampling down death by death, and upon those in the tombs bestowing life!

(Pentecostarion. Sunday of Pascha. Matins. Stichera of Pascha.)

The final sticheron is taken nearly verbatim from Saint Gregory the Theologian's first oration: "It is the day of resurrection and an auspicious beginning. Let us be made brilliant by the feast and embrace each other. Let us call brothers even those who hate us [Is 66.5]. . . . Let us concede all things to the resurrection. Let us pardon each other. . . ."[4]

According to the Typikon, the paschal greeting is performed after the singing of the sticheron. In the Pentecostarion it is described as follows:

. . . [T]he Superior taketh the precious Cross, and standeth outside, before the holy doors of the church. And all the Priests, as many as there are, and the Deacons, each taking up the holy Gospel-book and the precious icons, stand in order, each in his rank, along the right side of the Superior. And there approach first the most honored officers of the church, and the elders, one by one; and making a little bow before the Superior, each of them kisseth the precious Cross, and the holy Gospel-book, which a Priest holdeth, and the icons. Then, they kiss the Superior on the lips, saying: Christ is risen! And they kiss the Priests in the same way, and kiss each other according to their rank; and they stand beyond the Priests, along the right side. And after them come the layfolk, who likewise give and receive the kiss. The laborers of the community in the same manner kiss one another and stand in order. And great silence should reign over all. After the kiss, the catechetical homily of Saint John Chrysostom is read by the Superior or the Ecclesiarch. We do not sit down during this reading, but listen to it standing.[5]

Matins is concluded with the reading of the catechetical homily of Saint John Chrysostom, which was discussed in another volume in this series.[6] Next, the paschal hours are sung, including several hymns from matins. During the singing of

---

[4]Gregory the Theologian, *Orations* 1.1 (SC 246:72; Harrison, PPS).

[5]*The Pentecostarion of the Orthodox Church*, trans. Isaac E. Lambertsen (Liberty, TN: The St. John of Kronstadt Press, 2007), 9–10. In practice the paschal kiss normally takes place only among the clergy and servers in the sanctuary during the singing of the paschal stichera. The kissing "on the mouth" is replaced by threefold kissing on the cheek.

[6]See vol. 2, p. 368.

the hours, according to the custom of the Russian Orthodox Church, the revesting of the clergy from white vestments into red garments takes place. (This custom does not exist in the Greek Church or in the Russian Church Abroad).

Directly following the hours the paschal liturgy is celebrated. It begins with the singing of the troparion, "Christ is risen from the dead," together with verses from Psalm 67, many times. After the little entrance, the opening verses from the Acts of the Apostles are read, and then the Gospel according to John. The cycle of the year's readings from the Book of Epistles and the Gospel Book begins at the paschal liturgy. During the paschal period, in the days and weeks leading to Pentecost, the book of the Acts of the Apostles and the entire Gospel according to Saint John are read entirely. Furthermore, the reading of the apostolic epistles and the Gospel according to Saint Matthew begin after Pentecost. The prologue of the Gospel according to John is read at the paschal liturgy. The reading emphasizes that the risen Christ is the pre-eternal Word of God and the only-begotten Son of God. He is "the true light which gives light to every man coming into the world"

The Reading of the Catechetical Homily of Saint John Chrysostom.

(Jn 1.9), and the Church solemnly proclaims this on the night of Pascha. According to the tradition of the Russian Church, at the paschal liturgy the gospel is read in different languages, including Greek, the original language of the gospel.

A unique feature of the paschal service is that the royal doors and the side doors of the sanctuary remain open during its celebration, and when deacons exit to the ambon to pronounce the litanies, they exit not through the side doors, but through the royal doors. The doors to the sanctuary are not closed throughout the entire week of Pascha. The opened doors symbolize the Lord's tomb; during Christ's resurrection the angel cast the stone away from the doors of the tomb. The opened doors also remind us of the closeness of God's kingdom, whose gates are opened for everyone who believes in the resurrection of Christ and who lives according to his commandments.

The feast of Pascha, unlike other feasts of the Church, lasts not just one day but an entire week. The subsequent four and a half weeks constitute the afterfeast of Pascha. The leave-taking of Pascha is celebrated on the eve of the feast of the Ascension of our Lord, forty days after Pascha.

During Bright Week the divine services are performed in the same way as during the night of Pascha. Every day the liturgy of Saint John Chrysostom is celebrated, after which, according to custom, a cross procession takes place. Exiting the church with the gospel, the icon of the resurrection of Christ, and fans, singing the troparion "Christ is risen from the dead" and the irmoi of the Paschal Canon, the faithful give witness to the resurrection of the Savior to the world. In this same way the Church gives witness to the fact that its mission—to preach the risen Christ—is not limited to the walls of the church, but must envelop the entire world.

During the week of Pascha, all prayers for the departed are omitted during the liturgies. In non-liturgical services, prayers of commemoration of the departed (funerals, panikhidas) are performed according to a special paschal rite consisting mostly of hymns dedicated to Christ's resurrection.[7]

THE SUNDAYS FOLLOWING PASCHA

Each Sunday in the period between Pascha and Pentecost is dedicated to events or persons connected with the resurrection of Christ.

The *second Sunday after Pascha*[8] is called "Antipascha" (literally, "in place of Pascha.") Other names for the feast are "Thomas Sunday" and "New Sunday." On this day the gospel concerning Thomas' assurance in the risen Lord (Jn 20.19–31) is read, and many liturgical texts are dedicated to the events described in the gospel, which took place on the eighth day after Pascha:

> O strange wonder! Doubt bore certain faith. Thomas said: "Unless I see, I shall not believe." By touching his side, he blessed the incarnate Son of God who suffered in the flesh, and proclaimed the resurrected God by crying out with joy: "My Lord and my God, glory to thee!" (Pentecostarion. Sunday of Thomas. Great Vespers. Aposticha.)

Another theme of the divine services for Thomas Sunday is spiritual renewal, symbolized by the coming of spring. The canon performed at matins especially speaks to this theme:

[7]The commemorations of the departed during the paschal period will be discussed in the forthcoming final volume of this series.

[8]The reckoning of the "Sundays after Pascha" begins with the feast of Pascha itself. The next Sunday is considered the "Second Sunday after Pascha," and so forth. The reckoning of the "Sundays after Pentecost" does not begin with Pentecost itself, but rather from the first Sunday after the feast, which is called the "First Sunday after Pentecost."

Today is the springtime of our souls; for Christ, who shone forth from the tomb like the sun on the third day, has dispelled the dark winter of our sin. Let us praise Him for He has been glorified. (Pentecostarion. Sunday of Thomas. Matins. Canon. Ode 1.)

The queen of hours with splendor openly ministers to this light-bearing day, the queen of days, and gladdens the people received in the Church, as she unceasingly praises the risen Christ. (Pentecostarion. Sunday of Thomas. Matins. Canon. Ode 1.)

The troparia of the canon are connected with the theme of Homily 44 of Saint Gregory the Theologian, dedicated to New Week, in which he says:

The queen of seasons marshals her parade to honor the queen of days, distributing the sweetest and loveliest largess from her bounty. Now the sky has a greater clarity; now the sun stands higher and shines a more burnished gold; now the orb of the moon gleams more luminous and the chorus of stars twinkles more brightly. Now the waves clasp the shore in peaceful embrace, the clouds the sun, the earth the crops. . . . [I]n sum, a spring of the world, a spring of the spirit, a spring for souls, a spring for the body, a spring visible, a spring invisible; which may we, who have been richly blessed in this life, enjoy in the other as well, and be escorted new to the new life, in Jesus Christ our Lord. . . .[9]

The *third Sunday after Pascha* is called the Sunday of the Myrrh-bearing Women. On this day the Church remembers the women who stood at Jesus' cross, participated in his burial, and came to the tomb with myrrh and spices in order to anoint the body of the Savior (see Mk 15.43–16.8) on the first day after the Sabbath, early in the morning. Joseph of Arimathea, who performed the burial of Christ, is also remembered. Several hymns of this day are taken from the services of Holy Week and are dedicated to the final hours of the earthly life, death, and burial of the Savior. In particular, at matins, the hymn "O thou who puttest on light like a garment," sung at the burial rite on Great Friday, is added to the paschal stichera. The troparion "The Noble Joseph" is also sung, but the paschal ending is added to it: "But on the third day thou didst arise, O Lord, granting great mercy to the world."

The services of the following three Sundays after Pascha are thematically linked to pericopes from the Gospel according to John, which is read during the divine liturgies on those days.

[9]Gregory the Theologian, *Orations* 44.10, 12 (PG 45:617–621; Vinson, CUA).

The story of the Lord healing the paralytic at the pool of Siloam (see Jn 5.1–15) is read during the liturgy on the *fourth Sunday after Pascha*. The liturgical texts are dedicated to the interpretation of this event, as well as to the glorification of the Savior's death on the cross and resurrection. In particular, the first troparion of each ode in the canon at matins is dedicated to the Lord's death on the cross, the second troparion is dedicated to his resurrection, and the third troparion is dedicated to his healing of the paralytic; the fourth troparion is dedicated to the Archangel Michael, whom church tra-

Healing of the Paralytic. Mosaic. Church of Sant'Apollinare Nuovo. Ravenna. 6th c.

dition considers to be the angel who came down into the pool and stirred up the waters; the fifth troparion is dedicated to the Holy Trinity, and the sixth to the Theotokos.

Christ's conversation with the Samaritan woman (see Jn 4.5–42) is the theme of the divine service on the *fifth Sunday after Pascha*. This event is viewed in the liturgical texts as one of the stages of divine self-emptying (*kenōsis*), which began with the incarnation of the Son of God and ended with his death and resurrection:

> Let heaven and earth rejoice radiantly today, for Christ appeared as a man in the flesh, to deliver from the curse the whole race of Adam; and when he came to Samaria, he was made wondrous by wonders. He that was wrapped in the waters of the clouds stands near to a woman and seeks water. Wherefore, let all of us the faithful worship him, who willingly became poor for our sake in his compassionate counsel. (Pentecostarion. Sunday of the Samaritan Woman. Great Vespers. Stichera at the Litiya.)

The gospel narrative concerning the Lord's healing of the man blind from birth (see Jn 9.1–38) is read during the liturgy on the sixth Sunday after Pascha. This narrative inspires the authors of the liturgical texts to contemplate spiritual blindness, which is healed by faith in the risen Christ. Jesus Christ is light, as the Father and Holy Spirit are light: the Holy Trinity is "the one indivisible light who is known in three hypostases."[10] This divine light illuminates man, whose inner eyes Christ opens.

---

[10]Pentecostarion. Sunday of the Blind Man. Matins. Canon 2. Ode 9.

The Ascension of the Lord

On the fortieth day after Pascha the Church celebrates the feast of the Ascension of the Lord. This feast appeared no later than the end of the fourth century and is one of the most ancient feasts of the paschal cycle. The celebration is based on the event described in the Gospel according to Luke (see Lk 24.50–51) and in the Acts of the Apostles (Acts 1.9–11).

In the liturgical texts the ascension is perceived as the end of the earthly path of our Lord and Savior. His glorification is understood as the manifestation of the glory of God the Father through the Son:

> We praise the radiance of thy countenance, seeing thine Ascension upon the mount, O Christ, the splendor of the Father's glory. We bow in worship before thy Passion. We honor thy Resurrection. We magnify thy glorious Ascension. O Lord, have mercy on us. (Pentecostarion. Ascension of the Lord. Great Vespers. Stichera at "Lord, I call.")

The Son of God returns to his Father from whom he was never parted and ascends into heaven as the one who never left heaven. But while he was in heaven as God before the incarnation, now he carries up to the throne of God both his divine nature and the human nature joined to him. Having put on human nature, Christ completely deified it and opened up the path to deification for every person. The ascension is the conclusion and crowning of the path of deification on which God led human nature, which he himself had assumed:

> Thou hast renewed Adam's nature in thyself, which had gone down into the lower parts of the earth, and thou didst raise it up above every principality and authority today. For since thou didst love it, thou didst seat it together with thyself; since thou didst take compassion on it, thou didst unite it to thyself; since thou didst unite it to thyself, thou didst suffer with it; and enduring the passion, though thou art impassible, thou didst glorify it. . . . (Pentecostarion. Ascension of the Lord. Great Vespers. Stichera at Litiya.)

> God the unoriginate, who existed before all ages, and assumed man's nature, and mystically deified it, was taken up today. . . . (Pentecostarion. Ascension of the Lord. Matins. Sedalen after second kathisma.)

> Having come down from heaven to the things of earth as God, O Christ, thou didst resurrect Adam's form with thyself, which lay prostrate in the lower

reaches of hell's dungeon; in thine Ascension to the heights thou leddest it up to the heavens, and didst seat it upon the throne of thy Father, since thou art merciful, O Lover of man. (Pentecostarion. Ascension of the Lord. Matins. Sedalen after the Polyeleos.)

Returning to God the Father, Christ does not part with mankind, whose flesh he assumed; rather, he remains with his disciples and all those who love him and who make up his body—the Church. This is the theme of many hymns, including the kontakion of Saint Romanos the Melodist that is sung after the sixth ode of the canon:

When thou hadst fulfilled the dispensation for our sake, and united earth to heaven, thou didst ascend in glory, O Christ our God, not being parted from those who love thee, but remaining with them and crying: "I am with you and no one will be against you!" (Pentecostarion. Ascension of the Lord. Matins. Kontakion.)

Moreover, the Acts of the Apostles and certain liturgical texts speak of the ascension as a foretype of Christ's Second Coming, when he will come in glory to judge the living and the dead:

Thou didst leave peace to those on earth, O Christ, mounted upon heaven's clouds; and thou didst ascend and sit at the Father's right hand on high, since thou art one in essence with him and the Spirit, O Lord; for though thou hadst appeared in the flesh, thou didst never change. Wherefore thou dost now await the final fulfillment, when thou shalt return to judge all men upon the earth. . . . (Pentecostarion. Ascension of the Lord. Matins. Sessional Hymn after Ode 3 of the Canon.)

The afterfeast of Ascension lasts eight days; the leave-taking is performed on the Friday before the feast of Pentecost. During the days of the afterfeast, the liturgical texts combine the theme of the ascension with the theme of the anticipation of the descent of the Holy Spirit. In this way, the afterfeast of Ascension simultaneously becomes a type of forefeast of Pentecost:

At the sight of thine Ascension, O Giver of Life, the apostles mourned and wept: "O Master, do not leave us, thy servants, as orphans, whom thou hast loved in thy compassion, but send down on us thy Holy Spirit as thou didst promise, who will illumine our souls. (Pentecostarion. Thursday of the Ascension. Vespers. Stichera at "Lord, I call.")

Pentecost

The feast of Pentecost always falls on a Sunday and is preceded by a day commonly called "Soul Saturday" (in Russian, "Parents' Saturday"). On this day the Church commemorates all those who have departed throughout the ages. The service hardly differs in content from the service of Meatfare Saturday.

Descent of the Holy Spirit Upon the Apostles. Contemporary Icon.

On the day of the feast of Pentecost, the descent of the Holy Spirit upon the apostles is commemorated—an event described in the Acts of the Apostles (see Acts 2.1–13). Revealing the meaning of the feast in his homily on Pentecost, Saint Gregory the Theologian wrote:

We celebrate Pentecost and the dwelling with us of the Spirit and the appointed time of promise and the fulfillment of hope. The mystery is as great as it is venerable. What concerns Christ's embodiment is ended, or rather what concerns his bodily dwelling with us. . . . What concerns the Spirit is beginning. And what concerned Christ? A virgin, birth, a manger, wrapping in swaddling clothes, angels glorifying him, shepherds running to him, a star in motion, magi worshiping him and bearing gifts, Herod's murder of children, Jesus fleeing into Egypt, circumcised, baptized, receiving testimony from above, tempted, stoned for our sake—by which he had to be given as a model of suffering on behalf of the word—betrayed, nailed to the cross, buried, risen, ascended.[11]

The saint's words and ideas are reproduced in the liturgical texts. In them Pentecost is spoken of as a "post-festal" and "last" feast, since it concludes the long succession of feasts linked with the commemoration of all the major events in Christ's earthly life and his saving works, beginning with his nativity. Pentecost is the fulfillment of the promise and the beginning of the new life of the Church:

---

[11]Gregory the Theologian, *Orations* 41.5 (SC 358:324; Harrison, PPS).

We celebrate the feast of Pentecost and the coming of the Spirit, the appointed day of the promise, the fulfillment of hope. How majestic and great is the mystery! Therefore we cry aloud to you: "Glory to thee, O Lord and Creator of all!" (Pentecostarion. Sunday of Pentecost. Great Vespers. Stichera at "Lord, I call.")

O faithful, let us keep and celebrate this afterfeast and last feast most splendidly; this is the day of Pentecost, which fulfils the appointed time and the promise. For today the fire of the good Comforter came immediately upon the earth, in the form of tongues, and it illumined the disciples and showed them forth as heaven's initiates. Behold, the Comforter's light is come and hath enlightened the whole world. (Pentecostarion. Sunday of Pentecost. Matins. Sessional Hymn after the First Reading from the Psalter.)

While at the Mystical Supper, Christ promised his disciples that he would send them "another Comforter," who will guide them into all truth (Jn 16.13). This promise of the Comforter was fulfilled on the day of Pentecost. The descent of the Holy Spirit upon the apostles was the true "birthday" of the New Testament Church, because the Holy Spirit changed simple Galilean fishermen into apostles, granting them wisdom and boldness in preaching the crucified and resurrected Christ. Concerning the descent of the Holy Spirit, Saint Gregory the Theologian said:

This Spirit, who is most wise and most loving toward humankind, if he takes a shepherd makes him a harper subduing evil spirits by song and proclaims him king of Israel. If he takes a goatherd scraping mulberry trees, he makes him a prophet. Consider David and Amos. If he takes a youth with natural talents, he makes him a judge of elders, even beyond his years. Daniel testifies to this, who was victorious over lions in their den. If he finds fishermen, he catches them in a net for Christ, they who catch the whole world with the line of the Word. Take for me Peter and Andrew and the sons of thunder, thundering the things of the Spirit. If he finds tax collectors, he gains them as disciples and makes them merchants of souls. Matthew says this, who yesterday was a tax collector and today is an evangelist. If he finds fervent persecutors, he relocates their zeal and makes Pauls instead of Sauls and binds them to piety as much as they had been bound to evil.[12]

[12]Ibid. 41.14 (SC 358:346; Harrison, PPS).

Following Saint Gregory, the liturgical texts of the feast of Pentecost speak of the numerous grace-filled and miraculous activities of the Holy Spirit. He—Light of Light and Fire of Fire—was given in abundance to the apostles and through them to the entire Church, and through the Church to the entire universe:

> The Holy Spirit provides all things: he pours forth prophecies, he leads priests to perfection, he teaches unschooled people wisdom, he reveals fishermen as theologians, he confirms the Church. . . . (Pentecostarion. Sunday of Pentecost. Great Vespers. Stichera at "Lord, I call.")

> The Holy Spirit was, and is, and ever shall be, without beginning, without ending, always ranked and numbered with the Father and the Son; he is Life and Giver of life; he is Light and Giver of light; all good and the Fountain of goodness; through him the Father is known, the Son is glorified; through him all people proclaim one power, one order, one worship of the Holy Trinity. (Pentecostarion. Sunday of Pentecost. Matins. Praises.)

> Blessed art Thou O Christ Our God, who hast revealed the fishermen as most wise by sending down upon them the Holy Spirit. Through them Thou didst draw the world into Thy net, O Lover of Man, glory to Thee. (Pentecostarion. Sunday of Pentecost. Great Vespers. Troparion.)

The miracle of Pentecost is that people, divided by signs of nation, language, or race, are brought into unity by the activity of the Holy Spirit. The division of people into nations and the diaspora of nations took place, according to the Bible, as a result of the building of the tower of Babel (see Gen 11.6–8), which was a punishment for the sin of godless building, the attempt to attain the heavens by earthly means. The construction of the tower of Babel forever remains a symbol of building a social system without God. The unanimity of men in a godless enterprise will inevitably lead to division between them and the destruction of the enterprise itself. The task of the Church has always been to overcome all human divisions, and to attain unity with the help of the grace of the Spirit. Contrasting the construction of the tower of Babel with Pentecost, Saint Gregory the Theologian wrote:

> To be sure, the ancient division of tongues is praiseworthy—when those who in wickedness and impiety spoke the same language built the tower, as even now some dare to do—for the dividing of languages broke apart their oneness of intention and destroyed their undertaking. Yet the present miracle is more

praiseworthy. For being poured from one Spirit into many, the divided tongues bring them together again into one accord.[13]

The saint's thoughts are reflected in the liturgical texts. In them the descent of tongues of fire upon the apostles on the day of Pentecost are contrasted with the confusion of tongues at the construction of the tower of Babylon:

The arrogance of building the tower in days of old led to the confusion of tongues. Now the glory of the knowledge of God brings them wisdom. There God condemned the impious for their transgression. Here Christ has enlightened the fishermen by the Spirit. . . . (Pentecostarion. Pentecost. Great Vespers. Aposticha.)

When the Most High came down and confused the tongues, he divided the nations. But when he distributed the tongues of fire, he called all to unity. Therefore with one voice, we glorify the Most-holy Spirit. (Pentecostarion. Pentecost. Matins. Kontakion.)

On the feast of Pentecost a prayer to the Holy Spirit, which is not read over the course of the entire paschal period, is repeated many times. This prayer is one of exceptional significance in the Orthodox Church, because every divine service and every rule of prayer begins with it:

O heavenly King, the Comforter, the Spirit of Truth, who art everywhere and fillest all things, Treasury of blessings, and Giver of life: come and abide in us, and cleanse us from every impurity, and save our souls, O Good One.

The Church Typikon prescribes no prostrations for the entire paschal period. On the feast of Pentecost the faithful once again kneel, offering worship to all the persons of the Holy Trinity:

In Thy courts I will praise Thee, the Savior of the world. On bended knee I will worship Thine invincible might. In the evening, in the morning, and at noontime—at all times I will bless Thee, O Lord. (Pentecostarion. Sunday of Pentecost. Great Vespers. Stichera at "Lord, I call.")

All things kneel before the Comforter, and the Begotten of the Father, and he who is consubstantial with the Father; for they acknowledge in three persons the one, infallible, unapproachable and timeless essence; for the grace of the

[13]Ibid. 41.16 (SC 358:350; Harrison, PPS).

Spirit has shown forth illumination. (Pentecostarion. Sunday of Pentecost. Matins. Canon 2. Ode 4.)

In the Russian tradition the feast of Pentecost is called the "Day of the Holy Trinity" because on this day the Holy Trinity is glorified in a special manner in the service. The trinitarian dogma is most fully exposed in the sticheron "Come, ye people, and let us worship the Godhead in three hypostases," performed at vespers before the little entrance.[14] The worship of the Trinity is spoken of many times in other stichera and troparia:

Let us praise in song the consubstantial Trinity: Father, Son, and Holy Spirit. For this was the preaching of all the prophets, apostles, and martyrs. (Pentecostarion. Sunday of Pentecost. Great Vespers. Stichera at "Lord, I call.")

The Father is light, the Son is light, the Holy Spirit also is light! He was sent to the apostles in fiery tongues: through him the whole world is enlightened and adores the Holy Trinity. (Pentecostarion. Sunday of Pentecost. Matins. Exapostilarion.)

Pentecost—the day of the descent of the Holy Spirit upon the apostles and the "birthday of the Church"—is the conclusion of Christ's feat of the economy of the salvation of the human race. The cornerstone of the Church is Christ himself and the gates of hell cannot overcome his Church (see Mt 16.18). Founded by Christ on earth, the Church is called to continue his work: to lead people to salvation. Moreover, the Church is herself the body of Christ (see Eph 1.23; 4.12; Col 1.18), whose member every saved person becomes. The joining of the saved in the one, holy, catholic, and apostolic Church became possible because of the Savior's incarnation, sufferings, death, and resurrection. Christ's feat of redemption encompasses all of humanity and not only the chosen, because the Church exists not for the chosen only but for all people. She possesses a universal dimension. As Protopresbyter John Meyendorff wrote, "The Logos assumes *our* nature for the sake of the salvation *of all*. . . . Assuming and identifying himself with the poor, the weak, the persecuted and the dying—i.e. with fallen humanity as a whole—he leads them to life and joy . . . and the result of his resurrection is the "catholic" Church: *the gathering of all* into his risen body."[15]

---

[14]Concerning this sticheron, see vol. 2, pp. 121–122.

[15]John Meyendorff, "Christ's Humanity: The Paschal Mystery," *St Vladimir's Theological Quarterly* 31 (1987): 5–40, at 31 (author's italics).

Being ecumenical, universal, and all-encompassing, the Church encompasses in love and commemoration not only its own members, but also all who are outside her bounds. Like God himself, who does not leave anybody without his love, including those who are in hell, the Church of Christ is guided with love and prayer for every human being. All are alive in the Church and nobody is excluded from her memory. For this very reason, at the vespers of the feast of Pentecost, special kneeling prayers "for those confined in hades" are read:

> O ever-flowing Fountain of life and light, creative power coeternal with the Father, who hast most excellently fulfilled the whole dispensation of the salvation of mankind, Christ our God, who didst burst the indestructible bonds of death and the bolts of Hell, and hast trampled down the multitude of evil spirits . . . O Master of all, God our Savior . . . who also on this all-perfect and saving feast, dost deign to receive oblations and supplications for those bound in Hell. . . . Hearken to us, Thy humble and piteous ones who pray, and give rest to the souls of Thy servants who have fallen asleep before us, in a place of light, in a place of refreshment, in a place of repose, whence all sickness, sorrow, and sighing are fled away; and do Thou place their souls in the tabernacles of the righteous, and make them worthy of peace and repose. For the dead praise Thee not, neither do those in Hell dare to offer Thee confession. . . . (Pentecostarion. Sunday of Pentecost. Vespers. Kneeling Prayer 3.)

Praying "for those confined in hades," the Church proceeds from the understanding that God who "desires all men to be saved" (1 Tim 2.4) can change the lot of those who are in hell, since he already did this when he descended into the nether regions and brought the dead out with him. There are no obstacles to God's mercy other than the free will of man. Ultimately God himself "kills and makes alive; he brings down to hades and raises up" (1 Sam 2.6); therefore he can remove from hell those who are there. The Church draws its faith in this possibility primarily from the paschal tidings of Christ's victory over death and hell, which passes, like a *cantus firmus*, through the liturgical books of the Orthodox Church.

11

Divine Services from the Beginning of the Apostles' Fast to the End of the Ecclesial Year

The Apostles' Fast and Celebrations
in Honor of the Holy Apostles

T HE APOSTLES' FAST BEGINS on Monday of the second week after Pentecost (in Russian the fast is commonly called "Peter's Fast"). The duration of this fast differs from year to year because it begins according to the movable paschal calendar and always ends on the day of the commemoration of the apostles Peter and Paul. The maximum length of the Apostles' Fast is forty-two days, while the minimum length is eight days.[1] Having established the Apostles' Fast in this period of the ecclesial year, the Church emphasizes the exceptional role of the apostles in the work of spreading Christianity. Having received the gift of the Holy Spirit on the day of Pentecost,

Holy Apostles Peter and Paul.
Contemporary Icon

the apostles dispersed to various countries to preach Christ's doctrine. The Church is apostolic since it is built on the foundation of apostolic preaching and because the succession of the laying on of hands, dating back to the apostles, has been preserved up to the present day.

[1] This is true for those on the Old Calendar (and for the Orthodox Church of Finland). For those on the Revised Julian Calendar, the fast can fail to occur at all (when the commemoration of Sts Peter and Paul falls before the Monday after All Saints), and its maximum length is thirteen days shorter than the maximum length cited above. For more on the calendar, see pp. 20–25 in this volume.—*Ed.*

The day of the commemoration of the holy preeminent apostles Peter and Paul, June 29, belongs to the rank of great Church feasts, although it is not counted among the twelve great feasts. On this day the Church glorifies the "first-enthroned among the apostles and teachers of the whole world";[2] "they have closed the ever-gaping mouths of the ungodly, they are the dreadful swords of the Spirit, the splendid adornments of Rome, the nurturers of the whole world, the noetic and divinely graven tablets of the new covenant";[3] "the disciples of Christ and foundations of the Church, the pillars and ramparts of truth, the divine clarions of the teachings and sufferings of Christ."[4]

On the day following the commemoration of Saints Peter and Paul, a divine service in honor of the synaxis of the Twelve Apostles is celebrated. The eleven apostles chosen by Christ, and Matthias, chosen by the apostolic community to replace the betrayer Judas, are included in the ranks of the twelve apostles (see Acts 1.23–26).

THE TRANSFIGURATION OF THE LORD

The next of the twelve great feasts after Pentecost is the Transfiguration of the Lord, on August 6, which always falls during the period of the Dormition Fast.

The Transfiguration of the Lord. Contemporary Icon.

The date of the feast was selected, it appears, in connection with the feast of the Exaltation of the Cross of the Lord. In the opinion of several ancient authors, the transfiguration took place forty days before the crucifixion of the Savior. But if the celebration were to take place forty days before Great Friday, it would always fall during Great Lent. For this reason, it was decided to transfer the feast to the summer period and to celebrate it forty days before the Exaltation of the Cross, when the Church bows down before the cross of Christ and remembers the Lord's crucifixion.

The feast was established in honor of the event described by the synoptic Gospels (see Mt 17.1–8; Mk 9.2–9; Lk 9.28–36). In the eastern Christian tradition

---

[2]Menaion, June 29, Great Vespers, Troparion.
[3]Menaion. June 29. Great Vespers. Stichera at "Lord, I call."
[4]Menaion. June 29. Great Vespers. Stichera at the Litiya.

this event is seen as an appearance of the uncreated divine light and as a fore-shadowing of deification and the eschatological glory of human nature. In taking on human flesh, the Son of God divinized it and made it capable of becoming a receptacle of the glory of God. By being transfigured before his three disciples, the Savior revealed to them his divine essence, as well as the future glory that awaits the righteous in the kingdom of heaven.

The unbroken link between the transfiguration and the Savior's sufferings on the cross is noted in the liturgical texts. The Lord was transfigured so that his disciples, having seen him in all the brilliance of his divine majesty, would not doubt or waver when they saw him in the state of utmost humility, crucified on the cross:

> Before Thy Crucifixion, O Lord, the mountain became as heaven and a cloud spread itself out to form a tabernacle. When Thou wast transfigured and the Father testified unto Thee, Peter with James and John were there, who were to be present with Thee also at the time of Thy betrayal: that, having beheld Thy wonders, they should not be afraid before Thy suffering. . . . (Menaion. Transfiguration of the Lord. Great Vespers. Stichera at "Lord, I call.")

> Thou wast transfigured upon the mountain, O Christ God, and Thy disciples beheld Thy glory as far as they could see it; so that when they would behold Thee crucified, they would understand that Thy suffering was voluntary, and would proclaim to the world, that Thou art truly the Radiance of the Father. (Menaion. Transfiguration of the Lord. Matins. Kontakion.)

The appearance of Moses and Elijah to the Savior, transfigured on the mountain, and their conversation with him inspire the authors of the liturgical texts to reflect on the connection between the prophets and Christ. Events from the life of Moses and Elijah are seen as types of the transfiguration:

> Moses who saw God and Elijah who rode in the chariot of fire, passing across the heavens unconsumed, beheld Thee in the cloud at Thy Transfiguration, O Christ, and they testified that Thou art the maker and the fulfilment of the Law and the prophets. . . . (Menaion. Transfiguration of the Lord. Great Vespers. Stichera at the Litiya.)

> He who once spoke through symbols to Moses on Mount Sinai, saying, "I am He who is," was transfigured today upon Mount Tabor before the disciples;

and in His own person He showed them the nature of man, arrayed in the original beauty of the Image. . . . (Menaion. Transfiguration of the Lord. Great Vespers. Aposticha.)

Those with whom Thou hast conversed of old in fiery vapour, in darkness and the lightest of winds, stood before Thee in the manner of servants, O Christ our Master, and talked with Thee. Glory to Thy power, O Lord. (Menaion. Transfiguration of the Lord. Matins. Canon 1. Ode 4.)

The radiance of Moses' face after God revealed himself to him on Mount Sinai was one of the Old Testament types of the transfiguration. But, as Saint Gregory Palamas noted, "although [Moses] underwent transfiguration, he did not bring it about, in accordance with him who said, 'the humble light of truth brings me to the point where I see and experience God's radiance,'" while "[o]ur Lord Jesus Christ, however, possessed that radiance in his own right."[5] The liturgical texts indicate this distinction:

The face of Moses once shone with glory because of the divine voice he heard in the darkness; but Christ covers Himself with light and glory as with a garment. For He, who is by nature Himself the Author of light, shines upon those who sing: "O all ye works of the Lord, bless ye the Lord." (Menaion. Transfiguration of the Lord. Matins. Canon 1. Ode 8.)

Mount Tabor, on which Christ was transfigured, is compared with Mount Sinai, on which God revealed himself to Moses. This comparison was seen in the work of Saint Dionysius the Areopagite, who viewed the darkness on Mount Sinai and the light on Mount Tabor as one and the same appearance of the unspeakable glory of God:

The divine darkness is that "unapproachable light" where God is said to live [1 Tim 6.16]. And if it is invisible because of a superabundant clarity, if it cannot be approached because of the outpouring of its transcendent gift of light, yet it is here that is found everyone worthy to know God and to look upon him. And such a one, precisely because he neither sees him nor knows him, truly arrives at that which is beyond all seeing and knowledge.[6]

---

[5]Gregory Palamas, *Homilies* 34.2. Translation in *Saint Gregory Palamas: The Homilies*, trans. Christopher Veniamin (Dalton, PA: Mount Thabor Press, 2016), 271. [Palamas is quoting Saint Gregory the Theologian, *Oration* 38.11.—*Ed.*]

[6]Dionysius the Areopagite, *Letter 5* (PG 3:1073a; Luibheid, CWS).

The liturgical texts do not completely identify the gloom on Mount Sinai with the light on Mount Tabor, but they do emphasize that the appearance of God to Moses in the darkness was a type of the transfiguration. The cloud that covered the Old Testament tabernacle was also such a type:

> The mountain that was once gloomy and veiled in smoke has now become venerable and holy, since Thy feet, O Lord, have stood upon it. For thy dread Transfiguration, the mystery hidden before the ages, has been made manifest in the last times. . . . (Menaion. Transfiguration of the Lord. Great Vespers. Stichera at "Lord, I call.")

> The Glory that once overshadowed the tabernacle and spake with Thy servant Moses, O Master, was a figure of Thy Transfiguration that ineffably shone forth as lightning upon Tabor. (Menaion. Transfiguration of the Lord. Matins. Canon 2. Ode 3.)

The Transfiguration is a feast of the appearance of the divine light, and the significance of the feast for the Orthodox Church is in many ways defined by the central role that theology plays in the eastern Christian tradition.[7] According to Saint Gregory Palamas, Christ, transfigured on Mount Tabor, "did not manifest a radiance other than that which he already had invisibly. He possessed the splendor of the divine nature hidden under his flesh. This light, then, is the light of the Godhead, and it is uncreated." The light of Mount Tabor "is invisible, and those who behold it do so not simply with their bodily eyes, but with eyes transformed by the power of the Holy Spirit. The apostles were transformed, therefore, and saw that transformation which our human clay had undergone, not at that time, but from the moment in which it had been assumed, when it was deified through union with the Word of God."[8] The saints in the heavenly kingdom will be illumined with the very same light and will be changed and transfigured like Christ: "when they have all become divine light, they will behold, as children of that light, Christ's indescribable divine radiance. The glory that proceeds naturally from his divinity was shown on Tabor to be shared by his body as well, because of the unity of his person."[9]

This theology is reflected in the liturgical texts, which call the light of Mount Tabor "eternal," that is, it always abides in God and is inherent to him according to

---

[7]The theme of the divine light was discussed at length in Vol. 2, 158–168.

[8]Gregory Palamas, *Homilies* 34.13, in *Saint Gregory Palamas: The Homilies*, 272.

[9]Gregory Palamas, *Homilies* 34.11, in *Saint Gregory Palamas: The Homilies*, 271.

his nature. During the divine service on the feast of the Transfiguration of the Lord, the faithful turn to Christ asking that he illumine them with this divine light:

> Thou wast transfigured on the mountain, O Christ God, revealing Thy glory to Thy disciples as far as they could bear it. Let Thine everlasting Light also shine upon us sinners, through the prayers of the Theotokos. O Giver of Light, glory to Thee. (Menaion. Transfiguration of the Lord. Great Vespers. Troparion.)

> O Christ our God, who wast transfigured in glory on Mount Tabor, showing to Thy disciples the splendour of Thy Godhead, do Thou enlighten us also with the light of Thy knowledge. . . . (Menaion. Transfiguration of the Lord. Great Vespers. Stichera at the Litiya.)

> When they saw Thee, O Christ the eternal Light, shining forth in the glory of the Father, the disciples cried aloud to Thee: "Direct our paths in Thy light." (Menaion. Transfiguration of the Lord. Matins. Canon 1. Ode 5.)

The light of Christ is the light of God the Father. This was spoken of by the Cappadocian Fathers, who interpreted the words of the Psalter "in thy light we shall see light"(Ps 35.10) to mean that the light of God the Father is revealed through the light of the Son of God, owing to the operation of the Holy Spirit. According to Saint Gregory the Theologian, ". . . now we have both seen and proclaim concisely and simply the doctrine of God the Trinity, comprehending out of Light (the Father), Light (the Son), in Light (the Holy Spirit)."[10] We find this same theology in the liturgical texts of the Transfiguration:

> Come, let us ascend into the mountain of the Lord, even to the house of our God, and behold the glory of His Transfiguration, glory as of the Only-begotten of the Father. Let us receive light from His Light, and with uplifted spirits let us for ever sing the praises of the consubstantial Trinity. (Menaion. Transfiguration of the Lord. Great Vespers. Stichera at the Litiya.)

> Today on Tabor in the manifestation of Thy Light, O Word, Thou unaltered Light from the Light of the unbegotten Father, we have seen the Father as Light and the Spirit as Light, guiding with light the whole creation. (Menaion. Transfiguration of the Lord. Great Vespers. Matins. Exapostilarion.)

---

[10]Gregory the Theologian, *Orations* 31.3 (SC 250:280; *NPNF*[2] 7:318).

The transfiguration is understood as a witness to that deification of human nature that took place in the person of Christ, because of the union of his divine nature with human nature.[11] Deification extends to all people since, because of the incarnation, the possibility of attaining this state is revealed to every person:

Today Christ on Mount Tabor has changed the darkened nature of Adam, and filling it with brightness He has made it godlike. (Menaion. Transfiguration of the Lord. Little Vespers. Aposticha.)

Thou hast put Adam on entire, O Christ, and changing the nature grown dark in past times, Thou hast filled it with glory and made it godlike by the alteration of Thy form. (Menaion. Transfiguration of the Lord. Matins. Canon 1. Ode 3.)

When the infinite Light that knows no evening, even the brightness of the Father that gives splendour to creation, ineffably appeared in approachable glory on Mount Tabor, it made men godlike. . . . (Menaion. Transfiguration of the Lord. Matins. Canon 1. Ode 8.)

The Savior's transfiguration is viewed from the eschatological perspective as a foreshadowing of that reality that, according to Saint Paul, awaits the faithful at the Second Coming of Christ (see 1 Cor 15.51–52):

Thou wast transfigured upon Mount Tabor, showing the exchange mortal men will make with Thy glory at Thy second and fearful coming, O Saviour. . . . (Menaion. Transfiguration of the Lord. Matins. Sessional Hymn after the first kathisma.)

The Typikon prescribes the blessing of grapes at the end of the divine liturgy on the feast of the Transfiguration of the Lord. The date for blessing grapes was chosen because it was precisely on August 6, according to the Old Style, that grapes became ripe in Greece and were suitable for consumption. They were blessed primarily because they were used in the celebration of the Eucharist. In Rus' this custom was changed into the blessing of apples, from which the feast received the popular name "Apple-Savior."[12]

---

[11]Concerning deification, see vol. 2, pp. 371–385.

[12]In several places there is a custom of not eating apples until the feast of the Transfiguration, but there is no foundation for this tradition in the Typikon.

The Dormition of the Most-Holy Theotokos

The last of the great twelve feasts of the Church year is the Dormition of the Most-Holy Theotokos, celebrated on August 15.

Dormition of the Most-Holy Theotokos. Contemporary icon.

There is nothing said in the Acts of the Apostles or the epistles of the apostles about the death of the Theotokos. According to church tradition, her blessed death took place in Jerusalem and was marked by a special miracle: the apostles, who were located in various countries, were taken up upon the clouds and gathered at the deathbed of the Mother of God. Thomas was the only one who was not counted worthy of this honor. When, three days following the dormition of the most-holy virgin, he came to Gethsamane, where she was buried, the tomb was opened but the body of the most-pure one was not there, because she rose from the dead like her Son.

Telling of the events connected with the dormition of the most-holy Theotokos, Saint John of Damascus wrote:

> . . . this woman, holier than all things holy . . . [was] lying on a pallet. . . . What honors, then, were paid her by the one who has commanded us in the Law to honor our parents? The apostles were scattered everywhere on this earth, fishing for men and women with the varied and sonorous tongues of the Spirit. . . . The eye-witnesses, then, the servants of the Word, were there, ministering also to his Mother as they were bound to do and hoping to claim from her a blessing. . . . The companions and successors of the apostles were with them, too, to share in both their service and her blessing. . . . Nor was the company of the angels excluded. . . . But when they saw that the Mother of God was hastening towards the end of her life, even eager for it, they turned their minds towards hymns for the departing; for they were moved by divine grace. . . . Just then, it would seem to me, something must have happened that fit these circumstances and that would naturally follow them. I mean that the King must have come to the one who gave him birth, to receive her soul into his pure and holy hands, her soul so upright and spotless. And it seems likely that she would have spoken thus: "Into your hands, my Son, I confide my spirit! . . ." Then . . . she would have raised her hands, I imagine, and would have blessed those gathered there;

and she would have heard, "Come, my blessed Mother, 'into the place of my rest' (Ps 132.8). . . ." And having heard these words, the holy woman would have committed her soul to the hands of her Son.[13]

Saint John continues to recount that, after the most-holy Theotokos died, her body was transferred to Gethsamane and buried in a new tomb. But on the third day it ascended to heaven:

> For it was fitting that this worthy dwelling-place of God—the spring of the water of forgiveness, which no man ever dug; the wheatfield of the bread of heaven, which no man ever ploughed; the vine of the grape of immortality, which no man ever watered; the ever-blooming, richly fruitful olive-tree of the Father's mercy—should not be confined within the hollows of the earth. But rather, as the holy, spotless body which came from her, and which had its concrete existence in God the Word, rose on the third day from the tomb, so indeed it was right that she, his mother, should be taken out of her grave and joined with her Son. . . . It was fitting that she, who gave refuge to God the Word in her womb, should dwell in the tent of her own son. . . . It was fitting that she, who preserved her virginity undamaged by childbirth, should have her body preserved from corruption even in death. It was fitting that she, who held the creator in her lap as a baby, should rest in the tabernacle of God. It was fitting that the bride, whom the Father took for his own, should dwell in the bridal-chamber of heaven. It was fitting that she, who gazed at her own son on the cross, and who [there] received in her heart the sword of pain [Lk 2.35] that she escaped at childbirth, should look on him enthroned with his Father. It was fitting that the Mother of God should receive the blessings of her Son, and be reverenced by all creation as mother and servant of God.[14]

In the liturgical texts dedicated to the feast, the death of the most-holy Theotokos is glorified as a blessed dormition, an ascent not to death, but to life and to God, the source of life:

> In giving birth thou didst preserve thy virginity, in falling asleep thou didst not forsake the world, O Theotokos. Thou wast translated to life, O Mother of Life, and by thy prayers, thou deliverest our souls from death. (Menaion. Dormition of the Most-Holy Theotokos. Great Vespers. Troparion.)

[13]John of Damascus, *Homily on the Dormition* 2.4, 6, 9–10 (Daley, PPS).
[14]Ibid. 2.14.

O marvellous wonder! The source of life is laid in the tomb, and the tomb itself becomes a ladder to heaven. . . . (Menaion. Dormition of the Most-Holy Theotokos. Great Vespers. Stichera at "Lord, I call.")

The heavenly mansions of God fittingly received thee, O most holy, who art a living Heaven. Joyously adorned as a Bride without spot, thou standest beside our King and God. (Menaion. Dormition of the Most-Holy Theotokos. Matins. Canon 2. Ode 1.)

Thy death, O pure Virgin, was a crossing into a better and eternal life. It translated thee, O undefiled, from this mortal life to that which knows no end and is indeed divine: and so thou dost look in joy upon thy Son and Lord. (Menaion. Dormition of the Most-Holy Theotokos. Matins. Canon 1. Ode 4.)

Neither the tomb nor death had power over the Theotokos, who is ever watchful in her prayers and in whose intercession lies unfailing hope. For as the Mother of Life she has been transported into life by Him who dwelt within her ever-virgin womb. (Menaion. Dormition of the Most-Holy Theotokos. Matins. Kontakion.)

The story of how the apostles gathered in miraculous fashion at the deathbed of the most-holy Theotokos is again told in the liturgical hymns:

By the royal command of God, the divinely inspired apostles were caught up from over all the world into the clouds on high. Reaching thine immaculate body, the source of Life, they saluted it with mighty honour. . . . (Menaion. Dormition of the Most-Holy Theotokos. Great Vespers. Stichera at "Lord, I call.")

Carried to Zion as it were upon a cloud, the company of the apostles assembled from the ends of the earth to minister to thee, O Virgin. Thou art the swift cloud, from whom the Most High God, the Sun of Righteousness, shone forth upon those that were in darkness and shadow. (Menaion. Dormition of the Most-Holy Theotokos. Matins. Canon 1. Ode 5.)

On the icons of the Dormition, the Savior is depicted standing at the deathbed of the most-holy virgin and receiving her holy soul (depicted in the form of an infant wrapped in swaddling cloths) into his hands. This same image is encountered in the liturgical texts:

She who is higher than the heavens and more glorious than the cherubim, she who is held in greater honour than all creation, she who by reason of her surpassing purity became the receiver of the everlasting Essence, today commends her most pure soul into the hands of her Son. . . . (Menaion. Dormition of the Most-Holy Theotokos. Great Vespers. Stichera at the Litiya.)

He who, taking flesh, strangely made His dwelling in thy most pure womb, Himself received thine all-holy spirit, and as a Son paying His due, He gave it rest with Himself. Therefore we sing thy praises, O Virgin, and exalt thee above all for ever. (Menaion. Dormition of the Most-Holy Theotokos. Matins. Canon 2. Ode 8.)

In several churches and monasteries, on the second or third day after the feast of the Dormition, a special service called the rite of the burial of the Mother of God is performed. Its main component—the praises—is an imitation of the praises of Great Saturday. In this service a winding sheet with an image of the Virgin Mary's dormition is brought out for veneration into the middle of the church, and it is carried around the church in a cross procession at the end of the service, just as the winding sheet with the image of the Savior is carried around the church at the matins of Great Saturday. But it is necessary to note that the rite of the burial of the Mother of God is of rather late origin: it is found in Greek manuscripts beginning in the fourteenth century, and in Rus' it became widespread in the sixteenth century. The Typikon makes no mention of this service.

The two-week-long Dormition Fast is concluded with the feast of the Dormition of the Most-Holy Theotokos, and with it the whole yearly cycle of church feasts, which began with her Nativity, comes to an end.

Abbreviations

ACW   Ancient Christian Writers. Mahwah, NJ: Paulist Press, 1946–

ANF   *The Ante-Nicene Fathers.* Edited by Alexander Roberts and James Donaldson. 10 vols. Buffalo, 1885–1896. Reprint, Peabody, MA: Hendrickson, 1994.

CUA   The Fathers of the Church: A New Translation (Patristic series). Washington, DC: Catholic University of America Press. 1947–

CWS   Classics of Western Spirituality. Mahwah, NJ: Paulist Press, 1978–

LCL   Loeb Classical Library. Cambridge, MA: Harvard University Press, 1911–

NPNF¹   *The Nicene and Post-Nicene Fathers*, Series 1. Edited by Philip Schaff. New York, 1886–1889. 14 vols. Reprint, Peabody, MA: Hendrickson, 1994.

NPNF²   *Nicene and Post-Nicene Fathers*, Series 2. Edited by Philip Schaff and Henry Wace. New York, 1890. 14 vols. Reprint, Peabody, MA: Hendrickson, 1994.

PG   Patrologia Graeca [= Patrologiae cursus completes: Series graeca]. Edited by J.-P. Migne. 162 vols. Paris, 1857–1866.

PPS   Popular Patristics Series. Crestwood, NY [Yonkers, NY]: St Vladimir's Seminary Press, 1996–

SC   Sources Chrétiennes. Paris: Les Éditions du Cerf, 1942–

Select Bibliography

Afanasii (Sakharov). *O pominovenii usopshikh po ustavu Pravoslavnoi Tserkvi* [Concerning the commemoration of the departed according to the canons of the Orthodox Church]. St Petersburg: Satis, 1995.

Afanas'ev, Nikolai. *Tserkov' Dukha Sviatogo* [The Church of the Holy Spirit]. Paris: YMCA-Press, 1971.

Aleksii II. "O missii Russkoi Pravoslavnoi Tserkvi v sovremennom mire" [Concerning the mission of the Russian Orthodox Church in the contemporary world]. *Tserkov' i vremia* [Church and time] 4 (1998): 8–14.

Amvrosii (Pogodin). *Sviatoi Mark Efesskii i Florentiiskaia uniia* [St Mark of Ephesus and the Union of Florence]. Moscow: Posad, 1994. First published 1963 by Holy Trinity Monastery, Jordanville, NY.

Antonii (Bulatovich). *Apologiia very vo Imia Bozhie i vo Imia Iisus* [An apology for faith in the Name of God and the Name of Jesus]. Moscow, 1913.

Apostolic Constitutions. ANF 7:385–508.

Asmus, Mikhail. " 'O vsekh i za vsia' v anafore: utochnenie smysla" ["And all mankind" in the anaphora: a clarification of the meaning]. In *Ezhegodnaia bogoslovskaia konferentsiia PSTBI. Materialy 2000 g.* [Annual theological conference PSTBI. Materials for the year 2000], 65–73. Moscow, 2000.

Athanasius of Alexandria. *Commentary on Psalm 118. PG* 27:480–509.

Averintsev, Sergei. "Eusplanchnia." *Al'fa i omega* [Alpha and omega] 4 (1995):11–24.

———. *Poetika rannevizantiiskoi literatury* [The poetics of early Byzantine literature]. Moscow: CODA, 1997.

Balashov, Nikolai. *Na puti k liturgicheskomu vozrozhdeniiu* [On the path towards a liturgical rebirth]. Moscow: Kruglyi stol po religioznomu obrazovaniiu i diakonii, 2001.

Baldovin, John F. *The Urban Character of Christian Worship: The Origins, Development, and Meaning of Stational Liturgy.* Orientalia Christiana Analecta 228. Rome: Pontificio Istituto Orientale, 1987.

Barker, Margaret. *The Revelation of Jesus Christ.* Edinburgh: T & T Clark, 2000.

Basil the Great. *Ascetical Works.* Translated by Monica Wagner. Fathers of the Church 9. Washington, DC: Catholic University of America Press, 1999.

———. *Letter 93: To Caesaria, Concerning Communion. NPNF*[2] 8:179.

_____. *On the Holy Spirit.* Translated by Stephen M. Hildebrand. Popular Patristics Series 42. Yonkers, NY: St Vladimir's Seminary Press, 2011.

Bernardi, Jean. *La Prédication des pères cappadociens, le prédicateur et son auditoire.* Paris: Presses universitaires de France, 1968.

"Bogosluzhenie" [Worship]. In *Pravoslavnaia Entsiklopediia* [Orthodox Encyclopedia], 5:536–543. Moscow: Tserkovno-nauchnyi tsentr "Pravoslavnaia entsiklopediia," 2002.

Bolotov, Vasilii Vasil'evich. "Iz epokhi sporov o Paskhe v kontse II v." [From the epoch of controversies concerning Pascha at the end of the second century]. *Khristianskoe chtenie* [Christian reading] no. 1 (1900): 450–454.

Brock, Sebastian. *The Luminous Eye: The Spiritual World of Saint Ephrem the Syrian.* Kalamazoo, MI: Cistercian Publications, 1985.

Bulgakov, Sergii. "Evkharisticheskii dogmat" [The Eucharistic dogma]. *Put'* [The way] 20 (February 1930): 3–46 and 21 (April 1930): 3–33.

Christ, Wilhelm and Matthaios Paranikas. *Anthologia graeca carminum christianorum.* Leipzig: B. G. Teubner, 1871.

Clement of Alexandria. *The Instructor. ANF* 2:209–298.

_____. *The Stromata. ANF* 2:299–587.

Clement of Rome. *First Epistle to the Corinthians. ANF* 1:5–21.

Constantine VII. *The Book of Ceremonies.* Translated by Ann Moffatt and Maxeme Tall. 2 vols. Byzantina Australiensia 18. Canberra: Australian Association for Byzantine Studies, 2012.

Council of Laodicea. *Canons. NPNF*[2] 14:123–160.

Council of Trent. *The Canons and Decrees of the Sacred and Oecumenical Council of Trent: Celebrated Under the Sovereign Pontiffs, Paul III, Julius III, and Pius IV.* Translated by J. Waterworth. London: C. Dolman, 1848.

Cunningham, Mary. *Faith in the Byzantine World.* Downers Growe, IL: InterVarsity Press, 2002.

Cyprian of Carthage. *On the Lord's Prayer. ANF* 5:447–457.

Cyril of Jerusalem. *Lectures on the Christian Sacraments: the Procatechesis and the Five Mystagogical Catecheses.* Edited by F. L. Cross. Translated by R. W. Church. 1951. Reprint, Crestwood, NY: St Vladimir's Seminary Press, 1986.

Daley, Brian E., trans. *On the Dormition of Mary: Early Patristic Homilies.* Popular Patristics Series 18. Crestwood, NY: St Vladimir's Seminary Press, 1998.

Deianiia Vselenskikh Soborov [Acts of the Ecumenical Councils]. 4 vols. St Petersburg: Voskresenie, 1996.

Deianiia Soveshchaniia glav i predstavitelei Avtokefal'nykh Pravoslavnykh Tserkvei v sviazi s prazdnovaniem 500-letiia avtokefalii Russkoi Pravoslavnoi Tserkvi 8–18 iiulia 1948 goda [Acts of the Conference of heads and representatives of the Autocephalous

Orthodox Churches in connection with the celebration of 500 years of autocephaly of the Russian Orthodox Church, 8–18 July 1948] (Moscow: Moskovskaiia Patriarkhiia, 1948), 2:432–433.

Desnov, Nikolai. "Eshche neskol'ko slov ob izvestnykh raskhozhdeniiakh mezhdu russkimi i grekami v liturgiiakh sviatitelei Vasiliia Velikogo i Ioanna Zlatousta" [A few more words concerning well-known discrepancies between Russians and Greeks in the Liturgies of Saints Basil the Great and John Chrysostom]. *Bogoslovskie Trudy* [Theological Writings] 31 (1992): 86–96.

The Didache. Translated and edited by James A. Kleist. Ancient Christian Writers. New York: The Newman Press, 1948.

Dix, Gregory. *The Shape of the Liturgy.* London: A & C Black, 1960.

Dmitrievskii, Aleksei. *Bogosluzhenie v Russkoi Tserkvi v XVI v.* [Church services in the Russian Church in the 16th century]. Kazan, 1884.

Dmitrii of Rostov. *The Great Collection of the Lives of the Saints*, vol. 5. Translated by Thomas Marretta. House Springs, MO: Chrysostom Press, 2002.

Dorotheus of Gaza. *Teachings.* SC 92.

Dumoulin, Pierre, ed. *Khristianskoe verouchenie: Dogmaticheskie teksty uchitel'stva Tserkvi (III–XX vv.)* [Christian doctrine: Dogmatic texts of the teaching of the Church (3rd c. to 10th c.)]. Translated by Nataliia Sokolova and Iuliia Kurkina. St Petersburg: Izdatel'stvo Sv. Petra, 2002.

Dunlop, Beth Elise. "Earliest Greek Patristic Orations on the Nativity: A Study Including Translations." PhD diss., Boston College, 2004.

Egeria. *The Pilgrimage of Etheria.* Edited and translated by M. L. McClure and C. L. Feltoe. London: Society for Promoting Christian Knowledge, 1919.

Epistle of Barnabas. ANF 1:137–149.

Eusebius Pamphilius. *Church History. NPNF*[2] 1:81–387.

_____. *Life of Constantine. NPNF*[2] 1:481–560.

Evagrius Ponticus. *Homily on Spiritual Works.* SC 170; 171.

_____. *Homily on Prayer.* SC 170; 171.

Filaret (Drozdov). *Slova i rechi: v 5 tomax* [Sermons and speeches in 5 volumes]. Moscow, 1873–1885.

Florenskii, Pavel. *Sochineniia* [Writings], vol. 2. Moscow: Mysl', 1996.

Fokin, Aleksei. "Prelozhenie Sviatykh Darov v Tainstve Evkharistii" [The Change of the Holy Gifts in the Mystery of the Eucharist]. *Al'fa i Omega* [Alpha and Omega] 2/3 (9/10) (1996): 117–130.

Geerard, Mauritius, ed. *Clavis Patrum Graecorum. Volumen II: Ab Athanasio ad Chrysostomum.* Turnhout: Brepolis, 1974.

George Kedrenos. *Synopsis: Historiarum compendium.* PG 121:23–1165.

Georgievskii, Aleksei. "O voskresenii mertvykh v sviazi s Evkharistiei, v svete Svi-ashchennogo Pisaniia" [Concerning the resurrection of the dead in connection with the Eucharist, in light of Holy Scripture]. *Bogoslovskie Trudy* [Theological Writings] 16 (1976): 33–45.

_____. "Sviateishaia Evkharistiia v sviazi s ucheniem Tserkvi Pravoslavnoi" [The most holy Eucharist in connection with the teaching of the Orthodox Church]. *Zhurnal Moskovskoi Patriarkhii* [Journal of the Moscow Patriarchate] no. 6 (1977): 74–75 and 7 (1977): 75–78.

Gihr, Nikolaus. *The Holy Sacrifice of the Mass.* 6th ed. Freiburg im Breisgau: B. Herder, 1924.

Goar, Jacques. *Euchologion sive rituale graecorum.* Venice, 1730. Reprint, Graz: Akademische Druck- und Verlagsanstalt, 1960.

Gregory of Nyssa. *The Catechetical Oration of St. Gregory of Nyssa.* Translated by James Herbert Srawley. London: Society for Promoting Christian Knowledge, 1917), 110–111.

_____. *On the Ascension of Christ.* PG 46:689c–693b.

Gregory Palamas. *Saint Gregory Palamas: The Homilies.* Translated by Christopher Veniamin. Dalton, PA: Mount Thabor Press, 2016.

Gregory the Theologian. *Select Orations.* Translated by Martha Vinson. Fathers of the Church 107. Washington, DC: Catholic University of America Press, 2004.

_____. *Festal Orations.* Translated by Nonna Verna Harrison. Popular Patristics Series 36. Crestwood, NY: St Vladimir's Seminary Press, 2008.

_____. *Orations.* NPNF² 7:185–434.

Hackel, Sergii. "The Relevance of Western Post-Holocaust Theology to the Thought and Practice of the Russian Orthodox Church." In *Proceedings of the Second International Conference "Theology After Auschwitz and Its Correlation with Theology After the GULAG: Consequences and Conclusions" St. Petersburg, Russia, January 26–28, 1998.* Edited by Natalia Pecherskaya. St Petersburg: St Petersburg School of Religion and Philosophy, 1998.

Herman, Emil. "Die häufige und tägliche Kommunion in den byzantinischen Klöstern." In *Mémorial Louis Petit: mélanges d'histoire et d'archéologie byzantines,* 203–217. Bucharest: Institut français d'études byzantines, 1948.

Hilarion (Alfeyev). *Christ the Conqueror of Hell: The Descent into Hades from an Orthodox Perspective.* Crestwood, NY: St Vladimir's Seminary Press, 2009.

_____. *Orthodox Christianity.* Vol. 1, *The History and Canonical Structure of the Orthodox Church.* Translated by Basil Bush. Yonkers, NY: St Vladimir's Seminary Press, 2011.

_____. *Orthodox Christianity.* Vol. 2, *Doctrine and Teaching of the Orthodox Church.* Translated by Basil Bush. Yonkers, NY: St Vladimir's Seminary Press, 2012.

_____. *Orthodox Christianity*. Vol. 3, *The Architecture, Icons, and Music of the Orthodox Church*. Translated by Andrei Tepper. Yonkers, NY: St Vladimir's Seminary Press, 2014.

Hippolytus of Rome. *On the Apostolic Tradition*. Translated by Alistair Stewart. Popular Patristics Series 54. Yonkers, NY: St Vladimir's Seminary Press, 2015.

Iakimchuk, I. Z. "'Vsepravoslavnyi kongress'" ["All-Orthodox Congress"]. In *Pravoslavnaia Entsiklopediia* [Orthodox Encyclopedia], 9:680–683. Moscow: Tserkovnonauchnyi tsentr "Pravoslavnaia entsiklopediia," 2005.

Ignatius of Antioch. *The Letters*. Translated by Alistair Stewart. Popular Patristics Series 49. Yonkers, NY: 2013.

Ilarion (Troitskii). *Tvoreniia* [Works]. 3 vols. Moscow: Sretenskii monastyr', 2004.

Irenaeus of Lyons. *Against Heresies*. ANF 1:315–567.

_____. *Fragments from the Lost Writings of Irenaeus*. ANF 1:568–578.

Isaac the Syrian. *The Ascetical Homilies of Saint Isaac the Syrian*. Translated by Holy Transfiguration Monastery. 2nd ed. Boston, MA: Holy Transfiguration Monastery, 2011.

_____. *The Wisdom of Saint Isaac the Syrian*. Translated by Sebastian Brock. Oxford: S.L.G. Press, 1997.

John Cassian. *The Institutes of the Coenobia*. NPNF² 11:201–290.

John Chrysostom. *Homily IX on Repentance*. Translated by Andrew Maguire. Accessed December 5, 2016. http://earlychurchtexts.com/public/john_chrysostom_homily_ix_on_repentance.htm

_____. *Homilies on on 1 Timothy*. NPNF¹ 13:407–473.

_____. *Homilies on Hebrews*. NPNF¹ 14:333–522.

_____. *Homilies on 2 Corinthians*. NPNF¹ 12:271–420.

_____. *Homilies on Colossians*. NPNF¹ 13:257–321.

_____. *Homily on the Cemetery and the Cross*. PG 49.

_____. *Homilies on Matthew*. NPNF¹ 10:1–515.

_____. *Homilies on Romans*. NPNF¹ 11:335–564.

_____. *Letter to Monk Caesarius*. PG 52:753–760.

_____. *On the Ascension*. PG 50:441–452.

_____. *On the Betrayal of Judas*. PG 49:373–392.

_____. *On Holy Pentecost*. PG 50:453–470.

_____. *Six Books on the Priesthood*. Translated by Graham Neville. Popular Patristics Series 1. Crestwood, NY: St Vladimir's Seminary Press, 1996.

_____. *St. John Chrysostom: Eight Sermons on the Book of Genesis*. Translated by Robert Charles Hill. Brookline, MA: Holy Cross Orthodox Press, 2004.

John Climacus. *The Ladder of Divine Ascent*. Translated by Holy Transfiguration Monastery. Boston, MA: Holy Transfiguration Monastery, 2001.

John of Damascus. *Writings.* Translated by Frederic H. Chase. Fathers of the Church 37. Washington, DC: Catholic University of America Press, 1958.

John of Damascus, Germanos of Constantinope, Andrew of Crete, John of Euboea, and Kosmas Vestitor. *Wider than Heaven: Eighth-Century Homilies on the Mother of God.* Translated by Mary Cunningham. Popular Patristics Series 35. Crestwood, NY: St Vladimir's Seminary Press, 2008.

John of Euboea. *Homily on the Conception of the Theotokos.* PG 96:1460–1500.

John Moschus. *Spiritual Meadow.* PG 87/3:2851–3112.

Justinian. *Novellae Constitutiones.* In *Corpus Juris Civilis* III. Berlin, 1899.

Justin Martyr. *First Apology. ANF* 1:163–187.

Kallistos (Ware). *Through the Creation to the Creator.* London: Friends of the Centre, 1997.

_____. "The Meaning of the Great Fast," in *The Lenten Triodion*, trans. Mother Mary and Kallistos (Ware) (London: Faber & Faber, 1977), 40–43.

Karabinov, Ivan. "Anafora. Evkharisticheskaiia molitva. Opyt istoriko-liturgicheskogo analiza" [The Anaphora. The Eucharistic prayer. The experience of historical-liturgical analysis]. In *Sobranie drevnikh liturgii vostochnykh i zapadnykh* [Collection of ancient liturgies of the East and West], 817–1020. Moscow: Dar, 2007.

_____. "Sviataia Chasha na liturgii Prezhdeosviashchennykh Darov" [The Holy Chalice in the Liturgy of the Presanctified Gifts]. *Khristianskoe chtenie* [Christian reading] 6 (1915): 737–753 and 7–8 (1915): 953–964.

Khomiakov, Aleksei. *Polnoe sobranie sochinenii Alekseia Stepanovicha Khomiakova* [The complete works of Aleksei Stepanovich Khomiakov]. Vol. 2, *Sochineniia bogoslovskie* [Theological works]. 5th ed. Moscow, 1907.

Kuraev, Andrei. *Nasledie Khrista: Chto ne voshlo v Evangeliia?* [The legacy of Christ: What was not included in the Gospels?] Moscow: Fond "Blagovest," 1997.

Kyprian (Kern). *Evkharistiia* [The Eucharist]. 2nd ed. Moscow: Khram svv. bessr. Kosmy i Damiana na Maroseike, 1999.

_____. *Orthodox Pastoral Service.* Edited by William C. Mills and translated by Mary Goddard. Rollinsford, NH: Orthodox Research Institute, 2009.

Lake, Kirsopp, trans. *The Apostolic Fathers.* Vol. 1, *I Clement, II Clement, Ignatius, Polycarp, Didache, Barnabas.* Loeb Classical Library 24. Cambridge, MA: Harvard University Press, 1985.

Lauenstein, Diether. *Elevsinkie misterii* [The Eleusinian Mysteries], translated by N. Fedorova. Moscow: Enigma, 1996.

The Lenten Triodion. Translated by Mother Mary and Kallistos (Ware). London: Faber & Faber, 1977.

Louth, Andrew. *Greek East and Latin West: The Church, AD 681–1071.* Crestwood, NY: St Vladimir's Seminary Press, 2007.

_____. *St John Damscene: Tradition and Originality in Byzantine Theology.* Oxford Early Christian Studies. Oxford: Oxford University Press, 2002.

Luibheid, Colm, trans. *Pseudo-Dionysius: The Complete Works.* New York: Paulist Press, 1987.

Lukashevich, A. A. and A. A. Tkachenko. "Voznesenie Gospodne" [The Ascension of the Lord]. In *Pravoslavnaia Entsiklopediia* [Orthodox Encyclopedia], 9:197–230. Moscow: Tserkovno-nauchnyi tsentr "Pravoslavnaia entsiklopediia," 2005.

Macarius of Egypt. *Homilies.* PG 34:449–820.

Mango, Cyril. *Byzantium and Its Image: History and Culture of the Byzantine Empire and Its Heritage.* London, Variorum Reprints: 1984.

Mansvetov, Ivan. *Tserkovnyi ustav (Tipik), ego obrazovanie i sud'ba v grecheskoi i russkoi tserkvi* [The Typikon, its formation and fate in the Greek and Russian Church]. Moscow, 1885.

The Martyrdom of Saint Polycarp of Smyrna. ANF 1:39–44.

Mateos, Juan. "Evolution historique de la liturgie de saint Jean Chrysostome." *Proche-Orient Chrétien* 16 (1966): 3 ff.

Maximus the Confessor. *Maximus the Confessor: Selected Writings.* Translated by George Charles Berthold. Classics of Western Spirituality. New York: Paulist Press, 1985.

Maximus the Confessor. *Questions and Doubts.* PG 90:785–856.

Mazza, Enrico. *The Origins of the Eucharistic Prayer.* Collegeville, MN: The Liturgical Press, 1995.

Mensbrugghe, A. van der. "Prayer-Time in Egyptian Monasticism (320–450)." *Studia Patristica* 2, 435–454. Texte und Untersuchungen zur Geschichte der altchristlichen Literatur 64. Berlin: Akademie-Verlag, 1957.

Meyendorff, John. *Byzantine Theology: Historical Trends and Doctrinal Themes.* New York: Fordham University Press, 1979.

_____. "Christ's Humanity: The Paschal Mystery." *St Vladimir's Theological Quarterly* 31 (1987): 5–40.

_____. *Imperial Unity and Christian Divisions: The Church, 450–680 AD.* Crestwood, NY: St Vladimir's Seminary Press, 1989.

_____. *Orthodoxy in the Contemporary World.* New York, NY: Chalidze Publications, 1981.

_____. "Vremia Velikoi Subboty" [The time of Great Saturday]. *Zhurnal Moskovskoi Patriarkhii* [Journal of the Moscow Patriarchate] no. 4 (1992): 33–37.

Mirkovich, Grigorii. *O vremeni presushchestvleniia Sv. Darov. Spor, byvshii v Moskve, vo vtoroi polovine XVII veka. Opyt istoricheskogo issledovaniia* [Concerning the time of the change of the Holy Gifts. Controversy in Moscow in the second half of the 17th century. Experience of historical research]. Vilnius, 1886.

Mossay, Justin. *Les fêtes de Noël et d'Épiphanie: d'après les sources littéraires cappadociennes du IVe siècle.* Textes et études liturgiques 3. Louvain: Abbaye du Mont César, 1965.

Nicholas Cabasilas. *A Commentary on the Divine Liturgy.* Translated by J. M. Hussey and P. A. McNulty. Crestwood, NY: St Vladimir's Seminary Press, 2002.

Nicodemus the Hagiorite. *The Rudder.* Translated by Denver Cummings. Chicago, IL: Orthodox Christian Educational Society, 1957.

Niketas Stethatos. *The Life of Symeon the New Theologian.* Translated by Richard P. H. Greenfield. Dumbarton Oaks Medieval Library 20. Cambridge, MA: Harvard University Press, 2013.

_____. *Letters.* SC 81.

Nussbaum, Otto. *Die Handkommunion.* Cologne: Bachem, 1969.

Ogitskii, D. P. "Kanonicheskie normy opredeleniia paskhalii i problema datirovki Paskhi v usloviiakh nashego vremeni" [Canonical norms of the Orthodox Easter computation and the problem of the dating of Pascha in our time]. *Bogoslovskie Trudy* [Theological Writings] 7 (1971): 201–211.

Origen. *Against Celsus. ANF* 4:395–670.

_____. *Commentary on Romans.* PG 14:837–1292.

_____. *On Prayer.* PG 11:415–462.

Otzyvy eparkhial'nykh arkhiereev po voprosu o tserkovnoi reformie [Responses from the diocesan hierarchs on the question of church reform]. St Petersburg: Sinodal'naia tip., 1906.

Palladius of Aspuna. *The Lausiac History.* Translated by John Wortley. Collegeville, MN: Liturgical Press, 2015.

Paschal Chronicle. PG 92:69–1028.

Pashkov, Dmitrii. "O evkharisticheskom presushchestvlenii" [Concerning the Eucharistic Transubstantiation]. *Bogoslovskii Sbornik* [Theological Digest] 13 (2005): 381–391.

Pechatnov, Valentin. *Bozhestvennaia liturgiia v Rossii i Gretsii: Sravnitel'noe izuchenie sovremennogo china* [The Divine Liturgy in Russia and Greece: A comparative study of the contemporary order]. Moscow: Palomnik, 2008.

The Pentecostarion of the Orthodox Church. Translated by Isaac E. Lambertsen. Liberty, TN: The St. John of Kronstadt Press, 2007.

Petersen, William Lawrence. "The Dependence of Romanos the Melodist upon the Syriac Ephrem: Its Importance for the Origin of the Kontakion." *Vigiliae Christianae* 39, no. 2 (June 1985): 171–187.

_____. *The Diatessaron and Ephrem Syrus as Sources of Romanos the Melodist.* Corpus Scriptorum Christianorum Orientalium 475, Subsidia 74. Louvain: Peeters, 1985.

Podskalsky, Gerhard. *Griechische Theologie in der Zeit der Türkenherrschaft (1453–1821): die Orthodoxie im Spannungsfeld der nachreformatorischen Konfessionen des Westens.* München: C. H. Beck, 1988.

Probst, Ferdinand. *Liturgie des vierten Jahrhunderts und deren Reform.* Münster, 1893.

Proclus of Constantinople. *Homily on Tradition.* PG 65:850b–852c.

Protoevangelium of James. ANF 8:361–367.

Rochow, Ilse. *Studien zu der Person, den Werken und dem Nachleben der Dichterin Kassia.* Berliner byzantinistische Arbeiten 38. Berlin: Akademie-Verlag, 1967.

Rufinus. *Church History.* In Tiulenev, V. M. *Rozhedenie latinskoi khristianskoi istoriografii. S prilozheniem perevoda "Tserkovnoi istorii" Rufina Akvileiskogo* [The birth of Latin Christian historiography. With an appended translation of Rufinus of Aquileia's "Church History"], 230–284. St Petersburg: Izdatel'stvo Olega Abyshko, 2005.

Schmemann, Alexander. *The Eucharist: Sacrament of the Kingdom.* Translated by Paul Kachur. Crestwood, NY: St Vladimir's Seminary Press, 1987).

Sergii (Spasskii). *Polnyi mesiatseslov Vostoka* [Complete Menologion of the East]. 3 vols. Vladimir, 1901. Reprint, Moscow: Pravoslavnyi Palomnik, 1997.

Sergii (Troitskii). "Opyt izlozheniia sviatootecheskogo ucheniia" [Experience of Exposition of the Teachings of the Holy Fathers Concerning the Holy Eucharist]. In *Sviatootecheskaia khristologiia i antropologiia: Sbornik statei* [Patristic christology and anthropology: A collection of articles], 61–76. Moscow: Peresvet, 2003.

Skaballanovich, Mikhail. *Rozhdestvo Khristovo* [The Nativity of Christ]. Kiev, 1916.

_____. *Tolkovyi Tipikon* [The Typikon interpreted]. Moscow: Izdatel'stvo Stretenskogo monastyria, 2004.

_____. *Tolkovyi Tipikon: Ob"iasnitel'noe izlozhenie Tipikona s istoricheskim vvedeniem* [The Typikon Interpreted: An explanatory presentation of the Typikon with a historical introduction]. 1st ed. Kiev, 1910. Reprint, Moscow: Palomnik, 1995.

_____. *Tolkovyi Tipikon: Ob"iasnitel'noe izlozhenie Tipikona s istoricheskim vvedeniem* [The Typikon Interpreted: An explanatory presentation of the Typikon with a historical introduction]. 2nd ed. Kiev, 1913.

_____. *Vozdvizhenie Chestnogo i Zhivotvoriashchego Kresta Gospodnia* [The Exaltation of the Precious and Life-Creating Cross of the Lord]. Kiev: Prolog, 2004.

Sledstvennoe delo patriarkha Tikhona: Sbornik dokumentov [Investigatory matter of Patriarch Tikhon: Collection of documents]. Moscow: PSTBI, 2000.

Socrates Scholasticus. *Church History.* NPNF² 2:1–178.

Sozomen. *Church History.* NPNF² 2:239–427.

Symeon the New Theologian. *Catéchèses.* SC 96 (1963), 104 (1964), 113 (1965).

Symeon of Thessalonica. *Answers to Gabriel of Pentapolis.* PG 155:829–952.

Taft, Robert F. "Byzantine Communion Spoons: A Review of the Evidence." *Dumbarton Oaks Papers* 50 (1996): 209–238.

_____. *The Byzantine Rite: A Short History.* American Essays in Liturgy. Collegeville, MN: Liturgical Press, 1992.

_____. *The Great Entrance: A History of the Transfer of Gifts and other Preanaphoral Rites of the Liturgy of St. John Chrysostom.* Orientalia Christiana Analecta 200. Rome: Pontificium Institutum Studiorum Orientalium, 1975.

_____. *A History of the Liturgy of St. John Chrysostom.* Vol. 4, *The Diptychs.* Orientalia Christiana Analecta 238. Rome: Pontificium Institutum Studiorum Orientalium, 1991.

_____. *A History of the Liturgy of St. John Chrysostom.* Vol. 5, *The Precommunion Rites.* Orientalia Christiana Analecta 261. Rome: Pontificium Institutum Studiorum Orientalium, 2000.

_____. *The Liturgy of the Hours in East and West: The Origins of the Divine Office and its Meaning for Today.* Collegeville, MN: Liturgical Press, 1986.

_____. "The Pontifical Liturgy of the Great Church According to a Twelfth-Century Diataxis in Codex British Museum Add. 34060," pt. 1. *Orientalia Christiana Periodica* 45 (1979): 279–307.

Tertullian. *Apology. ANF* 3:17–55.

_____. *On Prayer. ANF* 3:681–691.

_____. *To His Wife. ANF* 4:39–49.

_____. *On Fasting. ANF* 4:102–114.

Tertullian, Cyprian of Carthage, and Origen. *On the Lord's Prayer.* Translated by Alistair Stewart-Sykes. Popular Patristics Series 29. Crestwood, NY: St Vladimir's Seminary Press, 2004.

Theodore the Studite. *Sancti patris nostri et confessoris Theodori Studitis Praepositi Parva catechesis.* Edited by Emmanuel Auvray. Paris, 1891.

_____. *Studite Constitutions.* PG 99:1703–1721.

_____. *Poenae monasteriales.* PG 99:1733–1757.

Theodoret of Cyrus. *Ecclesiastical History.* NPNF² 3:33–159.

Theodorus Lector. *Ecclesiastical History.* PG 86/1:165–225.

Thomas Aquinas. *Summa Theologiae.* 60 vols. and 1 index vol. New York: Blackfriars in conjunction with McGraw-Hill Book Co.; London: Eyre & Spottiswoode, 1963–1981.

Tkachenko, A. A. "Voskresen'e" [Sunday]. In *Pravoslavnaia Entsiklopediia* [Orthodox Encyclopedia], 9:448–454. Moscow: Tserkovno-nauchnyi tsentr "Pravoslavnaia entsiklopediia," 2005.

Tripolitis, Antonia ed. and trans. *Kassia: The Legend, the Woman, and her Work.* New York: Garland, 1992.

Usener, Hermann. *Religionsgeschichtliche Untersuchungen.* Bonn, 1911.

Uspenskii, Nikolai. *Vizantiiskaia liturgiia: istoriko-liturgicheskoe issledovanie. Anafora: opyt istoriko-liturgicheskogo analiza* [The Byzantine liturgy: a historical-liturgical study. The Anaphora: the experience of historical-liturgical analysis]. Vol. 2 of *Trudy po liturgike* [Works on liturgics]. Moscow: Izdatel'stvo Moskovskoi Patriarkhii, 2006.

———. *Pravoslavnaia liturgiia: Istoriko-liturgiheskie issledovaniia. Prazdniki, teksty, Ustav* [The Orthodox liturgy: Historical-liturgical studies. Feasts, texts, Ustav]. Vol. 3 of *Trudy po liturgike* [Works on liturgics]. Moscow: Izdatel'stvo Moskovskoi Patriarkhii, 2007.

———. *Pravoslavnaia vechernia: Istoriko-liturgicheskii ocherk. Chin vsenoshchnogo bdeniia na Pravoslavnom Vostoke i v Russkoi Tserkvi* [Orthodox vespers: A historical-liturgical overview. The order of the all-night vigil in the Orthodox East and in the Russian Church]. Vol. 1 of *Trudy po liturgike* [Works on liturgics]. Moscow: Izdatel'stvo Moskovskoi Patriarkhii, 2004.

Vaniukov, S. A., M. S. Zheltov, and K. Kh. Fel'mi. "Blagoveshchenie Presviatoi Bogoroditsy" [The Annunciation of the Most-Holy Theotokos]. In *Pravoslavnaia Entsiklopediia* [Orthodox Encyclopedia], 5:254–268. Moscow: Tserkovno-nauchnyi tsentr "Pravoslavnaia entsiklopediia," 2002.

Vasileios [Archimandrite of Stavronikita]. *Hymn of Entry: Liturgy and Life in the Orthodox Church.* Translated by Elizabeth Briere. Contemporary Greek Theologians 1. Crestwood, NY: St Vladimir's Seminary Press, 1984.

Vasilii (Krivoshein). "Nekotorye bogosluzhebnye osobennosti u grekov i russkikh i ikh znachenie" [Some liturgical peculiarities of Greeks and Russians and their significance]. *Messager de l'Exarchat du Patriarcat russe en Europe occidentale* 89/90 (1975): 71–88.

Vasil'ev, A. "O grecheskikh tserkovnykh pesnopeniiakh" [Concerning Greek church hymns]. *Vizantiiskii vremennik* [Byzantine chronicle] 3 (1896): 582–633.

Veilleux, Armand. *La liturgie dans le cénobitisme pachomien au quatrième siècle.* Studia Anselmiana 57. Rome: Herder, 1968.

Vissarion (Nechaev). *Tolkovanie na Bozhestvennuiu liturgiiu* [Commentary on the Divine Liturgy]. Moscow: Sviato-Troitskaia Sergieva Lavra, 1996.

Voronov, Liverii. "Kalendarnaia problema" [The calendar problem]. *Bogoslovskie Trudy* [Theological Writings] 7 (1971): 170–203.

"Vostochny" [Anatolian]. In *Pravoslavnaia Entsiklopediia* [Orthodox Encyclopedia], 9:484. Moscow: Tserkovno-nauchnyi tsentr "Pravoslavnaia entsiklopediia," 2005.

Wellesz, Egon. *The Akathistos Hymn,* Monumenta Musicae Byzantinae Transcripta 9. Copenhagen: Munksgaard, 1957.

_____. *A History of Byzantine Music and Hymnography*. 2nd ed. Oxford: Clarendon Press, 1961.

Wilson, Nigel G. "Books and Readers in Byzantium." In *Byzantine Books and Bookmen; A Dumbarton Oaks Colloquium*. Washington, DC: Dumbarton Oaks, 1975.

Wright, William. "An Ancient Syrian Martyrology." *Journal of Sacred Literature and Biblical Record* 8, no. 15 (October 1865): 45–56 and no. 16 (January 1866): 423–432.

Wybrew, Hugh. *The Orthodox Liturgy: The Development of the Eucharistic Service in the Orthodox Rite*. Crestwood, NY: St Vladimir's Seminary Press, 1990.

Zaitsev, Aleksei. "Evkharisticheskoe prelozhenie" [The Eucharistic Change]. *Tserkov' i Vremia* [Church and Time] 29 (2004): 208–226.

Zheltov, Mikhail. "Bogosluzhenie" [Worship]. In *Pravoslavnaia Entsiklopediia* [Orthodox Encyclopedia], 9:558–60. Moscow: Tserkovno-nauchnyi tsentr "Pravoslavnaia entsiklopediia," 2005.

_____. Foreword to *Vizantiiskaia liturgiia: istoriko-liturgicheskoe issledovanie. Anafora: opyt istoriko-liturgicheskogo analiza* [The Byzantine liturgy: a historical-liturgical study. The Anaphora: the experience of historical-liturgical analysis], by Nikolai Uspenskii, xxx–l. Vol. 2 of *Trudy po liturgike* [Works on liturgics]. Moscow: Izdatel'stvo Moskovskoi Patriarkhii, 2006.

_____. "Grigorii I Velikii" [Gregory I the Great]. In *Pravoslavnaia Entsiklopediia* [Orthodox Encyclopedia], 12:612–635. Moscow: Tserkovno-nauchnyi tsentr "Pravoslavnaia entsiklopediia," 2006.

Zheltov, Mikhail, A. A. Lukashevich, and A. A. Tkachenko. "Velikii Chetverg" [Great Thursday]. In *Pravoslavnaia Entsiklopediia* [Orthodox Encyclopedia], 7:464–471. Moscow: Tserkovno-nauchnyi tsentr "Pravoslavnaia entsiklopediia," 2004.

Zhivov, Viktor. Iz *tserkovnoi istorii vremen Petra Velikogo: Issledovaniia i materialy* [From church history in the time of Peter the Great: Research and materials]. Moscow: Novoe literaturnoe obozrenie, 2004.